Research Ideas for the Classroom

Middle Grades Mathematics

Research Ideas for the Classroom

Middle Grades Mathematics

DOUGLAS T. OWENS, *Editor*

**National Council of Teachers of Mathematics
Research Interpretation Project**

SIGRID WAGNER, *Project Director*

MACMILLAN LIBRARY REFERENCE USA

NEW YORK

Macmillan Library Reference
1633 Broadway
New York, NY 10019-6785

Library of Congress Catalog Card Number: 92-37478

Printed in the United States of America

printing number

9 10

Library of Congress Cataloging-in-Publication Data

Middle grades mathematics / Douglas T. Owens, editor ; National
   Council of Teachers of Mathematics, Research Interpretation Project,
   Sigrid Wagner, project director.
       p.   cm. — (Research ideas for the classroom)
     Includes bibliographical references and index.
     ISBN 0-02-895792-X—0-02-895795-4 (pbk.)
     1. Mathematics—Study and teaching (Elementary)   I. Owens,
Douglas T.   II. Wagner, Sigrid, 1942–   III. National Council of
Teachers of Mathematics. Research Interpretation Project.
IV. Series.
QA135.5.M53   1992
372.7—dc20   92-37478
                                                                          CIP

Contents

Series Foreword

Research Ideas for the Classroom (RIC) is a three-volume series of research interpretations for early childhood, middle grades, and high school mathematics classrooms. These books reflect the combined efforts of well over two hundred researchers and teachers to produce a comprehensive and current compilation of research implications in mathematics education. We hope these volumes will serve as a useful sequel to the popular Research Within Reach published a decade ago by the National Council of Teachers of Mathematics (NCTM). Much research activity has transpired in the past few years and whole new lines of inquiry have emerged, particularly in the area of technology. It is time to look again at what research has to offer in the way of ideas for the classroom.

The ultimate goal of research in mathematics education is to improve learning and teaching, and from this perspective the RIC volumes will serve as a valuable complement to the NCTM Research Agenda Project (RAP) monographs published in 1988 and 1989. The RAP monographs provide syntheses of several strands of existing research, as well as recommendations for future directions. The RIC volumes link the existing research to the classroom and provide ideas for teachers to explore with their own students.

From still another perspective, the RIC volumes should serve as an important supplement to the NCTM *Curriculum and Evaluation Standards* and *Professional Teaching Standards*. Chapter authors were asked to indicate where research supports recommendations in the *Standards* and where a research base is lacking. We hope these frequent citations will help guide implementation of the *Standards* and inform future recommendations.

A subtitle for the RIC volumes might be *Learning From Students*. Part of the value of research in mathematics education lies in the process itself, the process by which we learn from our students what they understand and how that understanding develops, how they feel about mathematics, and what factors affect those feelings. Any teacher who has ever asked a question or noticed an expression of puzzlement or delight has engaged in informal research. What we learn from students may cause us to question our assumptions, fortify our knowledge, investigate our reasoning, or rethink our methods of teaching.

Because research is a learning process, interpreting research becomes a multi-layered process of construction in which objective phenomena are filtered through the subjective inferences of researchers, editors, and readers. Yet, as with most learning, this individual process of construction leads, over time, to shared systems of beliefs that influence our behavior in remarkably similar ways. We may tend to regard the key elements of these belief systems as "truths" even though we know that truth is a function of the times, context, and people involved.

The authors of the chapters in *Research Ideas for the Classroom* have attempted to convey the key points suggested by research in their areas of specialization. We hope that you, the reader, will be intrigued enough by ideas described in these pages to do two things: (a) Go to the source of the authors' inspiration, the research reports listed at the end of each chapter (especially those marked with an *), and (b) go to the source of the researchers' inspiration, to students, and try some of these research activities yourself. By so doing, you can peel away several layers of subjective interpretation and come that much closer to learning the "truth" from your own students.

The NCTM Research Interpretation Project began in 1988 with a proposal to the National Science Foundation to produce an updated and comprehensive set of research interpretations for the mathematics classroom. The project was funded under NSF Grant No. MDR-8850572. The editorial panel and advisory board met in the spring of 1989 to structure the volumes and identify chapter topics. To enhance communication between teachers and researchers, as well as to insure the readability and practicality of the books, it was decided that chapters would be co-authored by a researcher and a teacher.

Without a doubt, the most crucial step in any writing project is picking the right authors. Researcher co-authors were chosen by the editorial panel for their knowledge of the research literature and their ability to interpret findings for the classroom. The researchers selected teacher co-authors for their expertise in teaching and the creativity of their ideas.

Authors agreed to an imposing array of requirements designed to guarantee comprehensive coverage, minimum overlap, and uniform format. They were given a long list of subtopics to be included in their chapters and then were told that they had to address all these topics in only twenty manuscript pages of text and five pages of references! They were asked to give some preference to easily accessible research reports, including research-based articles in *Mathematics Teacher, Arithmetic Teacher,* and *School Science and Mathematics.* They were asked to identify (*) articles that are especially rich in ideas for teaching.

Chapter development was a four-stage process. Editors and advisory board members reacted to chapter outlines and preliminary bibliographies from the standpoint of coverage and structure of the total volumes. First drafts of chapters were reviewed by researchers for breadth of coverage and balance of treatment within each chapter. Second drafts were reviewed by teachers for clarity of writing and practicality of suggestions for the classroom. Third drafts went to the publisher.

Each volume looks at research from the perspective of the learner, the content, and the teacher. Two chapters in each volume focus on the learner—one on cognition and one on affect. The content chapters vary according to the level, but each volume includes chapters on problem solving and technology. Four or five chapters in each volume focus on teaching—models of instruction, planning curriculum, classroom interaction, and evaluation. Each volume concludes with a chapter on teachers as researchers, which includes descriptions of research activities conducted by teachers within the constraints of the typical classroom environment.

The chapter structure makes each book easy to read selectively. References to accompanying chapters are included wherever appropriate, yet each chapter is quite comprehensible by itself. It is our sincere hope that most readers will enjoy an entire volume for its wealth of useful information and interesting ideas.

As comprehensive as the editors, authors, and reviewers have tried to be in a limited number of pages, the astute reader will surely note that some important themes are underrepresented. Some content topics (e.g., discrete mathematics, statistics, integers, inequalities), despite their importance in the mathematics curriculum, lack a substantial research base related to teaching and learning. Some themes, perhaps most notably that of gender and mathematics, have such a substantial research base that numerous books and monographs have been devoted to those single themes. Gender and mathematics is addressed in RIC in the chapters on affect, but we encourage the interested reader to consult other publications for further information. Other themes (e.g., multiculturalism or communication) have long histories of research but only recently within the field of mathematics education. We leave it to the next edition of NCTM research interpretations to report on these areas.

On behalf of the editorial panel, we thank the National Science Foundation, and especially Raymond J. Hannapel, for encouraging and supporting the project and for supplying copies of these books to mathematics supervisors across the country. We thank Lloyd Chilton for his help in launching the volumes and arranging for publication. We thank James D. Gates and Cynthia Rosso at NCTM and Philip Friedman and Michael Sander at Macmillan for helping in many ways throughout the project. We thank the advisory board—John A. Dossey, Mark J. Driscoll, Fernand J. Prevost, Judith T. Sowder, Douglas B. Super, and Marilyn N. Suydam—for their enthusiastic vision and willingness to share ideas. We thank the reviewers whose thoughtful comments and suggestions helped improve the quality of the final product. Most especially, we thank the authors for their considerable talents, their cheerful willingness to meet impossible constraints, and their patience in awaiting the final outcome.

I personally want to thank the volume editors—Robert J. Jensen, Douglas T. Owens, and Patricia S. Wilson—for the exceptional skills and tireless efforts they devoted to the project. It was an honor and a pleasure to work with them—they made a big job a lot of fun!

Sigrid Wagner

Introduction

Douglas T. Owens

This volume is the result of collaboration among middle school teachers and university teachers with experience and expertise in mathematics education in the middle grades. Each brings his or her own individual perspective. The co-authors of each chapter accepted the challenge of reading and synthesizing the research related to a specific topic. In fact, they have gone further to interpret the research in light of the trends and directions that mathematics teaching is headed. The authors have been asked to provide classroom implications wherever possible. However, this is not a methods text, and suggested activities tend to be presented as an idea which you will need to embellish and shape to your personality and your class.

The authors have also provided suggestions for classroom action research. The last chapter, written by two middle grades teachers, suggests how to conduct classroom inquiry. As a classroom teacher you have a unique opportunity to frame a question, systematically observe under ordinary classroom conditions, keep records, and then draw conclusions. We hope you will be motivated to conduct research in your own classroom and share what you have learned with your colleagues.

The middle grades volume follows the series format, placing chapters within separate broadly-identified sections: "Learning," "Processes and Content," "Teaching," and "Classroom Research." I will begin by giving a brief comment on each chapter.

Learning

In the first chapter, Kloosterman and Gainey present implications gleaned from the research on students' thinking. Constructivism and information processing theories are the most used theories. These theories incorporate the idea that students are not empty containers to be filled with unrelated bits of information; rather, they are thinking individuals who interpret and remember based on their past experiences and knowledge. The following suggestions are consistent with these views of learning.

- Continually listen to students and base instruction on what students already know.
- Help students make connections among various mathematical ideas.
- Help students make connections between concepts and procedures.
- Help students see connections among manipulative, pictorial, and abstract representations.
- Encourage students to think through a problem rather than rely on memorized procedures.
- Encourage students to talk to each other about math.
- Allow students to relate to mathematics concepts in their own way.
- Encourage students to make mental and written notes about their progress when solving problems.
- Encourage students to continually evaluate progress on a complex problem and consider alternative paths.

In Chapter 2, Hart and Walker present findings about the role of affect in learning mathematics. They hypothesize that self-confidence, perceived importance, fear of failure, etc., may be structured in long-term memory similar to the way cognitive knowledge is structured. A student's perception of the usefulness of mathematics is an important affective characteristic. It has a clear relationship to students' decisions whether to take optional mathematics courses and helps explain the gender and race differences in mathematics course election. On a questionnaire, students may view mathematics as useful, but when students are asked to elaborate, the perception of the useful of mathematics is found to be limited in scope and depth. Discussing with students how math is used in careers in all walks of life, not just by scientists, can expand students' perceptions.

Persistence has to do with continuing to work on a problem when the answer or even the method of solution is not apparent. Students seldom are allowed the opportunity to struggle with a mathematics problem. They are seldom taught how to deal with difficulty, except to ask for help.

Extrinsic rewards tend to focus student efforts on the aspects of the task to be evaluated. Also, performance on tasks requiring nonalgorithmic, creative, or insightful thinking, such as nonroutine problem solving, may be affected negatively. Four sources of intrinsic motivation have been identified: an appropriate level of challenge, an appeal to the sense of curiosity, sense of control, and encouragement to be involved in a world of fantasy.

Processes and Content

This section addresses the research on curriculum topics and processes. There is not an exact match with the curriculum of NCTM's *Curriculum and Evaluation Standards* (1) for several reasons. First, research has not yet been reported on all the standards. To help fill any void, the interpretation of previous research is made in light of the new standards. Second, much research has been reported on topics like rational numbers and their operations, which are extremely important in the middle grades. In this volume, we have emphasized these topics and interpreted the previous research in light of the *Curriculum and Evaluation Standards* and current trends.

Sowder and Kelin divide Chapter 3 into two distinct parts: research with implications and the teacher's point of view. Research is reviewed related to number sense, computational estimation, mental computation, number size, and evaluation of these number ideas. Some interesting research compares students' facility with the same numbers in school and with money out of school. How do people develop estimation skills? How can estimation skills be taught? What techniques do skilled mental calculators use? What kind of difficulties do students have with large numbers or small numbers close to zero? Middle school teacher Judith Kelin describes her involvement in a project with her class learning mental computation and estimation.

Researchers define a problem as a situation that requires resolution and for which the person sees no obvious path to solution. In Chapter 4, Kroll and Miller emphasize the importance of problem solving in middle grades mathematics. They explore what is involved in solving problems and why students have trouble. Sources of difficulty such as reading and a lack of knowledge of the concepts are explored. Beliefs that problems should be solved quickly and easily hamper students. Several suggestions are made for teachers to help students solve problems, such as ways to ask questions and hold discussions. Suggestions are made about creating a classroom climate, allotting sufficient time, and grouping students for effective problem solving.

Chapter 5 by Bright and Hoeffner contains several related topics. The research on measurement, probability, statistics, and graphing has been conducted separately, which necessitates the separate reviews. Students need hands-on experience developing formulas rather than applying them. Activities need to be organized in and beyond the classroom that allow movement for measuring and estimating measures. Students lack experience with situations that embody probability concepts. Instruction in probability must compete with students' intuitive beliefs that may be inconsistent with instruction. Increasingly, statistical skills are recognized as fundamental for mathematics literacy. Students need opportunities to be involved in a realistic problem solving process rather than only calculating statistical measures from fixed data. Teaching students to read and interpret graphs accurately is becoming increasingly important. Graphs are useful in communicating information from measurement, probability, and statistical activities. Measurement is important in interpreting graphs. These topics can be and should be integrated, and suggestions are made about how to integrate them.

As children progress to the middle grades, the operations change from addition and subtraction to multiplication and division, and the numbers change from the whole numbers to the rational numbers. Graeber and Tanenhaus in Chapter 6 focus on interpretations or models for multiplication and division. For example, repeated addition is an inadequate model for a complete understanding of multiplication. The chapter indicates relationships, such as connecting the groups model to the array model and to the area model. The Cartesian product model is explained. What children seem to know about division is that it undoes multiplication. This does not help students associate division with situations that are modeled by division. While division is usually introduced as repeated subtraction (measurement model), this model is later neglected in favor of the partitive (sharing) model. The division algorithm should be taught meaningfully, with difficult computations de-emphasized.

In Chapter 7 on common fractions, Bezuk and Bieck emphasize that our teaching should be meaning oriented rather than symbol oriented. Students should learn fraction concepts in the presence of manipulative materials using smaller denominators first. Once a concept is learned using one material, students can examine the same concept using another manipulative and thereby generalize the concept. Students can gain a qualitative understanding of the "bigness" of a fraction by estimation. For example, they can be asked to construct a fraction close but not equal to ½; then another still closer. They can be asked to estimate the answer to an addition or subtraction problem before learning the algorithm for finding the exact result.

In Chapter 8 on decimal fractions, Owens and Super conclude that decimal fraction instruction should be integrated with common fraction instruction to the extent possible. In order to be flexible and to have a fuller concept of fractions, students should know as early as possible that 0.25 is another name for ¼. Models used for whole number place value, notably Dienes' base-10 blocks, have been used successfully to help children learn decimal fraction concepts. Metric measure is a natural use of decimal fractions. This chapter examines many of the errors students make in using decimal fractions. Suggestions are made for overcoming the errors. A discussion of conceptual and procedural knowledge is presented, because much of the decimal fraction research has been reported in that theoretical context.

Ratio and proportion are among the most difficult content in the middle grades. Cramer, Post, and Currier (Chapter 9) point out that proportions involve multiplicative relationships. Many students try to use additive methods to solve proportion problems. Other student strategies are described in considerable detail. They describe proportional reasoning as being complex and give some components of it. They emphasize understanding and claim that it is impossible to explain the cross-product rule. They include two lesson tasks as models to show appropriate ways to develop proportional reasoning, including distinguishing proportional from nonproportional situations.

In the prealgebra chapter (Chapter 10), Kieran and Chalouh take the approach that algebra is a natural way of symbolizing what is sensible in arithmetic. There are two main thrusts in the chapter: the use of letters to represent numbers and an explicit awareness of the method or process rather than focus on the answer. In the first, they discuss the use of letters as unknowns versus using letters to represent given quantities. They discuss the forward operations of setting up an equation versus the "undoing operations" of solving by arithmetic. In the symbolization of method section, two projects are used to illustrate. The first uses a mathematics machine and the other uses graph paper multiplication which leads to algebraic multiplication. Negative numbers are explored and some additional resources are given. They deliberately avoid discussing teaching approaches aimed primarily at teaching algebraic symbol manipulation.

Geddes and Fortunato begin Chapter 11, "Geometry," with a discussion of psychological theories, primarily the van Hiele model of thinking in geometry. Research and teaching activities are given for the topics of concept formation, spatial visualization, reasoning, and higher-order thinking. Trends in geometry curriculum such as transformation geometry, use of technology, and problem exploration are discussed. Use of manipulatives and multicultural activities are cited as trends in teaching geometry. Each section in the chapter is organized by presenting the research or theory followed by sample activities.

Teaching

The NCTM *Professional Teaching Standards* (2) organizes the standards for teaching mathematics in four groups: mathematical tasks, classroom discourse, classroom environment, and analyzing teaching and learning. Chapter 12, "Technology," focuses primarily on worthwhile mathematical tasks (Standard 1) and tools for enhancing discourse (Standard 4). Chapter 13, "Models of Instruction," focuses primarily on the learning environment (Standard 5) and secondarily on worthwhile mathematical tasks (Standard 1). Chapter 14, "Planning and Organizing . . . Curriculum," focuses primarily on worthwhile mathematical tasks (Standard 1) and secondarily on learning environment (Standard 5). Chapter 15, "Classroom Interactions," focuses on the teacher's and students' roles in discourse (Standards 2 and 3). Chapter 16, "Assessment and Evaluation," focuses on analysis of teaching and learning (Standard 6).

In Chapter 12, Jensen and Williams discuss the implications of technology for middle grades mathematics. Fears that students will become less competent in mathematics as a result of calculator and computer use have proved to be ungrounded. When calculators are used in concert with traditional instruction, students maintain paper-and-pencil skills. The evidence is clear that calculators assist with problem solving tasks by decreasing the computational load. Students using calculators have a better attitude toward mathematics and a better self concept with regard to mathematics than those not using calculators. Computer assisted instruction (CAI), when used with traditional instruction, has proved to be more effective than traditional instruction alone. CAI is more effective in raising achievement among low or high achieving students than among average students. Computer microworlds provide a powerful arena for problem posing and playing "what if." Hypermedia computer technology can provide several windows simultaneously. The chapter looks forward to new technology on which little research has been reported.

In Chapter 13, Fitzgerald and Bouck give a brief historical overview of several funded projects that provided suggestions for excellent mathematics activities. Some of these projects have survived while some did not survive the "back-to-basics" movement of the 1970s. Several of the more recent projects are sources for excellent mathematics activities. Direct instruction is the most commonly used model of instruction in mathematics classrooms. Considerable detail is given on cooperative learning as a viable alternative model of instruction. Mathematics is seen as a human activity approached through cooperative groups. While cooperative skills such as decision making and conflict management must be taught, they can be learned and utilized in the mathematics context. One's view of mathematics affects classroom processes. Viewing mathematics as inquiry requires a new definition of the roles of the teacher, the students, and what it means to know mathematics. Using inquiry as a teaching model would seem to require a teacher to have a strong knowledge of the subject matter.

In Chapter 14, Madsen and Baker deal with two issues: planning to accommodate changing mathematics instruction, and reorganizing the curriculum to focus on a variety of mathematics topics and concepts. As mathematics teaching shifts from an authoritarian model to be more student centered, lesson presentations must be planned to include modeling the use of manipulatives, questions to promote students' thinking, and guided practice activities. In planning mathematics tasks, a teacher must consider how students are organized: pairs, threes, fours, or whole class. Challenging and interesting tasks must be developed to promote the understanding of concepts. Differential activities must be provided to allow for student work pace. Lesson summaries must be planned to encourage students to reflect on the lesson and make connections among the ideas. Suggestions for organizing the curriculum involve planning for strands (e.g., problem solving, communication reasoning, and technology) within the topics (e.g., rational numbers, algebra, and geometry).

In Chapter 15, Koehler and Prior deal with three aspects of teacher-student interactions. The first aspect is interactions and how they are studied. The second aspect is the influences on teachers and students that cause them to engage in an interaction. The third aspect is strategies for improving teacher-student interactions. Research in an earlier era was conducted by counting the number of questions or exchanges in a classroom to explain learning. Now, researchers want to understand why certain interactions occur. Teachers' beliefs about students and how they learn, about mathematics, and about teaching influence these interactions. Students' views of themselves and of mathematics influence these interactions.

In Chapter 16 by Webb and Welsch, evaluation is judging the value of a program while assessment is determining what an individual student can do. One reason for assessment is to direct student learning. This requires regular gathering of information and decision making. An obvious reason for assessment is grading or certifying students, but it is not clear whether "grading on the curve" or "grading for mastery" is the most effective reward structure. Informal assessment that creates interesting situations can build on intrinsic motivation and lead to a deeper understanding of mathematics. Some interesting ideas on assessing student disposition toward mathematics and evaluating program equity are reported. New forms of testing as well as questioning, making observations (performance assessment), student portfolios, and projects are explored. In some of these cases, a body of research has not been built up in order to reach consensus on the effectiveness of these as assessment and evaluation methods.

Classroom Research

Chapter 17, "Teacher as Researcher," was written by two middle grades teachers, Clouthier and Shandola, based on their experiences in doing research. They discuss teacher action research as well as the school-university model. They begin with a general classroom research theme and then zero in on mathematics. Each tells her story, one of an interview study, and the other of a classroom inquiry project. They report that teacher ownership and support groups are vital to classroom inquiry. Classroom inquiry empowers teachers and students. Classroom inquiry bridges the gap between theory and practice. Are you ready for it?

Summary

As I read the diverse chapters, I found some themes recurring in quite different settings. In fact, it seems that these can be summarized further in just four terms: connections, problem solving, reasoning, and communication (1). Interesting!

- Help students make connections among various mathematical ideas. Teach mathematics so that it is more integrated rather than compartmentalized.
- Teach mathematics so that it is more meaning oriented rather than symbol oriented. This includes teaching more contextualized mathematics.
- Whenever students learn rules or procedures, help them understand the concepts behind the procedures.
- Teach problem solving as a process within each unit or topic rather than as a separate topic.
- Encourage students to think through a problem rather than rely on memorized rules. Answers are not always immediate. Help students learn how to struggle with a problem.
- Encourage students to talk to each other about mathematics. Organize for students to work in pairs or small groups.
- Rely on student knowledge. Interpret mathematics as a human activity, investigated by a community of learners.
- Become involved in research in your own classroom.

Research has taught us a lot about teaching and learning mathematics in the middle grades. However, the task will never be finished. As our society changes, our needs change. We must continue to grapple with how to help an ever increasing portion of our population become more mathematically literate. Our goals as set out by NCTM in the *Curriculum and Evaluation Standards* (1) and the *Professional Teaching Standards* (2) are higher than ever before. New topics and methods are suggested and their effectiveness will need to be evaluated. As more teachers become active researchers, new interpretations will be made. All of this will add to the dialogue about teaching and learning mathematics. As you read this book you will have reactions. We hope you will share them with colleagues.

References

1. NATIONAL COUNCIL OF TEACHERS OF MATHEMATICS (1989). *Curriculum and evaluation standards for school mathematics.* Reston, VA: Author.
2. NATIONAL COUNCIL OF TEACHERS OF MATHEMATICS (1991). *Professional standards for teaching mathematics.* Reston, VA: Author.

Learning

Learning

CHAPTER 1

Students' Thinking: Middle Grades Mathematics

Peter Kloosterman and Patricia Haynes Gainey

During the first week of seventh grade, the following exercise is written on the board:

$$\begin{array}{r} .4 \\ \times\ .6 \\ \hline \end{array}$$

TEACHER: *Chris, what is .4 × .6?*
CHRIS: *2.4*
TEACHER: *That sounds a little high. Are you sure your answer is correct?*
CHRIS: *I think so. When you multiply two numbers, the result is always bigger. Besides, don't you just line up the decimal points?*

$\mathbf{I}$f you are like most middle school teachers, you probably start the school year with a number of "Chrises." Questions such as "Wasn't Chris taught to multiply decimals last year?" and "How can he think 2.4 is a reasonable answer?" quickly come to mind. You know that Chris was probably able to multiply decimals correctly when he was first taught, but you have to wonder why he has so much trouble remembering a few simple rules.

The purpose of this chapter is to look at recent research about students' cognition (i.e., how students think) and ask what it can tell us about how to teach mathematics. In particular, we want to know if theories of how students think can explain why the Chrises of the world are always getting confused and what can be done to help them remember. We will begin with the assumption made by most current cognitive theorists that learners actively construct their own knowledge. Known as *constructivism,*

3

> "Central to current theories is the view of the learners as active participants in learning. Learners construct their own meaning by connecting new information and concepts to what they already know." (*Professional Teaching Standards, 22,* p. 144)

this theory suggests that rather than simply accepting new information without question, students *interpret* everything they see and hear and then *remember* new information *in relation to what they already know* (6). Chris, for example, felt that 2.4 was a reasonable answer to 0.6×0.4 because he thought that "multiplication always

> A farm is in the shape of a rectangle. Its length is 1 km and its width is 1/2 km. How many kilometers of fence would be needed to enclose the farm?
>
> When fifth graders were interviewed about this problem, Wayne was perplexed by the "kilometers" measure, Jean misunderstood the word "enclose," and Mary was reluctant to draw a picture of the fence because she could not locate the barn or house. (27)

results in a bigger number." To understand why it is important to assume that students construct their own knowledge, we will look briefly at the shortcomings of theories of learning that do not make this assumption. Piagetian theory, which forms the basis of many constructivist ideas, will be discussed and followed by an examination of information-processing research. Information processing comprises a set of theories of learning that are distinct from, but generally compatible with, constructivism. After information processing has been explained, implications of constructivism and information processing for teaching will be explored. Finally, we will consider current research on thinking which, although potentially important to the teacher, is not cast in terms of constructivism.

Theories of How Children Think and Learn

While many of us are unaware of it, theories of how children think and learn have had an impact on mathematics texts and teaching throughout this century. These theories include associationism, meaning theory, Piagetian theory, and information processing.

Associationism

Drill and practice, a common feature of many mathematics programs, is based on the associationist theory of learning outlined by Thorndike (32) almost 70 years ago. The theory, based on the stimulus-response work of Pavlov and thus a forerunner of behaviorism, suggested that learning resulted directly from the establishment of a bond between a specific stimulus and a response (18). A middle school teacher needed only to continue drilling students to strengthen appropriate bonds. A major weakness of the theory, however, was that it treated students as "empty bottles" to be filled with knowledge rather than as thinking individuals who try to make sense of new information. Chris's notion that decimal points must be lined up when decimals are multiplied is probably the result of confusing multiplication and addition rules. Associationist theory, built on the assumption that drill is appropriate for establishing any necessary bond, does little to explain why Chris would confuse a new procedure with one previously learned.

Meaning Theory

Contrasting the drill philosophy of associationism, William A. Brownell (2) argued in the 1930s that children learn mathematics best if it is taught in a meaningful way. According to Brownell, "Meaning theory conceives of arithmetic as a closely knit system of understandable ideas, principles, and processes" (2, p. 19). While agreeing that drill is useful in certain situations, Brownell worried that excessive reliance on drill caused students to view mathematics as a set of unrelated facts and that the number of bonds needed for a good understanding of mathematics was so large that it was impossible to drill on all of them. If children saw the relations among various

---

"Drill does not develop meanings. Repetition does not lead to understandings." (William Brownell, 1935; 2, p. 10)

---

mathematical ideas, Brownell believed they would remember the mathematical concepts they were expected to master (18). For example, seeing division as the inverse of multiplication is an example of a mathematical structure we expect students to understand.

Piagetian Theory

In the latter half of the twentieth century, Piagetian theory has received considerable attention. According to this theory, children pass through four stages of cognitive development: sensorimotor (birth to about 2 years), preoperational (2 to about 7 years), concrete operational (7 to about 11 years), and formal operational (about 11 to adult) (see 8, 15, 23, 24). While knowledge of the concrete and formal operational stages provides useful background for middle school teachers, one aspect of Piagetian theory is especially important for this chapter: As children pass through the four stages

---

"The typical middle school class most likely contains a few students who are concrete operational, with the majority being in some transitional phase between the two stages [concrete operational and formal operational]." (15, p. 8)

---

of development, the way in which they think becomes progressively more complex and better suited for understanding the world around them. Piaget was interested in how children adapt to the world; he used the terms *assimilation* and *accommodation* to describe the process through which they overcome discrepancies between what they think should be true and what they see (9, 33). For example, Chris believed that multiplying two numbers always results in a product that is larger than the factors. When confronted with the possibility that 0.6×0.4 could be 0.24, he was forced to rethink that belief. Associationism does little to explain why beliefs based on prior learning should affect assimilation of new information. Piagetian theory, with its emphasis on how children reorganize their thinking to account for new information, clearly acknowledges the importance of prior beliefs. For this reason, it is often considered a forerunner of constructivism.

The stages of development identified by Piaget have implications for how children should be taught. Some researchers believe the mathematics curriculum should take into consideration the Piagetian stage of the students for whom the curriculum was designed. In a review of research of Piagetian stages applied to middle school mathematics, Juraschek (15) notes that many middle school students have not acquired formal operations, but they can understand abstract mathematical concepts on a concrete level. Students may be unable to grasp probability presented in terms of definitions and formulas (e.g., the probability of drawing a white marble from a bag containing p white marbles and q black marbles is $p / [p+q]$; see Fig. 1.1). However, the concept is fairly easy for them to master when they explore it through real experiments (e.g., actually drawing marbles from bags). Juraschek (15) suggests that middle school teachers can overcome the limitations of students who have not achieved formal·operational thought if they (a) proceed from concrete to abstract, (b) actively involve students in learning, and (c) use representations and ideas that are slightly more complex than those students are accustomed to seeing.

In a separate review of Piagetian-oriented research applied to mathematics instruction, Hiebert and Carpenter (12) note that many school mathematics tasks can be mastered by children who have not attained stages considered prerequisites for those tasks. They found that the problem is not with the measurement of Piagetian level

FIGURE 1.1   Concrete operational children often have trouble understanding
concepts that are presented without manipulatives

**Given two bags of marbles, from which bag would a white marble most likely
be drawn?**

The concrete operational child may say the first bag because it has fewer
marbles or the second bag because it has more white marbles. The *formal
operational child* will say the first bag based on a comparison of ratios or
in terms of common fractions of percents. (15)

or with Piagetian theory; rather, the skills measured by Piagetian readiness tests are not the skills necessary to complete school mathematics assignments.

Information-Processing Theories

Building on roots in both associationism and stage theories of learning, much recent research on human thinking is based on a set of related theories generally known as information processing. The term *information processing* arises from the notion that people take in, process (understand or fail to understand), and store or report information. Common to many information-processing theories is an analogy between human thought and computer programs: Both take in information, process it, and make decisions based on the data. As a simplistic example, both students and computers can be taught to solve routine one-step word problems by (a) finding the two numbers in the problem, (b) deciding, based on key words in the problem, to add, subtract, multiply, or divide, and (c) performing the appropriate computation. In fact, one common type of research in information processing is to try to write computer programs that solve certain types of mathematics problems (see 24).

A key component of information-processing theory is the importance of memory in learning. There is general agreement that humans possess at least two qualitatively different types of memory called short-term or working memory, and long-term or semantic memory (1, 24, 26, 29). Short-term memory can hold only a few pieces of information at a time, yet it is the system in which active thinking takes place. For

> "Students' problem-solving abilities might improve greatly if they could use working memory more efficiently, that is, if they learned to use automatic processing for the routine elements of an activity, and thus made resources available for the controlled processing of the novel aspects of solving the assigned problems." (29, p. 40)

example, many students can add 2.3 and 3.5 mentally, but few can multiply 2.3 by 3.5 without pencil and paper. From an information processing perspective, the partial products that must be remembered to perform two-digit multiplication exceed the capacity of short-term memory.

In contrast to the limitations of short-term memory, long-term memory appears to have virtually boundless capacity (1, 26, 29). From the information-processing perspective, the key to understanding learning is understanding how long-term memory is organized. Most information-processing theorists agree with the Piagetian notion that memory has a distinct structure. When asked to think of a telephone number, most individuals remember three distinct sets of numbers: the area code, the first three digits, and the last four digits. The last two parts of the number are stored in memory adjacent to the preceding digits; a person cannot access them without first thinking of those digits.

Mathematical knowledge is assumed to be stored, like other information, in some orderly system (1, 24). When a student is asked to define what is meant by parallel lines, he or she usually thinks of lines first and then what it means for lines to be parallel. In some cases, organization of memory depends on the individual. When asked to define a right triangle, some students think of a triangle and then the specific case of a right triangle. Others think of a right angle and then picture the rest of the triangle. The implication for teaching is that, unlike associationism which implies that bonds can be formed between any randomly chosen stimulus and response, mathematical concepts are best remembered if they are taught in relation to already stored information. Thus teachers should explain new information in terms of knowledge students already possess.

As a final example of what information-processing theories say about how children think, consider the human brain as a library. Long-term memory consists of all the books arranged on shelves in a specific order. Books, like information in long-term memory, are arranged in some logical manner to make them easy to find (i.e., there is a distinct organizational structure to the library). As the child grows, the card catalog system for keeping track of the books is expanded (Piagetian assimilation) and periodically reorganized (Piagetian accommodation) to make retrieval of books easier. Short-term memory can be thought of as the circulation desk for the library. Only a few books can go in or out at one time, and thus there are severe restrictions on the use of the books. Obviously, one goal of teaching should be to help students get information they need (stored in long-term memory) through the circulation system (short-term memory) as easily as possible.

Implications of Constructivism and Information Processing for Instruction

Information-processing theories, in connection with constructivist theory, form the basis of much current thought about students' thinking in mathematics. Many classroom teachers still use extensive drill as advocated by associationists. While most current learning theorists agree that some drill is appropriate, they also say that drill should be used only after extensive conceptual development of new ideas (11). They also claim that students need substantially less drill than is commonly required.

> "There is no question that for simple, one-step procedures, (e.g., addition and multiplication facts), practice promotes quick recall. But for more complex algorithms, such as computations with multidigit numerals, fractions, or algebraic expressions, it is not clear that large amounts of practice are necessary or even the best way to promote recall." (11, pp. 35–36)

The implications for teaching of information-processing and constructivist theories are fairly obvious. All incorporate the notion that students are thinking individuals who interpret and remember everything they see based on what they already know. The *Professional Standards for Teaching Mathematics* developed by the National Council of Teachers of Mathematics (NCTM) (22) contains numerous hypothetical classroom vignettes in which the teacher questions students to determine their understanding of concepts. The teacher then uses the information from this questioning to plan instruction. Additional ideas for teaching in a way that is consistent with constructivist and information-processing research can be found in the following suggestions.

> "The teacher consistently asks students to explain and to justify their answers. 'Why?' is a standard question, asked about apparently correct as well as about apparently wrong answers." (*Professional Teaching Standards,* 22, p. 37)

Listen to Students Continually and Base Instruction on What They Already Know. When teaching a topic, begin instruction by asking students what they remember from previous instruction on that topic. In the middle grades, there are few genuinely new topics to be covered, yet many textbooks present concepts as if students have never seen them before. By teaching as if the students have forgotten everything they have learned, we are encouraging them to store new information separately from old information in long-term memory. When students are doing problems, ask them to explain how they arrived at their answers. Such explanations show how previous

> "Students do not enter with a lack of knowledge, but rather children bring a great deal of knowledge to almost any learning situation. Some of the knowledge is correct, and some is incorrect. Some knowledge facilitates learning, and some hinders it. But learning is influenced by the knowledge that children start with." (4, p. 83)

knowledge has been properly or improperly integrated with the new concept. To help the student who is having difficulty, a teacher may often have to explain both the previously learned concept and the new concept to show the proper relationship between them.

Help Students Make Connections among Mathematical Ideas. In the NCTM *Curriculum and Evaluation Standards* the following claim is made:

> The mathematics curriculum should include the investigation of mathematical connections so that students can see mathematics as an integrated whole, explore problems and describe results using graphical, numerical, physical, algebraic, and verbal mathematical models or representations; [and] use a mathematical idea to further their understanding of other mathematical ideas. (21, p. 84)

Although the *Curriculum and Evaluation Standards* (21) was not intended to be a research document, the information-processing assumption that long-term memory has a distinct structure is certainly linked to the call for stressing mathematical connections. Students need to see that decimal fractions are merely a special case of common fractions and that place-value concepts learned for whole numbers apply to decimal fractions as well. They need to see that fractions can be interpreted as parts of a whole, parts of a set, and ratios. The list of examples is endless but the general

> "As students study one topic, relationships to other topics can be highlighted and applied." (*Curriculum and Evaluation Standards,* 21, p. 85)

> "Meaning or understanding in mathematics comes from building or recognizing relationships either between representations or within representations." (11, p. 32)

rule is clear: Students who have formed connections between various mathematical representations and concepts are able to remember because they have well-organized long-term memory structures that allow them to retrieve information from long-term memory easily.

Help Students Make Connections between Conceptual and Procedural Knowledge. Hiebert and Lefevre (13) define conceptual knowledge as that which is connected to and thus easily related to other knowledge. In contrast, procedural knowledge is based on symbols and memorized rules without regard for underlying understanding of those symbols and rules. Wearne and Hiebert (34) studied the extent to which seventh-grade students use procedural (rule-oriented) rather than conceptual knowledge on tasks involving decimal fractions. They found that 90% of the

> "Conceptual knowledge is . . . knowledge that is rich in relationships. It can be thought of as a connected web of knowledge, a network in which the linking relationships are as prominent as the discrete pieces of information. . . . A unit [of information] . . . is a part of conceptual knowledge only if the holder recognizes its relationship to other pieces of information." (13, pp. 3–4)

> "Procedural knowledge . . . is made up of two distinct parts. One part is composed of the formal language, or symbol representation system, of mathematics. The other part consists of the algorithms, or rules, for completing mathematical tasks." (13, p. 6)

students in their sample responded correctly to the problem $4.6 + 2.3$, but only 37% produced the right answer to $4 + .3$. Mathematically, the problems are very similar in difficulty. Most subjects in the Wearne and Hiebert (34) study, however, appeared to be applying rules they did not understand. In information-processing terms, they lacked well-structured knowledge about procedures for adding decimals. Students who can connect mathematical procedures with underlying concepts are likely to apply those procedures correctly rather than in an arbitrary, inappropriate fashion.

Encourage Students to Think Through a Problem Rather Than Rely on Memorized Procedures. As teachers, we all have students who say, "Don't tell me why it works, just tell me how to get the answer." All too often, we give in to such requests. When students memorize procedures, two problems occur. First, they are developing procedural knowledge without the related conceptual knowledge. Second, we are relieving them of the responsibility to search their long-term memory for ways of doing

> "Middle school students often can possess and follow mathematical procedures but as rules without reason. We can all think of examples of this kind: 'borrowing' in subtraction, 'turn it upside down and multiply' for division by a fraction, 'take it over to the other side and change the sign.'" (30, p. 9)

specific problems. Although we do want students to learn to solve problems with as little effort as possible, we also want them to have long-term memories that are structured so that they can find the information needed to solve nonroutine problems. There is no question that many students resist having to devise their own procedures to solve complex problems. However, such perseverance results in connections that will be useful for future problem-solving situations.

Teach Using a Variety of Manipulatives. Middle school students and teachers often view manipulatives as "play time," yet manipulatives are an excellent way to help students make connections between mathematical ideas. Dienes's (7) perceptual variability principle states that learning is enhanced when students are exposed to a concept in a variety of manipulative contexts. For example, seeing fractions represented with pattern blocks, fraction bars, fraction circles, and Cuisenaire rods helps students to understand the concept of fraction, independent of its physical representation.

> "It seems appropriate to urge that traditional instructional methods be replaced, or at least augmented, by activity-based teaching, incorporating manipulative materials wherever possible." (15, p. 9)

> I hear and I forget. I see and I remember. I do and I understand. (Chinese proverb)

When students have seen a concept explained using several different manipulatives, they are often able to build fractions using additional manipulatives they have never seen. Such demonstrations indicate a well-structured, conceptually based understanding of fractions that is unlikely to be forgotten. Teachers who treat manipulatives as serious mathematics find that their students learn to treat them that way also.

Help Students See Connections between Manipulative, Pictorial, and Abstract Representations of Concepts.   In addition to using various manipulative representations for new concepts, classroom activities should be oriented to help students make connections between concrete, pictorial, and abstract representations of ideas. Fraction shapes, fraction circles, and base-10 blocks for teaching decimals are the manipulatives most commonly pictured in textbooks. One fifth-grade student recently told us he had been asked to find the number represented by 5 "flats," 13 "longs," and 15 "ones" (see Fig. 1.2). First he was to assume that each flat (10-by-10 grid) represented the number one. He was then told to circle any hundredths that needed to be regrouped into tenths, any tenths that needed to be regrouped into ones, and then to identify the number represented. The student circled the group of 10 hundredths and the group of 10 tenths and then wrote 5.1315 as his answer, explaining that each group represented a "different decimal." Had he been taught to regroup decimal fractions using actual blocks rather than just these pictorial representations, he probably would have made the connection that 10 hundredths equals a tenth, that 10 tenths equals a one, and that the number represented was really 6.45.

Encourage Students to Talk with Each Other about Mathematics.   Another of the major themes of both NCTM's *Curriculum and Evaluation Standards* (21) and *Professional Teaching Standards* (22) is communication of mathematical ideas (Fig. 1.3). In addition to being an important on-the-job skill, communicating mathematically helps students construct a well-structured long-term memory because they

---

"Middle school students should have many opportunities to use language to communicate their mathematical ideas. . . . Opportunities to explain, conjecture, and defend one's ideas orally and in writing can stimulate deeper understandings of concepts and principles." (*Curriculum and Evaluation Standards*, 21, p. 78)

---

see how other students have integrated new information into what they already know. Piaget noted the importance of social interaction in helping students develop cognitively (9); thus student-to-student communication should be at least as important as teacher-to-student communication in the classroom.

Allow Students to Relate to Mathematics Concepts in Their Own Way.   Teachers should encourage students to think of their own methods of relating new concepts to previously acquired knowledge. When confronted with a nonroutine problem, students should be encouraged to attempt various methods of solution. In this way, they may see how the problem relates to other problems they remember how to do.

Encourage students to think of integer addition in terms of gain and loss of money, point scoring in a game, ascent and descent of a mountain, and rise and fall of the mercury in a thermometer.

FIGURE 1.2   A common textbook exercise for regrouping decimal fractions

Circle any hundredths that need to be regrouped into
tenths and tenths that need to be regrouped into ones.
Identify the number.

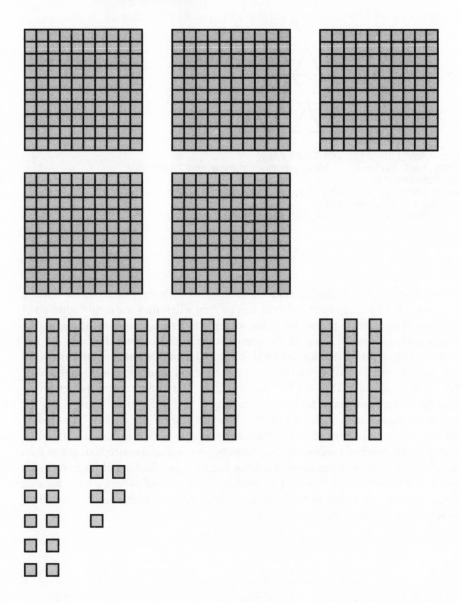

FIGURE 1.3   Student to student communication often leads to deeper understanding of a problem

Problem: How many triangles are in this picture?

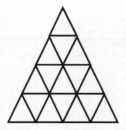

Bruce: Aren't there just 16? That's easy!
Kathy: Yeah, but look. . . . Here's another triangle and it's got four little triangles in it.
Bruce: I don't get it. . . . Oh, I see what you mean—here's another one that size and here and . . .
Kathy: Wait a minute. I better start keeping track of them all.

The benefits of encouraging students to think of their own methods for relating new concepts to already mastered ones can be seen when they are taught addition of fractions. The normal procedure is for students to find a common denominator, rewrite each fraction in terms of the common denominator, and then add the numerators (Fig. 1.4). When asked to add 2/3 and 1/5, one of our students discovered that multiplying the first numerator (2) by the second denominator (5) and adding the result to the product of the first denominator (3) and the second numerator (1) gave the correct numerator for the answer (Fig. 1.5). Furthermore, multiplying the two initial denominators gave the correct denominator for the answer. The student did this with a number of other examples and was able to explain how his procedure related to the standard method, leading us to believe he had a conceptual rather than merely procedural understanding of adding fractions. By thinking of fractions in his own way, the student had discovered a mathematically sound pattern which, because of the connections of that pattern with alternative methods of fraction computation, he was likely to remember.

FIGURE 1.4   Standard method for adding $\frac{2}{3}$ and $\frac{1}{5}$

$$\frac{2}{3}\left(\frac{5}{5}\right) + \frac{1}{5}\left(\frac{3}{3}\right) = \frac{10}{15} + \frac{3}{15} = \frac{13}{15}$$

FIGURE 1.5 An alternative method for adding $\frac{2}{3}$ and $\frac{1}{5}$

***Encourage Students to Make Mental and Written Notes About Their Progress
When Solving Problems.***   A limitation to complex thinking is that short-term memory can hold only a few pieces of information at a time. Students who write partial
solutions will not need to remember them consciously and thus will have more short-
term memory available for thinking. For example, when solving the problem "How
many different ways can you make change for a quarter?" some students try to keep
track of the possibilities in their heads. In many cases, they will forget some combi-
nations that they would have remembered had they made systematic written notes.
Limitations of short-term memory are also a major problem in estimation and mental
computation where the goal is for students to do all calculations in their heads. Front-
end estimation (25) is an effective estimation technique because it requires that
few numbers be remembered and thus frees short-term memory for computing
(Fig. 1.6).

Cognition-Related Topics

Although not directly related to learning theories per se, several cognitively oriented
topics currently being researched appear to have implications for instruction. Three
of these are dealt with here: learning styles, affect, and metacognition.

Learning Styles

Learning styles have been defined as "characteristic cognitive, affective, and physio-
logical behaviors that serve as relatively stable indicators of how learners perceive,
interact with, and respond to the learning environment" (16, p. 5). Obviously, educators are more interested in cognitive and affective factors than they are with phys-
iological factors.

The assumption underlying learning style research as applied to education is that
learning will be optimal when a student is placed in a classroom where instruction

FIGURE 1.6   Front-end estimation is effective because
it requires few mental notes

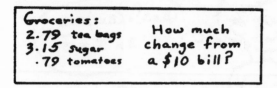

is compatible with the style in which he or she learns. Hodges (14) describes a fairly extensive list of learning styles ranging from preference for bright as opposed to dimly lit classrooms to preference for working alone as opposed to working in groups. Teachers should be aware of and try to adapt to the environmental and interpersonal preferences of their students, but to base major classroom or curricular changes on such learning styles will be very difficult in a class where every student could have a different learning style profile.

Smith and Holliday (31) addressed the issue of learning style in a somewhat different fashion when they administered a general learning style instrument to fourth-, fifth-, and sixth-grade students. The researchers found, among other things, that high achievers in mathematics were more independent and responsible than low achievers. Based on this finding, Smith and Holliday suggest that high achievers may benefit from self-directed activities while low achievers would benefit more from a structured schedule. We find this recommendation somewhat troublesome in that a characteristic of high achievement is self-direction. Teachers who fail to give low achievers the opportunity to practice self-direction may be depriving those children of the experiences they need to become high achievers.

One implication of learning style research with which we completely agree is that teachers need to listen to students' comments about how they learn best. Listening to discover students' previous knowledge and their learning styles is easy to do and, if nothing else, gives teachers a better understanding of factors that may be influencing how well students are learning mathematics.

Metacognition

All discussion thus far has been on cognition, or how students think. Research on problem solving in recent years has begun to include metacognition, or thinking about one's thinking. While the distinction between cognition and metacognition is not always clear, the notion that it helps to be aware of the thinking one does in mathematics is certainly important. A major component of metacognition involves regulation, or knowing when pursuing a specific solution path is no longer productive and it makes sense to try a different method of solving the problem (3, 19, 28).

Metacognition is particularly important in problem solving. Schoenfeld (28) has argued that many students, when given a challenging mathematical problem, have a tendency to spend long periods of time pursuing solution paths that show little

> "There is growing evidence that learning associated with problem solving is facilitated or enhanced by students' increased awareness of metacognitive aspects of the problem-solving process." (35, p. 68)

promise of success. For example, using unorganized guess-and-check on a problem with hundreds of possible answers can take hours. Students need to learn that persistence is a virtue only if it appears to be paying off. While it is not always possible to determine whether a potential solution path is worth pursuing, students need to be taught to stop what they are doing periodically and ask themselves if it makes sense to continue with their current plan of action (10, 19). Note that we are not saying teachers should discourage persistence on the part of students. Rather, teachers should encourage students to evaluate their progress on a complex problem continually and consider alternative solution paths when the ones they have chosen do not appear to be productive. Specifically, students should try to make connections between the current problem and solution strategies that have worked on similar problems in the past.

Cognition and Affect

Just as the distinction between cognition and metacognition is not always clear, neither is the distinction between cognition and affect (feelings and emotions). Whether a relationship exists between strong emotions (e.g., severe math anxiety) and cognition and whether strong emotions affect cognition are matters open to question. Students who are very upset usually have a hard time thinking or doing any work (20).

Kloosterman (17) has suggested that weaker feelings, such as self-confidence in learning mathematics, can be explained at least in part by other motivational variables. The important implication of research such as this is that students' feelings about mathematics are affected by their thinking. That is, affective variables including self-confidence, perceived importance of mathematics, and fear of failure may be structured in long-term memory in ways similar to those used to structure cognitive knowledge. Thus, how students will react emotionally to a novel mathematical task is probably dependent on how they see the task in relation to previous tasks. If students see a new problem as similar to one they enjoyed doing earlier, they are likely to be enthusiastic about undertaking the new problem.

Teachers may be able to build positive feelings about mathematics by relating it to some topics middle school students find enjoyable, such as

- geometry—try sports-related angle problems
- decimals/percents—figure television ratings or record discounts
- graphing/statistics—conduct surveys on favorite pizza toppings, video games, or skateboards

---

Constructivism: A Summary

Although human thought is incredibly complex, constructivist and information-processing theories provide a definite guideline for teaching: *Help students make connections*. The research of Piaget and the constructivists show us that children interpret new information based on what they already know (6). Information-processing research tells us that people store and retrieve knowledge by relating it to other knowledge. By helping students make appropriate connections, we are making it easier for them to understand and store new knowledge. Assisting them to relate two already

---

"All experience is an arch to build upon." (Henry Brooks Adams, 1838–1918)

"All our knowledge has its origins in our perceptions." (Leonardo da Vinci, 1452–1519)

---

learned concepts is important because it helps them access either concept. Research on metacognition tells us that we need to encourage students to monitor their own attempts to make connections.

One additional point that needs to be made involves problem solving. Most of the examples provided in this chapter deal with number concepts and computational skills as opposed to problem solving. Clearly, helping students make connections when solving problems is just as important as encouraging them to make connections when performing computations. We know that students who are good problem solvers see relationships more easily than do poor problem solvers (3). There has been considerable research on how young children think when solving word problems but much less research at the middle school level. Consequently this chapter has not been oriented toward problem solving. We firmly believe, however, that constructivist notions are just as powerful for problem solving as they are for other mathematical skills and thus hope you will use the suggestions we have presented in all of your teaching.

Looking Ahead . . .

The world around us is a very complex place. Researchers in fields from physics to medicine to sociology try to build models to make complex phenomena more understandable. Although we will never be able to know exactly how humans think, constructivism and information processing are models of thinking that are based on the knowledge we have available. NCTM's *Curriculum and Evaluation Standards* (21) and *Professional Teaching Standards* (22) are based on constructivist assumptions. We hope that understanding constructivist and information-processing models and their implications will make it easier for you to see the rationale behind many of the statements made in these documents. More important, we hope that understanding these models makes it easier for you to help students learn.

Peter Kloosterman

"We currently know a great deal more about how children learn mathematics than we know about how to apply this knowledge to mathematics instruction." (26, p. 859)

Schoen (27) and Charles, Lester, and O'Daffer (5) offer suggestions for interviewing students about mathematics. I challenge you, as teachers, to interview some of your students to learn whether you can understand how they have constructed knowledge about a single mathematical topic. Many times, informal observation of students or listening to students' conversations during group work provides almost as much information as a structured interview. Can you see evidence that your students have made questionable assumptions (e.g., "multiplication always makes larger")? To what degree are the questionable assumptions the same from one group of students to the next? What can you do to help them construct meaningful ideas about mathematical topics? Does understanding how your students think make it easier to individualize? If nothing else, I hope this chapter helps you spend more time considering these issues.

Patricia Haynes Gainey

About the Authors

Peter Kloosterman is an associate professor of elementary and mathematics education at Indiana University. His research focuses on how student's beliefs about mathematics and themselves as mathematics learners influence their thinking and motivation in mathematics. In addition to research, he works with preservice and inservice teachers at the elementary through high school levels.

Patricia Haynes Gainey is a seventh-grade mathematics teacher at Creston Junior High School in Indianapolis. She has taught remedial, average, and accelerated classes and is particularly interested in the affective, cognitive, and metacognitive benefits of cooperative learning for students at all ability levels.

References

1. BRIARS, D. J. (1982). Implications from information-processing psychology for research on mathematics learning and problem solving. In F. K. Lester & J. Garofalo (Eds.), *Mathematical problem solving: Issues in research* (pp. 39–51). Philadelphia: Franklin Institute Press.

2. BROWNELL, W. A. (1935). Psychological considerations in the learning and the teaching of arithmetic. In W. D. Reeve (Ed.), *The teaching of arithmetic* (Tenth Yearbook, pp. 1–31). New York: Teachers College Press.

*3. CAMPIONE, J. C., BROWN, A. L., & CONNELL, M. L. (1988). Metacognition: On the importance of understanding what you are doing. In R. I. Charles & E. A. Silver (Eds.), *The teaching and assessing of mathematical problem solving* (pp. 93–114). Hillsdale, NJ: Erlbaum; Reston, VA: National Council of Teachers of Mathematics.

4. CARPENTER, T. P., & PETERSON, P. L. (1988). Learning through instruction: The study of students' thinking during instruction in mathematics. *Educational Psychologist, 23*(2), 79–85.

*5. CHARLES, R., LESTER, F., & O'DAFFER, P. (1987). *How to evaluate progress in problem solving*. Reston, VA: National Council of Teachers of Mathematics.

6. DAVIS, R. B., MAHER, C. A., & NODDINGS, N. (1990). *Constructivist views on the teaching and learning of mathematics* (*Journal for Research in Mathematics Education* Monograph No. 4). Reston, VA: National Council of Teachers of Mathematics.

7. DIENES, Z. P. (1967). *Fractions: An operational approach*. New York: Herder & Herder.

8. FLAVELL, J. H. (1963). *The developmental psychology of Jean Piaget*. Princeton, NJ: Van Nostrand.

9. FLAVELL, J. H. (1968). *The development of role-taking and communication skills in children*. New York: Wiley.

*10. GAROFALO, J. (1987). Metacognition and school mathematics. *Arithmetic Teacher, 34* (9), 22–23.

*11. HIEBERT, J. (1990). The role of routine procedures in the development of mathematical competence. In T. J. Cooney (Ed.), *Teaching and learning mathematics in the 1990s* (1990 Yearbook, pp. 31–40). Reston, VA: National Council of Teachers of Mathematics.

12. HIEBERT, J., & CARPENTER, T. P. (1982). Piagetian tasks as readiness measures in mathematics instruction: A critical review. *Educational Studies in Mathematics, 13*(3), 329–345.

13. HIEBERT, J., & LEFEVRE, P. (1986). Conceptual and procedural knowledge in mathematics: An introductory analysis. In J. Hiebert (Ed.), *Conceptual and procedural knowledge: The case of mathematics* (pp. 1–27). Hillsdale, NJ: Erlbaum.

*14. HODGES, H. L. B. (1983). Learning styles: Rx for mathophobia. *Arithmetic Teacher, 30*(7), 17–20.

*15. JURASCHEK, W. (1983). Piaget and middle school mathematics. *School Science and Mathematics, 83*(1), 4–13.

16. KEEFE, J. W. (1987). *Learning style theory and practice*. Reston, VA: National Association of Secondary School Principals.

17. KLOOSTERMAN, P. (1988). Self-confidence and motivation in mathematics. *Journal of Educational Psychology, 80*(3), 345–351.

18. KROLL, D. L. (1989). Connections between psychological learning theories and the elementary mathematics curriculum. In P. R. Trafton (Ed.), *New directions for elementary school mathematics* (1989 Yearbook, pp. 199–211). Reston, VA: National Council of Teachers of Mathematics.

19. LESTER, F. K. (1988). Reflections about mathematical problem-solving research. In R. I. Charles & E. A. Silver (Eds.), *The teaching and assessing of mathematical problem solving* (pp. 115–124). Hillsdale, NJ: Erlbaum; Reston, VA: National Council of Teachers of Mathematics.

20. McLEOD, D. B. (1988). Affective issues in mathematical problem solving: Some theoretical considerations. *Journal for Research in Mathematics Education, 19*(2), 134–141.

*21. NATIONAL COUNCIL OF TEACHERS OF MATHEMATICS. (1989). *Curriculum and evaluation standards for school mathematics*. Reston, VA: Author.

*22. NATIONAL COUNCIL OF TEACHERS OF MATHEMATICS. (1991). *Professional standards for teaching mathematics*. Reston, VA: Author.

23. PIAGET, J., & INHELDER, B. (1969). *The psychology of the child*. New York: Basic Books.

24. RESNICK, L. B., & FORD, W. W. (1981). *The psychology of mathematics for instruction*. Hillsdale, NJ: Erlbaum.

*25. REYS, B. J. (1986). Teaching computational estimation: Concepts and strategies. In Schoen, H. L. (Ed.), *Estimation and mental computation* (1986 Yearbook, pp. 31–44). Reston, VA: National Council of Teachers of Mathematics.

26. ROMBERG, T. A., & CARPENTER, T. P. (1986). Research on teaching and learning mathematics: Two disciplines of scientific inquiry. In M. C. Wittrock (Ed.), *The third handbook of research on teaching* (pp. 850–873). New York: Macmillan.

*27. SCHOEN, H. L. (1979). Using the individual interview to assess mathematics learning. *Arithmetic Teacher, 27*(3), 34–37.

28. SCHOENFELD, A. H. (1985). *Mathematical problem solving*. Orlando, FL: Academic Press.

29. SILVER, E. A. (1987). Foundations of cognitive theory and research for mathematics problem-solving instruction. In A. H. Schoenfeld (Ed.), *Cognitive science and mathematics education* (pp. 33–60). Hillsdale, NJ: Erlbaum.

30. SKEMP, R. R. (1978). Relational understanding and instrumental understanding. *Arithmetic Teacher, 26*(3), 9–15.

31. SMITH, D. K., & HOLLIDAY, P. J. (1987). Learning style and academic achievement. *Focus on learning problems in mathematics, 9*(4), 15–24.

32. THORNDIKE, E. L. (1922). *The psychology of arithmetic*. New York: Macmillan.

33. WADSWORTH, B. J. (1971). *Piaget's theory of cognitive development*. New York: McKay.

34. WEARNE, D., & HIEBERT, J. (1989). Constructing and using meaning for mathematical symbols: The case of decimal fractions. In J. Hiebert & M. Behr (Eds.), *Number concepts and operations in the middle grades* (pp. 220–235). Hillsdale, NJ: Erlbaum; Reston, VA: National Council of Teachers of Mathematics.

35. WEAVER, J. F. (1987). What research says: The learning of mathematics. *School Science and Mathematics, 87*(1), 66–70.

CHAPTER 2

The Role of Affect in Teaching and Learning Mathematics

Laurie E. Hart and Jamie Walker

> *"Well, I felt confused when I first started reading the problem, and . . . especially, when I got to the end I felt real good about it. And when I got the answer I felt real good! You know, 'cause I got it." (Excerpt from an interview by Jamie Walker with an eighth-grade student in which the student had just solved a nonroutine mathematics problem.)*

$\mathbf{T}$his chapter will focus on affect and how it is connected with the teaching and learning of mathematics in middle grades classrooms. First, a discussion will be presented about why affect is important in mathematics teaching and learning. Second, what is meant by "affect" and "affective domain" will be explained. Next, some of the developmental characteristics of middle grades students will be described. Finally, research about the particular affective factors of confidence in learning mathematics, perceived usefulness of mathematics, persistence in the mathematics classroom, and student motivation to learn will be presented along with the relationship of each factor to mathematics teaching and learning.

Why Affect Is Important

Mathematics educators would like for students to view mathematics as useful, be interested in knowing and using mathematics, and feel positive about their mathematical ability. However, a positive attitude toward mathematics means little if a student does not understand mathematical ideas or cannot use mathematics to solve problems. We, as teachers, would like for students to view mathematics positively and be competent in mathematics.

What researchers are beginning to recognize is that both the cognitive and affective aspects of learning are present when students construct mathematical understandings, that focusing on one without the other limits what teachers and researchers know about the teaching and learning of mathematics (e.g., 8). When a student works on a mathematical task, he or she brings along a whole set of beliefs and attitudes about mathematics and what it means to do mathematics. These beliefs and attitudes form one part of the context in which the student does mathematics. As the student works on the mathematical task, his or her interest, frustration, excitement, or anxiety may rise and fall. The feelings experienced while working on the task may contribute to or detract from the student's performance. Thus, it makes sense for teachers and researchers to examine both the mathematics learning that occurs and the beliefs, attitudes, or emotions that accompany that learning.

> "AUTHOR: What's the thing you love to do the most?
> ROSALIE: Well, I guess it's writing, but also math, and reading.
> AUTHOR: Can you put your finger on why you like writing the best of those three?
> ROSALIE: Well, I can express my feelings. In reading a book, the feelings are already there, and you get to read the feelings of the author. But in math there isn't very much feeling, and in writing you get to express *your* feelings." (36,p. 88)

The affect of students also plays an important role in the teaching process. Teachers observe (perhaps unconsciously) the affective reactions of their students during instruction. These observations about the class and its individual members provide information for the teacher as he or she makes decisions about (a) how to structure the curriculum for the year, (b) how much and which content to teach on a particular day, (c) how well students understand the material during a class period, (d) whether to change the sequence of activities planned for the day when student behavior and/ or understanding indicates, (e) how long to spend on a particular section of a lesson, or (f) when to suggest that a particular student come in before or after school for some extra help and encouragement. In short, teachers' preactive (before instruction) and interactive (during instruction) thinking and decision making are based, in part, on the affective characteristics of students.

> "AUTHOR: Why is (math) fun?
> SEAN: . . . Probably because I use my mind a lot when I do math." (36, p. 144)

The importance of affect is reflected in the *Professional Teaching Standards* (35) and the *Curriculum and Evaluation Standards* (34). Standard 6 of the *Professional Teaching Standards* recommends that the teacher "should engage in ongoing analysis of teaching and learning" (p. 63). This analysis includes an examination of the effects of instruction on students' dispositions toward mathematics, that is, on students' confidence, interest, enjoyment, and perseverance. Also, in the *Curriculum and Evaluation Standards*, two of the five general goals for all students in grades K–12 are affective, that is, value mathematics and become confident of one's ability.

Definition of Affect

Finding a clear definition of what is meant by affect and affective domain has been a persistent problem in understanding the connections between affect and mathematics teaching and learning. The definition of affect most commonly used by educators stems from the *Taxonomy of Educational Objectives: The Affective Domain* (22). In this definition, the affective domain includes attitudes, beliefs, appreciations, tastes and preferences, emotions, feelings, and values. Similarly, McLeod (31) used *affective domain* "to refer to a wide range of feelings and moods that are generally regarded as something different from pure cognition" (p. 245) and included attitudes, beliefs, and emotions. A definition of affect that is narrower in scope includes feelings, emotions, and moods but not beliefs, attitudes, appreciations, and values (18). This narrower view of affect focuses on gut level emotional responses that rise quickly and spontaneously. In this chapter, the term *affective factors* will be used as Krathwohl et al. (22) defined it; that is, the definition will include not only feelings and emotions but also beliefs, attitudes, values, and appreciations.

"Mark described how he felt about his success with math problems: 'It made me feel peppy. . . . It made me want to laugh.'" (36, p. 192)

The Changes of Early Adolescence

During early adolescence (the period from age 10 to 14), students experience a number of transformations that affect them deeply. Physically, middle grades students change more than at any other time in their lives except infancy, although during infancy children are not nearly so aware of the growth and changes occurring in their bodies (46). Between the ages of 10 and 14, students begin to experience the physical changes associated with puberty. Early adolescents undergo a growth spurt in height and weight, they see their bodies change from child shapes to adult shapes, and they begin (and perhaps complete) the hormonal, glandular, and other physical changes that bring about adult reproductive capability. During early adolescence, students also change cognitively. They begin to develop formal operational thinking—the ability to think abstractly, hypothetically, and logically without access to concrete objects. However, the majority of seventh and eighth graders are still in Piaget's stage of concrete operations (5). (See the cognition chapter in this volume for a more detailed discussion of middle grades students' cognitive characteristics.) Related to these physical and cognitive changes, early adolescents also change socially and emotionally. Socially, middle grades students begin to focus more of their attention on the development of peer relationships and less on pleasing parents (12). This process of becoming detached from parents and established among peers can bring major changes in who the student talks to most frequently and how the student comes to see himself or herself as a student and as a person. Emotionally, early adolescents are in the process of adapting to the physical, cognitive, and social changes occurring in their lives as they try to understand the persons they are becoming.

Another important event in the lives of early adolescents that can affect their performance and attitudes in school is the move from an elementary school setting to a middle school or junior high setting. Although there is great variability in classroom and school organization in both elementary and middle grades schools, students typically have several different teachers daily in the middle school or junior high while they have one or two teachers for the majority of their academic instruction in the elementary school. Elementary schools usually provide a more protective environment while schools for early adolescents are often larger, more impersonal, and more departmentalized (7). There is a greater risk of students getting "lost in the crowd" in the middle grades than there was when they were in elementary school. There is evidence of a drop in self-esteem for some students as they adjust to the differences between the elementary school and the middle school (44). Students seem particularly susceptible to lower self-esteem if they are in the midst of the spurt in physical growth associated with puberty when they change schools (4). In addition, there is research evidence that girls struggle more than boys with the elementary to middle grades transition, probably because of the timing of puberty (43). (On the average, girls go through puberty 1½ to 2 years before boys.)

Based on what is known about 10- to 14-year-olds and the kind of school organization that supports them, mathematics teaching in the middle grades should take into account more than the cognitive characteristics and learning of students. The great cognitive, physical, social, and emotional changes early adolescents are experiencing, and the relationship of these changes to school success, add to the argument for the importance of attention to affect in middle grades mathematics teaching and learning.

Research on Specific Affective Factors

Confidence in Learning Mathematics

Confidence in learning mathematics has to do with how sure a person is of being able to perform well in mathematics, learn new topics in mathematics, and do well on mathematics tests. Confidence is one of the most important affective factors studied by mathematics education researchers. It plays a role in students' mathematics achievement and ability to solve nonroutine problems. There is also evidence of theoretical or empirical connections between confidence in learning mathematics and students' achievement motivation, intrinsic motivation, self-concept, and self-esteem. In addition, confidence in learning mathematics is helpful in explaining gender differences in mathematics achievement and course taking.

In the mid-1970s, Fennema and Sherman (14) developed paper-and-pencil instruments to measure both confidence in learning mathematics and mathematics anxiety. Since these two constructs are based on different theoretical frameworks, it was expected that the subscales would measure different characteristics of students. However, students' scores on the confidence and anxiety subscales were strongly correlated (14). Therefore, teachers will probably find it necessary to use only one of the two Fennema-Sherman attitude subscales. In situations where either subscale could be used, we recommend the confidence in learning mathematics subscale, both because it has been used more frequently and because of the more positive affective perspective it represents.

> **Excerpt from an eighth-grade student during a problem-solving interview done by Jamie Walker: "I'm having brain block."**

The data from each of the mathematics assessments of the National Assessment of Educational Progress (NAEP) included at least one item that was designed to measure the confidence in their own mathematical ability of the seventh-grade and 13-year-old students in the samples. In the 1986 NAEP, grade 7 and grade 11 students were asked to indicate their degree of agreement/disagreement with the statement: "I am good at mathematics" (10, p. 96). Sixty percent of the seventh graders indicated that they agreed or agreed strongly with the statement. This was about the same degree of confidence shown by the 13-year-old students in the 1982 NAEP, who were more confident of their mathematical abilities than the 13-year-old students in the 1978 NAEP. There is evidence of a drop in confidence in mathematical ability for both male and female students from age 13 to age 17. This result must be viewed with some caution, however, beause the data are not longitudinal (10).

Confidence in learning mathematics shows one of the strongest positive relationships with mathematics achievement of any affective variable (15, 33, 39). In a longitudinal study that followed students from grades 6 through 12, Meyer (32) found that confidence in learning mathematics was the best affective predictor of later mathematics achievement and course taking.

> **From grade 6 to grade 12, confidence in learning mathematics was a better predictor of mathematics achievement and mathematics course taking for females than for males. (32)**

Lester, Garofalo, and Kroll (28) studied confidence, interest, and beliefs as influences on the problem-solving behavior of seventh-grade students. They found that one of the groups of four students they studied was at times "almost helpless in solving mathematical problems" (p. 80) because of a lack of confidence. They hypothesized that confidence in learning mathematics, student beliefs about mathematics, and student beliefs about problem solving are "dominant forces in shaping" (28, p. 85) students' mathematical behavior.

"VIRGINIA: When I'm doing math, I'm really bored. . . . It's kind of dull because it's not words. . . . In writing, . . . you get to decide how it's going to end up, but in math it has to have one [right answer]. Otherwise, it's wrong." (36, p. 112)

Much of our knowledge about confidence in learning mathematics has come from research about gender-related differences in mathematics achievement and course taking. (See 33 and 39 for a more complete review.) When there is a gender difference in students' confidence in learning mathematics, the male students typically express greater confidence in their ability than do the female students (10, 15, 16). In addition, confidence is an important predictor of enrollment in optional high school mathematics courses for both male and female students (15, 24); however, it is a better predictor for female students than for male students (32). Thus, there is strong evidence of the relationship between confidence and gender-related differences in mathematics achievement and course taking.

Stanic and Reyes (45) studied a high-average seventh-grade mathematics class to understand the classroom process, cognitive, and affective factors related to student race and gender. They examined confidence in learning mathematics, enjoyment of mathematics, perceived usefulness of mathematics, and persistence in the mathematics classroom through paper-and-pencil measures (14), student interviews, teacher interviews, and classroom observations. They concluded that confidence was the attitude most related to achievement among the four race-gender groups (African American females, African American males, white females, and white males), although they found it difficult to separate confidence from usefulness and enjoyment. They also found evidence of differences in confidence among the four race-gender groups, with the white females and (to some degree) the African American males expressing less confidence.

Although white students consistently outperform African American and Hispanic students in mathematics achievement, African American and Hispanic students tend to enjoy mathematics more than white students do. (10)

During the middle grades, students are developing views of themselves that they will carry into high school and on into adulthood. There is evidence that students' confidence during these years has long-term implications for their mathematics achievement and decisions about what mathematics courses to take in high school. There is also evidence that a lack of confidence can undermine our attempts to involve middle grades students in problem solving. We suggest that teachers find ways to estimate how confident their students are in mathematics. The confidence subscale of the Fennema-Sherman Mathematics Attitude Scales (14) provides one good source of information. The confidence score along with information from teacher observations and conversations with students will help teachers determine how confident their students are and how this level of confidence contributes to students' achievement and future plans to take mathematics courses.

For female and minority students, we need to be particularly aware of the relationship between confidence and plans to take optional mathematics courses in the future. There is evidence that girls underestimate their ability in mathematics (15). Therefore, it may be necessary for teachers, parents, and counselors to provide more encouragement for girls and other students who are less confident of their ability to learn mathematics. The encouragement we provide to students who have more potential than they realize may be extremely important for their future.

Perceived Usefulness of Mathematics

Perceived usefulness of mathematics is another important affective factor. This is reflected by the inclusion of "learning to value mathematics" (p. 5) as one of the five major goals for all students in the *Curriculum and Evaluation Standards* (34). The logical rationale for why perceptions of usefulness are important is related to mathematics being seen as a difficult subject that students are required to take only through the ninth or tenth grade. Beyond that time, important mathematics courses are available, but students (with the help of their parents, teachers, and counselors) must decide whether to enroll in these optional courses. Students who do not like mathematics, who do not see themselves as able in mathematics, and who view mathematics as having little use for them in the future will be less likely to decide to take a difficult, optional mathematics course than students who perceive mathematics as useful for them. Students who see mathematics as necessary for their future career plans will probably enroll in optional mathematics courses even if they do not enjoy mathematics.

> "MARK: I just don't enjoy math as well as I enjoy writing and science and art and stuff like that.
> AUTHOR: So you go ahead and do math anyway?
> MARK: Yeah.
> AUTHOR: And why do you do that?
> MARK: Because I want to go to Harvard or Yale or a college like that and become a heart surgeon. And math does have something to do with heart surgery. But I don't enjoy it as much as I enjoy writing." (36, p. 172)

In the 1986 NAEP (10), seventh-grade and eleventh-grade students were asked to respond to statements about the usefulness of mathematics. Four out of five students in grades 7 and 11 agreed or strongly agreed with the statement: "Most of mathematics has practical use" (p. 100). About three out of four of the seventh- and eleventh-grade students agreed or strongly agreed with the statement: "Mathematics is useful in solving everyday problems" (p. 100). These results show a very positive view of the usefulness of mathematics by students. In another item students were asked, "When you think about what you will do when you are older, do you expect that you will work in an area that requires mathematics" (10, p. 100)? Forty-four percent of the seventh graders and 47% of the eleventh graders responded yes. On the first two items, there was no difference between the responses of the female and male students; however, on the third item, more male students than female students at both grade levels expected to work in an area requiring mathematics. Other studies have found that male high school students more than female high school students perceive mathematics as useful to them (6, 15). A comparison of the responses of white students, African American students, and Hispanic students on the same three NAEP items shows slightly lower perceptions of usefulness by African Americans and Hispanics at the seventh-grade level. The only large difference among the three racial groups for the seventh graders was on the third item; the Hispanic students indicated a lower expectation than the white students to work in an area requiring mathematics.

The role of perceived usefulness as a predictor of students' intentions and actual enrollment in optional mathematics courses has been examined. Perceived usefulness has been identified as the most important affective predictor (after controlling for prior achievement) of students' plans to enroll in additional high school mathematics courses (37, 3). Other studies have found usefulness to be important in prediction of enrollment plans but not as important as confidence (42).

Ask students once a week to write anonymously about the topics they had most difficulty understanding, understood most easily, enjoyed the most, and enjoyed the least. This will give you specific feedback about particular mathematics topics and instructional activities.

One study (45) compared seventh-grade students' perceptions of the usefulness of mathematics as shown in students' responses to a paper-and-pencil instrument and an individual interview. On the usefulness scale (14), the student ratings were uniformly positive although the white females' ratings were lower than those of the white males, African American females, and African American males. In the student interviews, researchers found a different picture. The seventh graders in the class could say very little on their own about the usefulness of mathematics. One African American female student with one of the highest scores on the paper-and-pencil usefulness scale could find virtually nothing to say in the interview about the usefulness of mathematics. She said she had not thought much about what she would do after high school, was not sure whether she would use mathematics, and was not sure why she had to study mathematics. All the other students either gave examples of how mathematics was useful or at least said that it was useful. However, most of their perceptions of the usefulness of mathematics were limited. For example, students said they needed mathematics to know how to count, or to be able to figure out the cost of something at the store, or to be able to balance a checkbook. Not one of the students was able to go beyond a shallow description of why mathematics is useful even though they responded positively on the paper-and-pencil measure.

In summary, student perception of the usefulness of mathematics is one of the most important affective characteristics. It has a clear relationship to students' decisions to take optional mathematics courses and helps to explain the gender and race differences in mathematics course election. Of particular interest are the results (10, 45) that students view mathematics as useful, but this perception is limited in scope and depth.

What can we do as teachers? There is evidence in the motivation literature (see later section of this chapter) that students will be more involved in mathematics problems they view as having uses beyond the classroom. It may be that by emphasizing real-world problems in the middle grades mathematics curriculum we can deepen students' understanding of the value and uses of mathematics. The current emphasis on computation of whole and rational numbers in the grade 6, 7, and 8 curriculum may contribute to a limited view of the ways

---

"DAVID: . . . in the math now you get kind of bored with it because you already know the stuff or you're just repeating what you're learning. . . . It's not real fun if you just have to repeat everything 'cause it's not like you're learning 'cause you already know how to do it. It's just that you're repeating and repeating and repeating." (36, p. 151)

---

mathematics is used in work and the role it plays in the functioning of our society. Discussing how mathematics is used in the careers of people in all walks of life, not just those who are viewed as mathematicians and scientists, can expand students' perceptions of the usefulness of mathematics.

Persistence in the Mathematics Classroom

Persistence has to do with continuing to work on a mathematics problem even when the answer or the method of solution is not apparent. A model of autonomous learning behaviors and problem solving (13) included persistence as one of the autonomous learning behaviors. Persistence was part of the model because of its importance in mathematical problem solving. The *Professional Teaching Standards* (35) also encourages teachers to foster students' persistence in Standard 5: Learning Environment. This standard recommends that teachers create a learning environment in which students have the "time necessary to explore sound mathematics and grapple with significant ideas and problems" (p. 57).

Excerpt from an eighth-grade student during a problem-solving interview conducted by Jamie Walker: "I don't like problems that take a long time."

Stanic and Reyes (45) studied the extent to which students in the seventh-grade class they observed persisted on mathematics problems during day-to-day classroom life. It was easier for them to find examples of students quickly giving up on a problem than it was to find positive examples of persistence in the face of difficulty. Students had only rare opportunities to demonstrate a willingness to work on something difficult on their own over an extended period of time. Continuing to struggle by themselves in the face of difficulty was rarely encouraged or observed. Neither the higher nor lower ability students in the class demonstrated persistence. The higher ability students had almost no opportunity to struggle with a mathematics problem because most of the work was easy for them; the lower ability students did face difficulties but had little opportunity to persist because of the pace of instruction. Furthermore, the students were never taught how to deal with difficulty other than to ask for help immediately. The goal in the class was clearly not to learn through extended efforts but to get answers and complete assignments. The students did not really have to persist to get an answer, especially on those tests and assignments that were presented in a multiple-choice format.

So, as teachers, we might ask ourselves how often we provide students with the opportunity to struggle with an appropriately difficult mathematics problem over a period of time. Because of the rarity of this experience for students, we may find it necessary to teach students strategies to use when they are working on a difficult problem over a period of several days. Also, we may find it valuable to evaluate the degree to which our interactions with students foster persistence. Does the student simply want to get an answer or is the student willing to struggle in order to understand a concept?

Student Motivation to Learn

Motivation has to do with "why people pursue certain goals instead of others" (2, p. xi). The research literature in mathematics education has examined only limited aspects of the psychological literature on achievement motivation. Leder (25) and Fennema and her colleagues (e.g., 17) have examined achievement motivation through the attributions of female and male students about why they are successful or unsuccessful in mathematics. Kloosterman (21) provides an extensive review of one portion of the literature on achievement motivation in order to set a clear theoretical context for his research on attributions, learned helplessness, and mastery orientation. The work of these three scholars is excellent and of interest to teachers. In this section, other areas of theory and research on achievement motivation are presented to highlight areas that are important to mathematics teachers yet have not been the focus of much research attention by mathematics educators.

Extrinsic Rewards and Punishments and Intrinsic Motivation. Extrinsic motivation and intrinsic motivation are concepts important to the understanding of motivation and classroom teaching. Intrinsic motivation exists when a student pursues a task because of the inherent value of the task rather than some external incentive. Extrinsic motivation exists when a student is involved in a task for reasons other than the nature of the task itself (e.g., grades, pleasing parents, avoiding punishment from the teacher). The use of extrinsic rewards to motivate students is based on principles of operant conditioning (20) and may involve rewards and punishments ranging from candies to check marks to verbal feedback. Rewards and punishments based on operant conditioning are used widely in classroom settings. It is assumed that behavior that is rewarded will increase in frequency and behavior that is punished will decrease in frequency.

There is support for the use of extrinsic rewards and punishments under appropriate conditions to aid in motivating students to be task oriented in learning situations (e.g., 9, 27). However, many teachers and administrators are not aware of the "hidden costs" of certain uses of extrinsic rewards to control student behavior and motivate learning (e.g., 9, 27, 29). Many studies using a wide variety of tasks, incentives, and subjects have shown that superfluous extrinsic rewards can actually decrease intrinsic motivation. When a person initially has strong intrinsic interest in an activity and when extrinsic rewards are salient, the extrinsic rewards can decrease the intrinsic motivation of the individual to engage in the activity again. In addition:

> When tangible rewards are based on task performance, . . . and convey to children clear positive information about their high competence and ability at an activity, the rewards will generally be less likely to undermine later intrinsic interest than when they are offered simply for task engagement. Similarly, rewards that have some integral . . . relationship to the activity for which they have been provided will be less likely to undermine interest than those that bear a more arbitrary . . . relationship to the task undertaken. (27, p. 78)

"Unnecessarily powerful extrinsic rewards, functionally superfluous temporal deadlines, and excessive adult surveillance all can be shown to have negative effects on children's later intrinsic interest in the activity." (27, p. 77)

When a student's intrinsic interest is reduced by unnecessary extrinsic rewards, there are both immediate and later effects. A number of these effects are of concern to teachers (27). Students tend to focus their energies only on the aspects of the task to be evaluated. Less effort is spent on any parts of the task that are seen by students as unnecessary for receiving the extrinsic reward. For example, in one study, the choice by students of which problems to attempt was affected when they were offered a reward only for the number of problems they solved correctly. Students selected easier problems than they would have if there had been no rewards, even though they found the more difficult problems more interesting (19).

Perhaps of even greater concern to mathematics educators, the use of unnecessary extrinsic rewards also undermines student performance on tasks requiring nonalgorithmic, creative, or insightful thinking. Performance on nonroutine problem solving and application tasks in mathematics is affected negatively. In addition, students are more likely to make more illogical guesses and work in a less systematic fashion when extrinsic rewards are given for a task that is already of intrinsic interest. Another effect of unnecessary extrinsic rewards is that students are less likely to choose an activity for which they were rewarded earlier when rewards are no longer available.

Sources of Intrinsic Motivation.   Researchers also have proposed ways of supporting students' intrinsic interest in learning activities. Malone and Lepper (30) identified four sources of intrinsic motivation in learning activities: (a) provide an appropriate level of challenge, (b) appeal to the sense of curiosity, (c) provide the learner with a sense of control, and (d) encourage the learner to be involved in a world of fantasy.

For an activity to be at an appropriate level of challenge it must be at a difficulty level that is neither so simple it is trivial nor so difficult it is viewed as impossible. In addition, the activity must present a goal that has meaning for the student and engages the student's self-esteem. Related to level of challenge is the need of students

> "... in relation to math problems.
> AUTHOR: Is it more fun if it's hard, or if it's easy?
> TOMMY: It's better if it's hard ... well ... not that hard.
> AUTHOR: Just the right amount of hard?
> TOMMY: Yeah. If it's too hard, I have to ask my Dad to help me." (36, p. 151)

to see themselves as competent. They can do this by exercising and extending their abilities. The competence students feel when they are successful helps motivate them. Yet this success cannot come from tasks that are too easy or familiar because intrinsic motivation depends on a continual process of learning new skills and ideas and thereby expanding the scope of what can be comfortably attempted (9, 47).

Curiosity is a crucial source of intrinsic motivation. Activities that stimulate curiosity highlight ideas that are surprising or discrepant from the student's current knowledge and understanding. Ideas that conflict with a student's present conception can lead to a search for information and explanations to resolve the inconsistency. However, as with level of challenge, disparities that are too large may be rejected and those that are too small may be ignored.

A third important source of intrinsic motivation is the student's sense of control over the environment, that is, a perception that outcomes are a result of the student's own actions (30). Deci and Ryan (9) go further and suggest that students need to be self-determining for intrinsic motivation to occur. With self-determination the student has a choice in deciding what to do. Learning activities that promote student

> "VIRGINIA: Unless you have a math problem that you make up yourself, and you get to answer in a different way. ... Then it gets fun, but if you're just doing problems like out of a book or something, it's not very fun." (36, p. 115)

involvement in a world of make-believe and fantasy can also promote intrinsic motivation. Fantasy situations may allow students to experience vicariously rewards and satisfactions that might not be available to them otherwise (27). Further, the introduction of fantasy in learning activities may provide relevance and meaningfulness in tasks that might be seen as mundane.

The Continuous Impulse to Learn.   Oldfather (36) developed the concept of the continuous impulse to learn, that is, the desire to go on learning. The source of the continuing impulse to learn is the pleasure of learning rather than seeking of approval

> "Certainly the material world is too diverse and too complex for a child to become familiar with all of it in the course of [a] school career. The best one can do is to make such knowledge, such familiarity, seem interesting and accessible to the child. That is, one can familiarize children with a few phenomena in such a way as to catch their interest, to let them raise and answer their own questions, to let them realize that their ideas are significant—so that they have the interest, the ability, and the self-confidence to go on by themselves." (11, p. 8)

or rewards from a parent or teacher or the avoidance of punishment. In a qualitative study of fifth and sixth graders, the continuing impulse to learn

> was linked, above all else, to activities involving self-expression. The depth of thought and feeling and action that were part of their experience of self-expression brought the meaning of self-expression to a new level: a level which involved deep engagement, self-discovery, and empowerment. *They found their own voices. . . . Not only did students gain their own voices: their voices were heard, taken seriously, acted upon, and honored.* (36, pp. 226–227)

There was considerable consensus among the students about the kinds of curriculum that were motivating to them (36). They preferred material that went beyond the surface level; material that was relevant to them and came from "real books" rather than textbooks; having some choice in what to do; and a level of challenge and pacing of the curriculum that fit them as individuals. The characteristics of a motivating teacher as described by the students in the study were "supportive, caring, understanding, sharing mutual trust and respect, listening to and respecting diverse opinions, offering choices, explaining things, not telling all the answers, being fun, humorous and enthusiastic, sharing interests, holding high expectations, giving specific feedback, and being accessible" (36, p. 234).

Conclusion

We should become more aware of the beliefs and attitudes our students hold about mathematics. One way to gain this information is to use formal instruments. Good instruments are available by Fennema and Sherman (14), Sandman (41), Fennema, Wolleat, and Pedro (17), and others. Space limitations prevent a full discussion of formal instruments and how to score them; however, excellent references are published elsewhere (23, 26, 33, 38, 40). Other ways to assess attitudes include interviewing students and having students keep journals about their experiences in mathematics (1). Some teachers ask students once a week to take a half sheet of paper and write anonymously about the topics they had most difficulty understanding, understood most easily, enjoyed the most, and enjoyed the least. This approach can provide helpful information for teachers and give students a safe way to let the teacher know what they are thinking and feeling. In addition, day-to-day interactions in the classroom will reveal some aspects of student affect; however, paper-and-pencil instruments, interviews, and journals can reveal much that might not be apparent under normal classroom circumstances.

In this chapter we have presented some results of research. It is our conviction that information about students' confidence in doing mathematics, perceptions of its usefulness, persistence, and motivation along with other affective topics (such as beliefs about the nature of mathematics, attributions of success and failure, fear of the consequences of success, performance following failure, mathematics anxiety, and emotional reactions to mathematics) can help teachers provide better mathematics instruction for middle grades students.

Looking Ahead . . .

Student affect in mathematics has been studied mainly through the use of paper-and-pencil instruments and individual interviews with students. There are few cases where affect has been studied in the context of instruction in mathematics classrooms. I think student attitudes and motivation differ based on characteristics of classrooms and instruction, such as the type of assignment, the mathematics topic, the classroom environment, the method of presenting material used by the teacher, and the way in which student interactions with their teacher and peers are structured. One way to move beyond our current understanding of the role of affect in mathematics teaching and learning is to study student affect in the classroom context, documenting the affect of individual students in particular classroom situations over an extended length of time. Classrooms in which there is a problem-solving environment (e.g., 8) might provide especially fruitful sites for such investigations.

Laurie E. Hart

I have learned a great deal about my students' problem-solving processes and affect by conducting interviews with individual students. I encourage teachers to select two or three students and find a time outside of class to conduct think-aloud interviews. I present the students with a nonroutine problem and ask them to solve the problem and, as they do so, tell me what they are thinking about. After the students have finished working on the problem, I ask them to go back and chart the positive and negative emotions they experienced as they worked. I have learned a lot about what my students know and how they feel about mathematics.

Jamie Walker

About the Authors

Laurie E. Hart is a faculty member in middle school education at the University of Georgia. She teaches courses about early adolescents and research on teaching and directs a project to evaluate the long-term effects of middle school organization on students' attitudes, motivation, and higher order thinking.

Jamie Walker teaches eighth-grade mathematics at Oconee County Intermediate School in Watkinsville, Georgia. She is a graduate student in middle school education at the University of Georgia. She is interested in having her students feel confident about their ability to think and develop strategies for solving problems.

References

1. ADAMS, V. M. (1989). Affective issues in teaching problem solving: A teacher's perspective. In D. B. McLeod & V. M. Adams (Eds.), *Affect and mathematical problem solving* (pp. 192–201). New York: Springer-Verlag.
2. AMES, R., & AMES, C. (Eds.). (1984). *Research on motivation in education: Vol. 1. Student motivation.* Orlando, FL: Academic Press.
3. ARMSTRONG, J. M., & PRICE, R. A. (1982). Correlates and predictors of women's mathematics participation. *Journal for Research in Mathematics Education, 13*(2), 99–109.
4. BLYTH, D. A., SIMMONS, R. G., & ZAKIN, D. F. (1985). Satisfaction with body image for early adolescent females: The impact of pubertal timing within different school environments. *Youth and Adolescence, 14*(3), 207–225.
5. BROOKS, M., FUSCO, E., & GRENNON, J. (1983). Cognitive levels matching. *Educational Leadership, 40*(8), 4–8.
6. BRUSH, L. (1980). *Encouraging girls in mathematics: The problem and the solution.* Cambridge, MA: ABT Books.
7. CARNEGIE COUNCIL ON ADOLESCENT DEVELOPMENT. (1989). *Turning points: Preparing American youth for the 21st century.* Washington, DC: Carnegie Corporation of New York.
8. COBB, P., YACKEL, E., & WOOD, T. (1989). Young children's emotional acts while engaged in mathematical problem solving. In D. B. McLeod & V. M. Adams (Eds.), *Affect and mathematical problem solving* (pp. 117–148). New York: Springer-Verlag.
9. DECI, E. L., & RYAN, R. M. (1985). *Intrinsic motivation and self-determination in human behavior.* New York: Plenum.
10. DOSSEY, J. A., MULLIS, I. V. S., LINDQUIST, M. M., & CHAMBERS, D. L. (1988). *The mathematics report card: Are we measuring up? Trends in achievement based on the 1986 national assessment.* Princeton, NJ: Educational Testing Service.
11. DUCKWORTH, E. (1987). *"The having of wonderful ideas" and other essays on teaching and learning.* New York: Teachers College Press.
12. ERIKSON, E. H. (1968). *Identity, youth, and crisis.* New York: Norton.
13. FENNEMA, E., & PETERSON, P. (1985). Autonomous learning behavior: A possible explanation of gender-related differences in mathematics. In L. C. Wilkinson & C. B. Marrett (Eds.), *Gender-related differences in classroom interaction* (pp. 17–35). New York: Academic Press.
14. FENNEMA, E., & SHERMAN, J. (1976). Fennema-Sherman Mathematics Attitude Scales. *JSAS: Catalog of Selected Documents in Psychology, 6*(1), 31. (Ms. No. 1225)
15. FENNEMA, E., & SHERMAN, J. (1977). Sex-related differences in mathematics achievement, spatial visualization, and affective factors. *American Educational Research Journal, 14*(1), 51–71.
16. FENNEMA, E., & SHERMAN, J. (1978). Sex-related differences in mathematics achievement and related factors: A further study. *Journal for Research in Mathematics Education, 9*(3), 189–203.
17. FENNEMA, E., WOLLEAT, P., & PEDRO, J. D. (1979). Mathematics Attribution Scale. *JSAS: Catalog of Selected Documents in Psychology, 9*(5), 26. (Ms. No. 1837)
18. HART, L. E. (1989). Describing the affective domain: Saying what we mean. In D. B.

McLeod & V. M. Adams (Eds.), *Affect and mathematical problem solving* (pp. 37–45). New York: Springer-Verlag.

19. HARTER, S. (1978). Effectance motivation reconsidered: Toward a developmental model. *Human Development, 1*(1), 34–64.

20. KELLER, F. S. (1969). *Learning: Reinforcement theory* (2nd ed.). New York: Random House.

21. KLOOSTERMAN, P. (1990). Attributions, performance following failure, and motivation in mathematics. In E. Fennema & G. C. Leder (Eds.), *Mathematics and gender* (pp. 96–127). New York: Teachers College Press.

22. KRATHWOHL, D. R., BLOOM, B. S., & MASIA, B. B. (1964). *Taxonomy of educational objectives: Handbook 2. Affective domain.* New York: David McKay.

23. KULM, G. (1980). Research on mathematics attitude. In R. J. Shumway (Ed.), *Research in mathematics education* (pp. 356–387). Reston, VA: National Council of Teachers of Mathematics.

24. LANTZ, A. E., & SMITH, G. P. (1981). Factors influencing the choice of nonrequired mathematics courses. *Journal of Educational Psychology, 73*, 825–837.

25. LEDER, G. C. (1984). Sex differences in attributions of success and failure. *Psychological Reports, 54*(1), 57–58.

26. LEDER, G. C. (1985). Measurement of attitude to mathematics. *For the Learning of Mathematics, 5*(3), 18–21, 34.

27. LEPPER, M. R., & HODELL, M. (1989). Intrinsic motivation in the classroom. In C. Ames & R. Ames (Eds.), *Research on motivation in education: Vol. 3. Goals and cognitions* (pp. 73–105). Orlando, FL: Academic Press.

28. LESTER, F. K., GAROFALO, J., & KROLL, D. L. (1989). Self-confidence, interest, beliefs, and metacognition: Key influences on problem-solving behavior. In D. B. McLeod & V. M. Adams (Eds.), *Affect and mathematical problem solving* (pp. 75–88). New York: Springer-Verlag.

29. MAEHR, M. L. (1976). Continuing motivation: An analysis of a seldom considered educational outcome. *Review of Educational Research, 46*(3), 443–462.

30. MALONE, T. W., & LEPPER, M. R. (1987). Making learning fun: A taxonomy of intrinsic motivations for learning. In R. E. Snow & M. J. Farr (Eds.), *Aptitude, learning, and instruction: Vol. 3. Conative and affective process analyses.* Hillsdale, NJ: Erlbaum.

31. McLEOD, D. B. (1989). Beliefs, attitudes, and emotions: New views of affect in mathematics education. In D. B. McLeod & V. M. Adams (Eds.), *Affect and mathematical problem solving* (pp. 245–258). New York: Springer-Verlag.

32. MEYER, M. R. (1986). The prediction of mathematics achievement and participation for females and males: A longitudinal study of affective variables (Doctoral dissertation, University of Wisconsin-Madison, 1985). *Dissertation Abstracts International, 47*, 819A.

33. MEYER, M. R., & KOEHLER, M. S. (1990). Internal influences on gender differences in mathematics. In E. Fennema & G. C. Leder (Eds.), *Mathematics and gender* (pp. 60–95). New York: Teachers College Press.

34. NATIONAL COUNCIL OF TEACHERS OF MATHEMATICS. (1989). *Curriculum and evaluation standards for school mathematics.* Reston, VA: Author.

35. NATIONAL COUNCIL OF TEACHERS OF MATHEMATICS. (1991). *Professional standards for teaching mathematics.* Reston, VA: Author.

36. OLDFATHER, P. (1991). *Students' perceptions of their own reasons/purposes for being or not being involved in learning activities: A qualitative study of student motivation.* Unpublished doctoral dissertation, Claremont Graduate School, Claremont, CA.

37. PEDRO, J. D., WOLLEAT, P., FENNEMA, E., & BECKER, A. D. (1981). Election of high

school mathematics by females and males: Attributions and attitudes. *American Educational Research Journal, 18*(2), 207–218.

38. REYES, L. H. (1981). Attitudes and mathematics. In M. M. Lindquist (Ed.), *Selected issues in mathematics education* (pp. 161–184). Berkeley, CA: McCutchan.

39. REYES, L. H. (1984). Affective variables and mathematics education. *Elementary School Journal, 84*(5), 558–581.

40. REYES, L. H., & STANIC, G. M. A. (1988). Race, sex, socioeconomic status, and mathematics. *Journal for Research in Mathematics Education, 19*(1), 26–43.

41. SANDMAN, R. The Mathematics Attitude Inventory: Instrument and user's manual. *Journal for Research in Mathematics Education, 11*(2), 148–149.

42. SHERMAN, J., & FENNEMA, E. (1977). The study of mathematics by high school girls and boys: Related variables. *American Educational Research Journal, 14*(2), 159–168.

43. SIMMONS, R. G., & BLYTH, D. A. (1987). *Moving into adolescence: The impact of pubertal change and school context.* Hawthorne, NY: Aldine de Gruyler.

44. SIMMONS, R. G., ROSENBERG, F., & ROSENBERG, M. (1973). Disturbance in the self-image at adolescence. *American Sociological Review, 38,* 553–568.

45. STANIC, G. M. A., & REYES, L. H. (1989, March). *Attitudes and achievement-related behaviors of middle school mathematics students: Views through four lenses.* Paper presented at the annual meeting of the American Educational Research Association, San Francisco.

46. THORNBURG, H. D., & ARAS, Z. (1986). Physical characteristics of developing adolescents. *Journal of Adolescent Research, 1*(1), 47–78.

47. WHITE, R. W. (1959). Motivation reconsidered: The concept of competence. *Psychological Review, 66,* 297–333.

PART II

Processes and Content

CHAPTER 3

Number Sense and Related Topics

Judith T. Sowder and Judith Kelin

> MYTH: *Arithmetic is the major goal of elementary school mathematics.*
> REALITY: *Number sense builds on arithmetic as words build on the alphabet.*
> *Numbers arise in measurement, in chance, in data, and in geometry, as well as*
> *in arithmetic. Mathematics in elementary school should weave all these threads*
> *together to create in children a robust sense of number. (22, p. 46)*

Part I: Research on Number Sense and Related Topics

Research related to number sense, computational estimation, mental computation, number size, and assessment is reviewed in this section; Part II explores number sense from a teacher's perspective.

Number Sense, In School and Out of School

"Children must understand numbers if they are to make sense of the ways numbers are used in their everyday world" (21, p. 38). This statement opens the discussion of the section from the *Curriculum and Evaluation Standards* focusing on number sense. According to the authors of this document, number sense is an intuition about numbers. Children with number sense will have developed meaning for numbers and number relationships, recognize relative magnitude of numbers and the effects of operating on numbers, and will have developed referents for quantities and measures.

NOTE: The preparation of this manuscript was partly supported by the National Science Foundation (Grant No. MDR 8751373). The opinions expressed here do not necessarily reflect the position, policy, or endorsement of the National Science Foundation.

"It may be more important, however, to consider all the activities of mathematical instruction as potential contributors to students' development of number sense. In addition to designing specific activities for the growth of number sense, we should think about how the rest of the activities of the curriculum can be designed and organized so they contribute positively to the growth of number sense." (9, p. 53)

If number sense is an intuition about numbers, then it might first be helpful to explore the topic of mathematical intuition. Resnick (28) has characterized mathematical intuition as self-evident to the person who has it and as easily accessible from the memory of that person. She proposes that concepts based on additive notions are acquired early and by almost everyone. However, when mathematics instruction focuses on symbol manipulation, poor students do not make appropriate associations between the symbols and their referents and are unable to develop new intuitions. Good students, on the other hand, correctly link symbols and concepts and spend time and energy trying to make sense of rules. In doing so, they develop intuitions about mathematics. Intuition provides "the basis for highly flexible applications of well-known concepts, notation, and transformational rules, . . . frees people from excessive reliance on fixed algorithms, and allows them to invent procedures for problems not previously encountered" (p. 188).

"Number sense is more related to intuitions and insights associated with numbers as quantities, rather than numbers as abstract, formal entities. There is a 'physical' aspect of responding to numbers; parts are 'tacked on' and 'knocked off' as needed." (44, p. 74)

Evidence that strong mathematical intuitions develop in out-of-school settings is accumulating. Carraher, Carraher, and Schliemann (2) interviewed Brazilian street vendors, ages 9–15 and all of whom had had at least 4 years of schooling, first during a normal sales transaction and later in a more formal setting. Children were consistently more successful during the sale than when the same problems were later presented to them. For example, when the examiner bought four coconuts at Cr $35.00 each (in Brazilian currency), the child said, "Three will be 105, plus 30, that's 135 . . . one coconut is 35 . . . that is . . . 140"; but in the formal interview, the child solved 35 × 4 as "4 times 5 is 20, carry the 2, 2 plus 3 is 5, times 4 is 20, 200" (p. 26). Saxe (35), also working in Brazil, compared the mathematical procedures of candy sellers of school age but with little or no schooling, candy sellers with up to 7 years of schooling, and school children who did not work in the streets. Schooling did not help sellers to get more correct answers. School children who were not sellers tended to use standard algorithmic strategies to solve problems and were less accurate than the sellers, who used street-learned regrouping strategies to solve problems. Investigations of mental computational methods of schooled and unschooled African children and adults (8) yielded similar results.

When calculations are performed out of school, people are continually engaged with the situation or objects and are unlikely to forget why they are doing the calculations, whereas in school, the calculation is highly symbolic and often without any meaningful context (29). Although the symbolization process is necessary, instruction that focuses on symbols without links to the concepts they represent leads to the kinds of errors noted in the Brazilian child's procedure for solving 35 × 4.

"To provide students with a lasting sense of number and number relationships, learning should be founded in experience related to aspects of everyday life or to the use of concrete materials designed to reflect underlying mathematical ideas." (*Curriculum and Evaluation Standards*, 21, p. 87)

How do we plan instruction that will allow children to attach meaning to symbols and assist them in developing strong intuitions about numbers? That is, how do we teach number sense? *Computational estimation* and *mental computation* are two ways of approaching number sense. Both can provide opportunities for flexible applications of concepts and operations, for inventing procedures to solve new problems, and for reflecting on numbers and their meaning within a problem. Exploration of *number size* through problems requiring comparing and ordering numbers can also lead to better number understanding. Research on these three topics is somewhat sparse but sufficient to provide evidence of the important role they should play in the mathematics curriculum.

Computational Estimation

In both the *Curriculum and Evaluation Standards for School Mathematics* (20) and in the position paper of the National Council of Supervisors of Mathematics, "Essential Mathematics for the Twenty-First Century" (21), there is a call for increased attention to estimation. These documents refer to three types of estimation. *Numeracy estimation* answers the question, "About how many?" Estimating the number of beans in a jar or the number of people in a stadium are examples of numeracy estimation. A second type of estimation requires finding a measurement without any measuring tools. This type of estimation, called *measurement estimation*, is covered in another chapter of this volume. A third type of estimation requires finding an approximate value for the result of a computation and is called *computational estimation*. Research on computational estimation is reviewed in this section.

How Do People Estimate? It is often helpful to look at the techniques used by people who have acquired a particular skill, especially if this acquisition is largely self-taught or at least not the result of instruction. These techniques should be quite natural and could form the basis for instruction for nonskilled individuals. This was the thinking behind a study undertaken by Reys, Rybolt, Bestgen, and Wyatt (31) who attempted to identify and characterize the computational processes used by good estimators. They found three key processes. The first was called reformulation and referred to changing the numbers to other numbers that were easier to manage mentally. Rounding was only one way of reformulating a problem used by good estimators. Another was to substitute "nice" numbers. For example, 79 ÷ 9 could be changed to 81 ÷ 9. Still a third way was to use equivalent (or nearly equivalent) forms of a number, like substituting 1/3 for 30%.

> "Is it more important for a student to be able to multiply 2507 × 4131 precisely or to be able to say that the result is about 10 million? Often, the approximate answer is not only sufficient, but it also provides more insight than the exact answer." (*Reshaping School Mathematics,* 23, p. 20)

A second process used by good estimators was called translation and referred to changing the structure of the problem so that the operations could be more easily carried out mentally. The problem (347 × 6) ÷ 43 could be changed to (350 × 6) ÷ 42 (reformulation) then to 350 × (6 ÷ 42) (translation). Now the problem is simply 350 × 1/7, or 350 ÷ 7, which is 50.

The third process good estimators used was compensation. Adjustments were made both during and after estimating. For example, 43 × 51 could be thought of as 40 × 50, or 2,000, but there are about three more 50s, so 2,150 would be a better estimate.

Looking at the work of poor estimators can also be very revealing. In one research study (43), children in grades 6–9 were given problems typical of those from the National Assessment of Educational Progress. Students who gave acceptable answers consistently demonstrated number sense, while those who gave unacceptable answers lacked understanding of the numbers in the problems.

> "INTERVIEWER: Can you estimate 0.52 × 789?
> STUDENT: Well, this (0.52) rounds to 1, and this (789) rounds to 800, and 1 × 800 is 800." (from a student interview by J. Sowder)

Good estimators have a good grasp of basic facts, place value, and arithmetic operations, are skilled at mental computation, are self-confident, tolerant of error, and flexible in their use of strategies (31). Three skills that seem particularly important in predicting performance on estimation are multiplying and dividing by powers of 10, choosing the larger or smaller of two numbers, and choosing which of two problems will yield a larger value (33). These three skills are not emphasized in most textbooks.

How Do Estimation Concepts and Skills Develop?   A small section on estimation might be found in current texts, but anyone who has been teaching for even a few years knows that it is a long-neglected topic. Yet we know that many people have learned to estimate.

Two recent studies provide some insight into the development of skills and concepts involved in the estimation process. In the first study (41), average-level students in grades 3, 5, 7, and 9 were presented with many examples of estimation done by hypothetical students and then asked questions about the estimation processes and solutions presented to them. Students at all grade levels preferred solutions obtained by computing first and then rounding to solutions obtained by rounding first and then computing. In fact, this preference increased with grade level. Apparently, the higher the grade level, the greater the students' concern was for getting as close to the exact answer as possible and knowing exactly how far the estimate was from the exact answer. Students at all levels were unwilling to accept two right answers, which, of course, are possible for estimation problems. As children became more proficient at rounding, they were less willing to deviate from the rounding rules they had learned even though other numbers clearly gave a better estimate. For example, estimating 4×267 as 4×250 gives a better estimate than 4×300, but children objected to rounding 267 to 250. Also, it was not until grade 9 that students seemed to understand the rationale for compensation.

> "Number sense is something that 'unfolds' rather than something that is 'taught' directly." (44, p. 75)

In the second study (4), the investigators first analyzed the cognitive demands of computational estimation. There are basically two components to estimation: approximating numbers and mentally computing with those numbers. According to Case's (3) theory of cognitive development, children cannot fully coordinate two such complex components until they are approximately 11 years old. After examining how children from kindergarten to twelfth grade approximate numbers, mentally compute, and estimate, the researchers concluded that we should not try to force estimation on children before they are ready. In lower grades, we should focus on mental computation and number size concepts. Any computational estimation problems introduced should be quite simple in nature, with limited memory requirements.

How Do Attitudes and Beliefs Affect Estimation Skills?　Most students believe that the exact answer is better than an estimate, and that, in fact, estimating is just guessing (41). It is difficult to become skilled at a process one does not understand or believe is useful. Good estimators have a good mathematical self-concept. They value estimation and are much less concerned about precision than are poor estimators (31).

These factors must be taken into account not only during instruction on estimation but also during instruction on other forms of computation. We cannot expect students to be willing to accept different processes and different solutions to the same problems that on the previous day had one correct process and one correct solution. We must demonstrate the value of estimation and, paradoxically, help students become more tolerant of error.

What Is Known about Teaching Estimation?　The strategies used by good estimators formed the basis for a middle school instructional program developed by Reys and his colleagues (32). Students in this program made progress toward a better understanding of estimation and of number concepts. The investigators concluded that for students to become really skilled at estimation, it had to be incorporated into their regular instruction over several years.

"I heard several participants counsel against the teaching of specific estimation strategies. I am in agreement that such teaching should not lead to a new set of algorithms (in this case, estimation algorithms) for the student to memorize. However, if the teaching is presented in a manner which promotes conversations among students as to the variety of approaches one might take to forming an estimate, then I believe these conversations could be extremely helpful to the learner. In this atmosphere, it would also seem appropriate for the teacher to propose strategies not highlighted by the students." (30, p. 71)

In a study limited to instruction on estimating with fractions, Mack (17) was quite successful in getting sixth-grade students to estimate sums and differences and then to use this knowledge to give meaning to the standard algorithms for adding and subtracting fractions. Mack suggests that all instruction on paper-and-pencil algorithms be postponed until students are able to form estimates for the operations. Owens (24) has made this same suggestion in the context of learning operations on decimal numbers.

Sowder and Markovits (39) investigated the effects of instruction on estimation where seventh-grade students had previously received instruction on mental computation and number size. Instead of directly teaching rules and strategies, the teachers provided students with carefully structured situations leading them to the discovery of rules and the invention of algorithms. Student responses to estimation problems in the concluding interview indicated that most had developed a better understanding of numbers and that they were able to use this understanding to solve many types of estimation problems.

Mental Computation

In an analysis of calculating, Plunkett (27) compared mental calculation algorithms with standard written algorithms. He showed that standard written algorithms are efficient, automatic, symbolic, general, and contracted; that is, they reduce several steps to one step. They encourage a person to carry out the steps without thinking about them. For all these reasons, they are excellent algorithms for written work, but they do not correspond to the ways people tend to think about numbers and, therefore, are not appropriate for mental computation. A mental algorithm is flexible and can be made up on the spot so it is appropriate for the problem. It requires understanding all along the way. It uses complete numbers rather than isolated digits.

"I returned to the counter, where a teen-age girl was now at the cash register. I counted the folders. 'Twenty-three at 12 cents each,' I said. 'That's $2.76 before tax.'
'You did that in your head?' she asked in amazement. 'How can you do that?'
'It's magic,' I said.
'Really?' she asked." (42, p. 93)

What Techniques Do Skilled Mental Calculators Use? A study of skilled and un-skilled mental calculators in secondary school (14) provides evidence that mental computation is related to understanding the structure of the number system. The students who were good at mental computation used a variety of strategies and, in particular, took advantage of the distributive property and of factoring. For example, many students distributed on 8×999 by thinking of 999 as $1,000 - 1$, $8 \times (1,000 - 1)$ is $8,000 - 8$, or $7,992$. To find 25×48, students used such factoring methods as $5 \times 5 \times 48$, so 5×48 is 240, and 5×240 is 1,200; or 25×48 is $100/4 \times 48$, which is $4,800/4$, which is 1,200. Skilled students showed other characteristics in their work. They avoided the carry operation because carrying required too many things to be remembered and led to errors. They kept a running total as they progressed. This technique was also less demanding on memory. They tended to work from left to right rather than right to left, as is required in the standard algorithms for addition, subtraction, and multiplication. Unskilled students, on the other hand, ignored obvious number properties and tried to carry out the pencil-and-paper procedures in their heads. For example, one student said she did 20×30 by putting the 30 on top and the 20 on the bottom, then began 0×0 is 0, and so on. She took 34 seconds to obtain the correct answer, but was unsure of it.

> "As I explained the testing procedures [to a highly skilled mental calculator], she remarked, 'I'm not very good at memorizing.' I commented that some people might regard her recall of squares as merely 'memorizing.' She exclaimed, 'But that's not memorizing. That's knowing and thinking.'" (13, p. 339)

How Should Mental Computation Be Taught? In order to maximize the development of number sense, instruction on mental computation should encourage students to explore different ways of doing problems, and discussions should include rationales for why one way is better than another or when it does not matter which way the problem is solved. For example, one student might think of $94 - 58$ as $96 - 60$, since adding the same thing to each number will not affect the difference. Another student might think $94 - 50$ is 44, minus 4 is 40, minus 4 more is 36. Still a third might count up: 2 to 60, then 30 to 90, and 4 more to 96, so $2 + 30 + 4$ is 36. A fourth might try $90 - 60$, then become confused and take $8 - 4$, arriving at 34. The class could discuss these four methods, and compare them with thinking $14 - 8$ is 6, cross out the 9, make it an 8, $8 - 5$ is 3, so 36. A well-guided discussion would result in the conclusion that the first three are all good ways, and if some students prefer one over the others, that is fine; but the fourth way leads to difficulties that are not easily solved. The last way is not too difficult to use here, but gets harder with problems like $834 - 695$, whereas the first and third methods would make this problem easy to solve mentally. In one research study, this type of instruction was given to fourth and sixth graders (19). Students moved away from using the paper-and-pencil analogue and used many different nonstandard methods. They also appeared to have a better understanding of place value, number decomposition, order of operations, and number properties.

Number Size

Research shows that children have great difficulties with concepts of number size. It is surprising how little time is spent teaching something so fundamental to number understanding. Of course, some attention is paid to number comparison, but it is often highly proceduralized and children either forget the rules or are unable to apply them to all cases.

How Are Fractions Compared?   To understand order and equivalence of fractions a student must have knowledge of ordering whole numbers (1). Children who do not understand the meaning of the fraction symbols focus on either the numerators or denominators when ordering and comparing. Only 10% of the fourth graders in one study (40) thought 5/6 was larger than 5/9. However, success at choosing the larger of these two fractions increased by grade level: 19% for sixth grade, 37% for eighth graders, and 95% for tenth graders. The extremely low scores before tenth grade indicate that children do not have mental representations for what the fractional symbol represents. Results are much worse for comparing fractions such as 2/3 and 3/4. Peck and Jencks (26) found several children who claimed these two fractions were equal because "there are the same number of pieces left over" (p. 344).

"Children's rules. I see nothing wrong any more with these children's attempts to find rules for working with fractions, even if some of those rules seem pretty wild. After all, Kepler, as he tried for about twenty-five years to find the laws governing the motion of the planets round the sun, made some wild guesses of his own. The trouble with the children was that they had no way of finding out whether their rules worked. They could not use either reality or internal logic and consistency as a way of checking them. Instead, they took their work to the teacher and said, 'Is this right?'" (12, p. 151)

Instruction focusing on the concept of fractional number size has proved to be quite successful (16,38). Sowder and Markovits (38) provided fourth grade teachers with an instructional unit containing eight lessons focusing on fractions as quantities and fraction comparison. Five weeks after they were taught the unit, students were able successfully to compare fractions such as 2/3 and 2/5, by reasoning that 2/3 is bigger than half, and 2/5 is smaller than a half, or that the pieces in 2/3 are bigger than the pieces in 2/5. Many of the children's answers demonstrated that they had begun to develop some intuitions about fractions. These understandings can later help children estimate solutions to operations on fractions.

How Are Decimal Numbers Compared?   To compare decimal numbers, children must be able to extend and generalize the notion of whole number place value. Hiebert and Wearne (11) point out that children have difficulty making the distinction between the conceptual features that generalize to decimal numbers, and the syntactic features that do not. For example, a syntactic feature of whole numbers that is useful in making comparisons is that "more digits make the number bigger." In their study, half of the sixth and seventh graders selected 0.1814 as the largest of

0.09, 0.385, 0.3, and 0.1814. Other children tend to compare decimal parts alone, as though they are whole numbers, as illustrated by fourth graders who selected 3.53 as the larger of 3.53 and 3.7 because 53 is larger than 7 (34).

The Sowder and Markovits study (38) also included a unit on comparing decimal numbers. After five preliminary lessons on using the base 10 blocks to represent whole numbers and then decimal numbers, students were given two lessons on comparing decimal numbers both with the blocks and with money. Eighteen of the 20 students interviewed 10 weeks after instruction could correctly compare and order decimal numbers and give reasonable explanations for their answers, such as 14.7 was larger than 14.26 because the 14.7 had a 7 in the tenths place, and the other had only a 2 in the tenths place.

How Are Large Numbers Perceived? Large numbers are usually introduced in fourth grade, but it takes experience working with large numbers to understand their magnitude. Many students in fourth, sixth, and eighth grades who were questioned about the number of people who could attend a Michael Jackson concert thought 5,000,000 was reasonable when asked to select possible estimates from 65, 300, 40,000, and 5,000,000 (40). Those who selected 40,000 related this number to the number of people they knew could fit into a local stadium, indicating that large numbers need to be related to familiar contexts before they make sense. Even unschooled children who work with the Brazilian currency system, in which bills are often of very high denominations because of Brazilian inflation, can work with large numbers that pertain to money (35). Some of the serious cultural consequences of a lack of understanding of large numbers have been dramatically illustrated by Paulos (25).

"A million dollars, a billion, a trillion, whatever. It doesn't matter as long as we do something about the problem." (25, p. 3)

Assessment Problems

The question of how to assess number sense is a particularly difficult one. If number sense calls for intuition about numbers, if it is a form of higher order thinking, then assessing number sense has all the inherent difficulties of testing intuition and higher order thinking. Yet recognizing number sense in a child's explanation is not really too difficult. For example, Markovits (18) had children place the decimal point in $15.24 \times 4.5 = 6858$ and explain their answers as one measure of number sense. Number sense exists, however, on a continuum and within realms of numbers. A child who says 1/3 is less than 1/4 exhibits some whole number sense, but not fractional number sense.

Estimation and mental computation are more well-defined topics, and attempts are being made in standardized tests to measure achievement in these areas. The 1990 National Assessment of Educational Progress (5) will assess children's ability to make estimates appropriate to a given situation with test items that measure children's abilities to recognize when to estimate, what form of an estimate to use (overestimate,

> "The goals implied by the term 'number sense' are not new for mathematics educators; good teachers, curriculum developers, textbook writers, and even test developers have long held them. Our best students have even achieved these goals. What is new is the term number sense and the emphasis on specific components such as estimation and reasonableness of results in settings within and outside mathematics, and a desire to emphasize these in instruction and assessment." (36, p. 67.)

underestimate, range of estimate), applications, and order of magnitude. Mental computation is addressed in items asking children to select the appropriate procedure to do a problem: pencil-and-paper, calculator, mental arithmetic.

Researchers studying estimation have tried to address the psychometric problems in a variety of ways. Group testing of estimation usually contains some sort of timing element to ensure that students have not actually computed the answer, but timing is not without pitfalls. Timing sends the message to students that efficiency is of paramount importance whereas this is not the case, particularly if we want the children to think about the numbers and appropriate strategies.

The format of computational test items has been found to affect performance. Rubenstein (33) found open-ended questions considerably more difficult than items asking whether an answer was reasonable, larger or smaller than a reference number, or of the proper order of magnitude.

An important issue for teachers is how to gauge whether an estimate is correct. Determining an appropriate range of answers can be helpful and has been used by researchers to determine whether answers are correct on group tests of estimation (31). However, when feedback is given to students, it is important to recognize that a range must be selected carefully. This will ensure that an answer obtained through an application of genuine number understanding is not tossed aside because it does not fall into the range, and that on the other hand, the range is not so large that poor estimates fall within its limits.

Part II: Number Sense from a Teacher's Perspective

Part I showed how the related areas of estimation, mental computation, and number size contribute to number sense, and conversely, how facility with these elements usually accompanies and demonstrates good number sense. The NCTM *Curriculum and Evaluation Standards* (21) states that number sense is an intuition about numbers. An important question then is whether this intuition is something that a student does or does not possess, and whether it can be enhanced through instruction. In Part II, I would like to describe my thoughts and experiences as a teacher teaching for number sense.

The Role of Number Sense in School Mathematics

After teaching mathematics in grades 7–12 for a dozen years and tutoring many students, from fourth graders through adults, I have become convinced that number sense plays an important role in learning. A source of major frustration to me is the number of students who are algorithmically trained and oriented and have no concept of the reasonableness of their answers. This flaw in their functioning is not a reflection of their capacity to think logically; many of these students are considered good mathematics students and receive good grades. I feel this lack of thinking about the solution process is the result of earlier training to do large sets of problems quickly. Students I have taught are always frustrated at the beginning of the year regardless of the level of difficulty of the work. They work out a problem, tell me the answer, and then I ask them to explain why they believe their answer is correct. Inevitably, students change their answers without giving the problem much additional thought. When confronted again with the same question of why, they become flustered and often resort to answering this question with an explanation of an algorithm. It usually takes a month or more for the students to become accustomed to examining whether their answers are reasonable and justifying what they have done from a logical point of view.

(Elwanger interviews Benny.)
"E: It (i.e., finding answers) seems to be like a game.
B: (Emotionally) Yes! It's like a wild goose chase.
E: So you're chasing answers the teacher wants?
B: Ya, Ya.
E: Which answers would you like to put down?
B: (Shouting) Any! As long as I knew it could be the right answer." (6, p. 216)

The reasonableness of an answer can take various forms. For example, if students are dealing with area or perimeter of any particular shape, a negative answer can be eliminated immediately; in doubling a recipe, no number should be the same size or smaller than the numbers in the original recipe; in deciding how many buses are needed for a trip, a mixed number is not an acceptable answer. In each of these cases, answers are eliminated or rejected for different reasons. In many other examples, estimation and mental computation play a large part in obtaining a "ballpark figure" or in simplifying the calculations in a problem. Figuring commission on a sale, the tip on a dinner check, and the total food bill at the grocery store are just some of the examples in which mental computation and estimation are very useful tools.

A Personal Teaching Experience

I was involved as the teacher in a study in my seventh-grade pre-algebra class (39) which included instruction on mental computation and estimation. For about

5 minutes or so at the beginning of every period students were asked to do mental computations. After providing answers to problems orally, they were asked to explain how they obtained their answers. At first, there was a wide range in students' attitudes toward the lessons. Some were very eager to do these exercises, some tried to come up with unique (although not always the most direct) ways of doing these problems, others thought they were to do a problem using an algorithm in their heads rather than on paper, and one or two felt that they were not good at mental computation and, therefore, did not even want to try. The problems ranged from addition of 2 two-digit numbers to multiplying 2 two-digit numbers to multiplying or dividing by powers or multiples of 10. As time went on, students' attitudes and strategies became more cohesive, and those who had avoided becoming involved in the beginning began volunteering by the middle of this study. Even after the study was completed, students were expected to use mental computation in many exercises, whether these were computational or story problems. I saw a marked improvement in the students' abilities to perform all sorts of calculations, even in those who were fairly adept at the beginning. Initially, I found that I too frequently relied on standard algorithms in my mental computations and that I had to stop and think several seconds about some of the alternate methods that students presented.

"INTERVIEWER: Will you estimate 53 × 27 for me?

STUDENT: 1500.

INTERVIEWER: Would the exact answer be less than, greater than, or equal to 1500?

STUDENT: Well, it won't be exactly 1500.

INTERVIEWER: Why not?

STUDENT: Because you estimated, and when you estimate you never get an exact answer.

INTERVIEWER: But here you've rounded down three and here up three . . .

STUDENT: But they're different numbers! If you round 27 to 30 you have three 27's left over. If you round this to 50 you'll have three 53's left over." (J. Sowder interviewing student)

Several different techniques were noted and used fairly regularly in these mental computation exercises. For example, in the problem 24 + 37, the use of adding from left to right (30 + 20 + 4 + 7 = 61), adding from right to left with no carrying (4 + 7 = 11, + 50 = 61), decomposition and recomposition (24 + 30 + 7 = 61), and use of "nice" numbers (24 + 40 − 3 = 61) were all easy for the students to use with little or no prompting from the teacher. They learned a lot from each other. They were able to keep track of place value in almost every exercise, and their use of properties, such as commutative, associative, and distributive, was consistent and appropriate. The distributive property was used often in multiplication and division problems. For example, 47 × 2 yielded (50 × 2) − (3 × 2) or (45 × 2) + (2 × 2), while 74 ÷ 2 yielded (70 ÷ 2) + (4 ÷ 2) or (60 ÷ 2) + (14 ÷ 2). "Counting up" was also used in division exercises: for 72 ÷ 4, 15 × 4 = 60 and 3 × 4 = 12, so 18 × 4 = 72, with 18 as the answer.

"I really enjoy math. I think it is neat the way there are so many ways of solving a problem without borrowing.

$6000 - 1$ 5999 That's hard when your borrowing. I probabling
$5416 - 1$ $\underline{5415}$ got it wrong lets see with an easyer way.
             584

             I got the other wrong this method is alot eas-
$- 5416$ yer." (student letter to Clare Clark, shared with
$\underline{5\ 4\ 1\ 6}$ J. Sowder)
    683

As mentioned earlier, an estimation unit was also taught. Ranges of estimates, deciding whether a problem would yield an answer bigger or smaller than a target number, comparing numbers, measurements, percent error versus absolute error, and ordering numbers were some of the topics covered in this unit. Throughout the unit, some students were concerned that there could be different estimates for the same problem (more than one "answer") and wondered how they were to be graded on a test if their answer was different from mine. However, most of them showed mathematical growth and increased flexibility during this unit. The concept that absolute error was not the sole determinant of a good estimate was difficult for them. They tended to feel that being "off" by 25 was equally good whether they worked a problem with numbers in the hundreds or in the millions. They had a good discussion, however, about numbers used in the newspaper—whether they were exact or estimates—although some were hard to convince that exact numbers are not always the best and that estimates are good and are not mistakes.

Another difficult concept for many of them was the notion of adjusting or compensating for an estimate. If 46×38 is viewed as 50×40, then the estimate of 2,000 should be adjusted downward somewhat since both numbers were rounded up before multiplying. This made some students anxious because they felt that an estimate should be just one step and adjusting only lengthened the time involved in working out the problem. Another difficulty involved decimals. Given an addition problem, for example, involving numbers such as 315.23, most students rounded the whole number portion but kept the decimal portion as it was. They came out with answers such as 1,200.31 and had difficulty understanding why the decimal part should have been dropped altogether. We made some progress in overcoming these difficulties, but it became clear to me that one short instructional unit on estimation was not sufficient.

Activity: Take the current year, 1992, and individually or in a group come up with as many mathematical bits of information as possible.

By the end of the unit, the students understood, rather than memorized, the "rule" that division by a number less than one would yield an answer greater than the original number while multiplying would yield an answer smaller than the original number. Their ability to analyze their answers also improved.

Activity: Decode the lines that appear on many envelopes to represent the zip code. The first and last long slash are check marks.

Answer:

‖₁₁₁ = 0		₁|₁|₁ = 5
₁₁|| = 1		₁||₁₁ = 6
₁|₁| = 2		|₁₁| = 7
₁||₁ = 3		|₁|₁ = 8
₁|₁₁| = 4		|₁|₁₁ = 9

In conclusion, the experimental estimation unit and the mental computation activities were very beneficial to me and to my students. As students gained better number sense, their self-confidence improved. This experience has firmly convinced me that all mathematics instruction should emphasize making sense of mathematics. Helping students develop a good number sense can go a long way toward reducing the frustration of both students and teachers.

Looking Ahead . . .

Instruction on number sense must enable students to relate number properties and operation properties for whole numbers, decimal numbers, and fractions, and to

---

"Number sense can be described as good intuition about numbers and their relationships. It develops gradually as a result of exploring numbers, visualizing them in a variety of contexts, and relating them in ways that are not limited by traditional algorithms. Since textbooks are limited to paper-and-pencil orientation, they can only suggest ideas to be investigated, they cannot replace the 'doing of mathematics' that is essential for the development of number sense. No substitute exists for a skillful teacher and an environment that fosters curiosity and exploration at all grade levels." (15, p. 11)

---

solve problems in flexible and creative ways. It must focus on making sense of the symbols used in mathematics. Mathematics becomes meaningful only when and where connections are made between symbols and related understandings (10). "Instruction that allows and encourages the invention of algorithms, promotes questioning of how numbers can be decomposed and recomposed and of how place value concepts can be applied, admits to multiple answers and procedures when appropriate, and demands reflection on reasonableness cannot help but develop quantitative intuition" (37). We know now that schooling needs to build on the intuitive knowledge children bring to the classroom, and that these intuitions can be used to develop new and more complex intuitions and understandings. There is evidence being gathered at the University of Wisconsin, Purdue University, Michigan State University, and other places that reasoned connections can be made between what students know and what we want them to know. Reports so far are very encouraging (7). We know it can be done.

Judith Sowder

Teaching the estimation and mental computation units and seeing the progress that was made in so short a period of time leads to new questions. What is the benefit of teaching estimation and mental computation in terms of retention and carryover into other topics? Research on how attitude affects development of number sense is also needed. Do students who perform well possess a positive attitude toward estimation and number sense, and do those with a poor attitude perform poorly? Finally, exposure to a variety of mental computation techniques, such as adding from left to right or using "nice" numbers to simplify calculations needs to begin early in a student's mathematics career. Perhaps this early exposure would encourage flexibility in thinking.

Judith Kelin

About the Authors

Judith Sowder is a Professor of Mathematical Sciences at San Diego State University. For a number of years she has been investigating students' learning of estimation and mental computation and their acquisition of number sense. She teaches both graduate and undergraduate courses in mathematics education.

Judith Kelin teaches middle school mathematics at San Diego Hebrew Day School. She and her seventh graders participated in a research study on estimation, mental computation, and number sense. She recently completed a master's thesis in which she investigated the use of estimation in a small business.

References

1. BEHR, M. J., WACHSMUTH, I., POST, T. R., & LESH, R. (1984). Order and equivalence of rational numbers: A clinical teaching experiment. *Journal for Research in Mathematics Education, 15*(5), 323–341.
2. CARRAHER, T. N., CARRAHER, D. W., & SCHLIEMANN, A. D. (1985). Mathematics in the streets and in the schools. *British Journal of Developmental Psychology, 3*(1), 21–29.
3. CASE, R. (1985). *Intellectual development.* Orlando, FL: Academic Press.
4. CASE, R., & SOWDER, J. T. (1990). The development of computational estimation: A neo-Piagetian analysis. *Cognition and Instruction, 7*(2), 79–104.
5. EDUCATIONAL TESTING SERVICE. (1989). *Mathematics Objectives: 1990 Assessment.* Princeton, NJ: Author.
6. ERLWANGER, S. (1975). Case studies of children's conception of mathematics, Part I. *Journal of Children's Mathematical Behavior, 1*(3), 157–283.
7. FENNEMA, E., CARPENTER, T. P., & LAMON, S. J. (Ed.). (1991). *Integrating research on teaching and learning mathematics.* Albany, NY: SUNY.
8. GINSBURG, H. P., POSNER, J. K., & RUSSELL, R. L. (1981). The development of mental addition as a function of schooling and culture. *Journal of Cross-Cultural Psychology, 12*(2), 163–178.

*9. GREENO, J. G. (1989). Some conjectures about number sense. In J. T. Sowder & B. P. Schappelle (Eds.), *Establishing foundations for research on number sense and related topics: Report of a conference* (pp. 43–56). San Diego: San Diego State University Center for Research in Mathematics and Science Education.

*10. HIEBERT, J. (1984). Children's mathematics learning: The struggle to link form and understanding. *Elementary School Journal, 84*(5), 497–513.

11. HIEBERT, J., & WEARNE, D. (1986). Procedures over concepts: The acquisition of decimal number knowledge. In J. Hiebert (Ed.), *Conceptual and procedural knowledge: The case of mathematics* (pp. 199–223). Hillsdale, NJ: Erlbaum.

*12. HOLT, J. (1982). *How children fail.* New York: Delta.

13. HOPE, J. (1987). A case study of a highly skilled mental calculator. *Journal for Research in Mathematics Education, 18*(5), 331–342.

14. HOPE, J. A., & SHERRILL, J. M. (1987). Characteristics of unskilled and skilled mental calculators. *Journal for Research in Mathematics Education, 18*(2), 98–111.

*15. HOWDEN, H. Teaching number sense. *Arithmetic Teacher, 36*(6), 6–11.

*16. KERSLAKE, D. (1986). *Fractions: Children's strategies and errors.* Windsor, Berkshire, England: NFER-NELSON.

17. MACK, N. K. (1988, April). *Using estimation to learn fractions with understanding.* Paper presented at the meeting of the American Educational Research Association, New Orleans, LA.

*18. MARKOVITS, Z. (1989). Reactions to the number sense conference. In J. T. Sowder & B. P. Schappelle (Eds.), *Establishing foundations for research on number sense and related topics: Report of a conference,* (pp. 78–81). San Diego: San Diego State University Center for Research in Mathematics and Science Education.

19. MARKOVITS, Z., & SOWDER, J. (1988). Mental computation and number sense. In M. J. Behr, C. B. Lacampagne, & M. M. Wheeler (Eds.), *Proceedings of the Tenth Annual Meeting of the North American Chapter of the International Group for the Psychology of Mathematics Education* (pp. 58–64), De Kalb, IL: Northern Illinois University.

*20. NATIONAL COUNCIL OF SUPERVISORS OF MATHEMATICS. (1989). Essential mathematics for the twenty-first century: The position paper of the National Council of Supervisors of Mathematics. *Arithmetic Teacher, 36*(9), 27–29.

*21. NATIONAL COUNCIL OF TEACHERS OF MATHEMATICS. (1989). *Standards for curriculum and evaluation in school mathematics.* Reston, VA: Author.

22. NATIONAL RESEARCH COUNCIL. (1989). *Everybody counts.* Washington, DC: National Academy Press.

*23. NATIONAL RESEARCH COUNCIL MATHEMATICAL SCIENCES EDUCATION BOARD. (1990). *Reshaping school mathematics.* Washington, DC: National Academy Press.

*24. OWENS, D. T. (1987). Decimal multiplication in grade seven. In J. C. Bergeron, N. Herscovics, & C. Kieran (Eds.), *Proceedings of the Eleventh International Conference, Psychology of Mathematics Education (PME-XI),* Vol. 2 (pp. 423–429), Montreal: University of Montreal.

25. PAULOS, J. A. (1988). *Innumeracy: Mathematical illiteracy and its consequences.* New York: Hill and Wang.

26. PECK, D. M., & JENCKS, S. M. (1981). Conceptual issues in the teaching and learning of fractions. *Journal for Research in Mathematics Education, 12*(5), 339–348.

*27. PLUNKETT, S. (1979). Decomposition and all that rot. *Mathematics in Schools, 8*(3), 2–5.

28. RESNICK, L. B. (1986). The development of mathematical intuition. In M. Perlmutter (Ed.), *Perspectives on intellectual development: The Minnesota Symposia on Child Psychology* (Vol. 19, pp. 159–194). Hillsdale, NJ: Erlbaum:

29. RESNICK, L. B. (1987). Learning in school and out. *Educational Researcher, 16*(9), 13–20.

*30. REYS, B. J. (1989). Conference on number sense: Reflections. In J. T. Sowder & B. P. Schappelle (Eds.), *Establishing foundations for research on number sense and related topics: Report of a conference* (pp. 70–73). San Diego: San Diego State University Center for Research in Mathematics and Science Education.

31. REYS, R. E., RYBOLT, J. F., BESTGEN, B. J., & WYATT, J. W. (1982). Processes used by good computational estimators. *Journal for Research in Mathematics Education, 13*(3), 183–201.

*32. REYS, R. E., TRAFTON, P. R., REYS, B. B., & ZAWOJEWSKI, J. (1984). *Developing computational estimation materials for the middle grades.* Final Report of NSF Grant No. NSF 81-13601.

33. RUBENSTEIN, R. N. (1985). Computational estimation and related mathematical skills. *Journal for Research in Mathematics Education, 16*(2), 106–119.

34. SACKUR-GRISVARD, C., & LEONARD, F. (1985). Intermediate cognitive organization in the process of learning a mathematical concept: The order of positive decimal numbers. *Cognition and Instruction, 2*(2), 157–174.

35. SAXE, G. B. (1988). Candy selling and math learning. *Educational Researcher, 17*(6), 14–21.

*36. SCHOEN, H. L. (1989). Reaction to the conference on number sense. In J. T. Sowder & B. P. Schappelle (Eds.), *Establishing foundations for research on number sense and related topics: Report of a conference* (pp. 67–69). San Diego: San Diego State University Center for Research in Mathematics and Science Education.

*37. SOWDER, J. T. (1992). Estimation and related topics. In D. Grouws (Ed.), *Handbook for research on mathematics teaching and learning* (pp. 371–389). New York: Macmillan.

38. SOWDER, J. T., & MARKOVITZ, Z. (1989). Effects of instruction on number magnitude. In C. A. Maher, G. A. Goldin, & R. B. Davis (Eds.), *Proceedings of the Eleventh Annual Meeting of the North American Chapter of the International Group for Psychology in Mathematics Education* (pp. 105–110). New Brunswick, NJ: Rutgers University.

39. SOWDER, J. T., & MARKOVITS, Z. (1990). Relative and absolute error in computational estimation. In G. Booker, P. Cobb, & T. de Mendicuti (Eds.), *Proceedings of the Fourteenth Annual Meeting of the International Group for Psychology of Mathematics Education* (pp. 321–328), Mexico City: Program Committee of the Fourteenth Psychology of Mathematics Education Conference.

40. SOWDER, J. T., & WHEELER, M. M. (1987). *The development of computational estimation and number sense: Two exploratory studies.* (Research report). San Diego: San Diego State University Center for Research in Mathematics and Science Education.

41. SOWDER, J. T., & WHEELER, M. M. (1989). The development of concepts and strategies used in computational estimation. *Journal for Research in Mathematics Education, 20*(2), 130–146.

42. STEIN, B. (May, 1990). Fable of the lazy teen-ager. *Reader's Digest*, pp. 93–96.

43. THREADGILL-SOWDER, J. (1984). Computational estimation procedures of school children. *Journal of Educational Research, 77*(6), 332–336.

*44. TRAFTON, P. R. (1989). Reflections on the number sense conference. In J. T. Sowder & B. P. Schappelle (Eds.), *Establishing foundations for research on number sense and related topics: Report of a conference* (pp. 74–77). San Diego: San Diego State University Center for Research in Mathematics and Science Education.

CHAPTER 4

Insights from Research on Mathematical Problem Solving in the Middle Grades

Diana Lambdin Kroll and Tammy Miller

> *A teacher of mathematics has a great opportunity. If he fills his allotted time with drilling his students in routine operations he kills their interest, hampers their intellectual development, and misuses his opportunity. But if he challenges the curiosity of his students by setting them problems proportionate to their knowledge, and helps them to solve their problems with stimulating questions, he may give them a taste for, and some means of independent thinking.*
> *(George Polya, 51, p. v)*

Mathematics educators have agreed for some time that problem solving is a very important, if not the most important, goal of mathematics instruction. Over 40 years ago, George Polya, the "father of mathematical problem solving," put it this way: "The first duty of a teacher of mathematics is to do . . . everything in his power to develop his students' ability to solve problems" (50, p. 2). More recently, the National Council of Teachers of Mathematics in its *Curriculum and Evaluation Standards*, reiterated many of its earlier recommendations by emphasizing once again that "problem solving should be the central focus of the mathematics curriculum" (44, p. 23).

Yet, problem solving is probably the most difficult aspect of mathematical performance for many students. Although most test results from the National Assessment of Educational Progress show that American students demonstrate acceptable mastery of computational skills, they also reveal that many of these same students are unable to apply these skills to anything other than the most routine of mathematical problem-solving situations (21,28). Furthermore, American students consistently rank near the bottom in international comparisons on mathematics tasks requiring higher order thinking or problem solving (38).

> In a study comparing American fifth graders with Chinese and Japanese children, the Americans had the lowest mean scores on both computation and word problems. In fact, 67 Americans were among the 100 lowest scoring fifth graders in the study which included 720 students. Only one American was among the 100 highest scoring students. (61)

What is problem solving? What do researchers know about why students have such difficulty in solving problems? How can middle grades teachers help their students become more proficient problem solvers? In this chapter, we present answers gleaned from research on mathematical problem solving, with special emphasis on the middle grades.

Problem Solving: What Is It?

For most teachers, the observation that students have difficulty with mathematical problem solving does not seem to be news. We know that many of our students have trouble with story problems. But it is important to realize that mathematics educators are talking about much more than routine story problems when they call for problem solving to be the central focus of the school mathematics curriculum.

In fact, most researchers would agree that the defining feature of a "problem" situation is that there must be some blockage on the part of the potential problem solver. That is, a mathematical task is a problem only if the problem solver reaches a point where he or she does not know how to proceed. For example, Krulik and Rudnick (30) define a problem as "a situation . . . that requires resolution and for

> "To solve a problem is to find a way where no way is known off-hand, to find a way out of a difficulty, to find a way around an obstacle, to attain a desired end, that is not immediately attainable, by appropriate means." (George Polya, 50, p. 1)

which the individual sees no apparent or obvious means or path to obtaining the solution" (p. 3). Many textbook story problems actually provide little practice in "problem solving" because no blockage exists: if students can recognize what strategy or operations to apply, the situation is not a problem but merely an exercise.

> "What is one student's problem is another student's exercise, and a third student's frustration." (25, p. 232)

Furthermore, mathematical situations that are mere exercises for some students can also be genuine problems for others. Here is an example of a genuine problem for most middle grades students who have not yet studied algebra:

> The Boys' Club held its annual carnival last weekend. Admission to the carnival was $3 for adults and $2 for children under 12. Total attendance was 100 people and $232 was collected. How many adults and how many children attended the carnival?

This problem requires no computational expertise beyond addition and multiplication of whole numbers. On the other hand, it cannot be solved merely by performing some operations on numbers plucked from the problem. In this respect it is different from many textbook story problems.

Of course, for a student who can write and solve systems of equations, a solution to the carnival problem may be routine. However, without algebra a more innovative approach is required. For example, a fifth grader might guess numbers of adults and children that sum to 100, check to see how much money would result, and systematically adjust successive guesses according to whether more or less money is required. Alternatively, students might make an organized list showing dollars collected from 1 child and 99 adults, 2 children and 98 adults, and so on. After completing a small number of entries, they might observe a pattern and use that observation to extrapolate the required result.

Problem Solving in Today's Classrooms

It is genuine problems like the above—problems in which students must do more than just apply a known procedure—that are receiving increased emphasis in today's mathematics curriculum. The NCTM *Curriculum and Evaluation Standards* (44) exhorts teachers to include a wide variety of problems in their teaching. For example,

---

"In grades 5–8, the curriculum should take advantage of the expanding mathematical capabilities of middle school students to include more complex problem situations involving topics such as probability, statistics, geometry, and rational numbers. . . . A balance should be struck between problems that apply mathematics to the real world and problems that arise from the investigation of mathematical ideas" (*Curriculum and Evaluation Standards,* 44, p. 75)

---

it is important to include process problems (those, like the carnival problem, in which the diverse processes students use are of more interest than the answer itself). Other types to include are puzzle problems, logic problems, spatial reasoning problems, and real-world application problems. Also important are project problems, which are chiefly distinguished by their open-ended nature and by the extended period of time they may require to complete.

Furthermore, as the NCTM *Curriculum and Evaluation Standards* makes clear, mathematics may actually be best taught through problem-solving situations (cf. 56). When students wrestle with problems that involve important mathematical concepts (e.g., area, perimeter, volume), they construct for themselves clearer understandings of these concepts and of the relationships among them.

> *An Application Problem:* A square cake is iced on the top and on the four sides. How can the cake be cut into five pieces so that five people can each get their fair shares of cake and of icing?

What Is Involved in the Problem-Solving Process?

By its very nature, problem solving is a complex process—one that Polya (51) suggested consists of four phases: *understanding the problem, devising a plan, carrying out the plan,* and *looking back.* Contrary to many students' expectations, experienced problem solvers do not always have an immediate plan in mind when they are confronted with a problem. In fact, experts often spend a considerable amount of time in the understanding phase, in planning their approach, and in checking their work

> "Mathematics today involves far more than calculation; clarification of the problem, deduction of consequences, formulation of alternatives, and development of appropriate tools are as much a part of the modern mathematician's craft as are solving equations or providing answers." (*Everybody Counts,* 45, p. 5)

both along the way and at the end of the problem (55). Inexperienced problem solvers, on the other hand, are more likely to plunge in without adequate time spent developing understanding or developing a plan.

Problem solving not only involves distinct phases but also requires individuals to coordinate their previous experiences, knowledge, and intuition whenever they attempt to resolve a problem situation. In particular, problem-solving performance seems to be a function of at least five broad, interdependent categories of factors: knowledge, beliefs, affects, control, and sociocultural contexts. In Figure 4.1 we provide a composite model that provides examples of categories within these factors (derived from the writings of several researchers: 36, 37, 48, 55).

Why Do Students Have Trouble with Problem Solving?

Most explanations proposed by teachers and researchers for students' difficulties with problem solving relate to one or more of the factors in our model (Fig. 4.1). In our study of the problem-solving research literature, we have identified seven major factors that have been posited as contributors to middle grades students' difficulties. Note

FIGURE 4.1   Factors involved in mathematical problem solving

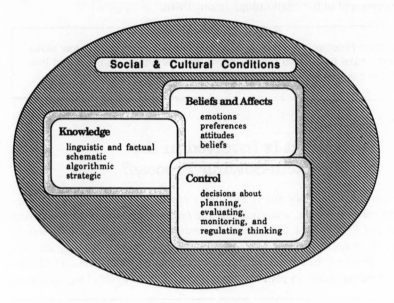

that although these factors may contribute individually, quite often it is an interaction among them that influences performance.

Knowledge Factors

To solve problems efficiently, students must possess appropriate knowledge and be able to coordinate their use of appropriate skills.

Algorithmic Knowledge.   Computational skills, one type of algorithmic knowledge, are a necessary but not a sufficient component of problem-solving proficiency. Clearly, students who cannot do basic computations will have difficulty solving problems. However, national test data seem to indicate that many students who are able to perform calculations accurately are nevertheless unable to solve problems successfully (8, 28); hence, there is a need for problem-solving instruction.

Data from the third National Assessment of Educational Progress revealed that although "almost 70 percent of the 13-year-olds correctly multiplied 2/3 × 2/5, fewer than 20 percent could solve a verbal problem similar to the following: 'Jane lives 2/3 mile from school. When she has walked 2/5 of the way, how far has she walked?'" (8, p. 10)

Linguistic Knowledge. Difficulties with reading skills have also been proposed as an explanation for students' trouble with mathematical problem solving. While it is certainly true that low verbal ability or lack of familiarity with the language used in problems may hamper children's understanding of word problems (19), it is an over-simplification to equate reading difficulties with problem-solving difficulties. Some

---

A Logic Problem: If Tom is twice as old as Dick will be when Harry is as old as Tom is now, who is the oldest, the next oldest, and the youngest?

---

researchers have claimed that reading ability is a key factor in problem-solving success (2), while others have maintained that reading plays a minor role, especially when students are familiar with the words used in the problems (3, 27). More recent research has investigated how reading skills and computational skills work together in successful problem solving (41, 43).

Conceptual Knowledge. Zweng (66) claims that neither computation skills nor reading skills is the major stumbling block when students have difficulty solving problems; rather, it is deciding what to do (often, which operations to perform). Studies

---

In one research study, one third of a group of sixth-grade students were unable to make up a story problem that correctly fit the number sentence $6 \times 3 = 18$. (49)

---

of the strategies used by sixth graders in problem situations reveal that many seem unsure in their understanding of the four basic operations. Although they may be competent in computing with whole numbers and successful in solving single-step problems, they may fall back on various mindless strategies when faced with more challenging problems (60). For example, instead of choosing numbers and arithmetic

---

"Bob (grade 8) offers the following as an explanation of how he decided to divide [to solve a word problem]:

BOB: I was thinking about the other ones, adding, subtracting, multiplying. . . . They didn't work.

INTERVIEWER: What do you mean, they didn't work?

BOB: They wouldn't work, 'cause . . . 'cause . . . it'd [the answer would] be lower than this, and multiplying would go higher.

INTERVIEWER: Uh-huh. Ok. So you wouldn't multiply, huh?

BOB: And adding would go higher. . . . And if you . . . if you subtract, it'd be . . . it wouldn't be that long." (60, pp. 229–230)

---

operations according to the meaning in a problem, students may use the very primitive strategy of simply trying all the basic operations (addition, subtraction, multiplication, division) on various numbers in the problem, then choosing the answer that seems most reasonable in size. Unless they are challenged with problems for which such approaches cannot be used successfully, students may continue to rely on these naive and unreliable strategies.

Difficulties such as these may be perpetuated by the emphasis in many middle grades classrooms on developing facility in calculation skills without concomitant attention to developing understanding. Many teachers spend considerably more class

> A simple math mistake—somebody added when he should have subtracted, or vice versa—caused the Hubble Space Telescope to miss its target stars and point to the wrong spot in the heavens. The telescope missed its target by one half of a degree—or about the width of a full moon as seen from earth.

time having students practice basic skills than having students work on solving genuine problems (24, 52). Furthermore, too much emphasis may be placed on teaching students to rely on key words to decide what operation to use (e.g., "in all" for addition or "of" for fraction multiplication). Many students rely extensively on key words (47), although such a strategy usually breaks down quickly as problems become more complex.

Schema and Strategic Knowledge.   Good problem solvers are more likely than poor problem solvers to remember information about the structure of problems they have solved previously (schema knowledge) and to be able both to learn from their mistakes and to relate work they have done on previous problems to the task at hand (57). Good problem solvers also usually have a wide range of strategies at their disposal (strategic knowledge) and demonstrate facility in choosing which of these strategies to apply in various situations.

Beliefs and Affective Factors

Another important difference between successful and unsuccessful problem solvers is their attitudes and beliefs about problem solving, about themselves as problem solvers, and about ways to go about solving problems (34, 39, 55). Many students develop the faulty belief that mathematics problems should be able to be solved

> A clipping posted on a classroom bulletin board depicts cartoonist Gary Larson's view of "hell's library." The devil, with an evil, gloating expression, shows a cowering newcomer through a room lined with bookcases overflowing with books. But the titles are all variations on the same theme: *Math Story Problems, More Story Problems, Big Book of Problems, Favorite Math Problems.* The cartoonist has successfully captured the feeling of dread many students experience when it's time for math problem solving again.

quickly. Students often develop images of themselves as incompetent problem solvers, with long-lasting consequences. Witness the many adults who are convinced that they are hopeless at doing mathematics. Furthermore, many students believe there is just one "right" way to solve any mathematics problem. Such students not

> It is impossible to teach rules for every problem, every situation. Students must be able to solve problems creatively.

only fail to appreciate the excitement that comes from finding different ways to solve problems but also become dependent on a teacher or an answer key for verification of their success.

Control Factors

In recent years, some researchers have linked work on metacognition with work on problem solving. The term *metacognition* is generally used to refer to two related constructs: (a) awareness of one's own knowledge and thinking processes and (b) the ability to monitor one's own thinking and progress when involved in a problem situation. Novice problem solvers are often unaware of their own thinking patterns. They also tend to spend little time reflecting on the productiveness of their approaches, either before or during problem solving (22, 34, 35, 55). While students are working on a problem it is often important for them to stop and consider alternative approaches, especially when their progress is slow. Although some research has attempted to help middle grades students become more metacognitively aware during problem solving (7, 35), it has not yet produced any simple prescriptions for teachers who want to help students become more aware of, and better able to monitor, their own thinking.

Sociocultural Factors

Problem-solving proficiency does not develop exclusively through experiences with textbook problems or school instruction. Studies have shown that children often develop their own solution strategies that are quite useful in problem-solving situations outside the classroom. But these same children are frequently unable to apply school-taught mathematics to solve similar problems (9). Teachers are encouraged to build

> *A Project Problem:* "Design a dog house that can be made from a single 4 ft. by 8 ft. sheet of plywood. Make the dog house as large as possible and show how the pieces can be laid out on the plywood before cutting." (*Everybody Counts*, 45, p. 32)

their classroom lessons on foundations already laid in students' out-of-class experiences whenever possible (33). Furthermore, the social context of the classroom should not be overlooked as a potent influence on students' achievement.

Components of a Problem-Solving Instructional Program

The best problem-solving instruction takes place over an extended period of time within the context of a problem-solving instructional program. Such a program has three essential components (12):

- suitable problem-solving tasks and materials
- clear roles for the teacher to play
- guidelines for organizing and implementing instruction

In the rest of this chapter, we comment on insights from research relating to each of these.

Suitable Tasks and Materials for Problem-Solving Instruction

Earlier we mentioned that the term *problem solving* is used to refer to a number of very different types of problems. Teachers should strive to include each of these types of problems in their problem-solving programs. Yet we must be concerned about more than just the variety of problem types to which we expose our students. The internal features of problems must also be carefully considered.

Problems That Are Motivating.   Real-life application problems often seem more meaningful and interesting to students. Furthermore, research suggests that when problem details are adapted to student interest—for example, by substituting names of students in the class or by using a popular context—students find the problems easier and more interesting (1, 54). Another way to increase interest is to give students regular opportunities to compose (and share) their own problems (19).

Problems with Missing, Extraneous, or Contradictory Information.   Students should be confronted with problems that offer missing, extraneous, or contradictory information because these are typical of real world problems (see Fig. 4.2). Research has confirmed that students find problems more difficult when extraneous information is included because they must think more carefully about the numbers to use, the number of steps needed, and the order in which to perform the steps (41, 42, 46). Similarly, encountering missing or contradictory information in a problem causes students difficulties (53). One suggestion for helping students learn to identify extraneous, missing, or contradictory information is to try integrating instruction on reading comprehension with mathematics lessons on problem solving. Teachers might also introduce students to specific strategies for identifying and organizing necessary problem information and for eliminating extraneous information (18).

Using Calculators, Computers and Other Technology.   Research findings are mixed concerning whether use of a calculator improves overall problem-solving achievement (63). However, one study found that some middle grade students who used calculators to complete the calculations in story problems were more successful

FIGURE 4.2 Problem (with extraneous information) by sixth grader Jeremy
Jeffers

At midnight, the wind over Jamaica started to increase as Hurricane Lucas came closer. Every 10 minutes from then on, the wind doubled, and five trees were pulled from the ground. At 12:30, the wind speed was 120 miles per hour. At what speed was the wind blowing at 12:00 midnight?

at using and selecting problem-solving strategies, and that students who used calculators had a more positive attitude (64). Another study suggested that use of a calculator stimulated pupils to think more about their approaches to problems (65). Perhaps just as important, permitting students access to calculators during problem solving means that they need not be limited to problems involving simple numbers. Thus, with the aid of a calculator students can learn more about mathematical concepts and can solve more realistic problems.

Computers seem to have great potential, not only as problem-solving tools but also as teaching aids in developing students' problem-solving skills. As tools, computers can quickly and accurately generate large data sets, sketch graphs, and perform mathematical simulations. Problem-solving skills may be taught via programming, spreadsheets, explore/conjecture software, or computer-controlled interactive video. Although little research seems to have been done to date in these areas, there is some information available showing how the use of technology may enhance middle grades problem-solving instruction (e.g., 5, 16).

Activities Focusing on Phases in Problem Solving.   A complete problem-solving program clearly must include instruction to help students know how to approach unfamiliar problems. It often helps to point out that there are identifiable phases in the problem-solving process and that it may be necessary to cycle back and forth among phases when working through a problem (12). Familiarity with Polya's phases allows both students and teachers to feel more comfortable in attacking unfamiliar problems.

Activities Utilizing a Variety of Problem-Solving Strategies.   Another way to help students deal with unfamiliar problem situations is to familiarize them with a variety of problem-solving strategies or heuristics. A heuristic is a general problem-solving

> *An Application Problem:* "A group of 8 people are going camping for 3 days and need to carry their own water. They read in a guide book that 12.5 liters are needed for a party of 5 persons for 1 day. How much water should they carry?" (51, p. 83)

approach, such as drawing a diagram, completing a table, or making a list, that is useful in a wide variety of problems. In his seminal work, *How to Solve It*, Polya (51) enumerates, explains, and illustrates a diverse collection of heuristics. Experience with using different heuristics gives students a better understanding of the problem-solving process and of possible strategy choices (32). Among heuristics that have resulted in better problem-solving scores are look for a pattern, guess and check, work backward, and draw a diagram. Researchers have also found that students who used strategies such as making a diagram or simplifying the problem showed greater flexibility in being able to choose other strategies when one strategy did not work (63).

> *A Spatial Reasoning Problem:* How can you use 6 toothpicks to form exactly 4 triangles (without breaking any)? [Answer:·construct a three-dimensional triangular pyramid].

For practical suggestions on teaching problem-solving strategies to middle grades students, see *Make It Simpler* (40) or *Solving Problems Kids Care About* (59).

Activities to Promote Fluency in Thinking About Mathematics. It is not uncommon for students to be unable to explain how they got their answers. Instead, they may simply exclaim, "I just knew it!" Students must be provided with specific vocabulary for mathematical operations and concepts if they are to be able to communicate about their mathematical understandings (66). And they must be afforded frequent opportunities to talk about their mathematical ideas.

One idea for developing understanding and verbal fluency is to ask students to make up questions for written or pictured data (4,10). Closely related are activities that require students to make up story problems for a given operation or for a given set of numbers. A final suggestion is to have students write and discuss their own story problems and solve or look for errors in problems written by others (19).

The Teacher's Role in Problem-Solving Instruction

Although the teacher's role in the classroom is clearly of paramount importance, until recently very little had been written about what teachers should do when teaching problem solving. In the last decade, however, some interesting research has been done in this area.

Teaching Actions. Charles and Lester have written widely about teacher actions during problem-solving instruction and have documented the effectiveness of their approach through a research study involving a large number of teachers in a variety of schools throughout the United States (11, 12). Table 4.1 provides a list of teaching actions recommended for use in teacher-directed problem-solving lessons. Note that the teaching actions are closely related to Polya's problem-solving phases.

Before students begin working on a problem, Charles and Lester recommend that the teacher lead a discussion to help students understand what the problem is asking, what constraints are given, and what assumptions they may need to consider. Next, to provide some assistance in the planning stage, the teacher should engage students in an open-ended discussion of possible problem approaches. While students are working on the problem (either individually or in small groups), the teacher should circulate throughout the room, offering carefully chosen hints at key points, and

TABLE 4.1 Teaching Actions for Problem Solving

Teaching action	*Purpose*
BEFORE	
1 Read the problem to the class or have a student read the problem. Discuss words or phrases students may not understand.	Illustrate the importance of reading problems carefully and focus on words that have special interpretations in mathematics.
2 Use a whole-class discussion about understanding the problem.	Focus attention on important data in the problem and clarify parts of the problem.
3 (Optional) Use a whole-class discussion about possible solution strategies.	Elicit ideas for possible ways to solve the problem.
DURING	
4 Observe and question students to determine where they are in the problem-solving process.	Diagnose students' strengths and weaknesses related to problem solving.
5 Provide hints as needed.	Help students past blockages in solving a problem.
6 Provide problem extensions as needed.	Challenge the early finishers to generalize their solution strategy to a similar problem.
7 Require studens who obtain a solution to "answer the question."	Require students to look over their work and make sure it makes sense.
AFTER	
8 Show and discuss solutions.	Show and name different strategies used successfully to find a solution.
9 Relate the problem to previously solved problems and discuss or have students solve extensions of the problem.	Demonstrate that problem-solving strategies are not problem-specific and that they help students recognize different kinds of situations in which particular strategies may be useful.
10 Discuss special features of the problem, such as a picture accompanying the problem statement.	Show how the special features of a problem may influence how one thinks about a problem.

(Table adapted from 35, p. 26)

> "There is a grain of discovery in the solution of any problem. Your problem may be modest; but if it challenges your curiosity . . . and if you solve it by your own means, you may . . . enjoy the triumph of discovery. Such experiences at a susceptible age may create a taste for mental work and leave their imprint on mind and character for a lifetime." (George Polya, 51, p. 1)

providing extension problems as appropriate. Finally, after the problem has been solved comes the most important teaching action: the teacher should encourage students to look back at their work; to check the reasonableness of their answers; to explain their solutions to each other; to relate the problem at hand to other, more familiar problems; and to reflect on what they have learned from both their successful and their unsuccessful attempts at a solution. (For further elaboration on teaching actions during problem solving, refer to the following works by Charles and Lester: 11, 14.)

Some researchers have suggested that it is also useful for teachers to model problem-solving behaviors for their students by thinking aloud while solving problems "cold" in front of the class (55). Students should be asked to observe carefully and,

> *The Voice of Experience:* "I approach each problem as if I didn't already know the conventional solution. The students are much more involved and excited. They become creators. It's as described by Felix Klein: The mathematician himself does not work in a rigorous, deductive manner, but rather uses fantasy." (Kenneth Cummins, quoted in 52, p. 83)

later, to discuss and critique the actions they observed. Researchers who have tried this idea in a seventh-grade class suggest that a better approach may be to use videotapes of more experienced students solving problems of the appropriate level of difficulty for the class (35).

> *A Seventh Grader Reacts:* "One thing that I really liked was that one time we got to watch someone else work the problem we had done for homework the previous night. It really helped to see someone else do the problem." (35, p. 112)

Questioning Techniques. An integral part of teaching children via the teaching actions described above is using higher level questioning techniques. Unfortunately, researchers have found that at least 80% of the questions typically asked by teachers are questions that require only general recall of information—for instance, the formula for area of a rectangle (62). Effective teachers, on the other hand, ask both recall questions and higher level questions—questions that call for explanations. For example, "If you have 100 feet of fence, what is the area of the largest rectangular garden you can enclose? Explain." Furthermore, effective teachers also ask follow-up questions after a correct answer is given. For example, "What if you had only 50 feet of fence instead? What if you could use a side of your house to enclose one side of the garden?" Such questioning allows children to reconsider their own thinking, to describe it, and to discuss how they might have answered differently or solved a problem more efficiently. Effective teachers realize that a problem is not truly solved until the learner reflects on and questions the appropriateness of his or her actions.

Organizing and Implementing Problem-Solving Instruction

The final component of a complete problem-solving program is consideration of guidelines for organizing and implementing whatever problem-solving instruction the teacher has planned. Among things that must be considered are classroom climate, grouping procedures, allocation of time, and evaluation procedures.

Classroom Climate. The ideal classroom environment for the teaching of problem-solving skills is a challenging one that accepts a wide range of explanations and ideas and that promotes communication about mathematics (17). Students should be willing to discuss their strategies and to defend their solutions. The teacher should be

---

Homemade Boat
This boat that we just built is just fine—
And don't try to tell us it's not.
The sides and the back are divine—
It's the bottom I guess we forgot . . .
(S. Silverstein, 58, p. 12)

---

tolerant of mistakes, should encourage persistence when initial solution attempts are not successful, and should maintain an open and accepting attitude in order to give students the opportunity to begin to make sense of their mathematical experiences.

Grouping Students for Problem-Solving Work. A complete instructional program for problem solving should probably include individual, small group, and whole class experiences since each of these requires students to use slightly different problem-solving behaviors. However, small group problem solving is particularly appropriate for promoting the classroom climate recommended above as well as for ensuring active participation and verbalization by all students. (For practical suggestions about small group work in mathematics see the following articles: 6, 20, 26.)

Allotting Time for Problem Solving. If students are to mature in their problem-solving abilities, they must be given sufficient time to solve problems. Problem solving is not a separate topic to be taught but a process that can be included in every aspect of the curriculum, and particularly in all mathematics lessons (24).

A Puzzle Problem: Fill in the cells of the magic square using each of the numbers 1–9 once, so that each row, each column, and each diagonal has a sum of 15.

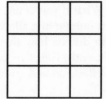

Since the problems presented should offer variety and depth, the time allotted for problem solving will vary with the project or problem. Not all problems can be solved during one mathematics lesson. In fact, research indicates that a great deal of time

"Students should be encouraged to explore some problems as extended projects that can be worked on for hours, days, or longer." (*Curriculum and Evaluation Standards,* 44, p. 77)

must be allotted for many problems, especially for the understanding phase of solving (23). And students also need time to discuss problems with one another if they are to consolidate and construct meaningful mathematical concepts (24).

Evaluating Problem-Solving Instruction

"How can I tell whether my students are doing better at problem solving?" Teachers who ask this question are aware of the difficulties inherent in grading problem-solving performance solely on the basis of correct or incorrect answers and are searching for more sophisticated ways of evaluating their students' growth. Although there has been very little research to date on the effectiveness of alternative forms of problem-solving evaluation, mathematics educators have begun to propose and recommend various evaluation alternatives (15, 31, 36, 44).

The NCTM booklet *How to Evaluate Progress in Problem Solving* (13) offers very practical suggestions for evaluating work on various types of problems, for considering students' facility with a variety of strategies and heuristics, and for documenting performance at various stages in the problem-solving process. Furthermore, this booklet also discusses evaluation of changes in students' beliefs, attitudes, and monitoring behaviors.

"In order to assess effectively within a mathematics curriculum that emphasizes applications and problem solving, we need assessment tools that are sensitive to process as well as product." (15, p. 118)

Looking Back

Successful teachers of problem solving recognize that students must be exposed to a wide variety of problem situations, that growth comes slowly, and that students must be taught to monitor their work throughout the various phases of problem solving. They also understand that students can be taught strategies for approaching problems and that it is important for students to develop positive beliefs about problem solving and about their own abilities. Perhaps just as important is that teachers encourage students to talk about their problem-solving efforts. Students should be expected to discuss relationships observed between old and new problems, to propose alternative strategies and justify their reasons for choosing or rejecting them, and to explain how they monitor and check their work. As Polya himself summarized: "There are two aims which the teacher may have in view. . . . First, to help the student to solve the problem at hand. Second, to develop the student's ability so that he may solve future problems by himself" (51, p. 3).

Looking Ahead . . .

Doing the research for this chapter has answered many of my questions about problem solving. However, I am still wondering how I can do a better job of integrating my textbook curriculum with problem solving and at the same time meet time requirements. It is important to teach both, but I have not found a clear answer to this dilemma. I would also like to know more about evaluation and performance assessment. As a teacher responding to so many needs, I find it difficult to assess while instructing. I would like to know more about effective methods of evaluating the process of problem solving rather than assessing only the product.

Tammy Miller

There are still many questions left unanswered by the research literature on mathematical problem solving. For example, how can computers best be used to improve problem-solving skills? How should teachers organize classrooms for cooperative work? How can writing help students be more reflective about their problem solving? I am convinced, however, that such questions should not be investigated only by "professional" researchers.

I am looking ahead to the day when many more teachers will initiate action research in their own classrooms. The best way to learn what works for real live kids, taught by typical teachers under actual school conditions, is to involve them in trying new approaches and in sharing their findings with others. *Conducting classroom action research is an example of real-world problem solving in the truest sense of the term.*

Diana Lambdin Kroll

About the Authors

Diana Lambdin Kroll, a former middle school and high school mathematics teacher, is an assistant professor in the School of Education at Indiana University in Bloomington, Indiana. Her special interests include problem solving and alternative assessment techniques.

Tammy Miller is a sixth-grade teacher at Clear Creek Elementary School in Bloomington, Indiana. Her teaching emphasizes problem solving related to the real world experiences of children. The authors met during a problem-solving project of the Indiana University Mathematics Education Development Center (Grant #NSF-TEI-8751478). The ideas expressed here are their own and do not necessarily reflect the views of the National Science Foundation.

References

1. ANAND, P. G., & ROSS, S. M. (1987). Using computer-assisted instruction to personalize arithmetic materials for elementary school children. *Journal of Educational Psychology,* 79(1), 72–78.
2. BALLEW, H., & CUNNINGHAM, J. W. (1982). Diagnosing strengths and weaknesses of sixth-grade students in solving word problems. *Journal of Research in Mathematics Education,* 13(3), 202–210.
3. BALOW, I. H. (1964). Reading and computation ability as determinants of problem solving. *Arithmetic Teacher,* 11(4), 18–22.
*4. BARNETT, J., VOS, K., & SOWDER, L. (1980). Textbook problems: Supplementing and understanding them. In S. Krulik (Ed.), *Problem solving in school mathematics* (1980 Yearbook, pp. 92–103). Reston, VA: National Council of Teachers of Mathematics.
5. BRANSFORD, J., HASSELBRING, T., BARRON, B., KULEXICA, S., LITTLEFIELD, J., & GOIN, L. (1988). Uses of macro-contexts to facilitate mathematical thinking. In R. I. Charles & E. A. Silver (Eds.), *The teaching and assessing of mathematical problem solving* (pp. 125–147). Hillsdale, NJ: Erlbaum; Reston, VA: National Council of Teachers of Mathematics.
*6. BURNS, M. (1981, September). Groups of four: Solving the management problem. *Learning81,* pp. 46–51.
7. CAMPIONE, J. C., BROWN, A. L., & CONNELL, M. L. (1988). Metacognition: On the importance of understanding what you are doing. In R. I. Charles & E. A. Silver (Eds.), *The teaching and assessing of mathematical problem solving* (pp. 93–114). Hillsdale, NJ: Erlbaum; Reston, VA: National Council of Teachers of Mathematics.
*8. CARPENTER, T. P., CORBITT, M. K., KEPNER, H. S., JR., LINDQUIST, M. M., & REYS, R. E. (1980). Solving verbal problems: Results and implications from national assessment. *Arithmetic Teacher,* 28(1), 8–12.
9. CARRAHER, T. N., CARRAHER, D. W., & SCHLIEMANN, A. D. (1987). Written and oral mathematics. *Journal for Research in Mathematics Education,* 18(2), 83–97.
*10. CHARLES, R. I. (1981). Get the most out of word problems. *Arithmetic Teacher,* 29(3), 39–40.
*11. CHARLES, R., & LESTER, F. (1982). *Teaching problem solving: What, why, & how.* Palo Alto, CA: Dale Seymour Publications.
12. CHARLES, R. I., & LESTER, F. K., JR. (1984). An evaluation of a process-oriented instructional program in mathematical problem solving in grades 5 and 7. *Journal for Research in Mathematics Education,* 15(1), 15–34.
*13. CHARLES, R., LESTER, F., & O'DAFFER, P. (1987). *How to evaluate progress in problem solving.* Reston, VA: National Council of Teachers of Mathematics.

*14. CHARLES, R., LESTER, F., & PUTT, I. (1986, November/December). How to teach problem solving: Step by step. *Learning, 86,* 63–66.

*15. CLARKE, D. J., CLARKE, D. M., & LOVITT, C. J. (1990). Changes in mathematics teaching call for assessment alternatives. In T. J. Cooney (Ed.), *Teaching and learning mathematics in the 1990s* (1990 Yearbook, pp. 118–129). Reston, VA: National Council of Teachers of Mathematics.

16. CLEMENTS, D. H. (1989). *Computers in elementary mathematics education.* Englewood Cliffs, NJ: Prentice-Hall.

*17. COBB, P., YACKEL, E., WOOD, T., WHEATLEY, G., & MERKEL, G. (1988). Creating a problem-solving atmosphere. *Arithmetic Teacher, 36*(1), 46–47.

18. COHEN, S. A., & STOVER, G. (1981). Effects of teaching sixth-grade students to modify format variables of math word problems. *Reading Research Quarterly, 16*(2), 175–199.

*19. DAVIDSON, J. E. (1977). The language experience approach to story problems. *Arithmetic Teacher, 37*(1), 28–37.

*20. DAVIDSON, N. (1990). Small-group cooperative learning in mathematics. In T. J. Cooney (Ed.), *Teaching and learning mathematics in the 1990s* (1990 Yearbook, pp. 52–61). Reston, VA: National Council of Teachers of Mathematics.

21. DOSSEY, J. A., MULLIS, I. V. S., LINDQUIST, M. M., & CHAMBERS, D. L. (1989). What can students do? (Levels of mathematics proficiency for the nation and demographic subgroups). In M. M. Lindquist (Ed.), *Results from the Fourth Mathematics Assessment of the National Assessment of Education Progress* (pp. 117–134). Reston, VA: National Council of Teachers of Mathematics.

22. GAROFALO, J., & LESTER, F. K. (1985). Metacognition and mathematical performance. *Journal for Research in Mathematics Education, 16*(3), 163–176.

23. GOOD, T., GROUWS, D., & EBMEIER, H. (1983). *Active mathematics teaching.* New York: Longman.

*24. GROUWS, D. A., & GOOD, T. L. (1989). Issues in problem-solving research. *Arithmetic Teacher, 36*(8), 34–35.

25. HENDERSON, K. B., & PINGRY, R. W. (1953). Problem solving in mathematics. In H. F. Fehr (Ed.), *The learning of mathematics: Its theory and practice* (Twenty-first Yearbook, pp. 228–270). Washington, DC: National Council of Teachers of Mathematics.

*26. JOHNSON, D. W., & JOHNSON, R. T. (1989). Cooperative learning in mathematics education. In P. R. Trafton (Ed.), *New directions for elementary school mathematics* (1989 Yearbook, pp. 234–245). Reston, VA: National Council of Teachers of Mathematics.

27. KNIFONG, J. D., & HOLTAN, B. D. (1977). A search for reading difficulties among erred word problems. *Journal for Research in Mathematics Education, 8*(3), 227–230.

*28. KOUBA, V. L., BROWN, C. A., CARPENTER, T. P., LINDQUIST, M. M., SILVER, E. A., & SWAFFORD, J. O. (1988). Results of the fourth NAEP assessment of mathematics: Number, operations, and word problems. *Arithmetic Teacher, 35*(8), 14–19.

*29. KRULIK, S. (Ed.). (1980). *Problem solving in school mathematics* (1980 Yearbook). Reston, VA: National Council of Teachers of Mathematics.

*30. KRULIK, S., & RUDNICK, J. A. (1980). *Problem solving: A handbook for teachers.* Boston: Allyn & Bacon.

31. KULM, G. (1990). *Assessing higher order thinking in mathematics.* Washington, DC: American Association for the Advancement of Science.

32. LESH, R., & ZAWOJEWSKI, J. S. (1988). Problem solving. In T. R. Post (Ed.), *Teaching mathematics in grades K–8: Research based methods* (pp. 40–77). Boston: Allyn & Bacon.

*33. LESTER, F. K. (1989). Mathematical problem solving in and out of school. *Arithmetic Teacher, 37*(3), 33–35.

34. LESTER, F. K., GAROFALO, J., & KROLL, D. L. (1989a). Self-confidence, interest, beliefs, and metacognition: Key influences on problem-solving behavior. In D. B. McLeod and V. M. Adams (Eds.), *Affect and mathematical problem solving: A new perspective* (pp. 75–88). New York: Springer-Verlag.

35. LESTER, F. K., GAROFALO, J., & KROLL, D. L. (1989b). *The role of metacognition in mathematical problem solving: A study of two grade seven classes.* (Unpublished final report: National Science Foundation Grant MDR 85-50346)

36. LESTER, F. K., & KROLL, D. L. (1990). Assessing student growth in mathematical problem solving. In G. Kulm (Ed.), *Assessing higher order thinking in mathematics* (pp. 53–70). Washington, DC: American Association for the Advancement of Science.

37. MAYER, R. E. (1982). The psychology of mathematical problem solving. In F. K. Lester & J. Garofalo (Eds.), *Mathematical problem solving: Issues in research* (pp. 1–13). Philadelphia, PA: Franklin Institute Press (subsequently Lawrence Erlbaum Associates).

38. McKNIGHT, C. C., CROSSWHITE, F. J., DOSSEY, J. A., KIFER, E., SWAFFORD, J. O., TRAVERS, K. J., & COONEY, T. J. (1987). *The underachieving curriculum: Assessing U. S. school mathematics from an international perspective.* Champaign, IL: Stipes.

39. McLEOD, D., & ADAMS, V. M. (EDS.). (1989). *Affect and mathematical problem solving: A new perspective.* New York: Springer-Verlag.

*40. MEYER, C., & SALLEE, T. (1983). *Make it simpler: A practical guide to problem solving in mathematics.* Menlo Park, CA: Addison-Wesley.

41. MUTH, K. D. (1984). Solving arithmetic word problems: Role of reading and computational skills. *Journal of Educational Psychology, 76*(2), 205–210.

42. MUTH, K. D. (1986). Solving word problems: Middle school students and extraneous information. *School Science and Mathematics, 86*(2), 108–111.

43. MUTH, K. D., & GLYNN, S. M. (1985). Integrating reading and computational skills: The key to solving arithmetic word problems. *Journal of Instructional Psychology, 12*(1), 34–38.

*44. NATIONAL COUNCIL OF TEACHERS OF MATHEMATICS. (1989). *Curriculum and evaluation standards for school mathematics.* Reston, VA: Author.

45. NATIONAL RESEARCH COUNCIL. (1989). *Everybody counts.* Washington, DC: National Academy Press.

46. NESHER, P. (1976). Three determinants of difficulty in verbal arithmetic problems. *Educational Studies in Mathematics, 7*(4), 369–388.

47. NESHER, P., & TEUBAL, E. (1975). Verbal cues as an interfering factor in verbal problem solving. *Educational Studies in Mathematics, 6*(1), 41–51.

48. NODDINGS, N. (1988). Preparing teachers to teach mathematical problem solving. In R. I. Charles & E. A. Silver (Eds.), *The teaching and assessing of mathematical problem solving* (pp. 93–114). Hillsdale, NJ: Erlbaum; Reston, VA: National Council of Teachers of Mathematics.

49. O'BRIEN, T. C., & CASEY, S. A. (1983). Children learning multiplication: Part I. *School Science and Mathematics, 83*(3), 246–251.

50. POLYA, G. (1949). On solving mathematical problems in high school. Reprinted in S. Krulik & R. E. Reys (Eds.), *Problem solving in school mathematics* (1980 Yearbook, pp. 1–2). Reston, VA: National Council of Teachers of Mathematics.

*51. POLYA, G. (1957). *How to solve it* (2nd ed.). New York: Doubleday & Co.

52. PORTER, A. (1989). A curriculum out of balance: The case of elementary school mathematics. *Educational Researcher, 18*(5), 9–15.

53. PUCHALSKA, E., & SEMADENI, Z. (1987). Children's reactions to verbal arithmetical problems with missing, surplus or contradictory data. *For the Learning of Mathematics, 7*(3), 9–16.

54. Ross, S. M., McCormick, D., & Krisak, N. (1986). Adapting the thematic context of mathematical problems to student interests: Individualized versus group-based strategies. *Journal of Educational Research, 79*(4), 245–252.

55. Schoenfeld, A. H. (1985). *Mathematical problem solving*. Orlando, FL: Academic Press.

*56. Schroeder, T. L., & Lester, F. K. (1989). Developing understanding in mathematics via problem solving. In P. R. Trafton (Ed.), *New directions for elementary school mathematics* (1989 Yearbook, pp. 31–42). Reston, VA: National Council of Teachers of Mathematics.

57. Silver, E. A. (1981). Recall of mathematical problem information: Solving related problems. *Journal for Research in Mathematics Education, 12*(1), 54–64.

*58. Silverstein, S. (1974). *Where the sidewalk ends*. New York: Harper & Row.

*59. Souviney, R. J. (1981). *Solving problems kids care about*. Glenview, IL: Scott Foresman.

60. Sowder, L. (1988). Children's solutions to story problems. *Journal of Mathematical Behavior, 7*(3), 227–238.

61. Stevenson, H. W., Lummis, M., Lee, S., & Stigler, J. W. (1990). *Making the grade in mathematics: Elementary school mathematics in the United States, Taiwan, and Japan*. Reston, VA: National Council of Teachers of Mathematics.

*62. Suydam, M. N. (1985). Questions? *Arithmetic Teacher, 32*(6), 18.

*63. Suydam, M. N. (1987). Indications from research on problem solving. In F. R. Curcio (Ed.), *Teaching and learning: A problem solving focus* (pp. 99–114). Reston, VA: National Council of Teachers of Mathematics.

64. Szetela, W., & Super, D. (1987). Calculators and instruction in problem solving in grade 7. *Journal for Research in Mathematics Education, 18*(3), 215–229.

65. Wheatley, C. L. (1980). Calculator use and problem-solving performance. *Journal for Research in Mathematics Education, 11*(5), 323–334.

*66. Zweng, M. J. (1979). The problem of solving story problems. *Arithmetic Teacher, 27*(1), 2–3.

CHAPTER 5

Measurement, Probability, Statistics, and Graphing

George W. Bright and Karl Hoeffner

Students at Westview Middle School are studying a pond in a nearby park so they can make recommendations to the city council about maintaining it as a city attraction. They stake out a rectangular region that includes the pond. A coordinate system is marked off with the origin at one corner and markers at constant intervals. A computer is used to generate 250 random-ordered pairs in the region. By determining how many points lie within the pond, they compute its approximate surface area. Then groups of students gather measurements several times each day over several weeks: water temperature at the bottom and on the surface, air temperature, size and number of microscopic organisms, composition of mud on the bottom, quantity and variety of plants, number of ducks in the pond, and so on. The data are analyzed, graphed, and interpreted, and a presentation is planned for the city council.

The importance of integrating measurement, probability, statistics, and graphing is illustrated in the project undertaken by the students at Westview Middle School. These topics are not only interdependent, but they also present some common challenges for students. First, middle grade students must deal with the content in several different forms: manipulation of objects (e.g., measuring), pictorial representation of information (e.g., graphs), symbolic presentation of ideas (e.g., formulas), and application to real-world events (e.g., presentation to the city council). If we attend to and relate these forms in our instruction, we may be able to help students construct useful concepts and maximize later learning. Second, students' backgrounds are likely to be incomplete, partly because of lack of attention to the content in previous classes. On the positive side this means that the content may be perceived as new and therefore exciting. On the negative side, it means you cannot assume understanding of even simple ideas. Third, many of the difficulties students encounter tend to persist even into adulthood. We hope this chapter will give both a frame-work within which to organize instruction and some immediately useful ideas for teaching this important content. While urging curriculum writers and teachers to integrate the topics of measurement, probability, statistics, and graphing, we face the reality that past research generally has dealt with them separately. We will discuss each in turn.

> "Mathematics instruction at the 5–8 level should prepare students for expanded and deeper study in high school through exploration of the interconnections among mathematical ideas." (*Curriculum and Evaluation Standards*, 31, p. 84)

Measurement

Enormous effort has been expended over many decades to understand the develop-ment of measurement concepts in children. Unfortunately, the most recent inter-national assessment of mathematics achievement (24) shows that for 13-year-olds in the United States performance is very low and far behind other nations. In the United States and many other countries, measurement is the content for which there is the most dramatic discrepancy between opportunity to learn and actual performance; that is, students are given instruction on measurement, but they do not learn the concepts well. Students must have opportunities to use measurement skills to solve real prob-lems if they are going to develop understanding. Hands-on instruction is difficult to provide on a printed page, so textbooks often compromise and emphasize symbolic rather than hands-on activities. Textbook programs need to provide hands-on activi-ties, and teachers must then take responsibility for implementing these real measur-ing opportunities.

> Have small groups of students compete in the cotton ball toss. Ask students to estimate and then measure each toss to the nearest centimeter.

Piaget's analysis of the development of measurement concepts is still a useful guide for instruction (38). Teachers must remember that students can be at very different levels of sophistication concerning measurement concepts. The assumption that stu-dents can and must learn about length concepts first, then area concepts, and then volume concepts frequently does not hold true (16). Measurement experience pro-vides opportunity for development of measurement concepts (e.g., conservation of quantities and iteration of units).

Units of Measure and Estimation

By middle grades some students still have difficulty recognizing the fundamental ideas of measurement: unit and the iteration of units. While most seventh graders were successful with simple problems involving use of measuring instruments, many could not determine the length of a segment that was not aligned with the zero mark on a ruler (Fig. 5.1). A common error seemed to be counting number marks on the ruler rather than units between those marks. Fortunately, performance seems to improve during middle grade years (15,26). But this confusion points up the need for an understanding of what the unit is and that the unit must be iterated.

One difficult idea is that the size of the unit and the number of units needed to measure an attribute are inversely related; as one increases, the other decreases. When told that 6 of one unit and 8 of another were required to measure a line segment (26), most seventh graders were unable to identify the larger unit. In contrast, knowledge of the impossibility of comparing measurements of two paths measured with two different arbitrary units increased substantially from age 12 to age 14 (15). You could present a similar situation to your students and share their responses with other teachers in your building. Context clearly influences the usefulness of understanding the inverse relationship. Perhaps more experience in analyzing problems would help. Since most measurement instruction is built around having students measure an object after the unit of measure is already identified, students typically do not have to reason about sizes of units. Practice at estimating measurements is one technique that helps students develop more flexible and useful concepts.

Estimation can begin either with an object for which an estimate will be generated (e.g., estimate the length of this page in centimeters) or with a measurement for which an object must be found to match (e.g., find a word on this page that is 7 mm long). For each type, both the object and the unit of measure may be present or absent from view (2). Most estimation instruction seems to be of the first type; it begins with a given object and a given unit, and the estimate is then generated. In contrast, many real world situations start with a measurement. For example, when packing a box you find objects to fit the available space (see Fig. 5.2). Estimating with a measurement as the starting point seems particularly useful for engaging students in comparison of units and helping them develop better understanding.

FIGURE 5.1   Line segments

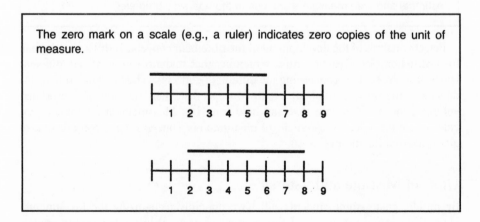

FIGURE 5.2   How many ways can you cover this grid with pentominoes?

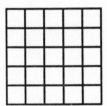

Most students' estimation skills are not well developed, especially for metric units; only 30% of 13-year-olds could estimate the length of a segment to the nearest centimeter (6). Performance was better for items in multiple-choice format (37% chose a correct metric estimate and 79% chose a correct customary estimate), but perhaps these latter items reflected familiarity with units of length rather than estimation skills. About 70% of seventh graders could choose the best estimate of the height of a tall man in feet, but only about 35% could do so in meters (26). More experience with estimation in both systems of measurement appears to be needed.

Teaching and Learning Formulas

Development of measurement formulas is an important part of middle grade mathematics. Formulas should be a product of exploration and discovery, especially in the context of geometry, and they should be developed as a convenient way to count iterated units. This is appropriate at middle grades for concepts like area and perimeter, if students have spent time measuring these in their own ways. There are many techniques for physically modeling formulas, especially those for area, but we know of no research on how such techniques affect learning. We do know that middle grade students are not terribly successful at applying even simple formulas for area and volume. Among seventh graders, 56% could compute the area of a rectangle with length and width given, but only 46% could compute the area of the same rectangle drawn on grid paper (Fig. 5.3) without the dimensions written in (26). Only 33% of students could compute the volume of a rectangular solid with the dimensions written in. You could ask your students to compute areas in situations similar to those in Figure 5.3 to find out how well area is understood in your class. Much more attention to developing understanding of and facility with measurement formulas is needed for middle grade students.

Equally apparent, however, is the confusion about the underlying concepts which are represented in the formulas (e.g., perimeter versus area). It has been repeatedly shown, for example, that middle grade students (and even preservice teachers) confuse perimeter and area in problem solving (26,42). This confusion may actually reflect serious difficulty with the concept of area. Only 40% of seventh graders and 55% of eleventh graders could choose the best estimate of the area of an irregular figure drawn on centimeter grid paper. About 25% at each grade chose an estimate

FIGURE 5.3 Labeled and unlabeled grids

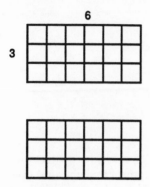

based on the total number of squares that overlapped the figure, and about 25% also said that when a figure was broken into parts, the areas of the separated parts could not be determined (Fig. 5.4). This performance is consistent with common errors in measuring area (18): focusing on length or width alone without accounting adequately for both dimensions, counting each unit that overlaps a region, counting corner units twice (for length and width), and counting perimeter instead of area units.

Summary

Students should have hands-on experiences with measuring, with emphasis more on understanding the underlying concepts than on applying formulas. Estimation seems helpful in this regard. Classrooms need to be organized so that students can move around and even beyond the room to make estimates and measurements. Limiting

FIGURE 5.4 Middle grade students need to
compare the areas of a figure
before and after cutting it apart

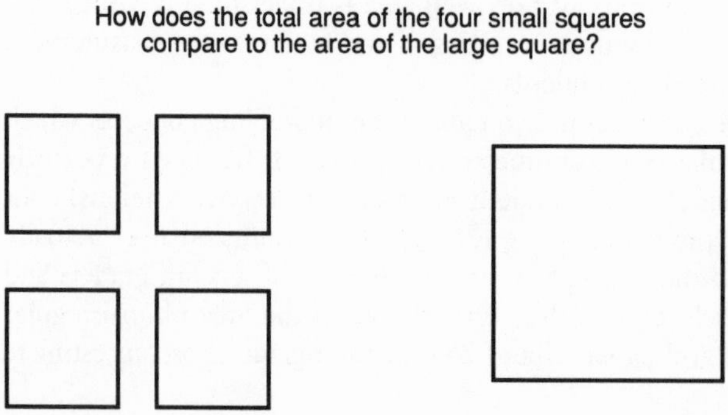

How does the total area of the four small squares
compare to the area of the large square?

experiences to a printed page restricts flexibility so that understanding cannot be generalized (37, 41).

> Have students work in groups to estimate the number of bricks needed to build the school building. Compare the strategies they use.

Probability

Much of what is known about how probabilistic thinking develops in students has been available for some time (10, 33). This base provides a beginning for improvement of instruction, even though research on model curriculum materials has been sporadic. One recent survey (19) begins to pinpoint the ways that a coherent theory might develop about what strategies adolescents are capable of learning from instruction or of generating themselves.

> "The young child goes through a first stage in which there is a failure to differentiate between the possible and the necessary, followed by a second stage in which there is the discovery of chance . . . as the antithesis of cognitive operations. The terminal third stage allows probabilistic composition by a synthesis of chance and deductive operations." (19, p. 117)

General Effects of Age

Studies of student understanding reveal an increase in knowledge with increased age, but age may be a simplistic explanation. In Britain, Green (14) noted a consistent improvement in performance across age, with boys outscoring girls on most items, but he concluded that general reasoning ability was more important than age in explaining performance. His follow-up interviews revealed that students had great difficulty talking about underlying probability concepts, suggesting both that backgrounds were deficient and that students had difficulty connecting their understanding of physical phenomena with representations of those events.

In the United States, about 25% of 13-year-olds could compute the probability of drawing a 4 out of a jar of Ping Pong balls with 2, 3, 4, 4, 5, 6, 8, 8, 9, 10 written on them (6). Only 18% of 13-year-olds responded correctly to a multiple-choice item for compound events (e.g., probability of two "heads" on a toss of two coins); 58% incorrectly answered 1/2. This overall low performance makes modest increases in performance from ages 9 to 13 to 17 (6) seem relatively insignificant.

Students' lack of experience with physical situations that embody probability concepts seems to be an important part of the explanation of poor performance. Students in grades 5, 6, and 7 who engaged in activities like generating sample spaces, calculating probabilities, and predicting events performed better on a direct measure of the instruction than did control subjects (11). But grade level seemed to be a more powerful influence than exposure to the instruction. Control subjects in grades 6 and 7 outperformed experimental subjects in grades 5 and 6, respectively. It is possible that the short period of instruction (12 lessons) simply torpedoed students' weak intuitions without replacing them with anything more useful. Consistent with this,

> Some important naive conceptions (e.g., that small sample distributions ought to match large sample distributions) seem more pronounced in older students and adults than in 13- to 15-year-olds. (19)

Green (14) noted that on some items (e.g., those involving random patterns) there was a decline or no change in performance across age. He hypothesized that increased exposure in other instruction to scientific and deductive thought may leave the impression that all actions are explainable by simple causal rules. Much school instruction in grades 4–7 tends to reduce phenomena to over-simplified rules that model some but not all aspects of real-world events. Young adolescents may try to impose simple rules on events that are, in fact, not simple and thus fail to recognize the complexity of events. When situations prevent simple modeling of outcomes (e.g., because of a large number of outcomes), adolescents fall back on intuitive strategies that often lead to inaccurate solutions.

> "It is the adolescent who balks at the unpredictable, and who looks for causal dependencies which would reduce uncertainty, even in situations where there can be no such dependencies." (10, p. 127)

Solutions to probability problems often seem counterintuitive even for teachers. Students (and adults) can simultaneously follow the logical reasoning needed to justify a solution yet be intuitively unwilling to believe or accept that reasoning. In such cases solutions often are erroneously remembered and then inaccurately or incompletely reconstructed when the need arises. Probabilistic paradoxes, too, are often explainable in terms of a mismatch between strongly held, but incorrect, intuitions and logical reasoning whose steps may be individually understood but whose holistic meaning is not accepted.

Students' Strategies

Improving instruction on probability requires that we understand how students deal with problems on their own. Situations involving equally likely outcomes are understandably the easiest for students. Instruction can increase performance (10, 12) even for students at the concrete stage of development. Lack of proportional thinking does not necessarily prevent development of understanding. Difficulty with part/whole relationships, however, will almost certainly hinder understanding (11). For example, when a red marble was removed from an urn, many fifth and sixth graders failed to decrease both the number of red marbles remaining and the total number of marbles, demonstrating a lack of "coordinating capacity" for part/whole relationships.

Similarly, distinguishing between additive and multiplicative situations causes difficulty even for seventh graders. One common error in dealing with sums of numbers on two dice (e.g., probability that the sum is divisible by 3) is assuming that the sums are equally likely. Students do not understand that the sample space is really 6 × 6 = 36 outcomes rather than the 11 sums they are dealing with directly.

> "The additive approach is still more 'at hand,' more intuitive, than the multiplicative one." (11, p. 10)

Similarly, Green (14) noted that for problems in which two bags of chips had to be compared in order to select the bag with the better chance of selecting a black chip there was a dramatic increase across age in the use of the black:white ratio as the selection strategy. Only 7% of the 11-year-olds used this strategy, but 42% of 16-year-olds did, with corresponding decreases in use of counting and difference strategies. Most students used a variety of strategies across several related problems, indicating that students' concepts are not stable and that teachers have to work hard to help students understand the similarity of such problems. By questioning your students, you might find which strategies they use. Then you could share these strategies with other teachers at professional conferences. Even college students demonstrate many misunderstandings (23). Consequently, teachers must expect that intuitions

> Only 10% of 15-year-olds could predict the probability of drawing out a number containing a digit 9 from a bag containing the numbers 1–100. (17)

will be difficult to alter. When dealing with content like probability that is so process oriented, it is essential that students discuss their thought processes. Processes are not likely to be changed unless they are explicitly examined and challenged by others.

Implications for Organizing Instruction

The apparent effects of both age and the acquisition of proportional thinking might suggest that instruction on probability be delayed until the end of middle grades when students know more. However, it seems equally plausible that the brevity of instruction in most studies may have unbalanced students' intuitively held concepts without providing enough experience to help them reorganize appropriate understanding. This is analogous to the unlearning of an inappropriate physical skill (e.g., typing with two fingers). Initially there is a decrease in skill (i.e., the product becomes poorer in quality or quantity) as the correct skill is learned, but ultimately the payoff is worth the temporary decrease. Because probabilistic thinking is initially developed intuitively, beginning formal instruction may seem to be counterproductive, when in fact that temporary decrease is necessary to set the stage for cognitive restructuring of underlying concepts. The current lack of attention in the curriculum to probability may need to be replaced with a much greater time commitment so that concepts can be fully developed.

With seventh graders (3) prior achievement was used as a means of forming groups to play games that embodied concepts of fair/unfair. Grouping by similar (homogeneous) and different (heterogeneous) prior achievement had no overall effect on learning. However, high-achieving students playing in heterogeneous groups improved more than high-achieving students playing in homogeneous groups, possibly because with heterogeneous grouping there is more chance for these students to consolidate their understanding during "tutoring" of low-achieving students. Providing situations for students to face faulty reasoning may be an effective way of forcing cognitive restructuring.

In a case study approach for teaching middle grade students to think probabilistically (1), scenarios were set forth, predictions and decisions were made by the students, and discussion of the reasoning behind those decisions was held. Students who received the instruction scored higher than students who did not, but again the

> "YOSSI: My cousin registered for pilot training. What are his chances of being accepted, higher than 50%, lower than 50%, or exactly 50%?
>
> DAVID: Why ask me? How should I know? I have never met your cousin and don't know anything about him.
>
> Question: Is David's answer right or wrong? If right, why? If wrong, should he answer more than 50%, less than 50%, or exactly 50%?" (1, p. 77)

effect was stronger for high-ability students than for low-ability students. While all students benefited from instruction, greater cognitive ability supported better development of thinking skills.

In two studies of students' understanding, sixth and eighth graders played pairs of games to determine whether one game was more fair or if they were equally fair (4). There was significant improvement noted on a test in which students were asked to choose the fairer of a pair of games when descriptions were accompanied by simulated plays of games; no effect was noted on a similar test in which the simulation data did not appear. In another pair of studies, seventh and ninth graders played a game in which a player rolls two dice, computes the sum, and then adds that sum to or subtracts it from a cumulative total in an attempt to reach a target number. A player's score for each target number is the number of rolls of the dice (analogous to strokes on a golf hole). There was significant improvement in performance on a test measuring knowledge of the more likely of two given sums of regular dice. However, there was no effect either on a test with dice numbered in nonstandard ways or on a test of selection of the best move in simulated plays of the game. These results speak to the need for helping students first make connections between physical problems and representations of those problems and then generalize their knowledge.

Summary

Unlike many other mathematics topics, probability instruction must compete with possibly strongly held intuitive beliefs and strategies that may be inconsistent with the instruction. Teachers need to be aware of their own conceptions of the ideas, and students need to be asked to explain their reasoning so that intuitions are openly discussed. Students need to be exposed to problems (32) for which intuitions alone are insufficient for finding solutions.

Statistics

Making decisions in today's world often requires the ability to analyze and interpret statistical information: for example, advertising claims, weather reports, statements of political candidates, and environmental impact reports. As a result, statistical skills are increasingly recognized as fundamental for mathematical literacy. Unfortunately, many students lack adequate comprehension even of basic statistical concepts such as *mean*.

Means and Weighted Means

The concept of a simple mean is more difficult for students to grasp than the simplicity the computational algorithm suggests. Apparently slight shifts in terminology cause great differences in performance (5, 6). For example, only about 6% of seventh-grade students were able to calculate a mean for given data. When the same data were presented in a problem that required finding an average, about 51% of the students were successful. Students seem more familiar with "average" than "mean." You could ask your students to compute an average and a mean to see if they also are more familiar with "average."

Specifically, of the seven identified properties of the mean (39), students had serious difficulty with three. The first was that the sum of the deviations from the average is zero; students scored only slightly above 50% on the test for this property. This property is important, for example, in estimating the mean of a set of data. Teaching this property effectively can be done by reversing the traditional sequence of instruction (4). Rather than providing students with data and having them compute a mean, provide students with a mean (say, 20) and have them construct data sets with that mean. With an even number of items in the data set, students will quickly discover a balancing strategy. For example, 18 is two less than 20 so it should be paired with 22, which is two more than 20. Constructing data sets with an odd number of items, then, provides a greater challenge.

The second difficult property was misunderstanding the impact that a zero can have on the mean; students scored slightly below 70% on the test for this property. Errors on this property center on the misunderstanding that zero means "nothing," when in fact it is a legitimate piece of data. Every middle grade teacher has probably had the experience of trying to explain to a student why he or she has received a lower than expected grade on a report card. Carefully entering the numbers into a calculator (particularly when one of the numbers is zero) and recomputing the average grade only results in a perplexed look on the student's face when the result in the display matches the grade on the report card. It is also interesting that 30% of preservice teachers thought that adding zero to a set of data would not change the value of the mean (29). Having students construct data sets for a given mean and requiring the inclusion of a zero can force students to consider the impact of zero.

Computer simulations may provide a method for helping students to overcome the misunderstandings they possess about the effect that particular values have on the mean. The BASIC program in Figure 5.5 generates interesting data for class discussion. Pressing the space bar alternately displays (a) a randomly generated whole number from 1 to 100 and (b) the cumulative average. The cumulative average is also plotted on a graph (Fig. 5.6) to provide students with a visual representation of the data. As the sample size increases, questions about the effect of each new number on the cumulative mean can be discussed. In addition, conjectures can be made about the shape the graph will take. For example, if the cumulative mean is 73.5 after three numbers, and a 2 is generated as the fourth number, how will the cumulative mean change? How will this affect the graph's shape? If the new number were 0, would the effect be different?

The third troublesome property of the mean is that the average is representative of the values that were averaged. Again, students scored slightly below 70% on the test for this property. This property is one of the most difficult for students to understand, but it is important because of its value in interpreting the computed mean of data. The mean is not necessarily part of the data it represents. Rather, it is an abstraction that may be troublesome to visualize. Only 40% of seventh graders knew that the average of two numbers must be halfway between the two numbers (5). You could show your students a number line with two points marked, and ask them to put a

FIGURE 5.5   Computer program for illustrating cumulative average

```
10 HOME: VTAB 23

20 HGR: HCOLOR=7

30 FOR J=1 TO 250 STEP 2

40 R=INT(RND(1)*100)+1

50 N=N+1: S=S+R: A=S/N

60 GET A$: PRINT N;"0";"NUM:";R

70 GET A$: PRINT "CUM.AVG:";A

80 HPLOTJ, 121-1

90 NEXT J

100 END
```

FIGURE 5.6   Sample output

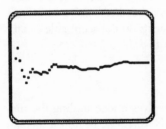

mark on the number line where the average of the two numbers should be. The responses might indicate how well they understand the concept.

Complete understanding of the mean may involve being able to picture the mean as a middle or balance point (34). A balance beam where the mean acts as a fulcrum balancing a distribution of weights may help some students understand the concept. A geometric analogy is the centroid of a triangle, that is, the point of concurrency of a triangle's medians (Fig. 5.7). Differently shaped triangles are analogous to differently shaped distributions of data. It may be useful for students physically to find the centroid of triangles cut out of some uniform material such as cardboard.

A concept that has great applicability in the real world is the weighted mean. Only 7% of 13-year-olds were able to solve weighted mean problems successfully (6). An analysis of errors showed that students attempted to apply an incorrect algorithm, indicating a lack of conceptual understanding. Later assessments reported similar results: 12% of seventh graders computed correctly. Surprisingly, 43% of students were able to choose the correct expression for computing the weighted mean (5).

There is evidence that misunderstanding of the weighted mean remains unresolved even for many adults: only 13% of college students solved weighted mean problems successfully (34). Middle grade teachers should expect that their students will have difficulty with such problems. The difficulty is typically in assuming that all infor-

FIGURE 5.7   Geometric models of the mean

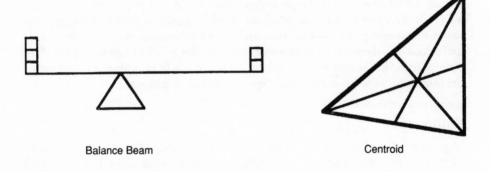

Balance Beam   Centroid

mation is equally important. For example, when asked to compute the grade point average (GPA) for a student who received a GPA of 2.7 on the first 60 credit hours and 3.5 on the next 20 hours, many college students act as if the 2.7 and 3.5 are equally important for solving the problem. These students do not seem able to take into account the larger number of credits associated with 2.7.

Other Descriptive Measures

More complete understanding of central tendency involves understanding the median and mode as well. Although 42% of 13-year-olds were able to find a median correctly, only 25% were able to derive a mode (6). When asked to choose an appropriate measure of central tendency involving a real-world application, only 12% of the students were able to make the correct choice (6). So, not only are middle grade students unable to compute measures of central tendency, they also lack a knowledge of applications of these measures. Unfortunately, there is little research on these concepts.

Measures of central tendency alone may be insufficient to represent a set of data adequately. The amount of variation or dispersion among values can help provide a more complete understanding of a data set. These measures are generally dealt with superficially at the middle grade level, and they have received very little research attention. Activities to use with students appear in professional journals (22), so teachers have a place to begin in their thinking about teaching these ideas.

Instruction Through Problem Solving

Providing students with meaningful and realistic problems is essential for developing statistical skills. Involving them actively in solving realistic problems is a successful teaching technique (35). In this method, students have participated in the entire process from problem formulation to collection, organization, representation, summarization, and interpretation of data. Planning instruction around questions has also been effective (30). Students in grades 4, 5, and 6 formulated questions, collected relevant data, and constructed representations of data to demonstrate what they found. Gains from pretest to posttest were approximately equal for each grade.

Having students make decisions about methods for collecting data rather than simply providing them with data sets helps further the general goal of developing problem solving skills. Organizing and representing data in tables and graphs help students get a feel for the shape of the data. Students should experiment with different types of representations (e.g., histograms, stem-and-leaf plots, and box plots) in order to help make decisions about which measure of central tendency might best be used to characterize a particular data set (27). These experiences will help students understand the limitations of any one particular representation of a data set.

Summary

More instructional time needs to be spent on the development of statistical skills. There is much more involved than the application of simple algorithms. We must actively involve students in the entire problem-solving process rather than simply providing them with fixed data for calculating statistical measures.

Graphing

Graphs are very effective for communicating information quickly, but there is a risk that the information will be communicated inaccurately. Even with lots of experience making graphs, students are not likely to be as good at it as graphics artists who have access to a wide range of technologies for translating information into pictorial form. Consequently, teaching students to read and interpret graphs accurately may be more important than teaching them to construct graphs (25).

Interpreting Graphs

Reading graphs is not a trivial task. Many graphs that are produced for commercial publications are in fact designed to magnify differences that may or may not be important. Students need to learn when information is accurately portrayed. For seventh-graders, prior knowledge of mathematics (e.g., 1 centimeter is less than 1 inch), of the topic of a graph (e.g., understand that height refers to "tallness" rather than "oldness"), and of graphical form (e.g., the tallest bar in a bar graph represents the greatest quantity) are all important for comprehending information in a graph (7). Significant predictors of graph comprehension were reading achievement, mathematics achievement, and prior knowledge of mathematics content. These results may not seem surprising, but they point up the complexity of graph comprehension as a cognitive task. Teachers must address the acquisition of supporting skills as graphing is taught.

One of the common mistakes that middle grade students make about graphs is to assume that a graph is always a realistic picture of a situation (8, 40). If students were asked to relate several graphs for a situation (e.g., height versus time and speed versus time of a roller coaster), the graphs will typically present quite different visual images. One of the graphs may represent a student's notion of "what the event ought to look like" but the others almost certainly will not. For the roller coaster, the height versus time graph will look much like the track, but the speed versus time graph will certainly not (Fig. 5.8). At the highest points on the track the speed will be low. The lack of match to a picture of the graph may be counter to the intuitive "expectations" of many students about the shape of any graph describing a roller coaster.

Similarly, 13- to 15-year-olds had great difficulty not only describing what type of "journey" was associated with a distance versus time graph but also knowing whether such a graph even represented a possible journey (15). Frequently, students act as if a graph is a map of the journey (8).

One technique useful for helping students understand that their mental image of an event is not necessarily what will show up on a graph is to have them deal with several graphs simultaneously. For example, the graphs in Figure 5.9 (40, p. 82) can be used as possible graphs for a variety of situations. Which one best represents the relationship between the circumference and diameter of a circle? Or between the

FIGURE 5.8   Graphs for roller coaster

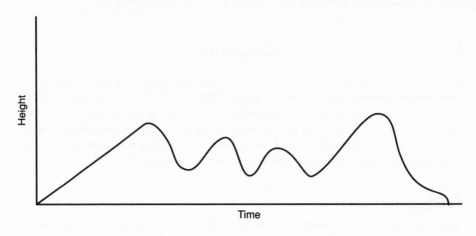

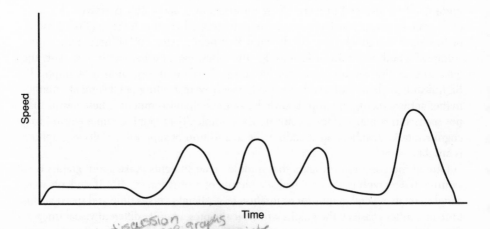

use a variety of graphs to extend discussion to why some graphs are more appropriate than others

area and diameter of a circle? Discussion of why one graph is better than another will expose both correct and incorrect conceptions of area, length, graphs, and functional relationships. This is an easy activity to do in class with your students. Students often know the formula for area of a circle, but they do not know what that formula means or how it translates into usable information about the relationship between area and diameter. Hands-on experimentation with models of circles (e.g., estimating and measuring diameters, circumferences, and areas of circles) would help students develop sufficient understanding to be able to apply formulas.

Problems requiring more than direct reading of graphical information are not often successfully solved (6). Seventh-grade students were approximately equally successful at using identical information presented in a bar graph or a table (5). Providing instruction like Swan's (40) or instruction that requires coordination of multiple presentations like tables and bar graphs or graphs and descriptions of events would seem

FIGURE 5.9 Graphs of functions

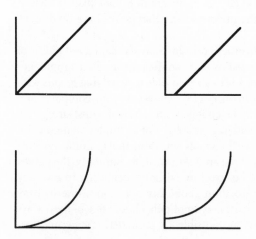

to be essential in helping students overcome deficits in being able to use information presented in graphs.

One of the difficult aspects of teaching graphing is scoring test questions dealing with graphs. One standardized test of graphing skills has been verified to discriminate well between high- and low-scoring students; middle and high school students answered only about half of the items correctly (28). Classroom teachers may, however, be somewhat more comfortable with less formal suggestions for marking students' graphs (40). For example, for the speed versus time graph of a roller coaster, one point might be awarded for each of the following aspects: (a) overall shape of the graph (e.g., correct number of "humps"), (b) correct identification of points of zero (or near zero) speed (e.g., beginning, each highest point, end), (c) slopes of rises and descents (e.g., increases in speed have steeper slopes than decreases in speed), (d) order of heights of humps (e.g., highest point is associated with bottom of steepest descent), and (e) smooth curve without any sharp corners. Teachers could make similar lists of critical features for graphs that they ask students to draw.

Graphs and Functional Relationships

One notion often associated with the term *graphs* is graphs of functions. Graphing functions is important because an understanding of functions is critical to much of advanced mathematics. Establishing a solid base of understanding in middle grades will serve students well in algebra and beyond. Two important concerns about how students interpret graphs of functions, especially in the context of the use of technologies, are notions of discrete versus continuous quantities and understanding of scale (13).

Some quantities are discrete (e.g., number of cars passing through an intersection each hour) while others are continuous (e.g., speed); students sometimes confuse characteristics of these quantities. This confusion is also manifest in the expectation by students that when a computer program zooms in on a graph, the points on that graph will be magnified; some students even expect the graph to look like a necklace of beads. Students need to internalize the understanding that points have no dimensions and lines have no thickness.

Because paper-and-pencil graphing instruction is done on standard sized pieces of paper, concerns of scale are rarely attended to in a significant way. In a simple pictorial exercise, from half to two-thirds of 13- to 15-year-olds realized that graphs with different scales displayed the same information (15). However, with computer and calculator graphing tools, scale can easily be changed, and students must struggle to understand how scale affects the presentation of graphs. For example, changing the scale for the graph of $y = 3x + 4$ makes the graph appear to move. Some students may see a left/right shift, while others will see an up/down shift. Similarly, the graphs of $y = 3x + 4$ and $y = 3x - 7$ could be transformed onto each other in a variety of ways: left/right slide, up/down slide, rotation about any point on a line halfway between the two graphs, and so on. Students may implicitly choose one of these ways without even acknowledging that others are possible. A particular choice may enhance or interfere with the instruction provided by the teacher.

Slope of lines, especially parallel lines, is related to notions of scale. Middle grade students have considerable difficulty comparing slopes of visually similar lines and even of different sections of the same line. Only about 30% of 13- to 15-year-olds were able to determine the slopes of two parts of a single line, and virtually none could correctly determine whether two lines with slopes of 1/3 and 4/11 were parallel (15). Interviews revealed confusion about both proportional thinking and parallelism.

Graphing calculators can soon be expected to be inexpensive enough that even middle grade students will be able to have access to them. Several software packages (e.g., science probes) allow students to change the form of representation of data (e.g., from graphs to tables or from line to bar graphs); thus, it is becoming increasingly important for students to develop cognitive linkages between various representations. We know little about how students actually relate representations. One characterization of representations is a multipointed, star-like iceberg (21). Only one point, representation, is in immediate memory at any time, but other points (other representations of the same idea) are presumably in cognition, ready to be brought to the surface at any time. Two unknowns are how to get students to move from one representation to another and how to help students realize when they need to make such moves. Students sometimes resist dealing with multiple representations because they do not find them helpful in solving problems (9). Rather, they see generating any representation as an end in itself, demanded by the requirements of the teacher or the text rather than by the needs of the problem. Changing students' attitudes about the usefulness and necessity of multiple representations is an important goal of instruction.

Conclusion

As illustrated in the opening scenario involving Westview Middle School, measurement, probability, statistics, and graphing can offer middle grade students opportunities to integrate mathematical topics and solve problems. Graphs, for example, are useful for communicating information from measurement, probability, or statistical activities. Measurement, in turn, is important for interpreting graphs, since most comparisons of information on graphs are based on length or area comparisons. Students must be comfortable with measurement if they are to be competent users of graphs.

Appropriate teaching of each of these topics requires a classroom climate that is open for experimentation. Discussion among students and between students and teachers is critical for the development of adequate understanding. Measurement, probability, and statistics are ideal topics for helping students learn to discuss mathematics, since problems can be solved in these areas even when students have had limited prior success in mathematics. Every student can contribute something (20).

"Although some [students] found the idea of discussion and open-ended questions very different from much that they were used to in mathematics lessons, they were quick to adapt, and many enjoyed their lessons all the more because of the different approach. One interesting feature was that those who often had great difficulty in the normal mathematics lessons were able to make a useful contribution to any discussion on the implications of the data with which they were faced." (20, p. 23)

Probability and statistics, however, seem to hold additional difficulties for understanding. Teachers must understand their own conceptions as well as their students' naive conceptions in order to design appropriate instruction. Emphasizing formalistic computation techniques may hide students' lack of a clear grasp of underlying concepts. "An initial formalistic approach to probability is unlikely to help students overcome misconceptions. However, if probability is introduced first through experiments, students appear to have more success in overcoming their probabilistic prejudices" (36, p. 95).

"There are difficulties inherent in the teaching of domains in which people are known to hold strong prior conceptions (or misconceptions) that are at odds with concepts central to the domain. . . . Beliefs students hold prior to instruction . . . in probability and statistics interfere with learning the concepts. . . . It is unfortunate that these misconceptions do not prevent many students from learning a host of the associated quantitative skills, because such skills can erroneously convince both teacher and student that the domain is being learned." (23, p. 92)

Measurement, probability, statistics, and graphing offer rich contexts in which problem solving can take place. Teachers can take advantage of a wide variety of excellent ideas to integrate content—for example, by using graphs to help students understand data generated in measurement activities. Students will surely benefit from such efforts.

Looking Ahead . . .

We are beginning to understand how students create personal embodiments of and intuitions about concepts in measurement, probability, statistics, and graphing. Advice that "students should be making hypotheses, testing conjectures, and refining their theories on the basis of new information" (31, p. 111) seems to apply broadly to all the content addressed in this chapter. Yet research is lacking on how such activities impact students' learning. Technology will cause us to rethink what is important to teach in mathematics as well as how mathematics ought to be taught. We cannot make those decisions without knowledge of how students learn, especially in the context of specific content, such as helping students predict changes in the mean and median when one data value changes.

George W. Bright

As we move deeper into the information age, good decision making requires increasing ability in interpreting data accurately. Why has so little attention been paid to how students learn important, fundamental concepts (e.g., measures of central tendency and dispersion)? The literature clearly indicates that it is insufficient for mathematics teachers to rely solely on textbook-based activities. Why is there so little direction for teachers in the research about the effects of actively involving students in their learning? Finally, why are there so few studies that validate appropriate curriculum materials for teaching concepts of measurement, probability, statistics, and graphing?

Karl Hoeffner

About the Authors

George W. Bright is a professor at the University of North Carolina at Greensboro where he coordinates mathematics education graduate programs. His interests include instructional technology (especially for mathematics teaching), mathematics inservice, statistics, and geometry. He has published a variety of professional articles as well as instructional materials for students.

Karl Hoeffner teaches mathematics and computer classes at Hartman Math-Science Academy in Houston, Texas. His interests include the use of technology in teaching mathematics, the development of curriculum materials that actively involve students in the exploration of mathematical ideas, and statistics. He also likes to fish.

References

1. BEYTH-MAROM, R., & DEKEL, S. (1983). A curriculum to improve thinking under uncertainty. *Instructional Science, 12*(1), 67–82.

*2. BRIGHT, G. W. (1976). Estimation as part of learning to measure. In D. Nelson (Ed.), *Measurement in school mathematics* (1976 Yearbook, pp. 87–104). Reston, VA: National Council of Teachers of Mathematics.

3. BRIGHT, G. W., HARVEY, J. G., & WHEELER, M. M. (1980). Achievement grouping with mathematics concept and skill games. *Journal of Educational Research, 73*(5), 265–269.

*4. BRIGHT, G. W., HARVEY, J. G., & WHEELER, M. M. (1985). Learning and mathematics games. *Journal for Research in Mathematics Education Monograph, 1*. Reston, VA: National Council of Teachers of Mathematics.

5. BROWN, C. A., & SILVER, E. A. (1989). Data organization and interpretation. In M. M. Lindquist (Ed.), *Results from the fourth mathematics assessment of the National Assessment of Educational Progress* (pp. 28–34). Reston, VA: National Council of Teachers of Mathematics.

6. CARPENTER, T. P., CORBITT, M. K., KEPNER, H. S., JR., LINDQUIST, M. M., & REYS, R. E. (1981). *Results from the second mathematics assessment of the National Assessment of Educational Progress.* Reston, VA: National Council of Teachers of Mathematics.

7. CURCIO, F. R. (1987). Comprehension of mathematical relationships expressed in graphs. *Journal for Research in Mathematics Education, 18*(5), 382–393.

8. DAYSON, G. (1985). *Children's concepts about the slope of a line graph.* Unpublished master's thesis, University of British Columbia.

9. DUFOUR-JANVIER, B., BEDNARZ, N., & BELANGER, M. (1987). Pedagogical considerations concerning the problem of representation. In C. Janvier (Ed.), *Problems of representation in the teaching and learning of mathematics* (pp. 109–122). Hillsdale, NJ: Erlbaum.

*10. FISCHBEIN, E. (1975). *The intuitive sources of probabilistic thinking in children.* Boston: D. Reidel.

11. FISCHBEIN, E., & GAZIT, A. (1984). Does the teaching of probability improve probabilistic intuitions? *Educational Studies in Mathematics, 15*(1), 1–24.

12. FISCHBEIN, E., PAMPU, I., & MĀNZAT, I. (1970). Comparison of ratios and the chance concept in children. *Child Development 41*(2), 377–389.

13. GOLDENBERG, E. P., HARVEY, W., LEWIS, P. G., UMIKER, R. J., WEST, J., & ZODHIATES, P. (1988). *Mathematics, technical, and pedagogical challenges in the graphical representations of functions* (Technical Report No. TR88-4). Cambridge, MA: Educational Technology Center, Harvard Graduate School of Education.

14. GREEN, D. R. (1983). A survey of probability concepts in 3000 pupils aged 11–16 years. In D. R. Grey, P. Holmes, V. Barnett, & G. M. Constable (Eds.), *Proceedings of the First International Conference on Teaching Statistics: Volume II* (pp. 766–783). Sheffield, England: University of Sheffield.

*15. HART, K. (Ed.). (1981). *Children's understanding of mathematics: 11–16.* London: John Murray.

*16. HART, K. (1984). Which comes first—Length, area, or volume? *Arithmetic Teacher, 31*(9), 16–18, 26–27.

17. HAWKINS, A. S., & KAPADIA, R. (1984). Children's conceptions of probability: A psychological and pedagogical review. *Educational Studies in Mathematics, 15*(4), 349–377.

*18. HIRSTEIN, J. J., LAMB, C. E., & OSBORNE, A. (1978). Student misconceptions about area measure. *Arithmetic Teacher, 6*(25), 10–16.

19. HOEMANN, H. W., & ROSS, B. M. (1982). Children's concepts of chance and probability. In C. J. Brainerd (Ed.), *Children's logical and mathematical cognition* (pp. 93–121). New York: Springer-Verlag.

*20. HOLMES, P., & TURNER, D. (1981). Teaching statistics to eleven- to sixteen-year-olds: An account of some development work in England and Wales. In A. P. Shulte (Ed.), *Teaching statistics and probability* (1981 Yearbook, pp. 18–24). Reston, VA: National Council of Teachers of Mathematics.

21. JANVIER, C. (1987). Representation and understanding: The notion of function as an example. In C. Janvier (Ed.), *Problems of representation in the teaching and learning of mathematics* (pp. 67–71). Hillsdale, NJ: Erlbaum.

*22. KELLY, I. W., & BEAMER, J. (1986). Central tendency and dispersion: The essential union. *Mathematics Teacher, 79*(1), 59–65.

23. KONOLD, C. (1989). Informal conceptions of probability. *Cognition and Instruction, 6*(1), 59–98.

24. LAPOINTE, A. E., MEAD, N. A., & PHILLIPS, G. W. (1989, January). *A world of differences: An international assessment of mathematics and science.* Princeton, NJ: Educational Testing Service.

25. LEINHARDT, G., ZASLAVSHI, O., & STEIN, M. K. (1990). Functions, graphs, and graphing: Tasks, learning, and teaching. *Review of Educational Research, 60*(1), 1–64.

26. LINDQUIST, M. M., & KOUBA, V. L. (1989). Measurement. In M. M. Lindquist (Ed.), *Results from the fourth mathematics assessment of the National Assessment of Educational Progress* (pp. 35–43). Reston, VA: National Council of Teachers of Mathematics.

*27. MAHER, C. A. (1981). Simple graphical techniques for examining data generated by classroom activities. In A. P. Shulte (Ed.), *Teaching statistics and probability* (1981 Yearbook, pp. 109–117). Reston, VA: National Council of Teachers of Mathematics.

28. MCKENZIE, D. L., & PADILLA, M. J. (1986). The construction and validation of the Test of Graphing in Science (TOGS). *Journal of Research in Science Teaching, 23*(7), 571–579.

29. MEVARECH, Z. R. (1983). A deep structure model of students' statistical misconceptions. *Educational Studies in Mathematics, 14*, 415–429.

30. MOKROS, J. R., & RUSSELL, S. J. (1989). What's typical? *Hands on! 12*(1), 8–9, 21.

*31. NATIONAL COUNCIL OF TEACHERS OF MATHEMATICS. (1989). *Curriculum and evaluation standards for school mathematics.* Reston, VA: Author.

*32. PHILLIPS, E., LAPPAN, G., WINTER, M. J., & FITZGERALD, W. (1986). *Middle grades mathematics project: Probability.* Menlo Park, CA: Addison-Wesley.

33. PIAGET, J., & INHELDER, B. (1975). *The origin of the idea of chance in children.* New York: Norton.

34. POLLATSEK, A., LIMA, S., & WELL, A. D. (1981). Concept or computation: Students' understanding of the mean. *Educational Studies in Mathematics, 12*(2), 191–204.

*35. RUSSELL, S. J., & FRIEL, S. N. (1989). Collecting and analyzing real data in the elementary school classroom. In P. R. Trafton (Ed.), *New directions for elementary school mathematics* (1989 Yearbook, pp. 134–148). Reston, VA: National Council of Teachers of Mathematics.

*36. SHAUGHNESSY, J. M. (1981). Misconceptions of probability: From systematic errors to systematic experiments and decisions. In A. P. Shulte (Ed.), *Teaching statistics and probability* (1981 Yearbook, pp. 90–100). Reston, VA: National Council of Teachers of Mathematics.

*37. SHROYER, J., & FITZGERALD, W. (1986). *Middle grades mathematics project: Mouse and elephant: Measuring growth.* Menlo Park, CA: Addison-Wesley.

*38. STEFFE, L. P., & HIRSTEIN, J. J. (1976). Children's thinking in measurement situations. In D. Nelson (Ed.), *Measurement in school mathematics* (1976 Yearbook, pp. 35–59). Reston, VA: National Council of Teachers of Mathematics.

39. STRAUSS, S., & BICHLER, E. (1988). The development of children's concepts of the arithmetic average. *Journal for Research in Mathematics Education, 19*(1), 64–80.

*40. SWAN, M. (1985). *The language of functions and graphs.* Manchester, England: Richard Bates.

*41. THOMPSON, C. S., & VAN DE WALLE, J. (1985, April). Let's do it: Learning about rules and measuring. *Arithmetic Teacher, 32*(8), 8–12.

42. WOODWARD, E., & BYRD, F. (1983). Area: Included topic, neglected concept. *School Science and Mathematics, 83*(4), 343–347.

CHAPTER 6

Multiplication and Division: From Whole Numbers to Rational Numbers

Anna O. Graeber and Elaine Tanenhaus

> *In the middle grades, the operations change from addition and subtraction to multiplication and division. And the numbers change, from whole numbers to rational numbers. Underneath all of the surface level changes is a fundamental change with far-reaching ramifications: a change in the nature of the unit. (16, p. 2)*
>
> *. . . Whereas additive situations need only involve . . . amounts that are derived from the environment and quantified by counting or measuring, multiplicative situations almost always require the manipulation of . . . relationships between quantities. . . . Again, the change . . . is not trivial. (16, p. 3)*

Among the NCTM *Curriculum and Evaluation Standards* directly related to this chapter is the statement that middle school students should "extend their understandings of whole number operations to fractions, decimals, integers, and rational numbers" (23, p. 91). This has frequently been thought to be a rather simple matter. Today's textbooks devote considerable attention to algorithms for multiplication and division with rationals, but they give little attention to the extension of the concepts of the operations themselves from whole to rational numbers.

The realization that the extension of concepts from whole numbers to rational numbers is neither quick nor easy has come from and led to research studies seeking to ferret out and build on students' early understandings of multiplication and division and the situations that can be modeled by these operations (5, 24, 26, 39, 40).

99

The availability of inexpensive handheld calculators and other calculating tools available at almost every work site has also shaped current goals. Emphasis on understanding, problem solving, estimation, and number sense replaces the former emphasis on mastery of algorithms for division or multiplication by multidigit numbers.

Concepts and Notation

Numerous recent studies indicate that students in the middle grades have gaps in their understandings of the meanings of the operations of multiplication and division and of the associated mathematical symbols. Since understanding of operations and symbolism are established goals for the middle grades, an understanding of students' difficulties and of methods for helping students build meanings for the operations are research outcomes that may be helpful to teachers.

Understanding and Symbolizing Multiplication

For many students, the repeated addition meaning of multiplication seems easiest to repeat and apply (6). In fact, Fischbein and his colleagues have called the repeated addition model the "primitive model" of multiplication. They claim that this model "tacitly affects the meaning and use of multiplication, even in persons with considerable training in mathematics" (6, p. 6). Steffe (34) has made us aware of the conceptual hurdles children face when struggling to master the sort of dual counting system required to make sense of repeated addition. Researchers (8, 26) have noted that a significant number of middle school students have difficulty producing concrete or pictorial representations of groupings from verbal descriptions (e.g., five boxes of six donuts or five boxes each with six donuts). For many students the interpretation results in a model similar to the one shown in Figure 6.1. As suggested by

---

Multiplication involves counting by units of a size other than one. Thus a child often needs to keep track of two counters running simultaneously. For example, when children are asked how many 3's there are in 15, more than a simple count to 15 is required. Children keep a second count to determine how many 3's are involved. Thus the count might be represented as 1, 2, 3, *1;* 4, 5, 6, *2;* 7, 8, 9, *3;* 10, 11, 12, *4;* 13, 14, 15, *5.* For examples of how children struggle with this see the work of Steffe (34).

Quintero (26, 27) student's proficiencies with these expressions can be diagnosed by having them make drawings or manipulative models of statements such as "five skateboards on each of the three shelves." The students who have difficulty interpreting the language "x sets each with y elements" or "x sets of y elements" may need instruction in the meaning of these phrases and practice both producing interpretations with drawings or manipulatives and formulating statements to describe drawings or groupings of objects.

FIGURE 6.1   Common interpretation of "five boxes each with six donuts"

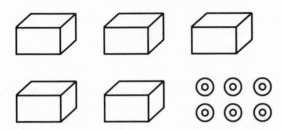

Expanding the Definition of Multiplication.   The repeated addition definition, while a useful link between multiplication and addition, is limiting if it is the students' only concept of multiplication. Since multiplication is first developed in the domain of whole numbers where, with minor exceptions, addition "makes bigger," students often conclude that "multiplication always makes bigger." Multiplication with nonintegral decimals or common fractions is not easily interpreted: first, because addition by a fractional amount is difficult; second, because the product is not always larger. (Think of 0.5×0.5. I add 0.5 to itself one half times? Think of $2/3 \times 3/4$. I add $2/3$ to itself $3/4$ths times?) Further, while the array, area, and cross product (or combination) models (see Figs. 6.2, 6.3, 6.4) may perhaps be teased out of the repeated addition conception, the relationships between these situations and multiplication is not immediately apparent. A number of researchers (24, 26, 29, 39) have investigated the difficulties students have in interpreting and generating examples of the cross-product and various other multiplicative situations. Here we concentrate on the means of seeing all the conceptual situations that are modeled by multiplication. This is not to suggest that the models be taught in the absence of real-life or problem settings. The need for an operation like multiplication should emerge from experience with genuine problems.

The array model can easily be tied to repeated addition. Students can be presented with a situation such as this: "Ana puts three baseball cards in a row in her scrapbook. Each page has room for four rows of cards. How many cards can she put on a page?" In response, they can make drawings that can be interpreted with repeated addition. The "tidy" arrangements that are called arrays can then be connected to the repeated

FIGURE 6.2   An array model for 2×3

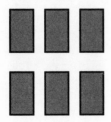

FIGURE 6.3   An area model for 2 × 3

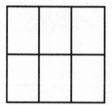

addition model for multiplication. Square tiles or cubes carefully arrayed on the overhead can also be used to illustrate arrays and the corresponding multiplication sentences. Finally, if the arrayed squares are pushed together, the repeated addition and array models can be connected to an area model. Grid paper is also useful in creating drawings of what might be termed "compact arrays" that can be seen as modeled by repeated addition and can be used to connect the repeated addition, array, and area models. Students will undoubtedly need a number of examples of how these models can be tied together as well as many experiences in modeling multiplication facts with stories or drawings and in modeling stories with multiplication sentences. Several authors present these models and techniques for making or reinforcing the transition between the models (10, 28, 35).

Since middle grades teachers are expected to extend multiplication to the rationals in a meaningful way, it is well worth the time for them first to develop the area interpretation of the operation with whole numbers. Then when the area model is used to make sense of expressions like 6 × 2/3, 2/3 × 3/4 or 0.5 × 0.5 (see Fig. 6.5), at least the model used in the interpretations will be a familiar one. The stu-

FIGURE 6.4   A cross-product model for 2 × 3

Four sets of three blocks can be used to generate 3 + 3 + 3 + 3 or 4 × 3.

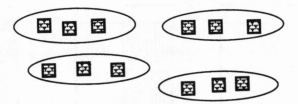

Or, we could arrange these boxes neatly, into a 4 × 3 array.

Or, we could close in the array forming a 4 × 3 area.

Relating the repeated addition model to the array model and the area model.

dents' hesitancy to accept 0.25 as the product of 0.5 × 0.5 is logical in light of the fact that multiplication (by whole number factors other than 0 or 1) has always resulted in a product greater than either factor. Thus it would seem beneficial if the students had some faith in the model as a means of realizing the product.

Other activities to lay the foundation for accepting that multiplication does not always "make bigger" might include explorations of products in patterns such as 6 × 6, 5 × 6, 4 × 6, 3 × 6, 2 × 6, 1 × 6, 0 × 6. Once decimals (fractions and mixed numerals) are understood, students can use their knowledge of the size of the non-integral factors and the information included in the set of products above to estimate boundaries for products such as 2.4 × 6, 1.7 × 6, and eventually 0.6 × 6. The actual products can be found using a calculator. Given such a set of examples, the class can discuss the pattern and the size of the product in relation to the constant factor. Students might also be encouraged to write about the pattern, describing it for other students, noting anything they consider to be strange, and telling why they consider the result strange. If this work is done against a real experience involving the "stretching and shrinking" of objects or the calculation of the area of a rectangle

FIGURE 6.5   Area model for 0.5×0.5 is 0.25

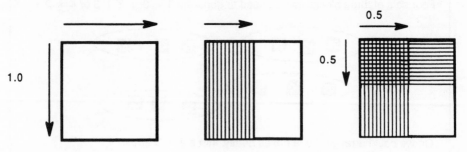

with the measure of one side held constant, the reasonableness of the results of the calculations may be even more evident.

Teachers should explore the "stretcher and shrinker" analogy for multiplication. A photocopying machine will enlarge or reduce by a range of factors. Students can explore what happens to a 10-cm line if it iss copied with a factor of 2, 1.5, 1.0 or 0.5. Computer graphics printing options that allow one to enlarge or reduce figures, maps, and other scale drawings provide additional settings for problem solving involving multiplication by factors less than or greater than one.

Notation for Multiplication.   Research suggests that middle school teachers need to take care in introducing and utilizing the various notations for indicating products. While 4×3 is probably quite clear to most middle school students, alternatives such as 4(3), $4 \cdot 3$, or related algebraic expressions such as $3m$ have been found to be readily misinterpreted. Matz (22) reported that many students interpret adjacency, or the chaining together, of symbols as either signaling place value notion or addition, not multiplication. They note that students have been taught to understand 43 as 40 + 3; so an interpretation of 4(3) as 40 + 3 or as 4 + 3 is not illogical to the student. This interpretation of chained symbols together with research on students' interpretation of variables (41) suggest that since "m" is the thirteenth letter of the alphabet, "$3m$" may be 30 + 13 or 43. To yet other students, expressions such as "$3m$" signal only a level in an outline or a company's trademark. Teachers will find it beneficial to talk about students' intuitive interpretations of these expressions and contrast them with the formal interpretations.

Understanding and Symbolizing Division

Again performance on simple division computational tasks may mask students' concepts of the operation. Graeber and Tirosh (8) reported that the most frequently given definition or explanation of division among fourth and fifth graders was that it "undoes multiplication." This may be an expression of the inverse operation concept or just the automatic repetition of an oft heard phrase. However, if it is the only concept students associate with division, they may not be able to match division with appropriate situations that are modeled by division.

> "I reviewed three text series that were fairly representative of those on the market. In one series, 9 pages of the grade 3 text, with roughly 56 demonstrated exercises and student exercises, could be said to give some conceptual background for multiplication, in the sense that it was possible to use given drawings to determine products. For division, the counts were 8 pages and 39 exercises. Very little additional work on concept development for multiplication and division, however, appeared in grades 4–6! Only two pages of the grade 4 text would allow the reader to attach meaning to multiplication by giving drawings which could show a meaning of multiplication, with about the same in the grade 5 and 6 texts. There was even less work for the concept of division in the grade 4–6 texts." (31, p. 3)

Middle grades students' primary level experiences in the whole number domain also lead them to place restrictions on division that are not necessarily true in the domains of rational and real numbers. Middle school students are unlikely to have encountered division by a divisor larger than the dividend (except perhaps in the context of money). Their insistence that "you can't write $4\overline{)2}$," seems to be based on a reaction to the mere appearance of a number in the divisor slot that is larger than the number in the dividend slot. The notion of 2 divided by 4 is not entirely foreign to them as most will readily agree that two pizzas can be shared by four people. What these students seem to miss is the connection or realization that a symbolic expression they know for the operation of division can be used to model this situation as $4\overline{)2}$.

There are a number of reasons that students may conclude that you cannot divide by a decimal, that is, that examples such as $0.25\overline{)2}$ are impossible. These include the following: experience restricted to the domain of whole numbers, the dominance of the sharing interpretation of division, the procedure for dividing by a decimal less than one ("change" the decimal to a whole number and divide as with a whole number), or some combination of these.

Expanding the Definition of Division.   Many elementary level textbooks introduce division as repeated subtraction—how many 2's are in 6? This interpretation, finding how many sets of a given size are contained in the total, has been called the measurement model of division (see Fig. 6.6). When using an alternative model, the partitive model, you are finding the size of each of a given number of equal sets as shown in Figure 6.7. Unfortunately, once the measurement model is introduced the frequency with which it is used in word problems in textbooks sometimes levels off (7); and the partitive model, which seems to dominate many adults' thinking about division, is reinforced. The division algorithm when taught using money or multibase blocks to model the algorithm is almost always interpreted with the partitive model. While this partitive model is certainly important, the partitive interpretation of 9 divided by 1.5 (how much is in each group if I share 9 equally among 1.5 groups?) is not easily imagined or represented with a drawing or manipulative. However, by using the measurement model, one can ask a question that has a more easily imagined answer, how many 1.5's are in 9? This interpretation also lends itself to

FIGURE 6.6   Measurement model for 6 ÷ 2

Two cupcakes are to be given out to each person.
There are six cupcakes. How many people will get cupcakes?

solution by drawing, by using manipulatives such as fraction pieces, or by measuring off segments of 1.5 cm along a 9-cm line.

The measurement and partitive division models are widely, although not universally, accepted as two early notions of division. Fischbein and his colleagues (6) have argued that there is a "primitive partitive" model of division and a "primitive quotative" (measurement) model. The primitive partitive model, based on experience in sharing, "demands" that the divisor be a whole number less than the dividend and, therefore, that the quotient be less than the dividend. These characteristics are typical of early elementary division problems in which division is confined to the set of whole numbers. In the primitive measurement model the only constraint "demanded" by the model is that the divisor be less than the dividend. Thus, some

FIGURE 6.7   Partitive model for 6 ÷ 2

Two people share six cupcakes.
How many cupcakes does each get?

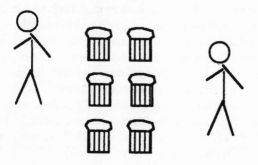

> "Put yourself in the place of a child who has divided thousands of times and on every occasion found the answer to be much smaller than the number divided— he has had 'make much smaller' as the one uniform associate of 'divide.' He now is told so to operate that 16 ÷ ⅛ gives a result far greater than 16. . . . There is a natural and, in a sense, a commendable reluctance to attach confidence to a procedure that produces a result so contrary to what he has always found previously to be the essence of division." (E. Thorndike, 1921; 37, p. 152)

researchers have argued that the naive conceptions associated with division are largely the result of experience with the primitive partitive model. Continued use of the measurement model permits students to interpret division by a rational number and, therefore, to encounter quotients greater than the dividend. For example, $2 \div 0.25$ can be thought of as how many one fourths in two? The resulting quotient, eight, is greater than the dividend, two.

> 0.10 ÷ 0.05
> (How many nickels in a dime?)
>
> 0.25 ÷ 0.05
> (How many nickels in a quarter?)
>
> 0.50 ÷ 0.10
> (How many dimes in a half-dollar?)
>
> Using the measurement interpretation and knowledge of coins to answer division exercises.

If students bring notions such as "you can't divide by a larger number," instruction must facilitate their construction of a new conception of the operation. Research by Bell and his colleagues at the Shell Centre in Britain (3, 36) suggests that it is important for students to (a) verbalize their expectations for the results of such problems, (b) argue the correctness of alternative solutions, (c) practice application of the concept or procedure, and (d) review how their expectations differed from their conclusions and why. Such engagement of students is thought to provoke the kinds of mental steps that facilitate conceptual changes or restructuring of conceptions. A small but growing number of research studies that utilized this technique to help students alter common naive conceptions suggests that the theory indeed has merit.

Notation for Division.   The symbolism and the language used to express division is much more varied and subtle than that used for multiplication. Word order, notational order, and the order in which one enters the numbers into a calculator certainly have no consistency. Although 12 divided *by* 3 is entirely different from 12 divided *into* 3, not all students attend to these subtleties. "Natural language" expressions also cause confusion. "Sue and I divided the three large cookies in half. How much do we each get?" does not translate as $3 \div 1/2$ or as $1/2 \div 3$. What students need is an understanding of the role of the dividend, divisor, and quotient, not the mere memorization of these terms as labels for various positions in the symbolic expressions. Such understanding seems to come from many experiences in modeling a wide variety of situations.

$3\overline{)12}$ $12 \div 3$ $12/3$
Different symbolic expressions that have the same meaning.

- Twelve divided by three
- Three divided into twelve
- Three into twelve
- Three goes into twelve

Different verbal expressions that describe the same computation.

The a/b notation for division offers a potential connection between the operation of division and the rational numbers. For example, if two small pizzas are shared by three people, each person receives $2 \div 3$, or $2/3$ of a pizza. The fact that the answer to the problem is given in the notation for the solution is rarely appreciated by students (8, 12). This connection may also help students who argue that one cannot divide a smaller number by a larger number. Teachers need to help students realize and make explicit the relationship between such real word situations, the division sentences, and the rational number answers.

Properties of Division.   If the complications of notation listed above are not enough, there is yet another related notion many students hold, namely that $2 \div 4$ is the same as $4 \div 2$. Overgeneralization of commutative properties of addition and multiplication, the notion that the "little number must be divided into the big number," and confusion about how to read division sentences probably all contribute to this naive conception. Students need to see the contrast between such demonstrable situations as "six meters of rope equally shared among two people" and "two meters of rope equally shared by six people." After acting out and then symbolizing both situations, students should discuss and perhaps write about how the contrast is reflected in the two expressions $6 \div 2$ and $2 \div 6$. First, writing the results as "each of two people would get three meters of rope" and "each of six people would get one third meter of rope" may help students realize the distinctions. Bell (2) has developed an exercise in which small groups of students sort cards. Each card contains one of the symbols 6/2, 2/6 $2\overline{)6}$, $6\overline{)2}$, 3, 1/3, "can't do," or one of the word problems suggested above. Students are asked to make two sets of four expressions that have the same meaning. The ensuing discussions help teachers assess students' understanding and require that students verbalize and defend their selections.

Solving Word Problems

Interpretations of the NAEP data (20) on problem solving suggest that (a) word problems are more difficult than the corresponding calculation alone, (b) problems with extraneous data are more difficult than those without, and (c) two-step word problems are more difficult than one-step problems.

Researchers (e.g., 32) who have probed students' word problem-solving strategies find that they frequently select the operation by guessing, by trying all operations and finding the one that gives a reasonable answer, by studying the number and digit length of the given pieces of data, or by taking cues from key words such as "more" or "times." While these strategies may hold some success for students solving routine textbook problems, they can quickly lead to errors in solving nonroutine or everyday life problems. Indeed, the routine textbook problems that most students encounter may foster these ill-considered strategies. Although textbooks with recent copyright dates do tend to mix problems requiring different operations, simple (having no more or no less than the needed data), one-step problems still dominate.

"Why do students use the immature strategies? . . . A computation-centered curriculum, and teachers so busy that checking consists most often of looking at what blanks contain, communicate that one thing is important in mathematics, the answer. Even before the choices of operation are problematical, we *must* routinely ask students to defend their choices, both to identify users of immature strategies and to shape what is recognized as an acceptable reason." (30, p. 236)

The precise strategy a student uses to solve problems can generally be determined only during an interview, but a rough assessment of student understanding of the operation can be obtained by asking students to select or write the number sentence for a word problem without carrying out the computation (33) or to write a word problem for a number sentence (5).

Varieties of Problems

Multiplication and division situations appear to be even more difficult for students to model with number sentences than are addition and subtraction situations. The many types of multiplication and division situations may be partially responsible for students' difficulties. Students' beliefs about the results of multiplying or dividing by numbers less than one also underlie many errors.

Schwartz (29) made the point that in addition and subtraction we take two like quantities and produce a third like quantity. (I walked 2 km and then ran 3 km. I traveled a total of 2 km + 3 km, or 5 km). Thus Schwartz called these operations referent (or unit) preserving operations. Generally in multiplication and division we take two quantities, either alike or different, and produce a third quantity that is often unlike either of the first two. Hence these operations are called unit transforming. For example, I have 8 T-shirts and 4 pairs of jeans. I can make 8 T-shirts × 4 jeans,

---

(A) A cheese weighs 3 kilograms.
One kilogram costs $8.00.
To find the price of the cheese,
which operation would you use?

8/3   8 × 3   8 + 3   8 + 8

(B) A piece of cheese weighs 0.92 kilograms.
One kilogram costs $8.50.
To find the price of the cheese,
which operation would you use?

8.5 + 0.92   8.5 ÷ 0.92   8.5 × 0.92   8.5 − 0.92

Most (83%) 12- and 13-year-old students correctly answered problem A. Given problem B a week later, only 29% answered correctly. Other students were given the problems one right after the other in an interview. Many answered A correctly but answered B incorrectly and either claimed that the problems were different or that they could not see how they were alike. Most of those who answered B incorrectly, selected division as the correct operation (problems adapted from Ekenstam and Greger, 5).

---

or 32 outfits. Or, she rode 40 km at an average speed of 10 km per hour (km/h). She bicycled for about 40 km ÷ 10 km/h, or 4 hours. In each of these examples the unit of measure of the answer is different from the unit of the other two quantities. Schwartz argued that when students build their concept of multiplication and division on the repeated addition and repeated subtraction models, they are led to believe that the calculated product or quotient will have the same unit as the quantities used in the calculation.

Schwartz's interest in the units of numbers is reflected in the classification scheme he chose for multiplication and division problems. Schwartz defined extensive quantities as measurements that tell how much of something—6 donuts, 4 cats, 13 years, 5 cm. Counting or a simple measurement gives us *extensive* quantities—direct measures of how much. *Intensive* quantities express relationships between two measures and are frequently expressed using the word "per" or some common language equivalent. Thus 40 km/h, 6 donuts in each box, and 10 cents for a stick of gum are examples of intensive quantities.

Schwartz categorized both multiplication and division problems according to the nature (intensive versus extensive) of the two factors and the product. He discussed the three cases shown in Table 6.1: one factor is intensive and the other is extensive, both factors are extensive, both factors are intensive.

Schwartz's scheme is of interest in light of findings about students' difficulties in interpreting rates. Bell (2) notes that middle grades students often believe that expressions such as "4 km per hour" and "4 hours per km" mean the same thing. The numerator and denominator roles of the quantities in a rate are not correctly recognized.

> Problems with several intensive quantities may be easier to solve if the intensive quantities are expressed as fractions. The method of unit analysis (sometimes called dimensional analysis) helps some students structure the computation. For example, given the problem,
>
> A car traveling $55 \frac{\text{miles}}{\text{hour}}$ uses gasoline at the rate of $33 \frac{\text{miles}}{\text{gallon}}$. How many gallons of gasoline does the car consume per hour?
>
> students may see
>
> $$\frac{\text{miles}}{\text{hour}} \times \frac{\text{gallons}}{\text{mile}} = \frac{\text{gallons}}{\text{hour}}$$
>
> $$\frac{55 \text{ miles}}{\text{hour}} \div \frac{33 \text{ miles}}{\text{gallon}} = ? \frac{\text{gallons}}{\text{hour}}$$

Vergnaud (40) also discusses the difficulties in moving from whole number operations to operations with rational numbers. He notes that when students add or subtract with fractions such as 1/2 + 1/4, the result makes sense only if the fractions are thought of as quantities (parts of wholes). Thus 1/2 of a dollar plus 1/4 of a dollar gives 3/4 of a dollar. On the other hand, multiplication and division of such fractions is interpretable only in terms of fractions as operations (as sharing). So 1/2 × 1/4 is thought of as follows: If I borrow one half of one fourth of your money, I will have one eighth of your money.

Yet other categorizations of problems may be found (14, 24, 38). Hendrickson (14) discusses change, compare, selection, and rate problems, briefly describing how each type might be illustrated with manipulatives or relatively easy to understand examples. Nesher (24) discusses only multiplication problems of the "mapping rule," compare, and Cartesian multiplication types (see Table 6.2). She focuses on the role language may play in developing multiplication concepts and questions whether repeated addition is necessarily a primitive model or an artifact of schooling. Usiskin and Bell (38) separate their categories of multiplication (size change, acting across, rate factor) and division (ratio, rate, rate divisor, size change divisor, and recovering factor) situations giving numerous, real-life examples of each type.

TABLE 6.1   Problem Types Discussed by Schwartz (29)

Problem type	Example
Intensive times extensive	At 3¢ per sticker, how much will five stickers cost? 15¢
Extensive times extensive	A card is 3″ wide and 5″ long. What is the area? 15 sq. in
Intensive times intensive	At 3¢ per sticker and five stickers per sheet, how much does a sheet cost? 15¢

TABLE 6.2   Types of Multiplication Problems

Type	Characteristic	Example
Mapping	Represented by repeated addition	There are five shelves. Each shelf has 6 books. How many books are on these shelves?
Compare	Involves idea of "times as many"	Juanita has five books. Demitri has six times as many. How many books does Demitri have?
Cartesian	Also called "cross product"	Reginald has 5 pairs of jeans and 6 sweatshirts. How many outfis can he make with these jeans and sweatshirts?

Suggestions for Teachers

The discussion above makes clear that the application of multiplication and division concepts is not an easy matter. Vergnaud (39) argues that the competency is not quickly achieved, but needs to be built over years of schooling for students ages 7–18. He warns against two options: (a) not teaching these applications because they are too difficult for students of some given age and (b) expecting that having once been taught the applications correctly, the students will have achieved mastery. Careful stretching of students' concepts seems necessary. Vergnaud (40) encourages teachers to examine their students' current level of understanding and look ahead at what their students will be asked to understand in the future.

In addition to helping them comprehend the various meanings of multiplication, teachers may need to help students wrestle with the phenomenon of changing labels and with the meaning of expressed ratios (such as km per hour, km per liter, and cost per kg). Textbook problems tend to be predominantly of the "mapping rule" type and provide very little experience with rational numbers less than one (7). Accepting the notion that multiplication does not always make bigger and that division does not always make smaller may come from studying these unexpected results when they do occur. Some of the sources listed (e.g., 14 and 38) will provide teachers with a variety of problems that can add richness to the concepts of multiplication and division.

Certainly teachers need to apply all the techniques advocated for good problem solving—avoiding reliance on key words, modeling their own thoughts in determining the structure of a situation, setting up information in tables that imply relationships, and so on. However, one reason that multiplication and division problems are often so complex is that many related ideas (such as understanding fractions as indicated division, rate, ratio, and proportion) are involved. Teachers will need to recognize what knowledge is required and what concepts their students know or need to know.

Algorithms for Multiplication and Division

Although relatively little recent research deals directly with the teaching of algorithms for multiplication and division of whole numbers, two trends are clear. First, whatever algorithms are taught should be taught meaningfully. Second, instruction ought to stress estimation, number sense, and skill in selecting the tool to perform a given calculation. When procedures are only memorized, the rules for the various operations for whole numbers, decimals, and common fractions often become confused, and the numerous systematic multiplication and division errors described by Ashlock (1) emerge. If students have no number sense or estimation skills, they cannot, even if they try, recognize their own faulty application of rules leading to "ridiculous" answers (15).

"Unfortunately, all of the fundamental operations of arithmetic are ordinarily taught as chains of rules. Usually the simplest case is taught first and the rules are firmly entrenched in children's minds with extended practice before other cases are explored. (Frequently the incorrect rule a child adopts is a modification of the first rule learned.) A child who knows the rules sifts through the chain to select one he thinks is appropriate for doing a particular problem. But then he cannot tell whether he picked the right rule or not because he has not been exposed to the underlying logic from which he can make intelligent decisions." (18, p. 40)

Understanding Algorithms

Wearne and Hiebert (42) interpret their work and the work of others on decimals to indicate that students are more likely to achieve semantic understanding (knowing why) of a process if that understanding is established before students gain a routinized syntactical understanding (knowing how) of the procedure. Further they argue that students need to have a meaningful grasp of the symbols (numbers and operations) involved before they can comprehend the procedures. There seem to be two main approaches to teaching algorithms meaningfully: a mapping approach and a rule elimination approach.

In the mapping approach, a model or manipulative is used in a manner that reflects the steps of the algorithm. Students then perform and eventually record each step—producing the algorithm as they go. Eventually the manipulatives or models are withdrawn, and the record or algorithm is generated on its own. Graph paper (9, 10), base-10 blocks (9, 10, 13, 17), and money (4, 25) have been used as models in mapping approaches. As with all instruction using manipulatives or models, unless care is taken in the instruction to ensure understanding, students may simply be memorizing two routines—one with a model and one with numerals. Also, the routine with the model may make sense but be totally disconnected from the routine with the symbols.

In the rule elimination approach, the student's understanding of the quantities and the operation are used to derive some written notation for the process. Understanding and reasoning are emphasized. A systematic routine with manipulatives is not demonstrated by the teacher, and the standard algorithm may or may not be derived from this process. Sometimes this approach is reflected in work that builds on what has been labeled children's intuitive methods. Weiland (43) expresses this point of view in writing about the standard division algorithm. She claims that children frequently express a rather intuitive understanding of the distributive property that undergirds the division algorithm. Hamic (11) also discusses examples of students' alternative algorithms and the insights they exhibit. As calculators become more accessible, educators may need to revisit the question of whether children's "inefficient" but understood methods of carrying out some algorithms are sufficient.

Estimation, Number Sense, and Tools

If results obtained from paper-and-pencil algorithms, calculators, or computers are to be established as sensible, students need skills in estimating products and quotients. They should also be reminded to reflect on the sensibility of their answers. The now infamous third NAEP item (21) involving army buses holding 36 soldiers each and 1,128 soldiers needing transportation was answered correctly by 24% of students who had no access to calculators and by only 7% of those who did. Although many textbooks stress estimation as a means of placing the first digit in the quotient, few encourage students to return to their estimate and check their calculated answer against it and to argue the sensibility of the answer (7). When using and teaching the algorithms in context, a teacher should not consider the work complete until the student interprets and justifies the reasonableness of the answer in the context of the problem situation. This implies something other than using the inverse operation to check computation—the usual interpretation children place on the direction to "check your work" (19).

> "No significant progress can be made until teachers put emphasis on helping students verify their thinking in the realm of their own experiences both in and out of school. That is, teachers need to put emphasis on building conceptual referents for the symbols and operations so children can use them to guide their thinking." (18, p. 40)

The habit of putting the answer back into the context of the original problem must be nurtured as the algorithms are extended to the domain of rationals. Students must understand for example that $0.5\overline{)2}$ indeed has 4 as the quotient. Understanding that it is reasonable to get 4, not 0.4, pieces of ribbon each 0.5m long from a 2m piece of ribbon may help those students who argue that while 4 is the quotient for $5\overline{)20}$, moving the decimal point to produce $5\overline{)20}$ from $0.5\overline{)2}$ requires that one "move" the decimal point back to obtain the quotient, 0.4, for the original question.

Looking Ahead . . .

Teachers may one day welcome students whose prior experiences have given them rich concepts of multiplication and division as well as facility with the notations for these operations. However, it is unlikely that the elementary schools will introduce these operations with other than whole numbers. Thus teachers will continue to face the challenge of helping students build new ideas as they use rational number factors and products, divide by numbers greater than the dividend, and find products less than one of the factors. Teachers and researchers working together can create and test new strategies and curricula designed to help students achieve such conceptual changes.

Anna O. Graeber

There are two issues I would like to see addressed. First, is there a model for multiplication of whole numbers that lends itself to multiplication of two negative numbers? None of the models I am familiar with are directly related to multiplication concepts; rather, they facilitate learning of the rules.

Second, what is the best time to encourage students who use primitive methods for finding simple products (e.g., $7 \times 8 = 8 + 8 + 8 + 8 + 8 + 8 + 8 = 16 + 16 + 16 + 8 = 32 + 16 + 8$) to rely on memorization of the basic facts? Furthermore, what do we do with students who seem unable to make this transition?

Elaine Tanenhaus

About the Authors

Anna O. Graeber teaches mathematics education courses at the University of Maryland at College Park. She has prepared teacher education materials on common misconceptions in secondary school mathematics. One of her current interests is in methods of teaching that help students overcome the influence of misconceptions.

Elaine Tanenhaus teaches mathematics and serves as the mathematics department head at Eastern Intermediate School in Montgomery County, Maryland. She has conducted numerous workshops on instructional strategies for preparing students for the state competency test. An Ohio State graduate in mathematics education, Ms. Tanenhaus holds a master's degree in human development from Fairleigh Dickinson University.

References

*1. ASHLOCK, R. (1990). *Error patterns in computation: A semi-programmed approach* (5h ed.). Columbus, OH: Merrill.
*2. BELL, A. (1986). Diagnostic Teaching: 2. Developing conflict-discussion lessons. *Mathematics Teaching, 116,* 26–29.
3. BELL, A., BREKKE, G., & SWAN, M. (1987). Misconceptions, conflict and discussion in the teaching of graphical interpretation. In J. Novak (Ed.), *Proceedings of the Second International Seminar on Misconceptions and Educational Strategies in Science and Mathematics* (Vol. 1, pp. 46–58). Ithaca, NY: Cornell University.
4. CHEEK, H., & OLSON, M. (1986). A den of thieves investigates division. *Arithmetic Teacher, 33*(9), 34–35.
5. EKENSTAM, A., & GREGOR, K. (1983). Some aspects of children's ability to solve mathematical problems. *Educational Studies in Mathematics, 14*(4), 369–384.
6. FISCHBEIN, E., DERI, M., NELLO, M. S., & MARINO, M. S. (1985). The role of implicit models in solving verbal problems in multiplication and division. *Journal for Research in Mathematics Education, 16*(1), 3–17.

7. GRAEBER, A. O., & BAKER, K. (1988). Curriculum materials and common misconceptions concerning division. In M. Behr, C. Lacampagne, & M. Wheeler (Eds.), *Proceedings of the Tenth Annual Meeting of the North American Chapter of the International Group for the Psychology of Mathematics Education* (pp. 79–85). De Kalb, IL: Northern Illinois University.

8. GRAEBER, A. O., & TIROSH, D. (1988, April). Extending multiplication and division to decimals: Insights fourth and fifth graders bring to the task. R. Shavelson (Chair), *Understanding situations modelled by multiplication and division*. Symposium conducted at the 65th annual meeting of the American Educational Research Association, New Orleans.

9. HALL, W. (1981). Using arrays for teaching multiplication. *Arithmetic Teacher, 29*(3), 20–21.

*10. HALL, W. (1983). Division with base-ten blocks. *Arithmetic Teacher, 31*(3), 21–23.

*11. HAMIC, E. (1986). Students' creative computations: My way or your way? *Arithmetic Teacher, 34*(1), 39–41.

12. HART, K. (Ed.). (1981). *Children's understanding of mathematics: 11–16.* London: John Murray.

13. HAZEKAMP, D. (1978). Teaching multiplication and division algorithms. In M. Suydam (Ed.), *Developing computational skills* (1978 Yearbook, pp. 96–128). Reston, VA: National Council of Teachers of Mathematics.

*14. HENDRICKSON, A. (1986). Verbal multiplication and division problems: Some difficulties and some solutions. *Arithmetic Teacher, 33*(8), 26–33.

*15. HIEBERT, J. (1984). Children's mathematics learning: The struggle to link form and understanding. *Elementary School Journal, 84*(5), 497–513.

16. HIEBERT, J., & BEHR, M. (1988). Introduction: Capturing the major themes. In J. Hiebert & M. Behr (Eds.), *Number concepts and operations in the middle grades* (pp. 1–18). Hillsdale, NJ: Erlbaum; Reston, VA: National Council of Teachers of Mathematics.

17. IRONS, C. (1981). The division algorithm: Using an alternative approach. *Arithmetic Teacher, 28*(5), 46–48.

*18. JENCKS, S., PECK, D., & CHATTERLEY, L. (1980). Why blame the kids? We teach mistakes! *Arithmetic Teacher, 28*(2), 38–42.

19. LESTER, F. (1985). Methodological considerations in research on mathematical problem-solving instruction. In E. Silver (Ed.), *Teaching and learning mathematical problem solving: Multiple research perspectives* (pp. 41–69). Hillsdale, NJ: Erlbaum.

20. LINDQUIST, M. (Ed.). (1989). *Results from the fourth mathematics assessment of the national assessment of educational progress.* Reston, VA: National Council of Teachers of Mathematics.

21. LINDQUIST, M., CARPENTER, T., SILVER, E., & MATTHEWS, W. (1983). The third national mathematics assessment: Results and implications for elementary and middle schools. *Arithmetic Teacher, 31*(4), 14–19.

22. MATZ, M. (1982). Towards a process model for errors in high school algebra. In D. Sleeman & J. Brown (Eds.), *Intelligent tutoring systems* (pp. 25–50). New York: Academic Press.

23. NATIONAL COUNCIL OF TEACHERS OF MATHEMATICS. (1989). *Curriculum and evaluation standards for school mathematics.* Reston, VA: Author.

24. NESHER, P. (1988). Multiplicative school word problems: Theoretical approaches and empirical findings. In J. Hiebert & M. Behr (Eds.), *Number concepts and operations in the middle grades* (pp. 19–40). Hillsdale, NJ: Erlbaum; Reston, VA: National Council of Teachers of Mathematics.

25. PETERSON, W. (1982). Sharing the wealth: Dividing with meaning. *Arithmetic Teacher,* 30(3), 40–43.

*26. QUINTERO, A. (1985). Conceptual understanding of multiplication: Problems involving combination. *Arithmetic Teacher,* 33(3), 36–39.

*27. QUINTERO, A. (1986). Children's conceptual understanding of situations involving multiplication. *Arithmetic Teacher,* 33(5), 34–37.

*28. ROBOLD, A. (1983). Grid arrays for multiplication. *Arithmetic Teacher,* 30 (5), 14–17.

29. SCHWARTZ, J. (1988). Intensive quantity and referent transforming arithmetic operations. In J. Hiebert & M. Behr (Eds.), *Number concepts and operations in the middle grades* (pp. 41–52). Hillsdale, NJ: Erlbaum; Reston, VA: National Council of Teachers of Mathematics.

30. SOWDER, L. (1988a). Children's solutions of story problems. *Journal of Mathematical Behavior,* 7(3), 227–238.

31. SOWDER, L. (1988b). *Concept-Driven Strategies for Solving Story Problems in Mathematics.* San Diego, CA: College of Sciences, Center for Research in Mathematics and Science Education.

32. SOWDER, L. (1989). Story problems and students' strategies. *Arithmetic Teacher,* 36(9), 25–26.

33. SOWDER, L., SOWDER, J., MOYER, M., & MOYER, J. (1986). Diagnosing a student's understanding of an operation. *Arithmetic Teacher,* 33(9), 22–27.

34. STEFFE, L. (1988). Children's construction of number sequences and multiplying schemes. In J. Hiebert & M. Behr (Eds.), *Number concepts and operations in the middle grades* (pp. 119–140). Hillsdale, NJ: Erlbaum; Reston, VA: National Council of Teachers of Mathematics.

35. STUART, M., & BESTGEN, B. (1982). Productive pieces: Exploring multiplication on the overhead. *Arithmetic Teacher,* 29(5), 22–23.

36. SWAN, M. (1983). *Teaching decimal place value: A comparative study of 'conflict' and 'positive only' approaches.* Nottingham, England: Shell Centre for Mathematical Education, University of Nottingham.

37. THORNDIKE, E. (1921). *The new methods in arithmetic.* New York: Rand McNally.

38. USISKIN, Z., & BELL, M. (1983). *Applying arithmetic: A handbook of applications of arithmetic: Part II Operations.* Chicago: University of Chicago, Department of Education. (ERIC Document Reproduction Service No. ED 264-088)

39. VERGNAUD, G. (1983). Multiplicative structures. In R. Lesh & M. Landau (Eds.), *Acquisition of mathematics concepts and processes* (pp. 128–175). New York: Academic Press.

40. VERGNAUD, G. (1988). Multiplicative structures. In J. Hiebert & M. Behr (Eds.), *Number concepts and operations in the middle grades* (pp. 141–161). Hillsdale, NJ: Erlbaum; Reston, VA: National Council of Teachers of Mathematics.

*41. WAGNER, S. (1983). What are these things called variables? *Mathematics Teacher,* 76(7), 474–479.

42. WEARNE, D., & HIEBERT, J. (1988). Construction and using meaning for mathematical symbols: The case of decimal fractions. In J. Hiebert & M. Behr (Eds.), *Number concepts and operations in the middle grades* (pp. 220–235). Hillsdale, NJ: Erlbaum; Reston, VA: National Council of Teachers of Mathematics.

43. WEILAND, L. (1985). Matching instruction to children's thinking about division. *Arithmetic Teacher,* 33(4), 34–35.

CHAPTER 7

Current Research on Rational Numbers and Common Fractions: Summary and Implications for Teachers

Nadine S. Bezuk and Marilyn Bieck

The data showed considerable confusion in students' algorithms for working with fractions. For example, an important source of error in adding fractions was simply adding numerators and denominators as follows: 3/4 + 5/2 = 8/6 or 3/8 + 7/8 = 10/16. (Lankford, cited in 38, p. 85).

This research finding probably does not surprise any middle grades mathematics teacher. A frequent concern and common complaint of middle grades teachers is that students cannot make sense of mathematics. One topic that is particularly difficult for students is fractions. A common observation is that "conventional middle grades instruction is producing students with overly simplistic conceptions of number and operations on number and overly mechanical strategies for solving problems" (15, p. 15). Kieren (20) summarized the feelings of many educators by saying "there has been a long-standing frustration with both teaching and learning about rational numbers" (p. 69).

What can teachers do to make learning about fractions less difficult for students? What help can research give us? This chapter will summarize research findings related to the teaching and learning of rational number and common fractions topics and discuss implications for classroom practice and for further research.

"Fractional numbers seem to cause more difficulties for primary school children than any other part of the curriculum. This may be because of the fundamental differences between the notation and operations with fractional numbers and those with whole numbers, with which children seem to be relatively at ease." (40, p. 215)

"Surveys in several countries suggest that, in general, current programs of instruction are not yielding a high, or even a reasonable, level of performance with rational numbers." (22, p. 177)

Hiebert and Behr (15) noted that existing research on middle school number concepts and operations "does not prescribe instruction in an exact way, but it does set parameters within which effective instruction is likely to fall" (p. 12). They made three comments about instruction: (a) instruction should be meaning oriented rather than symbol oriented; (b) instead of delivering knowledge in prepackaged form, instruction should encourage students to construct their own knowledge; and (c) instruction should provide students with structured learning experiences to help them acquire essential conceptual and procedural knowledge.

Hiebert and Behr recommended that increased attention be devoted to developing the meaning of fraction symbols, developing concepts such as order and equivalence that are important in fostering a sense of the relative size of fractions, and helping children connect their intuitive understandings and strategies to more general, formal methods. Instructional activities that support the process of linking symbols with concrete materials (including meaningful actions on these materials) and verbal interaction (e.g., talking about the mathematics students are doing) seem to be especially sucessful (15).

"Understanding of fractions as numbers, comparison of fractions, and conversions to decimals should have more emphasis while drill on addition, subtraction, and division of numerical fractions with large denominators should have less." (*Educating Americans for the 21st Century*, 28, p. 7)

Most research to date has focused on the development of fraction concepts, order, and equivalence. Although many of these topics are generally introduced in primary grades mathematics instruction, they usually receive only superficial attention and are often taught in a meaningless manner. It is crucial for middle grades instruction to strengthen students' understandings before progressing to operations of fractions, rather than assuming that students already understand these topics.

Developing Concepts

Fraction concepts include partitioning a whole into fractional parts and naming fractional parts. Other important aspects of instruction include interpretations of fractions, manipulatives, the use of language, and types of perceptual cues.

Various Interpretations of Fractions

Kieren (20) identified four basic ways in which rational numbers can be interpreted. The four, which he terms *subconstructs* are as a measure, a quotient or indicated division, a ratio, and an operator. The measure subconstruct involves measuring the area of a region by partitioning it and covering it with appropriately sized units (e.g., when 3/4 of a circle is shaded). The quotient subconstruct refers to using rational numbers as solutions to a division situation. For example, a 2/3 is the result of 2 objects shared by 3 people. A rational number is a ratio. For example, the fraction 1/4 can describe the ratio of one can of orange juice concentrate to four cans of water. A rational number also can be an operator or a mapping. For example, a 1/4 operator describes the relationship of filling packages of four cookies each; there are one-fourth as many packages as cookies.

> "Arithmetically, the fraction 2/3 becomes necessary as the only solution to the whole number problem 2 ÷ 3, such as in the real-world situation in which two pizzas are divided among three people." (*Curriculum and Evaluation Standards*, 26, p. 91)

These four subconstructs have similar mathematical properties, but they have been shown to elicit different types of responses from students. Kieren recommended that all four subconstructs be present in any well-designed mathematics curriculum. He insisted that true understanding of fractions requires both an understanding of each of these subconstructs and of their interrelationships.

Students often have difficulty in recognizing that a/b can mean $a \div b$. One researcher reported that many children thought the answers to 3 ÷ 4 and 4 ÷ 3 were the same, while several children thought one of the answers was zero (18). But when these children were presented with the task of sharing three cakes with four people, almost all of the children were able to solve it correctly, with some children even connecting the fraction 3/4 to the result.

> "It seems that the perception of a fraction as part of a whole shape, usually a circle or square, is so strongly held by some children that they find it impossible to adapt this model even to include the notion of 3 circles to be shared into 4 equal parts." (18, p. 261)

Recommendations for Instruction. Presenting a concept in different ways facilitates learning and teaches for understanding rather than rote memory. Related activities are suggested by Post, Behr, and Lesh (32) and Burns (12):

- Use more than one interpretation (or subconstruct) of fractions.
- Initially teach a concept using one subconstruct of fractions, such as part-whole. Once the concept is learned, introduce students to the same fraction in another subconstruct (e.g., as a ratio), having the students compare what is different and what is the same.

Use of Manipulatives and Other Models

NCTM's *Curriculum and Evaluation Standards* (26) recommends that students be able to represent fractions in a variety of meaningful situations, moving flexibly among concrete, pictorial, and symbolic representations.

"Mathematics instruction at all levels should foster active student involvement."
(*Reshaping School Mathematics,* 25, p. 39)

One study found that the use of manipulative materials (including circular and rectangular pieces, colored chips, paper folding, number lines, and Cuisenaire rods) as well as pictures, symbols, and words was of vital importance in developing students' understanding of fraction concepts and operations (2).

"Teachers must value and encourage the use of a variety of tools rather than placing excessive emphasis on conventional mathematical symbols. Various means for communicating about mathematics should be accepted, including drawings, diagrams, invented symbols, and analogies. The teacher should introduce conventional notation at points when doing so can further the work or the discourse at hand. Teachers should also help students to learn to use calculators, computers, and other technological devices as tools for mathematical discourse. Given the range of mathematical tools available, teachers should often allow and encourage students to select the means they find most useful for working on or discussing a particular mathematical problem." (*Professional Teaching Standards,* 27, p. 52)

Hunting (17) examined the effects of instruction on the fraction understandings of students. He used problems involving continuous quantities (e.g., cutting pizzas) and discrete quantities (e.g., colored chips). He found that students partition (i.e., subdivide) continuous quantities differently from discrete quantities. He concluded that students' "conceptions of fractions may therefore be quite different if restricted to either contextual material as a consequence" (p. 385). He also speculated that an understanding of fractions in continuous contexts may be prerequisite for understanding and being able to solve problems set in discrete contexts.

> "Actions used to subdivide continuous quantities are different from those used to subdivide discrete quantities. The goals may be identical but the means are not. Children's conceptions of fraction may therefore be quite different if restricted to either contextual material as a consequence" (17, p. 385).

Dienes's theory of perceptual variability, the multiple embodiment principle, suggests that concept learning is maximized when a concept is presented in a variety of physical contexts (35). Other researchers have recommended that "after a concept is introduced with a chosen manipulative aid, subsequent representations with manipulative aids which differ in perceptual features cause the child to rethink the concept, and learning is facilitated" (1, p. 208). In practical terms, if students see fractions represented in only one way, such as fraction circles, they may generalize incorrectly that fractions exist only with circles.

Mathematics concepts can have five different representations: real-world objects, manipulative materials, pictures, spoken symbols, and written symbols (23). For example, one half can be represented by a child holding one of two equal parts of an apple (real-world objects), by one of two equal-sized parts of a cardboard circle (manipulative materials), by drawing a circle cut into two equal parts with one part shaded (picture), by saying "one half" (spoken symbol), and by writing 1/2 (written symbol). Using a variety of modes in instruction and frequently asking students to switch among these modes enhanced their understanding of concepts. Students developed more flexible notions of fractions (23).

> "Children may have 'missing links' in their understanding. Links needing attention are those between symbols and their meanings, between natural knowledge structures and formal knowledge structures, and between syntactical structures and mathematical-logical structures." (22, p. 178)

Novillis reported that students' difficulties using region, set, and number line models to illustrate fractions may result from their lack of exposure to a sufficiently wide range of models to encourage them to generalize the fraction concept (29). For instance, many students were able to correctly associate the fraction 1/5 with a set of five objects, one of which was shaded, but most students were not able to associate the fraction 1/5 with a set of 10 objects, two of which were shaded (Fig. 7.1). This problem persisted even when the objects were arranged so that it was fairly easy to see that one of every five objects was shaded. Novillis also concluded that students do not see an adequate number of negative instances of the fraction concept. For example, students are rarely asked why 1/3 does not represent correctly the diagram shown in Figure 7.2 in which one of four equal parts is shaded and three are not shaded (hence the incorrect response of 1/3). This situation is common throughout mathematics curricula.

FIGURE 7.1 Two examples of one fifth

More students were able to associate the fraction
one fifth with Set A than with Set B

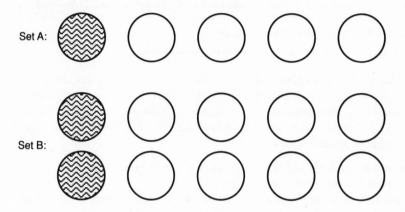

Set A:

Set B:

Another study examined children's understanding of fractions on the number-line model (30). Many students could locate fractions correctly on number lines that were one unit long and number lines with the number of segments equal to the denominator (i.e., divided into four segments when they were locating three fourths). However, tasks became much more difficult for students when number lines were two units long. Many students used the whole number line as the unit rather than the section from zero to one. These students seemed to be confusing the nubmer line model with the part-whole model; that is, they seemed to be finding a part of the number line segment shown rather than locating the nubmer on the number line. These difficulties indicate limitations in students' understanding of fractions.

FIGURE 7.2 A negative instance of
            one third

Students sometimes say that one third
of this rectangle is shaded, since
1 piece is shaded and 3 pieces are
not shaded. How would you respond?

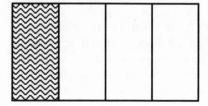

> "The mathematics tasks in which students engage—projects, problems, con-
> structions, applications, exercises, and so on—and the materials with which they
> work frame and focus students' opportunities for learning mathematics in
> school. . . . A central responsibility of teachers is to select and develop worth-
> while tasks and materials that create opportunities for students to develop these
> kinds of mathematical understandings, competence, interests, and dispositions."
> (*Professional Teaching Standards*, 27, p. 24).

Recommendations for Instruction. It is critically important to use a variety of manipulative materials in fractions instruction. Related activities are suggested by Bennett and Davidson (5), Berman and Friederwitzer (6), Bezuk (8), Bezuk and Cramer
(10), Burns (12), Charles and Roper (13), and Zulie (42). The following materials
are only a sample of possible teaching aids:

- Materials used to teach about fractional parts of whole objects:
  —teacher-made fraction circles, rectangles, and strips
  —purchased materials: pattern blocks, fraction bars, Cuisenaire rods
- Materials used to teach about fractional parts of a group of objects:
  —loose objects that can be sorted into fractional parts (e.g., beans)
  —purchased materials: colored tiles, lots-of-links, colored chips
- Number lines of different lengths and with different numbers of divisions
- Activities that reinforce fraction concepts:
  —fraction kits that teach equivalent fractions
  —paper folding that shows what happens when one multiplies fractions

Other recommendations:

- Use manipulatives, real-world materials, verbal expression, and written expression
  (symbols) for each fraction concept taught, being careful not to introduce symbols
  until students are familiar with the concepts and related vocabulary.
- Limit the size of denominators in initial concepts, order, and equivalence work to
  those that children are familiar with and can show with available manipulatives.
- Introduce a concept using one material, such as fraction circles. Once the concept
  is learned, students should examine the same concept with a different manipulative, such as colored chips, having the students compare what was different and
  what was the same.
- Use more than one mode of representation in instruction.
- Frequently ask students to switch among modes.

Generating Fractional Parts

Children progress through four levels of ability to partition (or cut) shapes into a
desired number of equal pieces: sharing, algorithmic halving, evenness, and oddness
(36). At the *sharing level*, children learn the halving process, drawing a line through
the middle of a region. A common misunderstanding at this level is that a "fair share"
is an equal number of pieces, regardless of their size. Children at the *algorithmic*

halving level are able to continue the halving process to obtain fourths, eighths, and sixteenths. Again, students sometimes do not produce equal-sized pieces, often because they use a correct procedure in inappropriate situations (such as cutting a circle into fourths with parallel vertical lines).

In the *third level*, evenness, equality of the pieces becomes critically important for students. Students can go beyond repeated halving to cut even numbers (that are not powers of two) of parts, such as sixths and tenths. A common error is that pieces that do not look the same are considered not equal; many students cannot recognize that shapes that are not congruent can have the same area. To be successful in the fourth stage, the *oddness stage*, students must realize that a different cutting procedure that is not based on the halving algorithm is/necessary to produce fractions with odd denominators, such as thirds and fifths. For example, rather than beginning with a vertical cut through the middle of the circle, to produce thirds one should begin with a cut along the radius of the circle. These researchers also hypothesized a fifth level, which they refer to as *composition*, in which children use a multiplicative strategy—to produce fifteenths, for example, by trisecting fifths.

Recommendations for Instruction.   Related activities are suggested by Pothier and Sawada (37).

• Provide students with opportunities to practice partitioning with physical objects, not just drawing (and trying to erase) lines on drawings of shapes. This can be done by positioning (and adjusting) coffee stirrers on top of uncut circles or rectangles, asking students to place the stirrers to show where the whole should be cut to make thirds, for example.

Naming Fractional Parts

In order to name a fractional part, the student must focus on the number of equal parts into which the whole has been partitioned (or cut) and the number of those parts that are being considered. It is important to help students attach meaning to fraction symbols by encouraging them to connect their knowledge of an arrangement of manipulatives to symbols. For example, students using fraction circles may show one half by displaying on a unit circle one piece of a colored circle that has been cut into two equal parts. These students can similarly describe the fraction one half as "1 piece of the 2 (equal) pieces the whole was cut into."

> "The language of instruction must build on naturally occurring language or children will not continue to use it." (22, p. 177)

Teachers should introduce word names, such as one half, for fractions before symbol names, such as 1/2. Word names seem to be more easily understood initially by students, perhaps helping them avoid part of the confusion of incorrectly applying whole number knowledge to fractions. Experiences of this sort help children connect their understanding of their work with manipulatives to the often confusing symbols used to name fractions and attempts to avoid or minimize the common meaningless reading of 1/2 as 1 over 2 or 1 "twoth."

> "During instruction, teachers should provide intuitive knowledge-building experiences with great attention to language use, mental imagery, and mathematical variety." (22, p. 178)

Recommendations for Instruction.

• Use word names before symbol names in fractions instruction.
• Help students connect word names and symbol names to displays of manipulatives, pictures, diagrams, and real-world objects.

Types of Perceptual Cues

The type of perceptual cues in circles, rectangles, sets, and number lines was found to be related to students' achievement on fraction concepts tasks (9). For example, students were asked to shade three fourths of rectangles divided into fourths, halves, and eighths, as shown in Figure 7.3.

Figures that were partitioned into the same number of parts as the denominator were easiest, followed by those cut into a number of parts that is a *factor* of the denominator requested (in this example, 2 is a factor of 4), followed by those cut into a number of parts that is a *multiple* of the denominator requested (in this example, 8 is a multiple of 4). This order of difficulty held for all four models (circle, rectangle, set, and number line) and for proper and improper fractions.

These results indicated that problems are more difficult for students when they must manipulate problem conditions. But manipulating given information is an important real-world skill; in out-of-school settings, problems rarely come in the perfect form usually found in school materials. Dealing with various types of perceptual cues is an important part of the conceptual development process as it requires the child to identify and distinguish between relevant and irrelevant variables (1).

Recommendations for Instruction.

• Include in instruction some tasks containing various types of perceptual cues.
• Do not always give tasks in "ready-to-use" form to students. Some should require modification to encourage students to think more carefully about the task. For example, ask students to find 1/2 of a cake that is cut into eighths.

Estimating Fractions

NCTM's *Curriculum and Evaluation Standards* (26) points out that an important aspect in fractions instruction is the integration of computation and estimation

FIGURE 7.3   Examples of rectangles divided into different numbers of pieces

Shade $\frac{3}{4}$ of each rectangle:

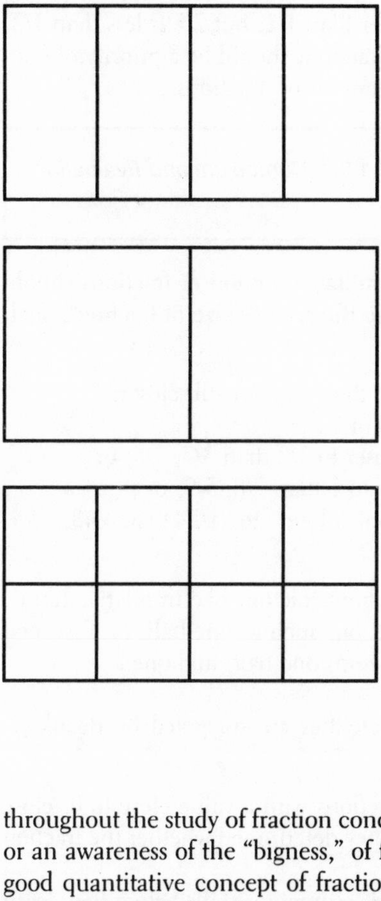

throughout the study of fraction concepts. The development of a quantitative notion, or an awareness of the "bigness," of fractions is very important. Students who have a good quantitative concept of fractions are able to estimate the relative size of fractions, find equivalent fractions, and estimate the location of a fraction on a number line.

"There should be heavy and continuing emphasis on estimation and approximation, not only in formal round-off procedures, but in developing a feel for numbers. Students need experience in estimating real world quantities as well as in estimating numerical quantities which appear in complicated form. . . . For example, many exercises on comparing complicated fractions with easy ones (e.g., 12/25 with 1/2, and 103/299 with 1/3 can be used to get students to think of complicated fractions as close to, but less than (or more than), easy fractions." (*Educating Americans for the 21st Century,* 28, p. 6)

Why is quantitative understanding important? It is crucial in evaluating the reasonableness of results of computation involving fractions. For example, many students will incorrectly report that $1/2 + 1/3 = 2/5$, by adding the numerators and the denominators. But students who understand something about the "bigness" of fractions will realize that $2/5$ is not a reasonable answer; the problem involves adding something to $1/2$, so the answer should be greater than $1/2$, but $2/5$ is less than $1/2$. The development of this quantitative notion of fractions should be a priority of fractions instruction, as well as a prerequisite to operations on fractions.

> **"Give examples of a number between 1/3 and 1/2."** (*Curriculum and Evaluation Standards*, 26, p. 80)

Instruction aimed at enhancing students' quantitative notion of fractions should include ample opportunities for students to judge the relative size of fractions, such as those in the following activities (3):

1. Construct a fraction close but not equal to 1, then another still closer;
2. Construct a fraction closer to 1 than 5/6, 7/8 or . . .
3. Construct a fraction not equal to 1/2, but closer to 1/2 than 3/7, 3/8, or
4. Construct a fraction greater than 1 but closer to 1 than 7/8, 5/9, or . . .
5. Construct a fraction greater than 1/2 but closer to 1/2 than 3/8, 2/5, or . . .

Exercises such as these force students to think about fraction size in relative terms, either in relation to a single reference-point fraction, such as one half, or to several reference-point fractions, such as those close to zero, one half, and one.

Recommendations for Instruction.   Related activities are suggested by Bezuk (7) and Burns (12).

• Lead students to discover characteristics of fractions with a value close to 0, close to 1/2, close to 1. Have students explain how they determined whether the fraction had a value close to 0, 1/2, or 1.
• Let students add and subtract fractions through estimation skills before they learn the process of adding and subtracting fractions.

Ordering Fractions

When examining the development of children's understanding of ordering fractions, also known as comparing, researchers (4) identified three classes of fractions: (a) fractions with the same numerators (such as 3/5 and 3/8), (b) fractions with the same denominators (such as 2/5 and 4/5), and (c) fractions with different numerators and denominators (such as 2/3 and 3/4). A typical ordering question asked the child to determine which of two (or three) fractions was the lesser (or least) and to give reasons for that decision.

Students used four types of reasoning strategies on comparison tasks: (a) considering both the numerator and denominator of each fraction, (b) referring to manipulative aids, (c) using a reference point (such as 1/2) to compare two fractions (for example, 1/3 is less than 3/4 because 1/3 is less than 1/2 and 3/4 is greater than 1/2), and (d) improperly using their knowledge of whole numbers. Whole number dominance, the fourth type of strategy listed, is a very common strategy, resulting in serious errors. For example, many students conclude that 1/3 is less than 1/4 because 3 is less than 4. This naive reasoning denotes students' inability to coordinate the number of pieces and the size of the pieces. Students using this reasoning do not understand or are not aware of the inverse relationship between the number of pieces into which the whole has been partitioned and the size of the pieces.

A common student misunderstanding centered on the words "more" and "greater." "More" can refer to more pieces in the whole or a larger area covered by each piece. Similarly, "greater" can refer to a greater number of pieces in the whole or a greater size of each piece. Students often were unclear of the meaning of a seemingly straightforward question such as "is 1/2 greater than or less than 1/3, or are they equal?" Many students had to ask the clarifying question, "Do you mean the size of the pieces or the number of pieces?" (34). Clearly, there is much to be considered when teaching ordering of fractions.

Recommendations for Instruction. Ordering activities are important in improving students' ability to determine the reasonableness of results of fraction computations. Related activities are suggested by Bezuk and Cramer (10), Burns (11), and Post and Cramer (34).

- Include the three classes of fractions listed above.
- Encourage students who are having difficulty to go back to a manipulative material or mental images of manipulatives in order to assist their reasoning.

Equivalence

Hunting (16) noted that "the absence of a stable operational basis for thinking effectively about fractions inhibits the success of children attempting to solve problems of equivalence of fractions" (p. 195). In other words, students who do not really understand what a fraction means will have a hard time finding another fraction equivalent to it.

Behr and his colleagues (4) also devoted much attention to the development of children's understanding of the equivalence of fractions. They examined the same three classes of fractions as in their work with ordering fractions. A common student error involved using additive rather than multiplicative reasoning. For example, a common incorrect solution to the problem 1/3 = ?/6 was 4; students often looked for the number they could *add* to 3 to get 6 (3 + ? = 6), and then *added* that same amount to the numerator (1 + 3 = 4), concluding that 1/3 was equivalent to 4/6.

As with other topics, one method for helping students avoid or eliminate these incorrect strategies is to teach the concept of equivalence and how to generate a set of equivalent fractions before teaching the symbolic algorithm. For example, students can use manipulatives (such as fraction circles) to generate a list of fractions equivalent to a fraction with which they are familiar, such as one half, finding other ways to cover the same amount of the unit circle. After this list (which is an equivalence class for one half) is generated, students should be encouraged to look for patterns in the list. The symbolic algorithm can be developed with meaning from this study of patterns.

Recommendations for Instruction.   Related activities are suggested by Bezuk and Cramer (10) and Burns (11).

* Discuss the meaning of "equivalent." Are there other instances in mathematics when we use equivalence? (Yes: regrouping one 10 for 10 ones, finding all the ways to make change for 39¢ from one dollar, etc.)
* Discuss how equivalent fractions are the same and how they are different.
* Help students generalize the symbolic algorithm from their experiences with manipulatives.
* Help students to understand ways in which fractions that appear to be very different, such as 1/2 and 512/1024, can be equivalent.

Operations

NCTM's *Curriculum and Evaluation Standards* (26) presents clear recommendations for operations on fractions:

> The mastery of a small number of basic facts with common fractions (e.g., $1/4 + 1/4 = 1/2$; $3/4 + 1/2 = 1\ 1/4$; and $1/2 \times 1/2 = 1/4$; . . .) contributes to students' readiness to learn estimation and for concept development and problem solving. This proficiency in the addition, subtraction, and multiplication of fractions and mixed numbers should be limited to those with simple denominations that can be visualized concretely or pictorially and are apt to occur in real-world settings; such computation promotes conceptual understanding of the operations. . . . Division of fractions should be approached conceptually. An understanding of what happens when one divides by a fractional number (less than or greater than 1) is essential. (p. 96)

"It is the intent . . . that computation be viewed not as a goal in itself but as a multifaceted tool for knowing and doing." (*Curriculum and Evaluation Standards,* 26, p. 97)

Research on students' understanding of and ability to perform operations on fractions has shown disappointingly poor results. For example, researchers reported that "children are going through the motions of operations with fractions, but they have not been exposed to the kinds of experiences that could provide them with necessary understandings" (32, p. 348). The emphasis in instruction must shift from learning the rules for operations to understanding fraction concepts.

"Operation sense should be expanded with such examples as, is 2/3 × 5/4 more or less than 2/3? More or less than 5/4?" (*Curriculum and Evaluation Standards,* 26, p. 89).

Kieren (21) recommended that instruction in operations on fractions be built on children's intuitive understanding of fractions and based on actions on objects rather than solely on the manipulation of symbols according to a set of rules and procedures. He pointed out that premature formalism leads to symbolic knowledge that children cannot connect to the real world, resulting in a virtual elimination of any possibility for children to develop number sense about fractions and operations on fractions. He also noted that symbolic knowledge that is not based on understanding is "highly dependent on memory and subject to deterioration" (p. 178).

Other researchers have documented common errors related to operations on fractions. The most common error on addition and subtraction problems is adding (or subtracting) the numerators and denominators, as in the introductory example to this chapter. A goal of instruction should be to enable students to determine the reasonableness of the results of operations on fractions.

"Hector got 4/6 when he added 3/4 + 1/2 (he confused the rules for adding fractions with those for multiplying fractions and added the numerators and then the denominators). His estimate suggested the answer should be greater than 1/2 + 1/2, or larger than 1." (*Curriculum and Evaluation Standards,* 26, p. 97)

Two common misunderstandings related to multiplication and division are that "multiplication makes bigger," meaning that students expect the product to be greater than both factors as in whole number multiplication; and "division makes smaller," meaning that students expect the quotient to be less than the dividend as in whole number division. For example, students often will report the answer to 6 ÷ 1/2 as 3, rather than the correct answer of 12. Many students think the correct answer of 12 is not a reasonable one. They believe that division makes smaller, so they think the answer should be less than 6.

Recommendations for Instruction. Students need help making sense of operations on fractions. Related activities are suggested by Burns (11) and Skemp (39).

- Introduce operations on fractions with manipulatives and pictures. Show the process of each operation with manipulatives before teaching the algorithm.
- Focus on the meaning of operations. Help students see it is possible to divide by a fraction, for example, and get a larger number.
- Connect operations on fractions to the real world. For example, determining how many one-half cup servings are in an eight-cup container involves dividing by a fraction.
- Help students connect meaning from procedures with manipulatives to symbolic

algorithms by encouraging students to look for patterns in data they collect with the manipulatives and generalize rules based on these patterns.

- Limit the size of denominators in computation with fractions to 12 and less.
- Stress reasonableness of results.

Other Research on Teaching Fractions

How have students experienced fractions in the real world? What do students already know about fractions? Mack (24) examined students' informal knowledge of fractions which she defined as "applied, real-life circumstantial knowledge constructed by an individual student that may either be correct and incorrect and can be drawn upon by the student in response to problems posed in the context of real-life situations familiar to him or her" (p. 17). She concluded that not only do students possess informal knowledge about fractions, but they often are able to connect this knowledge with formal symbols and procedures, attaching meaning to them.

> "Informal knowledge can provide a basis for developing understanding of mathematical symbols and procedures in complex content domains." (24, p. 29)

> "Teachers should be aware of pupils' viewpoints concerning fractions. The teacher should be like a consulting architect—knowing the ground of a pupil's knowledge and helping the pupil to build a knowledge structure on it." (22, p. 178)

> "It is possible for students to relate fraction symbols to informal knowledge in meaningful ways, provided that the connection between the informal knowledge and the fraction symbols is reasonably clear." (24, p. 29)

How do children best learn about fractions? Streefland (41) discussed the importance of students' constructing their own understanding of fractions by constructing the procedures of the operations, the language of fractions, rules, verbalization of rules, and problems and exercises involving fractions. He advocated valuing children's findings and using these findings as materials in further learning activities. "What comes in the first place is the appraisal of the work of the pupils, the methods and procedures they come up with, even if they are different from the formal procedures with regard to fractions" (p. 225).

> "As students build upon informal knowledge in meaningful ways, the development of their understanding may differ from the sequence in which fraction topics are traditionally taught." (24, p. 30)

What are promising methods for teaching fractions? Researchers found that 12-year-olds who were taught fraction and ratio topics by a concrete, process-oriented approach attained higher achievement and attitudes about fractions and ratios with enhanced development of general mathematics but no loss in computational facility (14).

> Students often come to instruction ". . . with a rich store of informal knowledge about fractions that they are able to build on to give meaning to formal symbols and procedures." (24, p. 29)

Payne (31) listed several difficulties that students have when learning about fractions: (a) recognizing the need for equal-sized parts, particularly with circles, (b) reversing numerator and denominator, (c) identifying a unit from a diagram when more than one unit was shown, (d) interpreting a/b as $a \div b$, (e) using the set model, and (f) using the number line model. He recommended that concrete objects be used for a longer period of time before diagrams are introduced and that more time be spent relating symbols to concrete materials. Payne noted that it takes much more time to teach any part of fraction work than has generally been allowed in curriculum guides.

Recommendations for Instruction. When teaching fractions there should be an emphasis on meaning, understanding, and reasonableness. Related activities are suggested by Bezuk and Cramer (10), Burns (12), and Skemp (39).

- Provide instruction that is concrete and process oriented rather than abstract and procedure oriented.
- Help students connect fractions to the real world.
- Help students connect their existing knowledge about fractions to instruction on fractions.
- Value children's findings.
- Use children's findings in further learning activities.

Looking Ahead . . .

Current work on fractions is striving to identify the components of instruction necessary to enhance students' understanding of the connections among multiplication, division, fractions, decimals, ratio, and proportion as well as ways to connect meaning to fraction concepts, symbols, and procedures. Teachers can expand the present knowledge base on teaching and learning fractions by trying some of this chapter's recommendations, sharing their findings with other teachers and researchers, raising additional questions, and assisting researchers in expanding current work. For example, what are good locations at which to connect students' real-world knowledge with fractions? Teacher-researcher interaction ultimately will benefit students.

Nadine Bezuk

There remain several unanswered questions. What previous skills and levels of understanding are needed before students can internalize the various fraction concepts? At what age should students be introduced to the various fraction concepts? What methods are best for helping students attach meaning to and determine the reasonableness of operations on fractions? What types of activities help students relate fractions to the real world?

Marilyn Bieck

About the Authors

Nadine Bezuk is a mathematics educator in the School of Teacher Education and the associate director of the Center for Research in Mathematics and Science Education at San Diego State University. Her research and writing interests include the effective teaching of fractions and ways to help all children learn mathematics.

Marilyn Bieck, math-science coordinator for Encinitas (California) Schools, teaches demonstration lessons, works with individual teachers to develop their math programs, and presents inservice workshops on the instructional delivery of math concepts. She is presently exploring the use of technology as an instructional tool in the areas of math and language arts.

References

1. BEHR, M. J., LESH, R., & POST, T. R. (1981). Construct analysis, manipulative aids, representational systems, and learning rational number concepts. In C. Comiti & G. Vergnaud (Eds.), *Proceedings of the Fifth International Conference for the Psychology of Mathematics Education* (pp. 203–209). Grenoble, France: Laboratorie I.M.A.G.
2. BEHR, M. J., LESH, R., POST, T. R., & SILVER, E. A. (1983). Rational number concepts. In R. Lesh & M. Landau (Eds.), *Acquisition of mathematics concepts and processes* (pp. 91–126). New York: Academic Press.
3. BEHR, M. J., WACHSMUTH, I., & POST, T. R. (1985). Construct a sum: A measure of children's understanding of fraction size. *Journal for Research in Mathematics Education, 16*(2), 120–131.
4. BEHR, M., WACHSMUTH, I., POST, T., & LESH, R. (1984). Order and equivalence of rational numbers: A clinical teaching experiment. *Journal for Research in Mathematics Education, 15*(5), 323–341.
*5. BENNETT, A. B., JR., & DAVIDSON, P. S. (1973). *Fraction bars.* Fort Collins, CO: Scott Resources.
*6. BERMAN, B., & FRIEDERWITZER, F. (1988). *Fraction circle activities: A sourcebook for grades 4–8.* Palo Alto, CA: Dale Seymour.
*7. BEZUK, N. (1984). *The effect of perceptual distractors and cognitive restructuring ability on performance on rational number tasks.* Unpublished master's thesis, University of Minnesota, Minneapolis.

*8. BEZUK, N. S. (1988). Fractions in the early childhood mathematics curriculum. *Arithmetic Teacher*, 35(6), 56–60.

9. BEZUK, N. S. (1989). Fractions—easy pieces. *Arithmetic Teacher*, 36(6), 3.

*10. BEZUK, N. S., & CRAMER, K. (1989). Teaching about fractions: What, when, and how? In P. Trafton (Ed.), *New directions for elementary school mathematics* (1989 Yearbook, pp. 156–167). Reston, VA: National Council of Teachers of Mathematics.

*11. BURNS, M. (1984). *The math solution: Teaching for mastery through problem solving.* Sausalito, CA: Marilyn Burns Education Associates.

*12. BURNS, M. (1987). *A collection of math lessons from grades 3 through 6.* New Rochelle, NY: Cuisenaire Company of America.

*13. CHARLES, L. H., & ROPER, A. (1990). *Activities for fraction circles plus.* Sunnyvale, CA: Creative Publications.

14. HARRISON, B., BRINDLEY, S., & BYE, M. P. (1989). Allowing for student cognitive levels in the teaching of fractions and ratios. *Journal for Research in Mathematics Education*, 20(3), 288–300.

15. HIEBERT, J., & BEHR, M. (1988). Capturing the major themes. In J. Hiebert & M. Behr (Eds.), *Number concepts and operations in the middle grades* (pp. 1–18). Hillsdale, NJ: Erlbaum; Reston, VA: National Council of Teachers of Mathematics.

16. HUNTING, R. (1983). Alan: A case study of knowledge of units and performance with fractions. *Journal for Research in Mathematics Education*, 14(3), 182–197.

17. HUNTING, R. P. (1984). Learning fractions in discrete and continuous quantity contexts. In B. Southwell, R. Eyland, M. Cooper, J. Conroy, & K. Collis (Eds.), *Proceedings of the Eighth International Conference for the Psychology of Mathematics Education.* Sydney, Australia: International Group for the Psychology of Mathematics Education.

18. KERSLAKE, D. (1986). Children's perception of fractions. In L. Burton & C. Hoyles (Eds.), *Proceedings of the Tenth International Conference for the Psychology of Mathematics Education.* London: University of London Institute of Education.

19. KIEREN, T. E. (1976). On the mathematical, cognitive, and instructional foundations of rational numbers. In R. Lesh (Ed.), *Number and measurement: Papers from a research workshop* (pp. 101–144). Columbus, OH: ERIC/SMEAC.

20. KIEREN, T. E. (1980). Knowing rational numbers: Ideas and symbols. In M. M. Lindquist (Ed.), *Selected issues in mathematics education* (pp. 69–81). Berkeley, CA: McCutchan.

21. KIEREN, T. E. (1988). Personal knowledge of rational numbers. In J. Hiebert & M. Behr (Eds.), *Number concepts and operations in the middle grades* (pp. 1–18). Hillsdale, NJ: Erlbaum; Reston, VA: National Council of Teachers of Mathematics.

22. KIEREN, T., & BEHR, M. (1985). Fractions: Summary. In A. Bell, B. Low, & J. Kilpatrick (Eds.), *Theory, research, and practice in mathematical education* (pp. 176–185). Nottingham, England: Shell Centre for Mathematical Education, University of Nottingham.

23. LESH, R., LANDAU, M., & HAMILTON, E. (1981). Applied mathematical problem solving. In T. Post & M. Roberts (Eds.), *Proceedings of the Third Annual Meeting of the North American Chapter of the International Group for the Psychology of Mathematics Education* (pp. 118–121). Minneapolis: University of Minnesota.

24. MACK, N. K. (1990). Learning fractions with understanding: Building on informal knowledge. *Journal for Research in Mathematics Education*, 21(1), 16–32.

25. MATHEMATICAL SCIENCES EDUCATION BOARD, NATIONAL RESEARCH COUNCIL. (1990). *Reshaping school mathematics: A philosophy and framework for curriculum.* Washington, DC: National Academy Press.

*26. NATIONAL COUNCIL OF TEACHERS OF MATHEMATICS. (1989). *Curriculum and evaluation standards for school mathematics.* Reston, VA: Author.

*27. NATIONAL COUNCIL OF TEACHERS OF MATHEMATICS. (1991). *Professional standards for teaching mathematics.* Reston, VA: Author.

28. NATIONAL SCIENCE BOARD COMMISSION OF PRECOLLEGE EDUCATION IN MATHEMATICS, SCIENCE AND TECHNOLOGY. (1983). *Educating Americans for the 21st century.* Washington, DC: Author.

29. NOVILLIS, C. F. (1976). An analysis of the fraction concept into a hierarchy of selected subconcepts and the testing of the hierarchical dependencies. *Journal for Research in Mathematics Education, 7*(3), 131–144.

30. NOVILLIS-LARSON, C. (1980). Locating proper fractions. *School Science and Mathematics, 53*(5), 423–428.

31. PAYNE, J. N. (1975). Review of research on fractions. In R. Lesh and D. Bradbard (Eds.), *Number and measurement: Papers from a research workshop* (pp. 145–187). Columbus, OH: ERIC/SMEAC.

32. PECK, D., & JENCKS, S. (1981). Conceptual issues in the teaching and learning of fractions. *Journal for Research in Mathematics Education, 12*(5), 339–348.

*33. POST, T. R., BEHR, M. J., & LESH, R. (1982). Interpretations of rational number concepts. In L. Silvey (Ed.), *Mathematics for the middle grades* (1982 Yearbook, pp. 59–72). Reston, VA: National Council of Teachers of Mathematics.

*34. POST, T. R., & CRAMER, K. A. (1987). Research into practice: Children's strategies in ordering rational numbers. *Arithmetic Teacher, 35*(2), 33–35.

35. POST, T. R., & REYS, R. E. (1979). Abstraction, generalization, and the design of mathematical experiences for children. In K. Fuson & W. Geeslin (Eds.), *Explorations in the modelling of the learning of mathematics* (pp. 117–139). Columbus, OH: ERIC/SMEAC.

36. POTHIER, Y. M., & SAWADA, D. (1983). Partitioning: The emergence of rational number ideas in young children. *Journal for Research in Mathematics Education, 14*(5), 307–317.

37. POTHIER, Y. M., & SAWADA, D. (1990). Partitioning: An approach to fractions. *Arithmetic Teacher, 38*(4), 12–16.

38. RESNICK, L. B., & FORD, W. W. (1981). *The psychology of mathematics for instruction.* Hillsdale, NJ: Erlbaum.

*39. SKEMP, R. (1989). *Structured activities for primary mathematics. Volume 2: For the later years.* London, England: Routledge.

40. SOUTHWELL, B. (1985). The development of rational number concepts in Papua, New Guinea. In A. Bell, B. Low, & J. Kilpatrick (Eds.), *Theory, research, and practice in mathematical education.* Nottingham, England: Shell Centre for Mathematical Education, University of Nottingham.

41. STREEFLAND, L. (1985). Basic principles for teaching and learning fractions. In A. Bell, B. Low, & J. Kilpatrick (Eds.), *Theory, research, and practice in mathematical education.* Nottingham, England: Shell Centre for Mathematical Education, University of Nottingham.

*42. ZULIE, M. E. (1975). *Fractions with pattern blocks.* Sunnyvale, CA: Creative Publications.

CHAPTER 8

Teaching and Learning Decimal Fractions

Douglas T. Owens and Douglas B. Super

INTERVIEWER: *Tell me how you did number three (2 + .8).*

STUDENT: *There is no decimal point in there so it would be after. You line it up with that (.8) and put your zero there (2.0), then you add down, then bring down the decimal point.*

INTERVIEWER: *So the 2 you can think of as 2.0? Does it make any difference if you put the zero in? Is it the same number?*

STUDENT: *Same number.*

INTERVIEWER: *Could you put another zero in?*

STUDENT: *Then it would be different.*

INTERVIEWER: *Why would that be different?*

STUDENT: *Well, it wouldn't really be different because after the decimal point, if there are zeros, they don't really have to be there.*

INTERVIEWER: *Would it change the answer if you used this number (2.00)?*

STUDENT: *Yes. (15, p. 207)*

$\mathbf{B}$ecause decimal fractions look similar to the familiar whole numbers, it seems reasonable to predict that children in the middle grades might understand them without much difficulty. However, appearance is deceiving. The research on

> Some students' conception of decimal numbers is as a point separating two whole numbers that can be operated on independently using the rules of whole number arithmetic. (9)

learning decimal fractions agrees on one point: There is a lack of conceptual understanding (13, 35). Some evidence indicates that students are being taught to compute with decimals before they fully grasp the basic decimal concepts (16, 6). This may result from (a) concepts being inherently more difficult than the computational procedures, (b) an instructional program slighting concepts assuming them to be straightforward, or (c) an instructional focus on the algorithms because they are perceived by teachers to be more important or easier to teach. In any case it seems useful to consider a distinction between conceptual and procedural knowledge—that which is understood versus routines or algorithms that are followed without understanding.

Conceptual Knowledge and Procedural Knowledge

Authors have used different terms to contrast rote and meaningful knowledge. Skemp (29) refers to instrumental understanding and relational understanding. Instrumental understanding involves the application of rules without reasons, whereas relational understanding involves why a rule works and its relationships to other concepts. Resnick (26) indicates that carrying out the steps of an algorithm by syntactic rules (symbol manipulation) may or may not reflect an underlying semantics (meaning). Researchers beyond the mathematics education community have identified three types of knowledge as important to monitoring and regulating one's own thinking: declarative (that, what), procedural (how), and conditional (when, why) (Paris, Lipson, & Wixson cited in 18).

Conceptual Versus Procedural Knowledge

Conceptual knowledge was defined by Hiebert and Wearne as "knowledge of those facts and properties of mathematics that are recognized as being related in some way. Conceptual knowledge is distinguished primarily by relationships between pieces of information" (15, p. 200). A piece of information becomes conceptual knowledge only when it is integrated into a larger network that is already in place.

For example, if children learn decimal position values (tenths, hundredths, etc.) only as verbal labels for isolated digits, then this learning does not qualify as conceptual knowledge. On the other hand, if numbers given by these names are related to whole numbers (e.g., when is a decimal less or greater than 1), to common fractions (e.g., what decimal names 1/4), or adjacent places are seen to be related by a factor of 10, then the knowledge becomes conceptual. Also, a decimal fraction that is associated with a diagram or is interpreted as a measure would be conceptually understood.

In this scheme, procedural knowledge is characterized by a lack of relationships and of connections to prior knowledge. Hiebert and Wearne (15) distinguish two types of procedural knowledge. One type is *knowledge about symbols* but not including what the symbol means. For example, a student could read 2.56 as "two point five-six," without realizing that it represents a number less than 3 and nearer to 2½. The second kind of procedural knowledge is a *set of rules or steps* that make up an algorithm or procedure. Computation algorithms are sometimes taught as rules for manipulating symbols. For example, computing a quotient is carried out by a series of steps in a specified order.

"To summarize the definitions, conceptual knowledge is knowledge that is rich in relationships, but not rich in techniques for completing tasks. Procedural knowledge is rich in rules and strategies for completing tasks, but not rich in relationships" (15, p. 201).

Connecting Conceptual and Procedural Knowledge

One significant research confirmation is that most students do not recognize connections between their conceptual knowledge of decimals and the symbol manipulation procedures they use (15). In a series of written tests and interviews, Hiebert and Wearne (14) verified that students generally operate according to a series of procedural rules with little reference to conceptual underpinnings. For example, students refer to "lining up the decimals" for addition and subtraction. Teachers need to help students support this rule by the understanding that this "lining up" results from adding like quantities, for example "tenths added to tenths." Thus, $3.7 + 5.35$ becomes

$$\begin{array}{r} 3.7 \\ + 5.35 \\ \hline \end{array}$$

in order to add 7 tenths to 3 tenths.

> It is more difficult for students to acquire conceptual understanding once they have learned rote procedures (35). Thus, it is essential to focus initial instruction on building conceptual understanding.

Hiebert (12) has described three types of connections between conceptual and procedural knowledge that can enhance student learning. First, meaning becomes attached to mathematical symbols. For example, in $2.53 \times 6.4 =$ _____ a student must have an understanding of 2.53, 6.4, $\times$, $=$, ., and _____. There must be referents for the decimal fractions: a diagram, a measure (2.53 cm, 6.4 cm), or the sense that 2.53 represents a number about midway between 2 and 3 and 6.4 a number midway between 6 and 7. Presumably, some meaning of symbols "$\times$," "$=$," and "_____" will carry over from a whole number context. Without conceptual connections to these symbols, the student will not be able to make sense of multiplication of decimals. In fact, for either numerical, operational, or relational symbols there is evidence that students often do not relate whole number and common fraction concepts that do apply to decimals (e.g., "add like quantities"), and yet many overgeneralize conventions that do not apply to decimal fractions (e.g., interpreting "$\times$" as "groups of" without realizing that 2.53×6.4 means taking 2 groups of 6.4 and part of a group of 6.4) (15).

By developing a robust understanding of the concepts and symbols, students can use their understandings to solve a variety of tasks not explicitly included in instruction (36). In one study, although students were not given instruction on the difficult concept of ordering decimal fractions, they were able to complete these tasks. In fact, "if students used the meanings of written symbols as a basis for solving problems immediately after instruction, they used these processes to solve problems one year later, regardless of entering achievement" (33, p. 545).

In developing computational procedures, it is recommended that connections to symbolism be made as objects are acted upon. In this way, each step of a symbolic procedure becomes associated with a concrete action.

In elementary and middle grades, a number of arithmetic procedures are introduced. This allows for building the second type of connections, those between the internal steps of the procedure and their conceptual underpinnings. For example, in $2.53 \times 6.4 = $ _____ we would want students to understand that the product would have three decimal places since hundredths times tenths is thousandths. Thus, the rule for placing the decimal point in the product by counting the decimal places in the factors is connected to the conceptual understanding of decimal place value.

An example of the third type of connection would be to realize that 2.53×6.4 must be somewhere between 12 and 21. Interpreting a computed answer with meaning is highly dependent on conceptual underpinnings of the number and operation symbols. It is also dependent upon a student's cognitive control to motivate the self-question, "Is the answer reasonable?" What Hiebert and Wearne found missing for students "was a link between their conceptual knowledge and a notion that written answers should be reasonable" (15, p. 220).

Many students believe the purpose of checking is to judge the exactness of answers, rather than to check the reasonableness of answers. (Osser, Durmin, & Sorensen cited in 12)

Representations of Decimals

Some research (27) has suggested that in certain instances whole number knowledge supports decimal fraction knowledge and in other cases whole numbers may interfere with students' learning decimal fractions. Table 8.1 shows whether whole number knowledge and fraction knowledge support or interfere with each other in the learning of decimals. We now turn to more specific examples of understanding decimal fraction concepts: reading and writing decimal fractions and applying decimal fractions in appropriate situations.

Language

In their struggle to find meaning with decimal place value, students display a variety of difficulties, including language difficulties. We have heard students saying "tens" for "tenths" and "hundreds" for "hundredths" (25, 27). In response to the task: Multiply the number 1 hundredth, 3 tenths, by the number 2 ones, 7 hundredths, Jo

TABLE 8.1 Comparison of Decimal Fraction and Whole Number Knowledge

Elements of decimal fraction knowledge	Corresponding elements of whole number knowledge	Similar (+) or different (−)
A. Column values:	A. Column values:	
1. Values decrease as move left to right	1. Values decrease as move left to right	+
2. Each column is 10 times greater than column to right	2. Each column is 10 times greater than column to right	+
3. Zero serves as a place-holder	3. Zero serves as a place-holder	+
4. Zero added to rightmost column does not change total value	4. Zero added to leftmost column does not change total value	−
5. Values decrease as move away from decimal point	5. Values increase as move away from decimal point	−
B. Column names:	B. Column names:	
1. End in -*ths*	1. End in -*s*	−
2. Start with tenths	2. Start with units	−
3. Naming sequence (tenths, hundredths . . .) moves left to right	3. Naming sequence (tens, hundreds . . .) moves right to left	−
4. Reading sequence is tenths, hundredths, thousandths	4. Reading sequence is thousands, hundreds, tens, ones	−
C. Reading rules:	C. Reading rules:	
1. The units must be explicitly specified and they vary	1. The ones implicitly serve as the units in all cases	−

Used by permission of NCTM (27, p. 10, Table 1)

wrote 130 × 702, a perfect translation of "hundred" for "hundredths" and "ten" for "tenths." Wanda, upon correcting her mistake said, "I always get confused on the endings. . . . I can't remember if it's the decimal or the other one, because they are so similar" (25, pp. 222–223). Learning activities developed by Skemp use the terminology "tenth-parts" and "hundredth-parts" to connect language and concepts (30).

Other examples of misinterpretation are (a) "11.9 miles per hour" read as "11 miles, 9 minutes per hour"; (b) "pork chops weighing 1.07 pound" read as "1 pound 7 ounces"; (c) a calculator result of a runner's time of 0.453852 reported as "0.45 hours or 45 minutes"; and (d) 0.8 estimated as "about an eighth" (2, p. 405).

Brown (4) asked students to write how they would say the number 0.29. About 1/3 of students ages 12–15 said, "point two nine"; about 1/3 said, "point twenty-nine"; and about 1/8 said "twenty-nine." What is surprising is that neither "twenty-nine hundredths" nor "two tenths, nine hundredths" was reported as being used. These latter ways of expressing 0.29 are conceptually oriented. In our experience, children have no difficulty using this language if they are encouraged to do so. Sometimes it is helpful for students to think of decimal fractions as the composition of tenths, hundredths, and so on. For the example 0.374, rather than the fraction name of 374 thousandths, students could think 3 tenths plus 7 hundredths plus 4 thousandths (27). We recommend that teachers be careful to use and require students to use meaningful language and avoid the use of the word "point."

You may have noticed that middle school teachers often employ the "point" language. Some possible conjectures explain this: (a) lengthy decimals become cumbersome to say, (b) for the relative expert the "point" language carries as much conceptual content as the fraction language since the more significant digits support a place value interpretation, (c) their teachers used the "point" language for the same two reasons.

Teachers generally think that students often have an implicit understanding before they can express it in words. However, "in some cases language may precede understanding and perhaps even direct it" (37, p. 334). For example, using base-10 blocks, one student made a connection between the language he was already using and the properties of physical representations. "He altered his behavior on several related tasks as he attempted to build representations that possessed correct 10-for-1 relationships" (37, p. 335).

Concrete Models and Regions

Wearne, Hiebert, and Taber (37) point out that decimal fractions have a continuous aspect like common fractions and a discrete aspect like whole numbers. They found that the continuous aspect of decimals was especially difficult for students to understand. To deal with continuous materials, one must select a unit and measure a quantity by applying the unit of measure. In seeing the discrete aspect, the unit is determined for you, especially when using base-10 materials. Base-10 materials in either the wooden or paper versions are particularly useful for showing decimal fractions (38).

In one study (34), the large cube is defined as one, the flat as one tenth, the rod as one hundredth, and the small cube as one thousandth. In most research, the flat has been defined as one whole unit (20, 36, 38). However, at various times we (20) have redefined the rod or the large cube to be one, depending on the application. We and others (37) have successfully varied the unit to emphasize the arbitrariness of the unit in an effort to encourage children to be flexible in their thinking. Figure 8.1 shows alternative ways of naming the blocks to show fractions.

Regions are used in most textbooks as models for common and decimal fractions, but the connections between the regions and the numbers are not always retained.

FIGURE 8.1 The representation of the unit may be changed

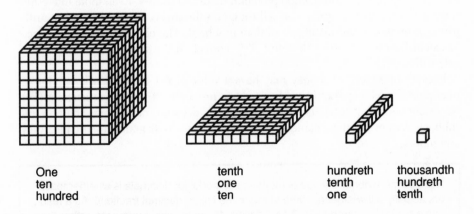

One	tenth	hundreth	thousandth
ten	one	tenth	hundreth
hundred	ten	one	tenth

Hiebert and Wearne (15) report that students were asked to write decimal fractions to represent the shaded part of a region. They summarize:

> One region was divided into 10 equal parts with three shaded; a second was divided into 100 equal parts with four shaded; and a third was divided into five equal parts with one shaded. Not more than half the students, even in grade nine, responded correctly to any of these items. The most frequent errors on the three tasks in all grades were 3.10, 4.100 and 1.5, respectively. The frequency of these errors declines from about 50% in grade five to about 15% in grade nine. (p. 209)

Apparently, the students recalled a common fraction response which they manipulated into an appropriate decimal form, which is conceptually unreasonable. Some suggestions are made later in this chapter for the effective use of models.

Money

Money is a familiar and engaging topic. It is an open question whether counting and calculating with amounts of money can be helpful in learning about place value and operations with decimal fractions. With money, two kinds of numbers are involved (5). One is the number of coins or the number of each kind of coin. Second, coins have value, and by choosing appropriately, we can choose those coins and bills that match the decimal system.

"The opportunity to relate decimals and money is too conceptually compelling to ignore. At the very least, after the notations are introduced separately, students could investigate in what ways the systems are analogous or not. For example, both use base 10, 42 cents is 42/100 of a dollar, and 0.42 is 42 out of a possible 100. On the other hand, $4.5 and $1.234, although meaningful, are not conventional." (D. Super)

Research in Brazil (5) has shown that adults who may not read or write numbers can solve addition and subtraction problems involving money. Even more interesting was the finding that children who sell things on the streets are much better at arithmetic computation outside of school than in school. The children were 98% correct in calculation in the streets, but only 37% correct on the same questions in school calculations.

Because one piece of money may have a value of 0.1 or 0.01, it is an abstract manipulative. Money should not be used first nor alone. To make connections (19), we recommend that teachers try using the same decimal fractions for addition and subtraction in two or three contexts: for example, base-10 diagrams, metric measures, and money.

> "One concern about the use of money as a model for decimals is whether teachers actually allow students time to make the link to decimal fractions. As a result some students interpret $7.42 as 7 dollars 42 cents, whole numbers, rather than 7 and 42 hundredths dollars." (D. Owens)

Equivalence and Order

Most teachers and textbook writers recognize the importance of students using correct procedures for examples like "0.25 has the same value as 0.250." We recommend that it be approached from the standpoint of "equivalence," two names for the same number, as it is for common fractions.

> 2 tenths, 5 hundredths is equivalent to 25 hundredths
> Using base-10 materials let the flat be one whole unit.
> Get 2 longs and 5 little ones.
>
>
> What is the name for this? (2 tenths, 5 hundredths.)
> Now trade the longs for little ones.
>
>
> What is the name for this? (25 hundredths)
> Right! So 2 tenths, 5 hundredths and 25 hundredths
> are two names for the same amount.

Equivalence of Decimal Fractions

Apparently, students overgeneralize whole number syntax rules concerning zero to decimal fractions (15). With whole numbers, annexing a zero to the right increases the number by a factor of 10 times, whereas attaching a zero to the left does not change the value. Contrary sorts of rules apply to decimal fractions. Fifth- through ninth-grade students were asked to select numbers equivalent to .8 from a list. About two thirds of fifth graders and one fifth of the others believed that only numbers with 0 to the left of 8 (on either side of the decimal point) were equivalent. On a written test item, "Write a number ten times as big as 437.56," the most frequent error was 437.560 (15, p. 206). Brown found conceptual inconsistencies to be typical. One student, for example, indicated that 4.90 is more than 4.9. In the next question she decided that 0.8 was bigger than 0.75 because, "Oh, it is eight tenths which equals 80 hundredths" (4, p. 52).

However, after conceptually based instruction on connecting decimal fractions with concrete referents (base-10 models), students in grade 4 were able to indicate equivalence or order without instruction directly on the topic. For example, Don was asked to identify the larger of .3 and .30. "He indicated they were equal . . . 'since this has got three tenths and this has got three tenths and it ain't got no hundredths, they would be equal'" (36, p. 509).

Whole Numbers as Decimals

Student understanding of the equivalence of decimals and whole numbers cannot be assumed. In one study, all interviewees who responded correctly to the task, "Take away $4 - 2.47$," wrote $4.00 - 2.47$ in vertical format (20). While it is easy to state a syntactic rule such as "You may 'add' (annex) zeros after the decimal point," the conceptual realization that 4 is equivalent to 4.00 is more difficult. Students have said, "4 doesn't have any places because it has no decimal point." Others agree that you can annex a decimal and zeros to whole numbers but then maintain that "4.00 is greater than 4." Even with instruction that the whole number 4 may have many decimal equivalents (e.g., 4.0, 4.00, 4.000), the substantive concept that whole numbers and decimals are a part of the same rational number system develops much later.

> Thoughtful practitioners and researchers (15) have noticed that students are often taught algorithms as indivisible procedures rather than as a collection of subprocedures. Hence, some students append zeros within the addition and subtraction algorithm and fail to see that the concept of equivalence is being applied.

Decimal and Common Fraction Equivalence

Common and decimal fractions are parallel symbol systems representing similar concepts. The fractions 0.7 and 7/10 are not only read alike—"seven tenths"—but both indicate seven tenths of some unit. In the Fourth National Assessment (16), about

60% of the seventh-grade students could express a simple common fraction as a decimal. Fewer could express a decimal fraction as a common fraction, and the difficulty was compounded when thousandths were introduced.

In Hiebert and Wearne's sample, about one fourth of the grade 5 students merely rearranged the digits to convert between fraction forms (e.g., ".09 = 0/9"). The errors made by older students suggest deeper conceptual understanding. For example, when asked to write a common "fraction for .09 the most frequent error was 9/10" (15, p. 209).

> That anything, especially a number, can have more than one symbol seems to be a difficult idea for students to grasp. "As one seventh grader said after denying that .6 is equivalent to 6/10, '.6 is six-tenths and 6/10 you say the same way, but it's different.'" (15, p. 210)

A conceptually oriented teaching experiment (25) demonstrated that common and decimal fractions can be taught concurrently as two symbols for the same situation. The example in Figure 8.2 calls for a decimal fraction (0.4) to be written for the common fraction 2/5. A similar diagram marked in hundredths can extend the possibilities to 40/100 and to 0.40. (Special care will be needed for children who have difficulty with spatial perception of "extra" lines.) Teaching these two symbol systems together as alternative forms for the same underlying concept will enhance students' ability to see decimal fractions and common fractions as belonging to the same rational number system.

Comparing and Ordering Decimals

In a national U.S. sample (16), students did worse on ordering decimal fractions than on all decimal items except the most difficult items on dividing decimals. In

FIGURE 8.2   Using a diagram to show equivalence of
                        common and decimal fractions

Shade 2/5 of the diagram below.

Write another common fraction name for the shaded part: _____
Write a decimal fraction name for the shaded part: _____

this assessment, about one half of grade 7 students could pick the decimal fraction representing the greatest number and about one third could identify a number between two given decimals.

Owens (20) found that after receiving conceptually oriented instruction 13 of the 16 students interviewed answered correctly to "Which is larger, 2.45 or 2.5?" Eight annexed a zero and concluded 2.50 is larger than 2.45. Four looked at the tenths place: "Because four is smaller than five." One student compared four and one-half tenths to five tenths. Of the three who answered incorrectly, one said "hundredths make it larger than tenths," and another "forty-five is bigger than five." Vance found some students in grades 6 and 7 making the common errors. However, "students who answered all five items correctly could state a valid rule for comparing decimals, and used appropriate place value language" (32, p. 56).

The apparent symmetry around the decimal point and the difficulty of distinguishing the whole number and fractional names can be expected to heighten children's tendency to apply whole number rules in comparing sizes of decimal fractions. Comparing decimals with the same numbers of digits encourages the "whole number mis-rule."

Children make few mistakes when comparing two decimals with different whole number parts, such as 12.7 and 15.56 (28), but they have difficulty comparing decimal fractions if there are different numbers of digits to the right of the decimal point and equal whole number parts (15). Students' errors such as .195 is greater than .2 are presumably a result of ignoring the decimal point and treating these as whole numbers (6).

Sackur-Grisvard and Leonard, refining these observations, found that students use several faulty generalizations to develop operational rules that are error prone. The most frequent error (made by 40% of fourth graders and 25% of fifth graders), called the "whole number rule" (27), is to select as smaller the number whose decimal portion would be a smaller whole number (e.g., choosing 11.7 as smaller than 11.14 because 7 is smaller than 14).

The next most frequent rule leading to error, called the "fraction rule" (27), is to select as smaller the number with more digits in the decimal part (e.g., choosing 11.723 as smaller than 11.41). As a student once said to one of the authors referring to the three decimal places right of the decimal point, "Thousandths are so tiny." Hiebert and Wearne report the percentage of students in grades 5, 7, and 9 choosing ".065 when asked to identify the smallest of 1.006, .06, .065, and .09" (15, p. 206) increases from 6% in grade 5 to 25% in grade 9. It seems that for one fifth of the students one faulty symbol-driven strategy is replaced by another. The fraction-rule error is more prevalent in countries like the United States and Israel where fractions are taught before decimals than in countries such as France where decimals are taught before fractions (27). Unfortunately, the fraction-rule error is still made by many students entering college (10).

The hidden numbers comparison task is one way to determine whether a student is using either the whole number mis-rule or fraction mis-rule. Ask, "Which is greater, 0.[ ] or 0.[ ][ ][ ][ ]? Of course, the answer is undetermined. For this question, a whole number mis-rule student selects 0.[ ][ ][ ][ ] and the fraction mis-rule student selects 0.[ ]. (27)

A third rule, more prevalent outside North America, is called the "zero rule": select as smaller the decimal that has a zero immediately after the decimal point, and otherwise choose as larger the number with more digits to the right of the decimal. In ordering 3.214, 3.09, 3.8, for example, the zero rule correctly chooses 3.09 as the smallest, but it chooses 3.214 as the largest. In cases with zeros it yields a correct answer and can mask the lack of complete understanding. In one study, this rule was used by about 8% of fourth graders and 14% of fifth graders (28, 27). The three rules together accounted for almost 90% of the mistakes in one study (28).

Write down a number that is:

	Correct	Responded "No Answer"
Larger than 3.9 but smaller than 4	37%	57%
Larger than 6 but smaller than 6.1	38%	49%
Larger than 0.52 but smaller than 0.53	20%	68%
Larger than 8.9 but smaller than 8.15	29%	
(66% responded 8.10, 8.11, . . . , 8.14)		

(Adapted from 9, p. 39)

If students have trouble comparing two decimal numbers, they have even more difficulty when ordering lists of decimals. It appears that teachers and textbooks adapt over time to student performance by avoiding exercises that are too difficult. Sackur-Grisvard and Leonard recommend giving lists of at least three numbers to be ordered so as to discriminate among levels of student understanding by identifying students who might order two numbers but not more.

The zero insertion task asks how the value of a decimal changes if a zero is inserted into different places (e.g., 2.35 altered to 2.305, 02.35, 2.035, 2.350) Response to this task also helps diagnose the use of mis-rules. (27)

In the previous sections, the focus is on establishing a conceptual understanding of decimal fractions: interpreting decimal notation, connecting decimals with appropriate models, ordering decimals, and determining equivalence. The sections that follow focus on operations. Most of the research has been on the use of computational algorithms. Some research is on applications or story problems, in particular choosing the correct operation for a particular situation. While the algorithms for addition and subtraction appear similar, performance is quite different. Subtraction is substantially more difficult. On the Fourth National Assessment a greater percentage of students was successful on addition and multiplication items than on subtraction and division (16).

Addition and Subtraction

Hiebert and Wearne (15) found that a significant portion of students align digits on the right rather than aligning decimal places or decimal points when adding and subtracting decimals. Among the most difficult items for students were $4 + .3$ and $7 - .4$. In the fall testing sessions, 84%, 85%, and 55% of fifth, sixth and seventh graders, respectively, aligned on the right for these two items. Only grade six students showed improvement by spring. Hiebert and Wearne (14) also found that students' errors were somewhat inconsistent. For example, in the fall testing sessions for grades 5 and 6, the most frequent error for $4.6 + 2.3$ was 69, with students ignoring the decimals. For the question $5.3 + 2.42$, the most frequent error was 2.95, aligning the right digits. In interviews, students who aligned the decimal points were asked to justify their use of the rule.

> The following percentages of students in each grade referred at *some* time during the interview, even vaguely, to the values of the numbers or other conceptual bases for the rule: 0%, 12%, 33%, 60%, in grades five, six, seven, and nine, respectively. It appears that if the link between rule and rationale is established at all, it is a late rather than an early development. (15, p. 213)

In summary, it appears that students are relying on rules about symbols rather than conceptual understanding when asked to add and subtract decimals. Using "ragged" decimals for computation tasks aids in a more precise assessment of whether students are using meaningful analysis or only rote rules in addition and subtraction (34).

Skemp describes a number of conceptually oriented games. One example is Target. To play the easier version you need two stacks of cards face down. One set of cards has tenth-parts written (.3, .7, etc.) and the other set are hundredth-part cards (.07, .08, etc.). Each player draws a card from each stack and chooses to use one, both, or neither of the cards to make a number. The player writes the number as chosen, and adds it to the previous total. The player who first reaches 1 unit exactly is the winner. (30)

During instruction (20) students were taught to add or subtract like quantities: "Add tenths to tenths," and so on. In subtraction, 8 of the 17 students interviewed were able to answer the item $4 - 2.47$ correctly. Each did so by rewriting vertically as $4.00 - 2.47$. Three others started this way but subtracted incorrectly. One of the three obtained 0.153 but concluded 0.1530, "Because there are four places in the question, I need to point off four in the answer." Two other characteristic errors were

$$
\begin{array}{r}
2.47 \\
-\quad 4 \\
\hline 2.43
\end{array}
\qquad \text{and} \qquad
\begin{array}{r}
4. \\
-2.47 \\
\hline 2.47
\end{array}
$$

Teachers must help children diagnose and overcome their errors in subtraction, which is more difficult than addition. Teachers should help children develop their conceptual understanding by using models and problem situations in instruction and setting tasks such as ragged decimals for computation.

Multiplication

It is common for middle grade students to become proficient with decimal multiplication algorithms without having an adequate conceptual understanding. Some students, when they multiply, confuse rote rules such as "lining up decimal points" and "counting the number of decimal places." However, their performance level with routine multiplication computation is usually judged to be nearly satisfactory. On the fourth NAEP assessment of mathematics, performance on simple decimal multiplication showed improvement from about 60% in grade 7 to over 75% in grade 11 (16). It is typical for student errors to be evenly split between the process of multiplication and the placement of the decimal (6). Teachers should give students feedback on whether student errors are in the (whole number) multiplication procedure or placement of the decimal point, which can be more conceptual.

Max (grade 7) said, "When you can't line up decimals you count." When asked to estimate the answer and place the decimal point in the given "answer": 7.342 × 0.5 = 3671, he concluded that 7.342 × 0.5 is .3671. (21, p. 221)

As evidence of understanding multiplication you could consider students' ability to compute a product such as 2.71 × 0.54. But what might be considered as indicators of conceptual knowledge? Three criteria have been investigated and are discussed below. First, the ability to estimate decimal products with flexibility (22, 24) requires a broad number sense with decimal fractions. Second, building and referring to appropriate models, whether concrete, pictorial or descriptive, may illustrate understanding (23, 24). Finally, choices made by students in solving application problems involving multiplication and division have been cited as evidence (1).

Estimation

There is evidence (22) to suggest that performance on estimating products (e.g., estimate the whole number closest to 3.5 × 4.52) is not related to performance on other multiplication tasks such as calculating products and solving routine multiplication story problems. A plausible explanation for this finding is that estimating products requires conceptual knowledge, while computation of products requires only procedural knowledge. Children's grasp of decimal product estimation depends on the particular decimal fractions.

The easiest estimation for students is with factors that have whole number parts. In an example like "Estimate the answer and place the decimal point in the given answer: $3.25 \times 5.52 = 1\ 7\ 9\ 4$," the factors can be rounded to 3 and 6, giving an estimate of 18. Students at grades 5 and 6 find these types of products to be relatively simple (24), assuming they actually attempt to estimate. Of course, some do not and apply the "count rule" arbitrarily and get 0.1794 as the answer. In general, products with ending zeros dropped (where one factor ends in a multiple of 2 and the other ends in 5) will cause more difficulty for students who do not estimate than for those who do estimate.

Students were asked to place the decimal point in an answer calculated by a malfunctioning calculator. The calculator "always forgot to insert the decimal point and it often added unnecessary zeros before or behind the correct non-zero digits (e.g., 3.20 divided by .08 = 00400000)" (15, p. 218). Sixth, seventh, and ninth grade students counted digits from the right on multiplication and division 27%, 59%, and 60% of the time, respectively. Only one student out of 45 consistently checked for reasonableness of results. Three students checked for reasonableness on at least one question. (15)

Another condition that affects performance and understanding is having one factor that is less than one. For example, when asked to estimate the product and place the decimal point in $7.342 \times 0.5 = 3\ 6\ 7\ 1$, few students referred to "one-half of seven" (21). The equivalence of 0.5 and 1/2 was overlooked or not seen as relevant. For products of this type it seems crucial for students to be able to apply equivalent common and decimal fractions. As another example, in trying to make sense of a product like 0.35×12.3, an effective strategy is to think "about 1/3 of 12."

Unlike the case for addition and subtraction, primitive notions of multiplication and division (i.e., based on equal groups) cannot be transferred wholesale from whole numbers to decimals. Performance data suggest that many students never extend the meanings of "×" and "÷" nor suppress their primitive conceptions. (15)

Models

When both factors are less than one, estimating is difficult and is unlikely to support conceptual understanding. The most commonly used meaning for products of numbers less than one is area. Unfortunately, for many students the meaning of multiplication is limited to repeated addition which is inappropriate for non-integral numbers (see Fig. 8.3). Only 60% of students in grades 4 and 5 used an area approach, even with examples as simple as 3×4 (8).

FIGURE 8.3   Area model for multiplication

"Area models are especially helpful in visualizing numerical ideas
from a geometric point of view. For example, area models
can be used to show... that 1.2 x 1.3 = 1.56." (19, p.88)

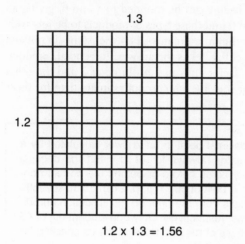

1.2 x 1.3 = 1.56

When grade 6 (24) and grade 7 (23) students were asked in an interview to find the product for .4 × .2, they invariably wrote 0.8 or .8. Later in the interview, they were asked to shade the 10 by 10 grid diagram to show 0.3 of 0.2 (see Fig. 8.4). With considerable prompting, students were able to interpret the diagram in terms of unit, tenth, and hundredth and to decide that 0.06 of the unit was to be shaded. They easily wrote a number sentence like 0.3 × 0.2 = 0.06. Near the end of the interview they were asked if they would like to reconsider the first question, .4 × .2 = _____. Every student was successful in correcting the earlier question without hesitation.

FIGURE 8.4   A graphic of $0.3 \times 0.2 = 0.06$

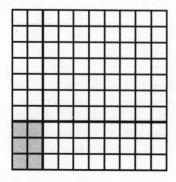

Choosing the Correct Operation

Knowing when to use multiplication can be seen as conceptual because of the relationships among the situations and the numbers involved. Most of the research related to choosing the operation uses a set of written story problems involving multiplication and division (1, 4, 7). One strong influence on students' choices as early as grade 4 is the common misconception that "multiplication always makes bigger, and division always makes smaller" (8). For example, students may be prone to divide in the following problem because they know a reduction is involved: "To fit a picture of a dress onto a page of a magazine, the picture has to be reduced to 0.14 of its original size. In the original picture the length of the dress was 2 m. What will its length be in the magazine?" (1, p. 132).

The other factor which seems to be important in selecting multiplication is the underlying situation. Thirteen-year-olds easily recognized a repeated addition situation as multiplication: "In the school kitchen the cooks use 0.62 kg of flour to make one tray of doughnuts. How much flour will it take to make 27 trays?" (1, p. 132). The same students found the rate situation much more difficult in a problem like "One gallon of petrol costs £1.33. How much will it cost to fill up a small tank which can only hold 0.53 gallons?" (1, p. 132). We recommend that teachers use many multiplication problems in a variety of different settings. Another suggestion is to assign tasks like "make up a multiplication problem for 1.4×2.7."

Division

Assessment results confirm what teachers of the middle grades know from experience: Division with decimals is particularly troublesome for students. On recent NAEP mathematics assessments, student performance with decimal computation was considerably below performance with the other operations. Further, division of a whole number or decimal by a decimal was more difficult for students than division of decimals by a whole number (3, 6). Division is especially difficult when the need arises for zeros as place holders in the dividend or quotient (4, 31). In fact, it has been noted that the low performance on decimal division items in the fourth NAEP mathematics assessment may be related to each item involving zeros in the dividends or quotients.

Put a circle around whichever statements are correct in the following:

The answer to 26.3×0.4 is
more than 26.3 / less than 26.3   Correct: 37%
The answer to $3.7 \div 8.6$ is
more than 1 / less than 1   Correct: 63%
The answer to $4.6 \div 0.6$ is
more than 4.6 / less than 4.6   Correct: 22%
(Quoted from 9, p. 39, Table 1)

Given the range of subskills required by the exercises shown in Table 8.2, it is surprising that the results are so consistent even by the grade 11 level (3). Comparable results have been reported by Brown (4) for students in England in the age range of 12 to 15.

Grossnickle observed that the "division process was not a dominant factor in the number of errors made" (11, p. 563) in the division of decimals; rather, the error occurred in the placement of the decimal point in the quotient. There is general agreement among researchers and mathematics educators that the method that converts a decimal divisor into a whole number divisor is preferred. The commonly suggested practice of multiplying divisor and dividend by a power of 10 (equal to the number of decimal places in the divisor) has more explanatory power than either rote adjustment of decimals or use of carets or subtractive methods for the placement of the decimal in the quotient (11). Grossnickle and Perry give five recommendations; the most important is to teach the procedure for understanding before teaching for computational skill. This can be accomplished by teaching estimation of the answer. Also with increased use of technology for calculation in society, estimation is more important than computational skill. Graeber and Tirosh (8) give several suggestions for teaching multiplication and division, including early estimation of whether the answer to a division word problem is greater than, less than, or equal to one.

Others have pointed out students' reluctance to allow division of whole number by a larger whole number or to predict such a division could result in a decimal fraction (4, 8). About one half of 12-, 13-, and 14-year-olds and about one fourth of 15-year-olds said there is no answer for 16 divided by 20 (4). Teachers can effectively use base-ten blocks to develop acceptance and understanding of this type division situation. Demonstration and student manipulation is recommended using the partitive (sharing) meaning of division with simple exercises such as 4 divided by 5.

"A car traveled for 25.6 miles at a steady speed of 37.8 miles per hour. Write down the calculation you would do to work out how long the journey took in hours."

Correct: 20%
Reversed division: 31%
Multiplication: 16%

(9, p. 40)

The conception that division "always makes smaller" is firmly ingrained in the minds of a large proportion of 12- to 15-year-olds (4, 8). It is important to discuss the effect of decimal size in multiplication and division, especially given the way in which students have been found to approach applications involving multiplication and division. Research by Owens (24) supports that by Fischbein et al. (7) that students often first develop an idea about the size of an answer relative to the numbers provided in an application, and then consistently let this idea influence the choice

TABLE 8.2 Percent Correct on Decimal
Division Computation Items

Item	Grade 7	Grade 11
$.3\overline{)9.06}$	52	67
$.02\overline{)8.4}$	46	67
$98.56 \div .032$	36	60
Divide .0884 by 3.4	36	55

(Adapted from 3, p. 246, Table 3. Used by permission of NCTM.)

of the operation. Clearly, the process does not serve well those with alternate conceptions or poor estimation monitoring skills.

Looking Ahead . . .

We look forward to the time when more students are able to make connections between decimal fractions and other number knowledge as suggested by the NCTM
Curriculum and Evaluation Standards (19). Teachers can make a beginning by
teaching decimal fractions in a context: a manipulative, a measure, a fraction, or
between two whole numbers. They can use calculators to help with basic notation
and multiplication and division concepts. Conceptually based instruction in decimal fractions pays big dividends in terms of helping students learn new content
(e.g., ordering or operations) and in terms of retention. Although common and
decimal fractions are discussed in separate chapters in textbooks and in this volume, it is now my conviction that these should be taught to whatever extent possible as different names for the same numbers. Teachers are encouraged to try integrating common and decimal fractions as an action research project. More
development is needed on contexts for teaching multiplication and division of decimal fractions. Research is needed on the relative ease or difficulty of understanding
multiplication and division following instruction that has developed a conceptual
understanding of the basic concepts.

Douglas T. Owens

In reviewing the research on decimal fractions, it is striking how much of it reinforces and clarifies what thoughtful teachers may already suspect. Thus, I add my
voice to the other teacher-contributors in this volume: Don't leave research to university researchers. Initiate action research in your classroom, in your school, and
in your district. Involve your students in thinking about and initiating alternative
approaches, methods, and resources. If you feel your research is of interest to a
wider audience, contact faculty in a college of education.

As a teacher-researcher with a class for the year, I would be tempted to explore
the effectiveness of a constructivist approach whereby decimal concepts are actively

created by students from what they know and believe about whole numbers and common fractions. The article by Wearne, Hiebert, and Taber (37) stimulated my imagination with numerous opportunities for critical study and classroom-based investigation. Think back over your reaction to ideas in this chapter: What might you and your colleagues be intrigued to investigate and share with others?

Douglas B. Super

About the Authors

Douglas T. Owens is Associate Professor of Mathematics Education in the Department of Mathematics and Science Education at the University of British Columbia where he teaches courses in teacher education and graduate courses in mathematics education. His research interests include classroom-based research on the teaching and learning of decimal and common fractions.

Douglas B. Super is supervisor of academic programs K–12 for the Vancouver School District in British Columbia. He is author of several elementary school mathematics programs including *The Mathematics Experience* and *Math Activities Courseware*, Levels 1–8.

References

1. BELL, A., FISCHBEIN, E., & GREER, B. (1984). Choices of verbal arithmetic problems: The effects of number size, problem structure and context. *Educational Studies in Mathematics, 15*(2), 129–147.
2. BELL, A., SWAN, M., & TAYLOR, G. (1981). Choice of operation in verbal problems with decimal numbers. *Educational Studies in Mathematics, 12*(4), 399–420.
*3. BROWN, C. A., CARPENTER, T. P., KOUBA, V. L., LINDQUIST, M. M., SILVER, E. A., & SWAFFORD, J. O. (1988). Secondary school results for the fourth NAEP mathematics assessment: Discrete mathematics, data organization and interpretation, measurement, number and operations. *Mathematics Teacher, 81*(4), 241–248.
4. BROWN, M. L. (1981). Place value and decimals. In K. M. Hart (Gen. Ed.), *Children's understanding of mathematics: 11–16* (pp. 48–65). London: John Murray.
*5. CARRAHER, T. N., & SCHLIEMANN, A. D. (1988). Using money to teach about the decimal system. *Arithmetic Teacher, 36*(4), 42–43.
*6. CARPENTER, T. P., CORBITT, M. K., KEPNER, H. S., LINDQUIST, M. M., & REYS, R. E. (1981). Decimals: Results and implications from national assessment. *Arithmetic Teacher, 28*(8), 34–37.
7. FISCHBEIN, E., DORI, M., NELLO, M. S., & MARINO, M. S. (1985). The role of implicit models in solving verbal problems in multiplication and division. *Journal for Research in Mathematics Education, 16*(1), 3–17.
*8. GRAEBER, A. O., & TIROSH, D. (1990). Insights fourth and fifth graders bring to multiplication and division with decimals. *Educational Studies in Mathematics, 21*(6), 565–588.
9. GREER, B. (1987). Nonconservation of multiplication and division involving decimals. *Journal for Research in Mathematics Education, 18*(1), 37–45.
10. GROSSMAN, A. S. (1983). Decimal notation: An important research finding. *Arithmetic Teacher, 30*(9), 32–33.

*11. GROSSNICKLE, F. E., & PERRY, L. M. (1985). Division with common fractions and decimal divisors. *School Science and Mathematics*, 85(7), 556–566.

*12. HIEBERT, J. (1984). Children's mathematics learning: The struggle to link form and understanding. *Elementary School Journal*, 84(5), 497–513.

*13. HIEBERT, J. (1987). Research report: Decimal fractions. *Arithmetic Teacher*, 34(7), 22–23.

14. HIEBERT, J., & WEARNE, D. (1985). A model of students' decimal computation procedures. *Cognition and Instruction*, 2(3 & 4), 175–205.

15. HIEBERT, J., & WEARNE, D. (1986). Procedures over concepts: The acquisition of decimal number knowledge. In J. Hiebert (Ed.), *Conceptual and procedural knowledge: The case of mathematics* (pp. 199–223). Hillsdale, NJ: Erlbaum.

*16. KOUBA, V. L., BROWN, C. A., CARPENTER, T. P., LINDQUIST, M. M., SILVER, E. A., & SWAFFORD, J. O. (1988). Results of the fourth NAEP assessment of mathematics: Number, operations and word problems: *Arithmetic Teacher*, 35(8), 14–19.

17. KOUBA, V. L., BROWN, C. A., CARPENTER, T. P., & SWAFFORD, J. O. (1989). Number and operations. In M. M. Lindquist (Ed.), *Results from the fourth mathematics assessment of the National Assessment of Educational Progress*. Reston VA: National Council of Teachers of Mathematics.

18. MARZANO, R. J., BRANDT, R. S., HUGHES, C. S., JONES, B. F., PRESSEISEN, B. Z., RANKIN, S. C., & SUHOR, C. (1988). *Dimensions of thinking: A framework for curriculum and instruction*. Reston VA: Association for Supervision and Curriculum Development.

*19. NATIONAL COUNCIL OF TEACHERS OF MATHEMATICS. (1989). *Curriculum and evaluation standards for school mathematics*. Reston, VA: Author.

20. OWENS, D. T. (1981). Children's thinking about addition, subtraction and order of decimal fractions. In T. R. Post & M. P. Roberts (Eds.), *Proceedings of the Third Annual Meeting of the North American Chapter of the International Group for the Psychology of Mathematics Education* (pp. 208–214), Minneapolis: University of Minnesota.

21. OWENS, D. T. (1985). Decimal concepts and operations: What do students think? In S. K. Damarin & M. Shelton (Eds.), *Proceedings of the Seventh Annual Meeting, North American Chapter of the International Group for the Psychology of Mathematics Education* (pp. 218–223), Columbus, OH: North American Chapter of the International Group for the Psychology of Mathematics Education.

22. OWENS, D. T. (1986). Estimating products of decimals. In G. Lappan & R. Even (Eds.), *Proceedings of the Eighth Annual Meeting, North American Chapter of the International Group for the Psychology of Mathematics Education* (pp. 84–89), East Lansing, MI: North American Chapter of the International Group for the Psychology of Mathematics Education.

23. OWENS, D. T. (1987). Decimal multiplication in grade seven. In J. Bergeron, N. Herscovics, & C. Kieran (Eds.), *Proceedings of the Eleventh International Conference, Psychology of Mathematics Education* (Vol. II, pp. 423–429). Montreal: University of Montreal.

24. OWENS, D. T. (1988). Understanding decimal multiplication in grade six. In M. Behr, C. Lacampagne, & M. Wheeler (Eds.), *Proceedings of the Tenth Annual Meeting, North American Chapter of the International Group for the Psychology of Mathematics Education* (pp. 107–113). De Kalb, IL: Northern Illinois University.

25. OWENS, D. T. (1990). Thinking on rational number concepts: A teaching experiment. *Final Report to Social Sciences and Humanities Research Council of Canada Grant #410-88-0678.*

26. RESNICK, L. B. (1982). Syntax and semantics in learning to subtract. In T. P. Carpenter, J. M. Moser, & T. A. Romberg (Eds.), *Addition and subtraction: A cognitive perspective* (pp. 135–155). Hillsdale, NJ: Erlbaum.

27. RESNICK, L. B., NESHER, P., LEONARD, F., MAGONE, M., OMANSON, S., & PELED, I. (1989). Conceptual bases of arithmetic errors: The case of decimal fractions. *Journal for Research in Mathematics Education, 20*(1), 8–27.

28. SACKUR-GRISVARD, C., & LEONARD, F. (1985). Intermediate cognitive organizations in the process of learning a mathematical concept: The order of positive decimal numbers. *Cognition and Instruction, 2*(2), 157–174.

*29. SKEMP, R. R. (1978). Relational understanding and instrumental understanding. *Arithmetic Teacher, 26*(3), 9–15.

*30. SKEMP, R. R. (1989). *Structured activities for primary mathematics: Volume 2*. London: Routledge.

*31. TRAFTON, P. R., & ZAWOJEWSKI, J. S. (1984). Teaching rational number division: A special problem. *Arithmetic Teacher, 31*(6), 20–22.

32. VANCE, J. M. (1986). Ordering decimals and fractions: A diagnostic study. *Focus on Learning Problems in Mathematics, 8*(2), 51–59.

33. WEARNE, D. (1990). Acquiring meaning for decimal fraction symbols: A one year follow-up. *Educational Studies in Mathematics, 21*(6), 545–564.

34. WEARNE, D., & HIEBERT, J. (1988). A cognitive approach to meaningful mathematics instruction: Testing a local theory using decimal numbers. *Journal for Research in Mathematics Education, 19*(5), 371–384.

35. WEARNE, D., & HIEBERT, J. (1988). Constructing and using meaning for mathematical symbols: The case of decimal fractions. In J. Hiebert & M. Behr (Eds.), *Number concepts and operations in the middle grades* (pp. 220–235). Hillsdale, NJ: Erlbaum; Reston, VA: National Council of Teachers of Mathematics.

36. WEARNE, D., & HIEBERT, J. (1989). Cognitive changes during conceptually based instruction on decimal fractions. *Journal of Educational Psychology, 81*(4), 507–513.

*37. WEARNE, D., HIEBERT, J., & TABER, S. (1991). Fourth graders' gradual construction of decimal fractions during instruction using different physical representations. *Elementary School Journal, 91*(4), 321–341.

*38. ZAWOJEWSKI, J. (1983). Initial decimal concepts: Are they really so easy? *Arithmetic Teacher, 30*(7), 52–56.

CHAPTER 9

Learning and Teaching Ratio and Proportion: Research Implications

Kathleen Cramer, Thomas Post, and Sarah Currier

> *Consider this problem: Sue and Julie were running equally fast around a track. Sue started first. When she had run 9 laps, Julie had run 3 laps. When Julie completed 15 laps, how many laps had Sue run? Thirty-two out of 33 preservice elementary education teachers in a mathematics methods class solved this problem by setting up and solving a proportion: $9/3 = x/15$; $3x = 135$; $x = 45$. While these students knew a procedure for solving a proportion, they did not realize that this particular problem did not represent a proportional situation. Therefore, the traditional proportion algorithm was not an appropriate strategy to use.*

"The fact that many aspects of our world operate according to proportional rules makes proportional reasoning abilities extremely useful in the interpretation of real world phenomena." (15, p. 79)

$\mathbf{T}$he problem above was one of two problems given to these students as part of the introduction to teaching ratio and proportion ideas. The other problem involved a money exchange context: 3 U.S. dollars can be exchanged for 2 British pounds. How many pounds for 21 U.S. dollars? This is a proportional situation, and all the students correctly solved this problem using the traditional proportion algorithm. But no one could explain why this problem reflected a proportional situation while the running laps problem did not.

Superficially the two problems are similar; each contains three pieces of information with one number unknown. That structure does lend itself to a proportion: $a/b = c/x$ where a, b, c are the known quantities and x is the unknown quantity. The deeper differences between the two tasks highlight what is special about proportional situations. The next section will discuss these differences. At this point it is sufficient to conclude that we cannot define a proportional reasoner as simply one who knows how to set up and solve a proportion. The research on proportional reasoning helps expand our view of what it means to be a proportional reasoner. Having a better understanding of what proportional reasoning entails should influence our classroom instruction.

> "Being able to perform mechanical operations with proportions does not necessarily mean the students understand the underlying ideas of proportional thinking ... the ability to firmly understand proportionality is a turning point in mental development." (6, p. 293)

Mathematical Relationships in Proportional Situations

The critical component of proportional situations is the multiplicative relationship that exists among the quantities that represent the situation. In the running laps problem, the relationship between the number of laps Sue ran and the number of laps Julie ran can be expressed through addition or subtraction: Sue's laps = Julie's laps + 6; Julie's laps = Sue's laps − 6. In the money exchange problem the relationship between U.S. dollars and British pounds can be expressed through multiplication: pounds = 2/3 U.S. dollars or U.S. dollars = 3/2 British pounds. The running laps problem is not a proportional situation while the money exchange situation is proportional.

Gerard Vergnaud is a French psychologist and mathematics educator who for many years has directed a center for research in Paris. Vergnaud (19) has used a model based on the concept of *measure space* to assist in clarifying the nature of the multiplicative relationships that exist in proportional situations. A measure space can be thought of in terms of physical magnitudes such as length, weight, money, or children. When the type of physical magnitude is quantified as with 2 cm, 3 kg, or 5 dollars, these values are known as quantities. *A proportion then can be viewed as a multiplicative relationship between the quantities in two measure spaces.* Vergnaud's notation is as follows:

M1	M2
a	b
c	d

M1 and M2 represent any two measure spaces and *a*, *b*, *c*, and *d* are the quantities that form the rates in a proportion. For example, let us record the money exchange situation using the measure space notation: If 3 U.S. dollars can be exchanged for 2 British pounds, then at this rate 21 U.S. dollars can be exchanged for 14 British pounds. Translating to measure space notation we have the following:

Dollars	Pounds
3	2
21	14

In proportional situations the quantities between or across measure spaces (3:2, 21:14) always are related by multiplication. If we multiply the number of U.S. dollars by 2/3 we obtain the corresponding number of British pounds. If we extend the table using this multiplication rule, some of the other entries would include the following:

Dollars	Pounds
3	2
6	4
9	6
12	8

In each case the number of British pounds can be found by multiplying the number of U.S. dollars by 2/3 ($6 \times 2/3 = 4; 9 \times 2/3 = 6; 12 \times 2/3 = 8$). This constant factor can be used to write an algebraic rule for this proportional situation: $y = 2/3 x$ where y = British pounds and x = U.S. dollars. This constant factor also describes the number of pounds per one dollar: 2/3 pound per 1 dollar. This is called the *unit rate*.

The graph for this situation is shown in Figure 9.1. Note that the line is straight, leans toward the right and passes through the origin. This is true of graphs of all proportional situations.

Another interesting characteristic of proportional situations can be shown by recording the different rates as fractions. In the example above, the relationship of British pounds to U.S. dollars can be expressed as 2/3, 4/6, 6/9, 8/12. These fractions are equivalent and reduce to the same number: 2/3. All rate pairs in proportional situations always reduce to the same fraction, the unit rate.

A different multiplicative relationship exists among the elements within each measure space. Starting with 3 U.S. dollars for 2 British pounds, if we multiply the number of dollars by 2 and correspondingly multiply the number of pounds by 2 then we obtain another rate pair in the table: 6:4. If we triple the number of dollars we must triple the number of pounds. This rate pair, 9:6, is also in the table. Intuitively, we can easily see this number pattern going down the table (within a measure space). Note that the factor relating any two quantities within the same measure space

FIGURE 9.1   Graph of proportional situation: money exchange

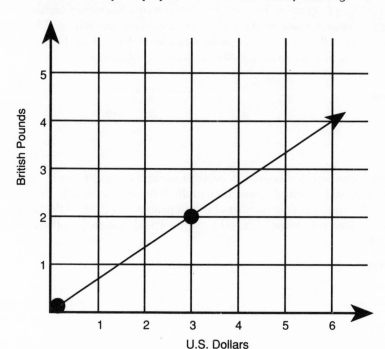

is not a constant while the factor relating quantities between or across the measure spaces is a constant.

A proportional relationship is just one type of relationship that can exist between two sets of quantities. It is a special class in which multiplication defines the relationship. Another example of a nonproportional situation highlights this point (see Fig. 9.2). A taxicab charges $1.00 plus 50 cents per kilometer. The cost for one kilometer is $1.50; the cost for 2 kilometers is $2.00. Though a relationship between cost and kilometers exists and can be written using a function rule ($y = .50\,x + 1.00$, $y = $ cost, $x = $ kilometers), it is not proportional because both addition and multiplication define the relationship. The graph of this function does not go through the origin.

Methods of Assessing Proportional Reasoning

Research has used students' achievements in solving missing value problems as an important index of their ability to think proportionally (8,13,14,15,17).

FIGURE 9.2   Graph of taxicab problem: nonproportional

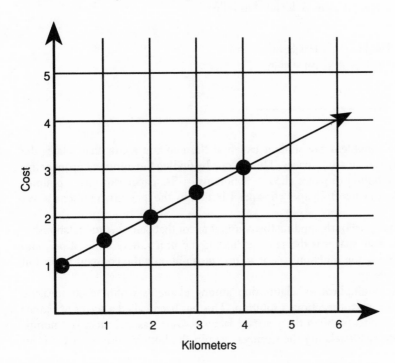

"The acquisition of proportional thinking skills in the population at large has been unsatisfactory. Not only do these skills emerge more slowly than originally suggested but there is evidence that a large segment of our society never acquires them at all." (6, p. 285)

In a missing value problem three pieces of information are given. The task is to find the fourth or missing piece of information. The measure space notation can be used to describe missing value problems and the solution strategies presented in the research. The well-known "Tall Man Short Man" problem (7) has been a popular research task. In this problem subjects are given a picture of a figure labeled Mr. Short and a chain of paper clips. They are told that Mr. Short's height is four buttons. After measuring the height of Mr. Short as six paper clips, the subjects were told that there was another figure not shown, a Mr. Tall, who was six buttons high. They were asked to find the height of Mr. Tall in paper clips. At this point the subjects had three pieces of information: the height of Mr. Short in paper clips and in buttons, and the height of Mr. Tall in buttons. The missing information was the height of Mr. Tall in paper clips. The problem is depicted as follows:

	Height in buttons	Height in paper clips
Mr. Short	4	6
Mr. Tall	6	x

To solve this problem the student can find the constant factor that relates the quantities between measure spaces. This is done by finding the number of paper clips that equal one button (6 paper clips ÷ 4 buttons = 3/2 paper clips per 1 button). Multiplying this factor, 3/2 paper clips per 1 button by the quantity 6 buttons solves the problem.

As mentioned previously, finding the constant factor that describes the relationship across two measure spaces is the same as finding the *unit rate* or amount per one. When considering the function rule $y = mx$, m is not only the constant factor but also the unit rate.

Finding the multiplicative relationship among elements within each measure space is another way of reaching a solution. This has been called a *factor of change* method. In the next problem the constant factor across measure spaces is a noninteger while the factor relating the numbers within the button measure space is an integer.

	Height in buttons	Height in paper clips
Mr. Short	4	10
Mr. Tall	12	x

Students can reason that if the number of buttons is tripled, then the number of paper clips must also be tripled. Knowing that both within and between relationships exist offers students alternative strategies. Research has shown that students often look for the whole number relationship and solve the task using this integer factor.

When the multiplicative relationship between and within measure spaces are both noninteger, students have more difficulty. In this type of missing value problem incorrect additive strategies often occur.

	Height in buttons	Height in paper clips
Mr. Short	3	7
Mr. Tall	5	x

Students often reason that $x = 9$ because $3 + 4 = 7$ so $5 + 4 = 9$ or because $3 + 2 = 5$ so $7 + 2 = 9$. This is an incorrect fallback strategy and is probably utilized because of an inability to deal with the noninteger relationships. This is an example of what Karplus called the "fraction avoidance syndrome" (8).

"Children's responses to missing value problems with noninteger answers reflect their belief that fractions are not numbers. A common answer to $3/4 = ?/9$ is to say that a number cannot be found to satisfy the equality." (16, in press)

Understanding of proportional situations must eventually involve generalizing beyond the numerical aspects of the problem to the point that all solutions are based on either the multiplicative relationship within or between measure spaces. Problems without integer relationships seem more difficult but in fact have the same mathematical structure as the integer problems and are solved by identical types of solution strategies.

Missing value tasks are just one type of problem used in the research on ratio and proportion. Numerical comparison problems requiring the comparison of two rates also have been used to assess proportional reasoning ability. Noelting's (13) orange juice problems are well-known examples of this problem type. Figure 9.3 shows Noelting's problem types. Subjects were to determine the relative strength of orange juice given the number of glasses of juice and the corresponding number of glasses of water that were mixed. In each picture the orange juice is presented first. Students were to imagine that the liquid in each set of glasses was poured into a jug and mixed well; they were then asked to identify the jug whose liquid would have the stronger "orangey" taste. In the specific example shown, 3 parts orange juice to 4 parts water is stronger than 2 parts orange juice to 3 parts water so the box under the stronger mixture is shaded.

FIGURE 9.3   Noelting's Orange Juice Task (13, p. 219). Reprinted by permission of Kluwer Academic Publishers

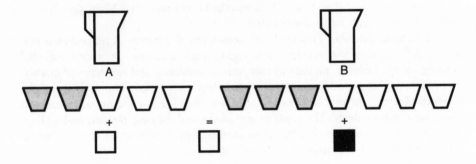

The numbers used in orange juice tasks were varied to include integer (whole number) and noninteger relationships. For example:

Orange juice	Water
3	12
5	20

In this example, there is 4 times as much water as orange juice in each rate so the mixtures taste the same. Here there is an integer relationship between each measure space comparison. If the tabular entries are as follows,

Orange juice	Water
3	7
6	14

the integer relationship would be within each measure space.

As with missing value tasks, the numerical comparison tasks with rates having noninteger relationships were more difficult for students than rates with integer relationships. This body of research also showed that the comparison of two unit rates such as 1 to 3 and 1 to 5 made the tasks easier. Comparing unequal rates was more difficult than comparing equal ones.

Qualitative prediction tasks and qualitative comparison tasks have also been used to assess proportional reasoning ability (4,15). These problems contain no numerical values but require the counterbalancing of variables in measure spaces. An example of a qualitative prediction task follows: If Devan ran fewer laps in more time than she did yesterday, would her running speed be (a) faster, (b) slower, (c) exactly the same, (d) not enough information to tell.

The following is a qualitative comparison task: Mary ran more laps than Greg. Mary ran for less time than Greg. Who was the faster runner? (a) Mary, (b) Greg, (c) same, (d) not enough information to tell.

The Rational Number Project (RNP) administered a survey of proportional reasoning tasks to over 900 seventh- and eighth-grade students. Questions included missing value problems, numerical comparison problems, and two types of qualitative problems. Integer and noninteger relationships were tested. The study varied the contexts in which the problems were embedded while keeping the numerical aspects the same across contexts. The contexts included speed, buying, density, and scaling. The researchers predicted that the more familiar buying and speed contexts would be easier than the less familiar density and scaling contexts.

Students' Solution Strategies

Information from the RNP study is shown in Table 9.1. The types of correct solution strategies for the missing value and numerical comparison problems are shown as well as the percentage correct for each strategy.

Although seventh-grade students had no prior instruction in the standard algorithm (cross-multiply and divide), eighth graders had received such instruction a few weeks prior to the survey. Note the much larger incidence of the algorithmic approach with missing value problems for eighth graders. Also note that eighth-grade students performed better on both the missing value and numerical comparison problems. Other results not depicted here show that there was almost no difference (5%) between the groups on the qualitative questions, an area for which neither group received specific instruction.

The *unit rate* approach was the most popular strategy and one that was responsible for the largest number of correct answers (15). This approach is characterized by finding the multiplicative relationship *between* measure spaces. The unit rate is found through division. For example, if 3 apples cost 60 cents, find the cost of 6 apples. The cost for 1 apple is found by dividing: 60 cents ÷ 3 apples = 20 cents per apple. This unit rate is the constant factor that relates apples and cost. To find the cost of 6 apples, you simply multiply 6 apples by 20 cents per apple. This method was especially popular with seventh-grade students who were uninstructed in the usual cross-multiply and divide algorithm. This result should not be surprising. Children have made purchases and have had the opportunity to calculate unit prices and other unit rates. It seems a natural way to approach these problems.

TABLE 9.1 Percentages of Correct Solutions by
Strategies for Missing Value (MV)
and Numerical Comparison (NC)
Word Problems

| Strategy | Seventh grade $n = 421$ | | Eighth grade $n = 492$ | |
	MV	NC	MV	NC
Unit Rate	28* (15)**	48 (26)	14 (6)	30 (18)
Factor	17 (5)	12 (5)	7 (3)	8 (2)
Algorithm	3 (4)	1 (1)	33 (45)	10 (15)
Fraction	2 (1)	8 (10)	12 (2)	26 (25)
Incorrect	50 (75)	31 (57)	35 (44)	32 (40)

*The first entry is an average of 3 problems—all numerical values
are integral multiples of one another.
**The entry in parentheses is an average for single problems whose
numerical values are not integral multiples of one another.

A student using the *factor of change* method might reason as follows: "If I want twice as many apples, then the cost will be twice as much." The factor of change method is a "How many times greater" approach and is equivalent to finding the multiplicative relationship within a measure space (15).

A small number of seventh-grade students employed what we have called a fraction strategy. This strategy was used by a much larger percentage of eighth-grade students. The fraction strategy is applied devoid of problem context. That is, rate pairs would be treated as fractions by disregarding the labels. A student using this strategy would calculate the answer, applying the multiplication rule for generating equivalent fractions as follows:

$$\text{If } \frac{3}{60} = \frac{6}{?} \quad \text{then} \quad \frac{3}{60} \times \frac{2}{2} = \frac{6}{120}$$

The percentage of correct responses for the single item that did not use integral multiples was significantly lower than problems with integer relationships. In this problem, one number of a rate pair was 1.5 times the other. Although this is still not a particularly difficult situation, differences in the results obtained were rather dramatic.

Apparently the presence of a noninteger relationship does two things: first, it significantly decreases the level of student achievement and second, it actually changes the way in which students think about a problem. This is evidenced by the significantly lower percentage of students who used the unit rate and factor methods.

As denoted by the last row in Table 9.1, large percentages of seventh and eighth graders were unable to solve these problems correctly. Data not reported here suggest that scaling problems were significantly more difficult than the buying, speed, or density problems (4).

Summary

"Conceptual knowledge is characterized most clearly as knowledge that is rich in relationships." (5, p. 3)

Proportional reasoning involves an understanding of the mathematical relationships embedded in proportional situations. These relationships are always multiplicative in nature. Algebraically, proportional relationships can be expressed through a rule with the form of $y = mx$. This again emphasizes the multiplicative relationship inherent in all proportional situations. Graphically proportional situations are depicted by a straight line passing through the origin. Recalling an idea from algebra, the "m" in the equation $y = mx$ designates the slope of the line. This slope m is also the unit rate and the constant factor that relates quantities between two measure spaces. All rate pairs for that situation appear on the line $y = mx$.

Proportional reasoning also involves the ability to solve a variety of problem types. Missing value problems, numerical comparison problems, and two types of qualitative situations are among the types of problems that are important for children to understand. Proportional reasoning involves the ability to discriminate proportional from nonproportional situations. A proportional reasoner ultimately should not be influenced by context nor numerical complexity. That is, students should be able to overcome the effects of unfamiliar settings and cumbersome numbers.

The understandings underlying proportional reasoning are complex. We should expect this type of reasoning to develop slowly over several years (18).

> "The ability to reason proportionally develops in students throughout grades 5–8. It is of such great importance that it merits whatever time and effort must be expended to assure its careful development. Students need to see many problem situations that can be modeled and then solved through proportional reasoning." (11, p. 82)

A Look at the Curriculum

Proportional reasoning abilities are more involved than textbooks would suggest. Textbooks emphasize the development of procedural skills rather than conceptual understandings. This approach often encourages rote learning and inhibits meaningful understanding of proportional tasks.

The following example is typical of a grade 5 text.

> In Marcia's class two out of every three students live in an apartment building. There are 27 students. How many live in apartments?

To solve this problem type, ratios are identified and a proportion is set up. The equation $2/3 = n/27$ is written and solved by noting that $3 \times 9 = 27$ and $2 \times 9 = 18$. Many questions arise: What does 18 mean? How is it related to 27? Why not multiply 2/3 by 27?

> "We should note that the difficulty children have with rational numbers should not be surprising, considering the complexity of ideas within this number domain and the type of instruction offered by the textbooks." (16, in press)

Why should students assume a multiplicative relationship between the numbers? In other words, why is this a proportional situation? Students need to see examples of proportional and nonproportional situations so they can determine when it is appropriate to use a multiplicative solution strategy. If such issues are not raised, how can students be expected to be aware of and understand them?

> "Although it can be effectively argued that students need to automatize commonly used processes, it can be likewise argued that the most efficient methods are often those that are the least meaningful." (15, p. 81)

In the textbooks for grades 6–8, the traditional cross-multiply and divide algorithm is used to determine whether two rates are equal. This algorithm is also used to set up and solve missing value problems. To solve the apartment problem, for example, the following proportion is set up:

$$\frac{\text{students in}\atop 2 \text{ apartments}}{3 \text{ students}} = \frac{\text{students in}\atop x \text{ apartments}}{27 \text{ students}} \quad 3x = 54 \quad x = 18$$

While the cross-product algorithm is efficient, it has little meaning. In fact, it is impossible to explain why one would want to find the product of contrasting elements from two different rate pairs. The labels are normally excluded. What meaning does "2 students in apartments × 27 students" have? The cross-product rule has no physical referent and therefore lacks meaning for students and for the rest of us as well (15).

Teachers need to step outside the textbook and provide hands-on experiences with ratio and proportional situations. Initial activities should focus on the development of meaning, postponing efficient procedures until such understandings are internalized by students. The RNP developed such a curriculum and used it with seventh-grade students.

> The *Curriculum and Evaluation Standards* calls for an instructional emphasis on building a strong conceptual framework on which to base the development of skills (11).

Rational Number Project Teaching Experiment

Since 1979 the Rational Number Project (RNP) has been conducting research on children's learning of rational number concepts (part whole, ratio, decimal, operator and quotient or indicated division) and proportional relationships.

One of the teaching experiments conducted by the Rational Number Project dealt with seventh-grade students' learning of ratio and proportional concepts. A teaching experiment is a research model that focuses on the process of concept development rather than on achievement as measured on a written test of some sort. It is normally conducted with a small number of students, involves observation of the instructional process by persons other than the instructor, and controls the instruction by providing detailed lesson plans, activities, written tests, and student interviews. Data come primarily from student interviews.

Instructional materials and interviews developed for these experiments reflected what has been gained from the research discussed in the previous sections of this chapter. We hope the description of the curriculum that follows will influence mathematics teachers in grades 5 through 8 to reconsider how they might approach this topic.

The RNP lessons reflected the belief that proportional reasoning involved more than simply setting up and solving a proportion. The lessons emphasized the mathematical characteristics of proportional situations. To do this, students' initial experiences involved physical experiments with proportional and nonproportional situations in which students collected data, built tables, and determined the rule for relating the number pairs in the tables. Proportional situations were defined as those whose rule could be expressed in the form $y = mx$. Coordinate graphs were used to depict the data from these experiments showing that proportional situations had straight-line graphs through the origin.

The lessons addressed the issue of context and numerosity. Problem contexts evolved from familiar to less familiar ones. Early emphasis focused on problem situations with whole number multiples within and between the elements of the proportion. Students' understanding evolved to see that the strategy they used did not depend on the presence of whole number multiples. Students had opportunities to solve a variety of problem types including missing value problems, quantitative comparison problems, and qualitative reasoning problems.

Multiple strategies for solving problems involving proportional relationships were taught. These included building tables to see number patterns, a unit-rate approach, a factor of change approach, and a fraction approach. The unit-rate strategy was stressed initially because earlier survey results suggested that this interpretation was not only the most natural with students but also the solution strategy that resulted in the greatest percentage of correct responses. Relationships among the different approaches were emphasized.

"When concepts and procedures are not connected, students may have a good intuitive feel for mathematics but not solve the problems, or they may generate answers but not understand what they are doing." (5, p. 9)

Since the standard algorithm (cross-multiply and divide) is not meaningful, its use was postponed until more meaningful, although less efficient, strategies were developed.

Observations from this teaching experiment include the following:

1. Students were able to learn to solve problems involving proportional reasoning using different strategies.
2. There were marked differences in preferred strategy. No one strategy seemed to be preferred by all students.
3. Even with the use of calculators students had trouble with noninteger relationships.
4. Additive strategies were often used with noninteger rates.
5. Students using a unit-rate approach often had difficulty determining which unit

rate to use as a factor. For example, 3 apples for 24 cents can be interpreted as 8 cents per apple or as 1/8 apple for 1 cent.

6. One strategy based on the unit rate was to use a calculator to generate both unit rates, propose two answers, and then reason from the context of the problem as to which answer was most reasonable.

"Proportional reasoning is generally regarded as one of the components of formal thought acquired in adolescence. Relatively few junior high students of average ability use proportional reasoning in consistent fashion." (15, p. 78)

The next section presents sample lessons that demonstrate the type of initial concrete experience possible for modeling the mathematical characteristics of proportional situations.

Teacher Notes for Sample Lessons

These lessons represent the types of initial experiences with proportional reasoning that students should have. The activity pages found at the end of the chapter present students with proportional and nonproportional situations. For each problem they construct a table based on the particular situation, generalize a rule to describe those data, and then plot the data on coordinate axes. From the tables, students have the opportunity to see the different number patterns within and between measure spaces that are inherent in proportional situations. The graphing aspect of the lesson highlights the idea that the graphs of all proportional situations will form a straight line through the origin. By comparing the number patterns and graphs of proportional and nonproportional situations students can see what makes proportional situations unique. These activities can be extended to highlight the relationship between the quantities across measure spaces and the unit rate. For suggestions and for other lessons similar to the two presented here, readers are referred to the *Mathematics Teacher* (1, 3).

"Representations can be viewed as the facilitators which enable linkages between the real world and the mathematical world." (17, p. 223)

Materials.   Red and green Cuisenaire rods, graph paper and activity sheets 1 and 2 for each student (see Figures 9.4 and 9.5). Teachers will need to make a sheet showing four stick figures 6 cm, 12 cm, 18 cm, and 24 cm in height. Label the figures Ms. Adams, Mr. Barton, Ms. Crane, and Mr. Dahl.

Objectives.

1. Students generate data by translating information from a story problem to a table of data, and write a rule for the number pattern discovered in the table.

2. Students plot a set of data points and connect the points to form a graph of the rule.
3. Students learn to discriminate proportional from nonproportional situations on the basis on the formulas and graphs used to describe these situations.

Directions. For each of the activity sheets, the teacher should introduce the problem in a large group setting and discuss the solution plan. Students complete the activity in small groups and discuss the questions. The teacher should then discuss the questions in a large group. Each activity may take more than one class period.

For activity 1 (Fig. 9.4) students measure the figures using a 2-cm red rod and a 3-cm green rod. The rule developed finds the number of greens given the number of red rods: $G = 2/3 R$. A teacher can draw the figures to develop a rule with an integer relationship. The graph drawn is a straight line through the origin.

For activity 2 (Fig. 9.5) the students should use play money to act out the relationship between kilometers and cost of the limousine. The rule developed finds the cost given the number of kilometers: $C = 50 + 2K$. The graph is a straight line through (0, 50).

Students compare the results of the two problems. The teacher should lead students to discover that proportional relationships, which form a special class of problems, always have a straight line graph going through the origin. Only one of the two problems represents a proportional situation. The teacher should also point out that the rule describing the proportional relationship involves only multiplication or division.

To reinforce these two ideas, students should be given an opportunity to do similar activities and asked to identify the proportional situations.

Looking Ahead . . .

Curriculum to develop the deeper understanding of the mathematics taught in the middle grades needs to be developed. Research on various middle school content areas supports the value of a conceptually oriented curriculum over a procedurally based curriculum. Since textbooks are generally procedurally oriented, textbook-dominated programs should become less frequent.

There is currently a mismatch between how and what teachers are encouraged to teach and what skills are evaluated. More valid ways to evaluate student outcomes must be found. Evaluating what students are thinking and how they solve problems is more important than a numerical score reflecting the number of items correct.

"At present, very large numbers of teachers appear to be in need of a rather substantial updating of their mathematical and methodological skills." (16, in press)

As teachers are encouraged to teach toward deeper understandings of the content in the middle grades, we need to determine whether they have the necessary

FIGURE 9.4   Activity sheet 1: Modeling a proportional situation

Problem: Ms. X measures 33 red rods tall. How tall is Ms. X using green rods? Clues are hidden in a packet of materials containing red and green rods and pictures of Ms. Adams, Mr. Barton, Ms. Crane and Mr. Dahl.

Solution Plan: Measure each figure with the red and green rods. Build a table to show your results.

Person	Height in red rods	Height in green rods
Ms. Adams		
Mr. Barton		
Ms. Crane		
Mr. Dahl		

Questions:

1. It is possible to determine the height in green rods if you know the height in red rods. If Mr. Edwards is 15 red rods in height, how tall is he in green rods? _____

2. Write a formula that can be used to determine the height of a figure in green rods given the height in red rods. Use R to stand for height in red rods and G for height in green rods: $G =$ _____

3. Test your formula using the number pairs in the table. Use your formula to determine the number of green rods for Ms. X. _____

4. Graph the data from the table on a pair of coordinate axes and connect the data points.

5. Describe what the graph looks like: _____

FIGURE 9.5   Activity sheet 2: Modeling a nonproportional situation

Problem: The Classy Limousine Company hired you to make a sign showing the cost of hiring its limos. Your sign needs to show the cost for 1, 2, 3, 4, 5, 20, and 100 kilometers. The cost is $50 plus $2 per km.

Solution Plan: Using play money show the cost for 1 through 5 km. Build a table to show your results.

Kilometers	Cost
1	
2	
3	
4	
5	

Questions:

1. It is possible to determine the cost if you know the number of km. If you rented the limo to drive 20 km, what would it cost?_____

2. Write a formula that can be used to determine the cost of a limo given the number of km. Use C to stand for cost and K for km: $C = $_____

3. Test your formula using the number pairs in the table. Use your formula to determine the cost for 100 km._____

4. Graph the data from the table on a pair of coordinate axes and connect the points.

5. Describe what the graph looks like:_____

understandings of the content. Research with preservice and inservice elementary school teachers on rational numbers suggests that many teachers do not have this understanding (2, 10). We may be seeing mathematics specialists in the middle grades in the future. This is an idea supported by the National Council of Teachers of Mathematics in the *Curriculum and Evaluation Standards* (11) and its *Professional Standards for Teaching* (12).

Kathleen Cramer and Thomas Post

Teachers who support the need for change in how ratio and proportion ideas should be taught may wonder how they can institute such changes in their classrooms. Questions arise that inhibit change: Am I not required to cover what is in the textbook? If I do something different in fifth grade, will my students have trouble in sixth grade? Will not students need to know the standard algorithm in fifth grade because it is tested on the standardized tests? Teachers hoping to change need the support of other teachers at their own grade level and of those at other grade levels. They also need the support of principals and parents.

"The assessment of students' knowledge and understanding of mathematical concepts should provide evidence that they can . . . identify and generate examples and nonexamples; use models, diagram and symbols to represent concepts; translate from one mode of representation to another." (11, p. 223)

We hope that teachers reading this chapter will be encouraged to use techniques involved in teaching experiments. Finding time to interview small numbers of students after instruction will be a worthwhile activity. Interviews are the major data source for research in mathematics education, and teachers will find interesting interview questions in the professional literature.

Sarah Currier

About the Authors

Kathleen Cramer is an associate professor in the College of Education at the University of Wisconsin-River Falls. Dr. Cramer teaches mathematics methods classes for undergraduate and graduate students. She is currently working on a National Science Foundation (NSF) grant revising the curriculum from RNP teaching experiments.

Thomas Post is a professor in mathematics education at the University of Minnesota. Besides teaching graduate and undergraduate courses in mathematics education, Dr. Post has been a co-director of the NSF-sponsored Rational Number Project since 1979.

Sarah Currier is on leave from her sixth-grade teaching responsibilities in the Minneapolis Public Schools. She is currently working on a master's degree in mathematics education at the University of Minnesota. She particularly enjoys teaching geometry and incorporating cooperative learning techniques in her mathematics classes.

References

*1. CRAMER, K., BEZUK, N., & BEHR, M. (1989). Proportional relationships and unit rates. *Mathematics Teacher*, 82(7), 537–544.

 2. CRAMER, K., & LESH, R. (1988). Rational number knowledge of preservice elementary education teachers. In M. Behr & C. Lacampagne (Eds.), *Proceedings of the Tenth Annual Meeting of the North American Chapter of the International Group for the Psychology of Mathematics Education* (pp. 425–431). De Kalb, IL: Northern Illinois University.

*3. CRAMER, K., POST, T., & BEHR, M. (1989). Interpreting proportional relationships. *Mathematics Teacher*, 82(6), 445–453.

*4. HELLER, P., POST, T., BEHR, M., & LESH, R. (1990). The effect of two context variables on quantitative and numerical reasoning about rates. *Journal for Research in Mathematics Education, 21*(5), 388–402.

 5. HIEBERT, J., & LEFEVRE, P. (1986). Conceptual and procedural knowledge in mathematics: An introductory analysis. In J. Hiebert (Ed.), *Conceptual and procedural knowledge: The case for mathematics* (pp. 1–27). Hillsdale, NJ: Erlbaum.

*6. HOFFER, A. (1988). Ratios and proportional thinking. In T. Post (Ed.), *Teaching mathematics in grades K–8: Research based methods* (pp. 285–313). Boston: Allyn & Bacon.

 7. KARPLUS, R., KARPLUS, E., FORMISANO, M., & PAULSON, A. (1979). Proportional reasoning and control of variables in seven countries. In J. Lochhead & J. Clement (Eds.), *Cognitive process instruction* (pp. 47–103). Philadelphia: The Franklin Institute Press.

 8. KARPLUS, R., PULOS, S., & STAGE, E. (1983). Proportional reasoning of early adolescents. In R. Lesh & M. Landau (Eds.), *Acquisition of mathematical concepts and processes* (pp. 45–89). New York: Academic Press.

 9. KURTZ, B., & KARPLUS, R. (1979). Intellectual development beyond elementary school VII: Teaching for proportional reasoning. *School Science and Mathematics, 79*(5), 387–398.

10. LACAMPAGNE, C., POST, T., HAREL, G., & BEHR, M. (1988). A model for the development of leadership and the assessment of mathematical and pedagogical knowledge of middle school teachers. In M. Behr & C. Lacampagne (Eds.), *Proceedings of the Tenth Annual Meeting of the North American Chapter of the International Group for the Psychology of Mathematics Education* (pp. 418–424). De Kalb, IL: Northern Illinois University.

*11. NATIONAL COUNCIL OF TEACHERS OF MATHEMATICS. (1989). *Curriculum and evaluation standards for school mathematics*. Reston, VA: Author.

*12. NATIONAL COUNCIL OF TEACHERS OF MATHEMATICS. (1991). *Professional standards for teaching mathematics*. Reston, VA: Author.

13. NOELTING, G. (1980). The development of proportional reasoning and the ratio concept. Part I: The differentiation of stages. *Educational Studies in Mathematics, 11*(3), (pp. 217–253).

14. NOELTING, G. (1980). The development of proportional reasoning and the ratio concept Part II—Problem structure at successive stages: Problem-solving strategies and the mechanism of adaptive restructuring. *Educational Studies in Mathematics, 11*(3), 331–363.

15. POST, T., BEHR, M., & LESH, R. (1988). Proportionality and the development of prealgebra understanding. In A. Coxford (Ed.), *Algebraic concepts in the curriculum K–12* (1988 Yearbook, pp. 78–90). Reston, VA: National Council of Teachers of Mathematics.

16. POST, T., CRAMER, K., BEHR, M., LESH, R., & HAREL, G. (in press). Curriculum implications from research on the learning, teaching and assessing of rational number

concepts: Multiple research perspectives. In T. Carpenter & E. Fennema (Eds.), *Learning, teaching and assessing rational number concepts: Multiple research perspectives.* Madison: University of Wisconsin.

*17. POST, T., & CRAMER, K. (1989). Knowledge, representation and quantitative thinking. In M. Reynolds (Ed.), *Knowledge base for beginning teachers* (pp. 221–232). Elmsford, NY: Pergamon Press.

18. TOURNAIRE, F., & PULOS, S. (1985). Proportional reasoning: A review of the literature. *Educational Studies in Mathematics, 16*(2), 181–204.

19. VERGNAUD, G. (1983). Multiplicative structures. In R. Lesh & M. Landau (Eds.), *Acquisition of mathematics concepts and processes* (pp. 127–174). New York: Academic Press.

CHAPTER 10

Prealgebra: The Transition from Arithmetic to Algebra

Carolyn Kieran and Louise Chalouh

> *Algebra can and should arise as a by-product of making arithmetic sensible. (32, p. 85)*

Prealgebra, what is it? The perspective we take in this chapter is that prealgebra is the transition from arithmetic to algebra. Most algebra courses begin immediately with the use of letters as mathematical objects and then proceed to the operations that can be carried out on these objects. Links between the use of numbers in arithmetic and the use of letters in algebra are rarely accorded more than a passing nod in high school algebra. In general, students are not given the opportunity to construct explicit connections between these two domains (26). Thus, we have chosen to consider as prealgebraic that area of mathematical learning in which students

> "It is essential that in grades 5–8, students explore algebraic concepts in an informal way to build a foundation for the subsequent formal study of algebra." (*Curriculum and Evaluation Standards*, 29, p. 102)

construct their algebra from their arithmetic, that is, building meaning for the symbols and operations of algebra in terms of their knowledge of arithmetic. At the core of this perspective on prealgebra there are two aspects that we consider crucial: (a) the *use of letters* to represent numbers, and (b) explicit awareness of the *mathematical method* that is being symbolized by the use of both numbers and letters. Before looking at teaching approaches that have been researched and found to be helpful in developing student understanding of these two aspects of prealgebra, we offer a few general remarks that provide some background on the focus we have chosen to adopt.

The Use of Letters in Algebraic Symbolism: Historical Considerations

The historical development of algebra as a symbol system suggests potentially fruitful avenues to be followed in the teaching of prealgebra. In a very interesting and readable account of the three evolutionary stages through which the development of algebraic symbolism has passed, Harper (13) provides some evidence that students appear to go through the same stages in developing their ability to handle algebraic symbolism. The rhetorical stage, which belongs to the period before Diophantus (c. 250 A.D.), was characterized by the use of ordinary language descriptions for solving particular types of problems and lacked the use of symbols or special signs to represent unknowns. The second stage, which extended from Diophantus to the end of the sixteenth century, involved the use of abbreviations for *unknown* quantities. Harper points out that the concern of algebraists during these centuries was exclusively that of discovering the value of the letter(s), as opposed to an attempt to express the general. The third stage was initiated by Vieta's use of letters to stand for *given*, as well as unknown, quantities. At this point it became possible to express general solutions by means of symbols and, in fact, to use algebra as a tool for proving rules governing numerical relations.

This brief historical synthesis of the development of algebraic symbolism draws out the importance of language as a first step in the process of expressing one's thinking by means of symbols. It also highlights the distinction between (a) using letters to represent unknowns in, for example, equation solving or the representation of word problems by equations, and (b) using letters to represent givens in, for example, the specification of a general solution or the generalization of numerical patterns or the expression of numerical properties and formulas. The order in which these two uses of letters developed historically suggests that the use of letters as unknowns may be more accessible to early learners than the use of letters as givens. However, as stated in the NCTM *Curriculum and Evaluation Standards*, both of these usages are important for students in grades 5–8:

> Students need to be able to use variables in many different ways. Two particularly important ways in grades 5–8 are using a variable as a placeholder for a specific unknown, as in $n + 5 = 12$, and as a representative of a range of values, as in $3t + 6$. (29, p. 103)

Awareness and Symbolization of Method: Cognitive Considerations

The historical evolution of the use of letters from representing unknown numbers to representing general numbers was accompanied by a shift in attention from purely numerical solutions to considerations of method or process. That shift brings us to the second aspect of prealgebraic learning which we wish to emphasize here, that is, a focus on method or process instead of on the answer. A related issue concerns the awareness of the nature of the operations that are being represented.

Thinking about the Method Itself, Not the Numerical Answer.   The teaching of arithmetic is often answer oriented. Unfortunately, this answer-driven approach leads students away from thinking about the methods of arithmetic and what they might mean. Booth (5) has pointed out, for example, that if students in elementary school do not recognize that the total number of objects in two sets containing 5 and 8 objects, respectively, can be written as 5 + 8 (rather than 13), it is highly unlikely that they will recognize that $a + b$ represents the total number of objects in the sets containing a and b objects.

The Nature of the Operations That Are Being Represented.   Usiskin (34) has emphasized that

> in solving problems such as "When 3 is added to 5 times a certain number, the sum is 40," many students have difficulty moving from arithmetic to algebra. Whereas the arithmetic solution involves subtracting 3 and dividing by 5 [i.e., using undoing operations], the algebraic form $5x + 3 = 40$ involves multiplication by 5 and addition of 3 [i.e., using forward operations]. That is, to set up the equation, you must think precisely the opposite of the way you would solve it using arithmetic. (p. 13)

This shift from thinking about the undoing or solving operations to focusing on the forward operations required in setting up an equation is one of the crucial steps in the transition from arithmetic to algebra. Another example illustrating what we

> "The algebraic sentence that most naturally describes . . . a problem situation does not immediately fit an arithmetic computation procedure. This possibility of 'first describing and then calculating' is one of the key features that makes algebra different from arithmetic." (27, p. 657)

mean by forward-operations thinking involves representing the problem "Blue jeans increase in price from \$33.95 to \$39.95; what is the amount of increase?" by $33.95 + n = 39.95$ rather than by $39.95 - 33.95 = n$. In this case, addition is the operation suggested by the text of the problem ("increase"); on the other hand, subtraction is an undoing operation that is the inverse of the suggested operation.

We conclude this introductory section by stressing that what we mean by prealgebra is not a preparation for the traditional ninth-grade algebra course where the emphasis is usually on learning to manipulate meaningless symbols by following rules learned by rote. What we mean is an exploration of some key algebraic ideas in which students (a) think about the numerical relations of a situation, (b) discuss them explicitly in simple everyday language, and (c) eventually learn to represent

> "Middle school students should have many opportunities to use language to communicate their mathematical ideas, . . . to reach agreement about the meanings of words, and to recognize the crucial importance of commonly shared definitions [and notation]." (*Curriculum and Evaluation Standards*, 29, p. 78)

them with letters or other nonmisleading notation (9). The research we discuss in the sections that follow illustrates approaches that have provided such learning experiences and have been found to facilitate the transition from arithmetic to algebra.

Using Letters as Unknowns

Even though the use of letters as givens (in Harper's sense, 13) is the more neglected aspect of variable use in mathematics instruction, we begin with the use of letters as unknowns because this practice preceded the other historically. Typical situations involving letters as unknowns are those dealing with equations and equation solving. Our first example below describes an equation-solving approach that emphasizes thinking about forward operations—a way of seeing the problem that is crucial in setting up algebraic equations. Whitman (36, 37) has shown how this kind of thinking can be fostered in an equation-solving context.

The Cover-Up Equation-Solving Procedure

Whitman began her instructional sequence with equations containing one operation (e.g., $\square + 17 = 21$). She made sure that students became comfortable with these by asking questions such as, "What number plus 17 gives 21?" Next, students were given practice with two-operation equations (e.g., $2 \cdot \square + 5 = 47$, $3 \cdot \triangle - 8 = 31$, $48 - 3 \cdot \S = 6$). During this period much time was spent verbalizing questions such as, for the first example, "What number plus 5 is 47?" (response: 42); "two times what number is 42?" (response: 21).

Whitman points out that this approach helped students learn to associate the product of a number and a frame as a single number. She also emphasizes that this "cover-up" procedure illustrated in Figure 10.1 aided students in seeing the overall structure of equations and in unpacking this structure in a systematic way. Another component of Whitman's study was the teaching of formal solving techniques, that is, performing the same operation on both sides of the equals sign. She found that students who had been taught the cover-up equation-solving procedure followed by formal techniques were more successful at equation solving than were students who had learned only formal techniques.

Forward Operations Versus Undoing Operations

Another study illustrates how a one-dimensional focus in elementary school mathematics classes on "undoing operations" can sometimes be counterproductive to students' developing an understanding of (a) an equation as a balanced entity and (b) the solving procedure of performing the same operation on both sides of the equation. By a *one-dimensional focus on undoing operations*, we mean an undue emphasis on interpreting open sentences, such as $\square + 7 = 15$, not as the "number that when added with 7 gives 15" but rather as the number that results from subtracting 7 from 15. In other words, the focus is on the undoing operation of subtraction, not on the given operation of addition.

FIGURE 10.1   Teacher-student interaction using the cover-up technique for solving the equation $69 - 96/(7 - \Delta) = 37$. (Adapted from 37, p. 202, with permission)

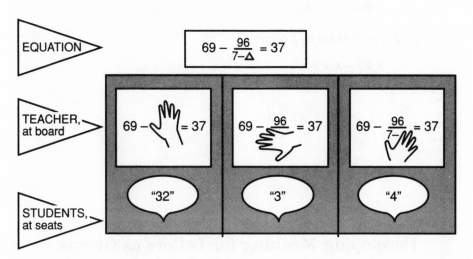

Kieran (20) asked seventh graders what the letter means in $5 + a = 12$ and $2 \times c + 15 = 29$. One typical response for the first equation was, "An answer—12 minus 5 is 7." For these students, an equation had to be reversed—that is, undone—for the letter to have some meaning; they had transformed $5 + a = 12$ into $a = 12 - 5$. Other students responded that the letter means the number that should be added to 5 to equal 12; that is, they viewed the operations of an equation in the left-to-right sequence in which they were presented. These latter students also relied on substituting trial values into equations in order to solve them and spoke explicitly of the balance between the two sides of an equation.

All of the students were then taught to construct "arithmetic identities" such as $7 \times 2 - 3 = 5 \times 2 + 1$ (see reference 19 for more details). To transform these identities into equations, one of the numbers was hidden. This hiding was done first by a finger, then by a box, and finally by a letter (see Fig. 10.2). Last, by means of parallel representations of both arithmetic identities and equations involving boxes, students were shown how to solve equations by performing the same operation on both sides of the equality symbol.

Students who preferred to reverse the form of the equation using undoing operations had great difficulty making sense of doing the same operation on both sides of the equation. They had problems with the procedure even though it had been taught by relating the operations carried out on the equations to the same operations carried out on the arithmetic identities. This solving procedure seemed most accessible to those students who had interpreted equations such as $5 + a = 12$ as "the number that should be added to 5 to equal 12." For students to grasp the "same operation on both sides" procedure, they may require a good deal of prior development in forward-operations thinking similar to that used with Whitman's cover-up technique.

FIGURE 10.2   Hiding a number of the arithmetic identity $7 \times 2 - 3 = 5 \times 2 +$
1 to arrive at the algebraic equation $7 \times a - 3 = 5 \times 2 + 1$.
(Adapted from 19, p. 322. Reprinted by permission of Kluwer Academic Publishers)

The hiding was done at first by a finger:

$$7 \times - 3 = 5 \times 2 + 1 \, ,$$

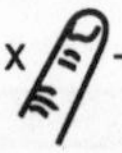

then by a box:

$$7 \times \square - 3 = 5 \times 2 + 1 \, ,$$

and finally by a letter:

$$7 \times \; a \; - 3 = 5 \times 2 + 1 \, .$$

Developing Meaning for Letters as Givens

We believe that the use of letters to specify a range of values in representing numerical relationships is not given enough consideration in most mathematics classes or
textbooks. Familiarity with this usage of letters should be developed gradually in
students before they take a formal algebra course.

Using One Letter in Expressions of Numerical Relations

To help students begin thinking about using letters to express general relationships,
problems such as the following are appropriate:

• A girl multiplies a number by 5 and adds 12. She then subtracts the original number and divides the result by 4. She notices that the answer she gets is 3 more than
the number she started with. She says, "I think that would happen, whatever number I started with." Using algebra, show that the girl is right.
• Take three consecutive numbers. Now calculate the square of the middle one,
subtract from it the product of the other two. . . . Now do it with another three
consecutive numbers. . . . Can you explain it with numbers? . . . Can you use
algebra to explain it?

In a study that involved problems like these, Lee and Wheeler (25) found that most
students did not use an algebraic solution but produced numerical examples and
concluded from these examples. However, the students appreciated the algebraic solutions, even if they could not produce them themselves. Lee and Wheeler point out
that classroom experiences with problems similar to the ones above can help students
see algebra as generalized arithmetic and give sense to the letters of algebra.

"As students progress from grade 5 to grade 8, their ability to reason abstractly matures greatly. Concurrent with this enhanced ability to abstract common elements from situations, to conjecture, and to generalize—in short, to do mathematics—should come an increasing sophistication in the ability to communicate mathematics. But this development cannot occur without deliberate and careful acquisition of the language of mathematics." (*Curriculum and Evaluation Standards,* 29, p. 78)

Mulligan (28) has also promoted the idea among students that algebra is a tool for generalization and justification in mathematics with her collection of "amazing facts." She usually begins her course by introducing the Fibonacci sequence 1, 1, 2, 3, 5, 8, 13, 21, . . . and telling students that much of mathematics consists of making observations, looking for patterns, and generalizing. Students try to determine the pattern in the Fibonacci sequence after they have discovered the rules for some simple arithmetic and geometric sequences. Another of her "amazing facts" is "If you multiply any four consecutive integers and add 1, the result is always a perfect square" (p. 208). Although proving this is beyond the intended student-age range of this chapter, Mulligan's work illustrates both the richness and potential of her approach.

Another study dealing with the use of letters to represent a range of values was a teaching experiment carried out by Chalouh and Herscovics (7) with a group of sixth- and seventh-grade students. The tasks of this study involved three different geometric representations, each of which had some hidden component (see Fig. 10.3). In one episode, after having ensured that the students knew how to find the area of a rectangle when the measures of both the length and width were provided, Chalouh and Herscovics asked the students to write the area of a rectangle whose width was 8 units and whose length was hidden, but represented as *c* units. They found that the majority viewed the expression 8 × *c* to be incomplete and wrote an equal sign after

FIGURE 10.3   The first type of problem involved determining the total number of dots in a rectangular array; the second, finding the length of a line segment; the third, finding the area of a rectangle. (Adapted from 7, p. 34, with permission)

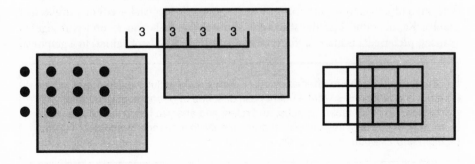

it or wished to express it as "Area $= 8 \times c$." Such answers provide some evidence of the difficulty experienced by beginning algebra students in holding unevaluated operations in suspension—an ability that Collis (8) has named "Acceptance of Lack of Closure." These responses also illustrate that for some students the use of a letter to represent a range of values in an algebraic expression is more foreign to them than the use of a letter to represent an unknown in an equation. Furthermore, the students' answers suggest that they may have been interpreting the letters used in certain geometric figures as specific unknowns rather than as representatives of a range of values. In all, the findings of these studies indicate that we ought to be providing students with a richer range of experiences involving the use of letters as givens. See Küchemann's (24) analysis of the different ways in which students interpret letters.

"In grades 5–8, the mathematics curriculum should include exploration of algebraic concepts and processes so that students can understand the concepts of variable, expression, and equation." (*Curriculum and Evaluation Standards,* 29, p. 102)

Using Two Letters in Functional Situations

The examples presented above were based on problem situations involving only one variable quantity and, thus, single-letter expressions. In this section, we look at functional situations involving the use of two letters.

An introduction to the use of letters as pattern generalizers in functional situations is suggested by W. W. Sawyer's *Guess My Rule* game, described by Davis (9). The game presented to students is this: "Make up a rule, we'll tell you a number, you'll use your rule on that number and tell us the answer, and we'll try to guess what your rule is" (p. 201). For example, the "rule" might be "Whatever number you tell us, we'll double it and add eight." If $\square$ represents the number given to the student, and $\triangle$ represents the student's response, the table shown in Figure 10.4 might be generated, followed by the writing of the rule: $(\square \times 2) + 8 = \triangle$. Notice the use of nonletter symbols as an intermediate representation.

Kaput (18) has described a study that involved a computer game modeled after the above activity (2). In this game, the computer has a "secret" function that the student is to guess on the basis of the computer's response to the student's numerical inputs. The student can choose the form of the computer's feedback—either numbers or graphs. Kaput found that the students, who were in first- and second-year algebra courses, preferred a numerical form of feedback (i.e., a table of values) to a graphical

---

"In grades 5–8, the mathematics curriculum should include explorations of patterns and functions so that students can describe and represent [properties and] relationships with tables, graphs, and rules; and analyze functional relationships to explain how a change in one quantity results in a change in another." (*Curriculum and Evaluation Standards,* 29, p. 98)

FIGURE 10.4 Table of values for the rule, "Whatever Number You Tell Us, We'll Double It and Add Eight." (Adapted from 9, p. 202)

□	△
0	8
10	28
1	10
5	18
100	208

one. Significant teaching and prompting were needed to get them to use the graphically represented information. While a table-of-values approach is sufficient for middle school curricular goals, graphical representations form a critical base for the concept of slope necessary in later mathematical development. The advent of graphing calculators and computer graphing utilities now makes it possible to devise alternate approaches to the teaching of graphs and functions—approaches accessible to the prealgebra student. (For suggestions on teaching these topics using technology, see references 3, 14, and 22.)

> "Computers and calculators are powerful problem solving tools. The power to compute rapidly, to graph a relationship instantly, and to systematically change one variable and observe what happens to other related variables can help students become independent doers of mathematics." (*Curriculum and Evaluation Standards,* 29, p. 75)

One "nontech" teaching approach that has been quite successful in enabling students to see the relationships between tables and graphs is detailed in a lesson described by Davis (10). The teacher's goal was to have his fourth- and fifth-grade students see the arithmetic, algebraic, and geometric meanings of the numbers known as *slope* and *y-intercept* (see Fig. 10.5). All these students had had extensive experience with the noncomputer version of the *Guess My Rule* game.

Three different sheets were given to the students. On the first sheet (see Fig. 10.6), functions were represented by formulas. Students were required to make a table and a graph. The hidden agenda was for them to discover the correspondences between the arithmetical (table), algebraic (formula), and geometric (graph) representations of a function, that is, to discover the meanings of slope and *y*-intercept.

Davis states that many students quickly saw the roles of these two key numbers. For those who were not sure, the second sheet contained "blank" forms (see Fig. 10.7) on which students could test personal conjectures by making up functions. The critical test of each student's theories came with the third sheet (see Fig. 10.8).

FIGURE 10.5 Arithmetic, algebraic, and geometric representations of y-intercept and slope. (Adapted from 10, p. 116)

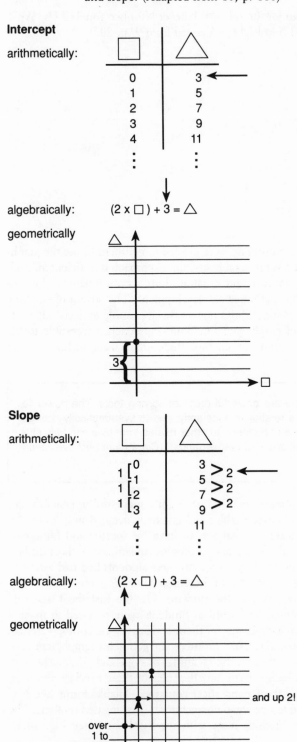

FIGURE 10.6   Students were to make a table and graph for each of the given formulas. (Adapted from 10, p. 117)

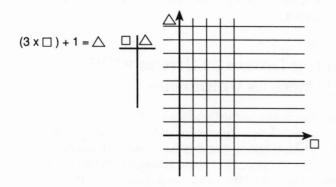

$(3 \times \square) + 1 = \triangle$

FIGURE 10.7   Students tested their conjectures with "blank sheets" such as this one. (Adapted from 10, p. 118)

$(\_\_ \times \square) \div \_\_ = \triangle$

FIGURE 10.8   The task was to find the formulas corresponding to the given graphs. (Adapted from 10, p. 119)

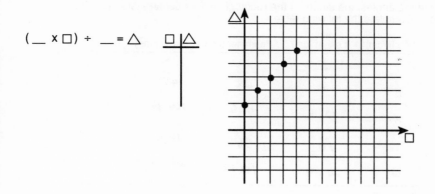

$(\_\_ \times \square) \div \_\_ = \triangle$

Here students were given the graph and their task was to find the formula. Davis reports that this approach was successful with most of the students. The success he observed is noteworthy for it is well known that working with Cartesian graphs is an activity that students find difficult.

Combining Letters as Givens with Letters as Unknowns

Some research studies have focused on instructional approaches that combine letters representing a range of values with letters representing unknown numbers. Demana and Leitzel (11) describe a problem setting that they have tried with middle school students. They began with the problem, "For some rectangles, the length of the rectangle is four centimeters more than the width," and then helped the students complete the table shown in Figure 10.9. For the perimeter entry in the last line of the table, different students wrote other expressions. Within the numerical setting, they realized that an expression could have several forms.

Demana and Leitzel suggest that tables containing both numerical data about a problem situation and a variable describing the general case provide an excellent opportunity for introducing prealgebra students to equations and solutions to equations. Using the completed table, shown in Figure 10.9, the researchers asked questions such as, "Find w if $w^2 + 4w = 45$" and "Find w if $4w + 8 = 41.6$." Since these numerical values were already in the table, students had all the information they needed to "solve" the equations. The next step was to ask the students to solve for numerical values not in the table. Many students developed their own solving methods, such as substituting different values of w into the equation until the left and right sides balanced. We have seen from the Kieran (20) study that use of the substitution procedure provides a good conceptual basis for later development of the formal procedure of doing the same operation on both sides of the equality symbol.

FIGURE 10.9   Students completed this table, as illustrated. (Adapted from 11, p. 65, with permission)

For some rectangles, the length of the rectangle is four centimeters more than the width. Complete the follwing table:

Width (cm)	Length (cm)	Perimeter (cm)	Area (cm^2)
1	5	12	5
5	9	28	45
8.4	12.4	41.6	104.16
12	16	56	192
w	$w+4$	$4w+8$	$w^2 + 4w$

Symbolization of Method

In our introductory remarks, we argued that two major components of prealgebra are the gradual use of letters and the symbolization of method. Each of the two studies we have included in this section suggests interesting and viable approaches for helping students develop an ability to symbolize method.

The "Mathematics Machine"

Booth (5) has argued that for teaching to be effective in addressing students' difficulties in learning to symbolize method, it ought to attend to the structure of problems and to the unambiguous representation of the methods used in solving problems. Thus, she designed a teaching sequence around the context of "giving instructions to a machine to solve given problems"—a "mathematics machine" for which all instructions could be written using the language of mathematics (see Fig. 10.10).

FIGURE 10.10   Model of the "Mathematics Machine" whose cells were to be filled using the "Language of Mathematics." (Adapted from 5, p. 40, with permission)

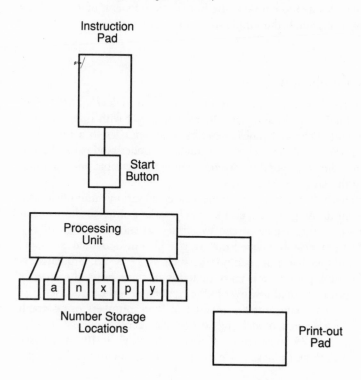

The teaching sequence was divided into six components; each of these is described below with an example.

- Introduction—"If I want the machine to add 15 and 8, how will I write the instructions?"
- Number operations—"A fat man wants to lose 25 kg of weight; so far he's lost 13 kg; how many more kilograms must he lose?" (The student's task is to write the instructions for solving each problem, giving all alternative forms where appropriate.)
- Generalization I—"I want the machine to add 5 to any number I give it. How will I write the instructions?" (introduction of the use of letters to represent a range of values and the notion of the indeterminate answer).
- Generalization II—"Find the area of any square" (discussion of the difference between $a \times a$ and $a \times b$, etc.).
- Notation—"Find the perimeter of a six-sided shape that has all the sides the same length" (discussion of the equivalence of expressions such as $a + a + a$ and $3 \times a$ and $3a$, in contrast with $3 + a$).
- Consolidation—"Tick the correct statement: Divide 8 by any number I give [$x/8$ or $8/x$]."

For many of the 12- to 15-year-old students in Booth's study, symbolizing the method used to solve even simple problems was not a trivial task. Nevertheless, her results indicated a significant improvement in success, especially with the 13-year-olds. She concluded that the 12-year-olds would probably have benefited even more if they had been able to devote more time to the first two components of the teaching program, that is, those in which the emphasis was on representing the arithmetic method using numbers.

"Graph Paper Multiplication"

A study by Peck and Jencks (32) is important for its attention to developing student understanding of method in arithmetic prior to symbolizing it with nonnumerical notation. In their report, Peck and Jencks describe some episodes in a fifth-grade arithmetic classroom where children, who were taught "to understand parts of arithmetic in depth, found the corresponding algebra completely sensible and a natural product of their own thinking" (p. 85).

Rather than have children simply compute the answers to various multiplications, the teacher asked them to use graph paper and small masking strips to show operations such as "2 times 3" (three squares seen two times, as shown in Fig. 10.11). Later, special graph paper heavily marked on every tenth line was used to model multiplications the children had not memorized, such as 24×26. Students explained shortcuts for multiplying such pairs in terms of transposing the rows of squares below the last heavily lined row over to the right-hand vertical end (see Fig. 10.12). Experiences with working out the product of these numbers using graph paper eventually led to a general model and written statements such as $(\Box + 4)(\Box + 6) = \Box^2 + 10\Box + 24$ and even $(x + 4)(x + 6) = x^2 + 10x + 24$ (see Fig. 10.13). Note that Peck and Jencks made extensive use of squares and triangles

FIGURE 10.11   Graph paper covered with small masking strips to represent "2 times 3." (Adapted from 32, p. 86)

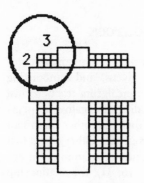

FIGURE 10.12   A student explained the multiplication of 24 by 26 as follows: "If I cut all the forties off down here and paste them over here, then I have two rows of three hundred, so $(2 \times 3) \times 100 = 600$. Now there are 4 rows of six left in the corner, so $4 \times 6 = 24$. So altogether, there are 624." (From 32, p. 87, with permission)

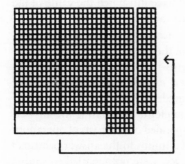

FIGURE 10.13   An instance of the general model of multiplication. (Adapted from 32, p. 88)

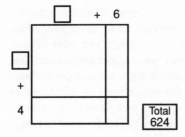

as early symbols for general numbers. You are urged to refer to their report (32) for details of the teaching approach.

Additional Topics and Resources

Thus far, we have discussed research related to what we consider two important components of prealgebra: using letters as unknowns and as givens, and symbolizing method. Clearly, there are other conceptual areas that the prealgebra teacher must also address. One of these is developing student understanding of negative numbers and the operations carried out with them. Even though there are other important issues, we have had to limit our remaining discussion to this one. Other topics that we would like to have discussed include the role of computer programming in enriching middle school students' understanding of variables (16, 31), the relationship between procedural and structural approaches in algebra learning (21), distinctions between semantic and syntactic understanding (6), the nature of the cognitive obstacles encountered in learning various algebraic concepts (15, 35), and so on.

Negative Numbers

Few research studies have addressed the difficulties experienced by students in operating with negative numbers. Some studies have emphasized the importance of introducing negative numbers to younger students and have illustrated the value of the "zero-pairs" approach using such models as positive and negative chips (12, 33). Kohn (23), however, questions the introduction of integers by means of thermometers, countdowns, and number lines because none of these models aids in the teaching of operations involving integers. Related concerns have been expressed by Human and Murray (17) who conducted a teaching experiment focusing on the thermometer model with several classes of seventh graders. They found that the students generally chose not to think about the thermometer in calculating the answers to questions such as $^-12 - {}^-4$ or $^-8 - 3$. They responded on the basis of operations with whole numbers (e.g., "8 − 3 is 5 and you add a minus to the answer bcause of the minus before the 8"). Errors such as this, however, were not reported in studies using variations of positive and negative chips as models.

Other Sources

We could not include in this chapter every study related to the issues involved in teaching prealgebra. In general, we restricted ourselves to research carried out since 1980 that illustrates viable approaches to teaching concepts we think are crucial for students' later understanding of algebra. Nevertheless, we would not want to conclude the chapter without mentioning three resources we consider important. One of these is Bell, Costello, and Küchemann's summary of algebraic and prealgebraic research carried out prior to 1980 (4). In addition, the British journal, *Mathematics in School*, is a valuable source of excellent teaching ideas that should not be overlooked. Last is a set of curriculum materials, called *Algebridge* (1), designed to bridge the gap between arithmetic and algebra. These materials are intended to help teachers both teach and assess prealgebraic thinking within the context of arithmetic.

We hope the research presented in this chapter will give the reader a different perspective on prealgebra and a few new teaching ideas. We have deliberately avoided discussing teaching approaches whose primary objective was students' learning of algebraic symbolism as an end in itself or the development of so-called manipulative skill. In fact, we believe that such approaches contribute to student misunderstanding of the power of algebra. If algebraic notation could be viewed by the middle school student as a natural way of expressing what is sensible in arithmetic, we as teachers would be building a strong foundation not only for the understanding of algebra but for mathematics in general.

Looking Ahead . . .

Algebra is a field that is undergoing drastic changes in terms of what can and should be taught to students. The advent of technology has led many mathematics educators and others to begin questioning how computers, symbolic and graphing calculators, and other tools might be used to alter the emphases of current algebra curricula and allow inclusion of topics that were simply not feasible before. Clearly the old definitions and boundaries of algebra are changing. Thus, you may ask

---

"From the accountant who explores the consequences of changes in tax law to the engineer who designs a new aircraft, the practitioner of mathematics in the computer age is more likely to solve equations by computer-generated graphs and calculations than by manual algebraic manipulations. Mathematics today involves far more than calculation; clarification of the problem, deduction of consequences, formulation of alternatives, and development of appropriate tools are as much a part of the modern mathematician's craft as are solving equations or providing answers." (*Everybody Counts*, 30, p. 5)

---

whether the perspective we have adopted in this chapter is relevant to a future, but as of yet undecided, conception of school algebra. I believe it is. The need for a good sense of variables and how they are used to symbolize general mathematical relationships and methods will continue to be important—in fact, they might be more important than ever. In the past, algebra students could camouflage their weak conceptual understandings by memorizing rules for symbol manipulation. It is likely that the effective use of technology will require students to have an even greater understanding of the notational links between arithmetic and algebra.

Carolyn Kieran

Researchers have concentrated on developing meaning for algebraic symbolism and operations. However, integers, an important topic in prealgebra, appear to be somewhat neglected. For some students the positive ($+$) and negative ($-$) signs have only operational definitions (addition and subtraction). Thus, computing with integers often results in conflicts with these preconceived ideas. Some commonly

heard frustrations are "There are two 'minus' signs and you want me to ADD!?!";
"Aren't we doing addition $(-7+3)$, but you say I must SUBTRACT!?!" These difficulties are further aggravated by the seemingly contradictory rules associated with
integers [e.g., $(-)\times(-)=(+); (-)+(-)=(-)]$ and are compounded even more
when the rules for operating with integers are applied to letters. Future research
should attempt to provide teachers with findings that not only give them a better
understanding of these learning difficulties but also help them to respond to such
student questions.

Louise Chalouh

About the Authors

Carolyn Kieran teaches in the Mathematics and Computer Science Department of the University of Quebec at Montreal. In addition to working with preservice and inservice teachers,
she is an active researcher in mathematics education and has in the past taught secondary
school mathematics. One of her current interests is the use of technology in school algebra.

Louise Chalouh is the head teacher of a small high school in Montreal. Her experience teaching mathematics ranges from elementary school to junior college. She has done research on
developing new methods to introduce algebra and has made written contributions on this topic
in journals and books. She is currently engaged in writing a grade 11 mathematics textbook.

References

*1. *Algebridge*. (1990). Providence, RI: Janson.
2. BARCLAY, T. (1985). *Guess my rule* [Computer program]. Pleasantville, NY: HRM
   Software.
*3. BARRETT, G., & GOEBEL, J. (1990). The impact of graphing calculators on the teaching
   and learning of mathematics. In T. J. Cooney (Ed.), *Teaching and learning mathematics
   in the 1990s* (1990 Yearbook, pp. 205–211). Reston, VA: National Council of Teachers
   of Mathematics.
4. BELL, A. W., COSTELLO, J., & KÜCHEMANN, D. (Eds.). (1983). *A review of research in
   mathematics education; Part A: Research on learning and teaching*. Windsor, England:
   NFER-Nelson.
*5. BOOTH, L. R. (1984). *Algebra: Children's strategies and errors*. Windsor, England:
   NFER-Nelson.
6. BOOTH, L. R. (1989). A question of structure. In S. Wagner & C. Kieran (Eds.), *Research issues in the learning and teaching of algebra* (Vol. 4 of *Research agenda for
   mathematics education*, pp. 57–59). Hillsdale, NJ: Erlbaum; Reston, VA: National
   Council of Teachers of Mathematics.
*7. CHALOUH, L., & HERSCOVICS, N. (1988). Teaching algebraic expressions in a meaning-
   ful way. In A. F. Coxford (Ed.), *The ideas of algebra, K–12* (1988 Yearbook, pp. 33–
   42). Reston, VA: National Council of Teachers of Mathematics.
8. COLLIS, K. F. (1974, June). *Cognitive development and mathematics learning*. Paper
   presented at the Psychology of Mathematics Workshop, Centre for Science Education,
   Chelsea College, London.
*9. DAVIS, R. B. (1985). ICME-5 Report: Algebraic thinking in the early grades. *Journal of
   Mathematical Behavior*, 4(2), 195–208.

*10. DAVIS, R. B. (1987). Theory and practice. *Journal of Mathematical Behavior*, 6(1), 97–126.

*11. DEMANA, F., & LEITZEL, J. (1988). Establishing fundamental concepts through numerical problem solving. In A. F. Coxford (Ed.), *The ideas of algebra, K–12* (1988 Yearbook, pp. 61–68). Reston, VA: National Council of Teachers of Mathematics.

*12. DUNCAN, R. K., & SAUNDERS, W. J. (1980). Introduction to integers. *Instructor*, 90(3), 152–154.

13. HARPER, E. (1987). Ghosts of Diophantus. *Educational Studies in Mathematics*, 18(1), 75–90.

*14. HEID, M. K. (1990). Uses of technology in prealgebra and beginning algebra. *Mathematics Teacher*, 83(3), 194–198.

15. HERSCOVICS, H. (1989). Cognitive obstacles encountered in the learning of algebra. In S. Wagner & C. Kieran (Eds.), *Research issues in the learning and teaching of algebra* (Vol. 4 of *Research agenda for mathematics education*, pp. 60–86). Hillsdale, NJ: Erlbaum; Reston, VA: National Council of Teachers of Mathematics.

*16. HOYLES, C., SUTHERLAND, R., & EVANS, J. (1985). *The Logo Maths Project: A preliminary investigation of the pupil-centred approach to the learning of Logo in the secondary mathematics classroom. 1983–4.* London: University of London, Institute of Education.

*17. HUMAN, P., & MURRAY, H. (1987). Non-concrete approaches to integer arithmetic. In J. C. Bergeron, N. Herscovics, & C. Kieran (Eds.), *Proceedings of the Eleventh International Conference for the Psychology of Mathematics Education* (Vol. III, pp. 437–443). Montreal: Univesité de Montreal.

*18. KAPUT, J. J. (1988, April). *Translations from numerical and graphical to algebraic representations of elementary functions.* Paper presented at the annual meeting of the American Educational Research Association, New Orleans, LA.

*19. KIERAN, C. (1981). Concepts associated with the equality symbol. *Educational Studies in Mathematics*, 12(3), 317–326.

*20. KIERAN, C. (1988). Two different approaches among algebra learners. In A. F. Coxford (Ed.), *The ideas of algebra, K–12* (1988 Yearbook, pp. 91–96). Reston, VA: National Council of Teachers of Mathematics.

*21. KIERAN, C. (1992). The learning and teaching of school algebra. In D. A. Grouws (Ed.), *Handbook of research on mathematics teaching and learning.* (pp. 390–419). New York: Macmillan.

*22. KIERAN, C. (in press). Functions, graphing, and technology: Integrating research on learning and instruction. In T. A. Romberg, E. Fennema & T. P. Carpenter, (Eds.), *Integrating research on the graphical representation of function.* Hillsdale, NJ: Erlbaum.

*23. KOHN, J. B. (1978). A physical model for operations with integers. *Mathematics Teacher*, 71(9), 734–736.

24. KÜCHEMANN, D. (1981). Algebra. In K. M. Hart (Ed.), *Children's understanding of mathematics: 11–16* (pp. 102–119). London: John Murray.

*25. LEE, L., & WHEELER, D. (1987). *Algebraic thinking in high school students: Their conceptions of generalisation and justification* (Research report). Montreal: Concordia University, Department of Mathematics.

*26. LEE, L., & WHEELER, D. (1989). The arithmetic connection. *Educational Studies in Mathematics*, 20(1), 41–54.

*27. LESH, R., POST, T., & BEHR, M. (1987). Dienes revisited: Multiple embodiments in computer environments. In I. Wirszup & R. Streit (Eds.), *Developments in school mathematics education around the world* (pp. 647–680). Reston, VA: National Council of Teachers of Mathematics.

28. MULLIGAN, C. H. (1988). Using polynomials to amaze. In A. F. Coxford (Ed.), *The ideas of algebra, K–12* (1988 Yearbook, pp. 206–211). Reston VA: National Council of Teachers of Mathematics.

29. NATIONAL COUNCIL OF TEACHERS OF MATHEMATICS. (1989). *Curriculum and evaluation standards for school mathematics.* Reston, VA: Author.

30. NATIONAL RESEARCH COUNCIL. (1989). *Everybody counts: A report to the nation on the future of mathematics education.* Washington, DC: National Academy Press.

*31. OPREA, J. M. (1988). Computer programming and mathematical thinking. *Journal of Mathematical Behavior, 7*(2), 175–190.

*32. PECK, D. M., & JENCKS, S. M. (1988). Reality, arithmetic, algebra. *Journal of Mathematical Behavior, 7*(1), 85–91.

*33. THOMPSON, F. M. (1988). Algebraic instruction for the younger child. In A. F. Coxford (Ed.), *The ideas of algebra, K–12* (1988 Yearbook, pp. 69–77). Reston, VA: National Council of Teachers of Mathematics.

*34. USISKIN, Z. (1988). Conceptions of school algebra and uses of variables. In A. F. Coxford (Ed.), *The ideas of algebra, K–12* (1988 Yearbook, pp. 8–19). Reston, VA: National Council of Teachers of Mathematics.

35. WAGNER, S., RACHLIN, S. L., & JENSEN, R. J. (1984). *Algebra Learning Project: Final report.* Athens: University of Georgia, Department of Mathematics Education.

*36. WHITMAN, B. S. (1976). Intuitive equation solving skills and the effects on them of formal techniques of equation solving (Doctoral dissertation, Florida State University, 1975). *Dissertation Abstracts International, 36,* 5180A. (University Microfilms No. 76-2720)

*37. WHITMAN, B. S. (1982). Intuitive equation-solving skills. In L. Silvey (Ed.), *Mathematics for the middle grades (5–9)* (1982 Yearbook, pp. 199–204). Reston, VA: National Council of Teachers of Mathematics.

CHAPTER 11

Geometry: Research and Classroom Activities

Dorothy Geddes and Irene Fortunato

> *"Let no one destitute of geometry enter my doors"*—so read the inscription over the entrance to Plato's academy.

But what is geometry? Why study geometry? What is the role of geometry in the mathematics curriculum? What aspects of geometry should middle school students study?

Frequently geometry is referred to as the mathematics of space. It is a way of connecting mathematics and the real world. In a survey of professional and lay groups by the Priorities in School Mathematics Project, two of the main goals for teaching geometry were to develop logical thinking abilities and to develop spatial intuitions about the real world (31). Learning geometry can be fun and challenging for middle school students when they engage in activities and spatial experiences organized around physical models, modeling, mapping, and measuring, discovering geometric relationships through use of mathematical procedures (e.g., drawing, sorting, classifying, transforming, finding patterns), and developing geometrical fantasies and mathematical creativity through problem solving (32, 33).

"Children are not vessels to be filled but lamps to be lighted." (Henry Steele Commager)

Geometry is an integral part of the mathematics curriculum in the middle grades. Geometric concepts and representations contribute effectively to students' learning of number and measurement (e.g., length, area, and volume) ideas. There are numerous examples of these: (a) the number line provides a way of representing whole numbers, fractional numbers, integers, and a probability scale; (b) regions are used in developmental work with multiplication, fractional numbers, percent, and area; (c) number and geometry are closely connected in developing the function concept, the coordinate plane, and graphs; and (d) similar triangles are used to develop concepts of ratio and proportion. These examples clearly show the connections between geometry and other areas of the mathematics curriculum and partially illustrate the spirit of the NCTM *Curriculum and Evaluation Standard*, Mathematical Connections.

In this chapter research on the learning and teaching of geometry is discussed and some research-based ideas and activities to enrich your students' geometry experiences are presented.

Learning Geometry: Cognitive Development

Cognitive development in the learning of geometry was a major focus of the research and theories developed by Piaget (37) and the van Hieles (47). These theories and recent studies on concept formation, levels of thinking, spatial visualization, reasoning, and higher order thinking as they relate to the learning of geometry are discussed in this section.

Piaget: On Space and Geometry

Piaget's research, resulting in a theory of intellectual development, did not explicitly study the development of mathematical concepts and skills, although much writing and many investigations have hypothesized implications of Piaget's theory for mathematics learning. Three themes characterize Piaget's research on children's space concepts: (a) the acquisition of spatial concepts and intellectual development, (b) the building up of spatial representations through active manipulation of the spatial environment, and (c) the characterization of acquiring spatial concepts according to the type of geometry involved—topological, projective, Euclidean. Piaget claimed that children's concept of space invariably begins with simple topological types of relationships long before it becomes projective or Euclidean in nature (37) (see Fig. 11.1).

Certain Piagetian tasks have been suggested as providing a sound basis for determining students' readiness to learn certain aspects of mathematics—geometry in particular. However, the available evidence suggests that this is not always so; many students who fail Piagetian tasks are able to learn mathematics concepts and skills (17). This observation is not to refute Piaget's theory of intellectual development, but it is an indication that more research, perhaps of a different type, is needed.

van Hiele Model of Thinking in Geometry

Two Dutch teachers, Dina van Hiele-Geldof and Pierre van Hiele, were concerned about the difficulties their students encountered with geometry. They believed that the geometry they were teaching in grades 7–9 involved thinking at a relatively high

FIGURE 11.1 Representations of topological, projective, and euclidean geometry

Topological aspects: open/closed, inside/outside, stretching

open   closed

By stretching, triangle, square, and circle are topologically equivalent on balloon surface

Projective: viewing objects from different perspectives

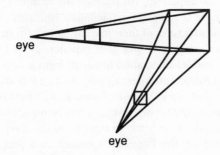

eye

eye

Euclidean: distance, measurement

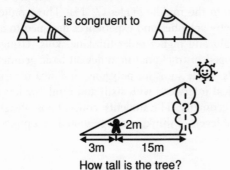

is congruent to

2m

3m   15m

How tall is the tree?

level, and that their students had not had sufficient experience in thinking at prerequisite lower levels. They were interested in finding ways to develop insight in their students. Thus their research focused on levels of thinking in geometry and the role of instruction in helping students move from one level to the next. The van Hiele model, designed to help students gain insight into geometry, uses five levels to describe student thinking—Level 0: Visual (e.g., judges shapes by their appearance); Level 1: Analysis (e.g., sees figures in terms of their components and discovers properties of a class of shapes); Level 2: Informal deduction (e.g., logically interrelates previously discovered properties); Level 3: Deduction (proves theorems deductively); and Level 4: Rigor (e.g., establishes theorems in different postulational systems (10, 14, 47). The levels have specific characteristics: they are sequential, each level has its own language and set of symbols, what is implicit at one level is explicit at the next level, and levels are subject to "reduction" by substituting a rote procedure for thinking.

For middle grade students, attention must be focused on levels 0, 1, and 2 of the van Hiele model. If students are having trouble learning geometry, one might hypothesize according to this model that they are being taught at a higher level than they have attained. Moreover, two individuals (perhaps teacher and student or student and textbook author) who reason at different levels cannot understand each other because differing linguistic symbols and relationships are used; thus communication is difficult.

To move students from one thought level to the next within a topic, the van Hieles proposed a sequence of five phases of learning. These phases provide a prescription for organizing classroom instruction in geometry and are described as (a) inquiry (discussion/questions on the topic to be explored), (b) directed orientation (careful sequencing of activities for student explorations), (c) explicitation (students express explicit views/questions about inherent structures of their investigations), (d) free orientation (students now encounter multistep tasks and gain experiences in finding their own way of resolving the tasks), and (e) integration (students form an overview in which objects or relationships are unified and internalized into a new domain of thought) (13, 14, 19). The phases are not usually accomplished in a linear fashion; students frequently cycle through some of the phases several times before attaining a new domain of thought and thus reach the next level. In comparing the level structure to Piaget's stages, van Hiele considers the Piagetian approach as a process of maturation while the level approach is experienced based and as such is a process of apprenticeship for the student (47).

In recent years several research projects have investigated and verified aspects of the van Hiele model in relation to the middle grades (7, 14). These projects have developed van Hiele-type geometry activities and experiences designed to assist students in developing greater insight and higher order thinking skills. Using the van Hiele model, one project developed instructional modules on basic geometric concepts, properties of quadrilaterals, angle sums for polygons, and area measurement. The modules were used in clinical interviews with sixth and ninth graders to determine their levels of thinking in geometry. The students' conceptions, insights, difficulties, and successes in terms of levels of thinking are presented in a project monograph that provides the reader with many insights into learning and teaching geometry (14).

Sample Classroom van Hiele-type Activities.

1. Sorting activities help students to develop classifying skills, to recognize properties of shapes, and to discover subclass relationships.

Example: Give groups of 4–6 students sets of quadrilaterals. Ask them to sort the quadrilaterals into three or four piles in any way they wish and to give a rule that describes their sort. The teacher's role is to raise questions in each group, such as, Using your rule, could this shape go in this pile? Why or why not? Then the teacher asks the students to sort their set of quadrilaterals using a different rule (see Fig. 11.2).

2. Clue games are designed to help students distinguish between necessary and sufficient conditions in describing a shape; this leads to the development of a good definition.

Example: If you want to challenge your friend to identify a square by only giving a set of clues, which minimum set of clues would you select from those listed below? Explain your selection. Is it possible to select a different minimum set of clues? Explain.

FIGURE 11.2   Quadrilateral sort

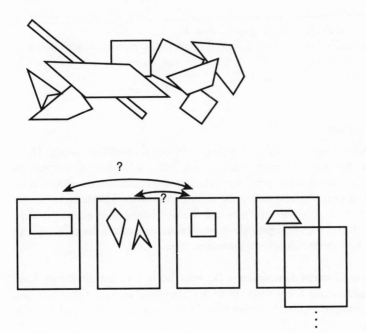

1. There are 4 angles.
2. All angles are right angles.
3. There are 4 sides.
4. All sides are congruent.
5. It is a simple closed curve.
6. Opposite angles are congruent.
7. Opposite sides are congruent.
8. Opposite sides are parallel.

   3. Many properties of geometric shapes can be discovered and verified by reading a grid. In a parallelogram grid (see Fig. 11.3) can you find congruent angles? What can you discover about alternate interior angles and corresponding angles of parallel lines and about opposite angles of a parallelogram?

In a triangular grid (see Fig. 11.4), can you find congruent triangles, similar triangles, different shaped parallelograms, trapezoids, pentagons, hexagons? By reading this grid, what can you discover about the line joining the midpoints of two sides of a triangle? How do the areas of two similar triangles compare? Can you discover and verify the angle sum for a triangle or the relationship of an exterior angle of a triangle to the two opposite interior angles? Do your discoveries hold true when you read other parallelogram and triangular grids?

   4. After developing a topic, it is useful to have students look back and discover interrelationships among what might have seemed to be a set of disjointed ideas. By building "family trees," students need to determine "ancestor" relations between or among relations/properties and place them in a logical hierarchy.

   Example: a. Build a family tree (Fig. 11.5 [p. 207]) to show a logical relationship of ideas that led to the angle sum for a quadrilateral.

   b. Complete a family tree to show a logical relationship among quadrilaterals in a given set as in Figure 11.6 (p. 207). Additional van Hiele-type activities can be found in references 6, 10, 13, 14, and 43.

Concept Formation

Geometric concepts are vital for understanding our three-dimensional world. However, studies show that geometry instruction in elementary schools tends to focus on recognition of shapes and development of vocabulary rather than on development of concepts (14). Work with concrete materials, pictures, drawings, images in computer microworlds, and other resources can promote the development of geometric concepts. Pictures and drawings that provide examples and nonexamples of a concept can give students an intuitive grasp of a geometric idea.

Sample Activity on Concept Formation.   An effective way to familiarize students with a concept and to make them aware of its distinguishing characteristics is to use the example-nonexample approach, sometimes referred to as a concept card, like the one shown in Figure 11.7 (p. 208).

FIGURE 11.3 Reading a parallelogram grid

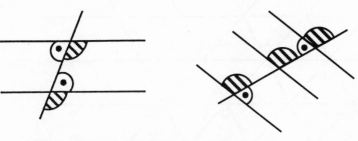

⊙ Alternate interior angles of parallel lines are congruent.

◉ Corresponding angles of parallel lines are congruent.

Informal deduction: Level 2

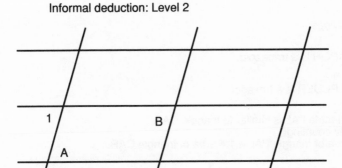

In parallelogram grid:

angle A is congruent to angle 1,
angle B is congruent to angle 1,
so angle A is congruent to angle B.
Thus, in a parallelogram a pair of
    opposite angles is congruent

Each student should work on a concept card independently. This nonverbal approach allows students to compare and contrast different characteristics, to make conjectures and test them, and to arrive at a working description/definition of the concept. Concept cards can be developed for many geometric and other mathematical topics. Students enjoy the concept card approach. They can be challenged to develop their own concept cards and then try them out on their peers.

FIGURE 11.4   Reading a triangular grid

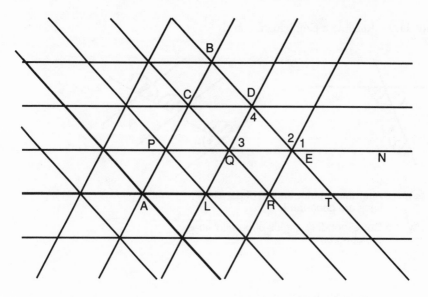

Readings:

- APQR is a trapezoid.

- LPCDER is a hexagon.

- Triangle PAL is similar to triangle CAR.
  By counting,
  area of triangle PAL = 1/4 area of triangle CAR.

- angle DEN is exterior angle of triangle QED.
  angle 1 is congruent to angle 3,
  angle 2 is congruent to angle 4,
  so m (angle DEN) = m (angle 3) + m (angle 4).
  Thus the measure of an exterior angle of a triangle
  is equal to the sum of the measures of the opposite interior angles.

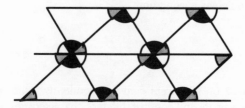

- **The sum of the measures of the angles
  of a triangle is equal to the measure
  of a straight angle.**

206

FIGURE 11.5 Ancestors of a polygon angle sum

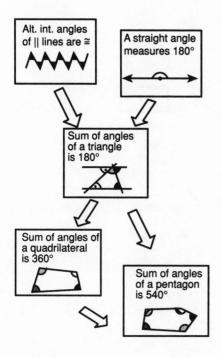

FIGURE 11.6 Family tree

The arrow ——————▶ means "is a special."

Select from the following to fill in the blanks
and correctly complete the family tree:

rhombus, square, kite rectangle, trapezoid

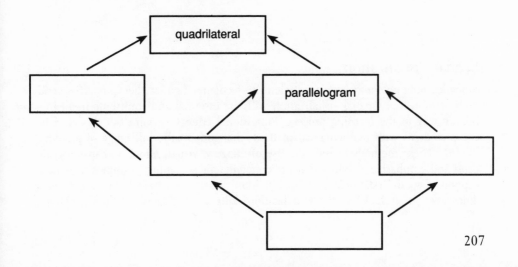

FIGURE 11.7   Concept card

These are larps:

These are not larps:

Which of these are larps?

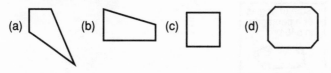

Draw some larps.

Draw some non-larps.

What is a larp?

Spatial Visualization

Since learning geometry requires students to recognize figures, their properties, and their relationships, spatial visualization skills are essential and contribute in an important way to the learning process. Professional educators point out the need to equip students with mathematical methods that support the full range of problem solving. These methods include the use of imagery, visualization, and spatial concepts and emphasize activities that use concrete representations to improve the perception of spatial relationships (26, 49). Many researchers have hypothesized that differences in students' spatial visualization skills are one cause of their problem-solving difficulties. Two studies investigated the interaction of middle grade students' spatial visualization ability and their performance on mathematical problems. Major findings indicated a strong correlation between spatial ability and problem-solving performance, suggesting that spatial visualization skill is a good predictor of general problem solving (45).

Studies that investigated the effect of instruction in spatial skills showed that spatial skills of middle school students can be improved through instruction. Boys and girls gained similarly from instruction in spatial visualization in spite of initial sex differences favoring boys (3); also, instruction in spatial skills significantly improved the mathematics performance of girls (2).

Do visual representations influence a student's intuitive grasp of a geometric concept? Studies investigating this issue indicate that students form visually biased concepts in favor of upright figures even when instruction focused on tilted figures (12); students tended to view a drawing in terms of a single concept even when the drawing included several concepts (52).

What are the effects, if any, of cultural differences in the process of spatial visualization? Several studies suggest that visualization and perception are culturally dependent (4, 30). As examples, (a) individuals from some African and Polynesian cultures do not perceive rectangular shapes in drawings in the same way as individuals from most Western cultures (42); (b) African languages contain relatively few words for shapes or spatial relationships whereas the Inuit not only have a rich spatial language but most of their spatial work focuses on a circle (30, 51); (c) the average level of students' spatial ability is lower in developing than in industrialized countries (30).

Sample Classroom Spatial Visualization Activities. A number of curriculum projects have developed innovative activities designed to develop students' spatial visualization skills (20, 28, 48). A few sample activities are presented below.

1. In a project in the Netherlands (19), a pictorial puzzle similar to this one is given. From a cruising ferryboat, a series of photographs of some landmarks (a lighthouse, a water tower, and a steeple) was taken. The resulting pictures shown in Figure 11.8 were dropped and mixed up. Can you determine the order in which the pictures were taken? The map shows the coastal region (15).

2. In a 2-week unit on spatial visualization in the Middle Grades Mathematics Project (48), students engage in concrete activities, building and drawing solids made of cubes. The students learn to relate a solid to the drawing of it, to make an isometric drawing of a solid, and to build a solid from an isometric drawing. The types of representations used are two-dimensional flat view, three-dimensional corner view, and map plan, which includes the description of the base of the building by squares and numbers in each square to tell how many cubes are to be placed on that square. A sample item from the project's spatial visualization test is given in Figure 11.9 (25).

3. The California mathematics model curriculum guide (8, pp. 93–96) presents lessons on emphasizing geometry by developing spatial visualization. The tasks in-

FIGURE 11.8 In what order were the pictures taken? (15, p. 1)

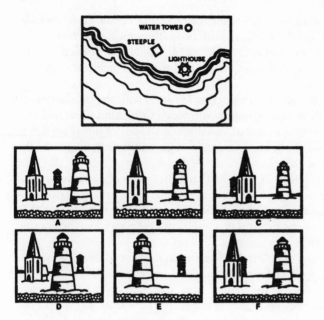

FIGURE 11.9 View of a building

You are given a picture of a building drawn from the FRONT-RIGHT corner. Find the BACK VIEW.

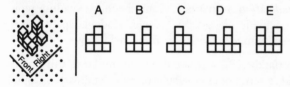

FIGURE 11.10 From pentominoes to milk cartons

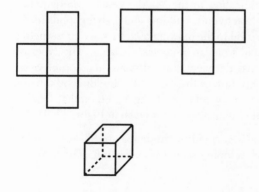

clude work with milk carton pentominoes (see Fig. 11.10) and the computer software program, The Factory (23).

Reasoning, Higher Order Thinking

Geometry provides a vehicle for developing mathematical reasoning abilities of students. The NCTM *Curriculum and Evaluation Standard*, Mathematics as Reasoning, calls for middle grade students to be able to recognize and apply deductive, inductive, and spatial reasoning, and to make and evaluate conjectures and arguments to validate their own thinking.

"Reasoning shall permeate the mathematics curriculum so that students can appreciate the pervasive use and power of reasoning as a part of mathematics." (*Curriculum and Evaluation Standards*, 32, p. 81)

The van Hiele model described earlier outlines a procedure a teacher might follow when planning and organizing instruction to develop higher order thinking skills. Activities such as example and nonexample concept cards, sorting problems, clue games, classifying, finding patterns, reading grids, validating, and building family trees provide a rich environment for developing and using reasoning skills (6, 14, 43).

Students need to be aware of the reasons for the skills and procedures they are learning and be expected to reflect on the reasonableness of their solutions. A mathematics classroom should offer students opportunities to explore new ideas, to develop thinking skills, to experience the fun of solving real-world problems and asking "what if" questions, to view mathematics as the "queen of the sciences" (e.g., requiring the power of reasoning), and to reflect on their own mathematical thinking.

Sample Geometry Activities to Foster Reasoning.

1. This classroom activity (Fig. 11.11) should be done in small groups (25, p. 26). Each student is given a straw that is 8 cm long. The straw can be bent in two places, but only at a centimeter mark. Ask how many different triangles can be made. (Surprise, only one triangle!) Why? Extend the problem by using a 9-cm straw and a 10-cm straw. Students should report on their observations, conjectures, discoveries, and generalizations.

FIGURE 11.11   Straws to triangles

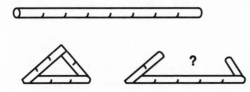

2. Given a cut-out parallelogram, can it be cut up and the parts arranged into a shape that makes it easy to determine the area? (See Fig. 11.12.) Can the same thing be done for a trapezoid? How does this help explain the area formulas for these figures? (8)

FIGURE 11.12 Parallelogram to ____?____.

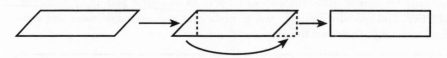

Trends in Geometry Curriculum

The middle grades curriculum in geometry is designed to develop student insight and intuition into spatial-visual aspects of geometry. It includes an inductive approach to investigate patterns, build models, make and verify conjectures, examine geometry as a mode of representation for other mathematical topics, explore transformation (motion) geometry, and use technology in learning geometry.

Informal Geometry

Informal geometry is an integral part of the mathematics curriculum for the middle grades although the content of the informal geometry units varies considerably around the world. Proof to middle grades students usually does not mean deductive proof. Rather, a "proof" can consist of testing more examples that seem to verify a conjecture being tested or "disproof" can be attained by finding a counterexample. Proving then must be thought of as a final objective along a road that contains elements such as guessing, conjecturing, arguing, and reasoning (36, 46). These apprentice elements are what the van Hiele model calls for in order to assist students in reaching thinking at Level 3 (Deduction).

In North America, all commercial texts for middle grades mathematics contain one or two chapters on informal geometry. However, teachers frequently delay teaching geometry until the end of the school year if there is time. Why does this occur? Perhaps teachers do not consider geometry of equal importance to other topics in the mathematics curriculum. As a result many middle grades students could be described as geometry deprived. This type of deprivation may be a critical factor in students' progress in mathematics since many mathematical concepts are developed by using geometric representations. A wide variety of informal geometry activities for the middle grades is described in several publications (11, 18, 28).

Transformation Geometry

Although transformation or motion geometry—that is, translation (slide), reflection (flip), rotation (turn), and dilation (stretch or shrink)—is a relatively new approach in

FIGURE 11.13   Slides, flips, turns

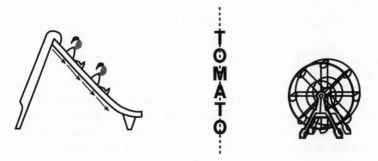

the mathematics curriculum in North America, it has been a standard part of informal geometry taught in the middle grades in many parts of the world (see Fig. 11.13).

Why teach transformation geometry? Transformations bring a spatial-visual aspect to geometry that is as important as logical-deductive aspects. Also, transformation geometry has important real-world applications such as fabric patterns, mirrors, symmetry in nature (see Fig. 11.14), record turntables, photos and enlargements (40).

Since transformations can be defined in terms of actions (sliding, flipping, turning) and their results represented easily by drawings, the topic is ideally suited for student investigations. In two studies with eighth graders that investigated two methods of instruction (student activity-centered and teacher demonstration-centered) on the learning of transformation geometry, one study found that the two approaches were equally effective in terms of student achievement (39). The other study found that students in activity-centered groups performed significantly better than those taught by the teacher-centered approach (34), thus supporting the view that an inductive approach to instruction that allows students to experiment with objects by actively manipulating them helps foster students' understanding of the transformations of objects (4).

FIGURE 11.14   Symmetry in nature

       Protozoa

Sample Activities in Transformation Geometry.

1. "Living in a World of Transformations" (40)
2. Symmetry and motion activities in "Graph Paper Geometry" (5)

Teaching Geometry with Technology

Computer microworlds hold exciting potential for improving students' learning of geometry. A microworld can be described as an ideal environment composed of objects, relationships among objects, and operations that transform objects and relationships. One area of research on the use of technology in teaching geometry in the middle grades is the use of Logo, a computer microworld with a programming language developed for children, which focuses on "turtle geometry."

One study, conducted over a 4-week period with two eighth-grade classes, used Logo turtle graphics to investigate the way students respond to questions at different van Hiele levels (1). The experimental class studied geometry through the use of Logo; the other class studied geometry from the regular classroom textbook. Major findings of the study were that students in the experimental group showed a tendency to respond at a relatively high van Hiele level, became less dependent on irrelevant features of geometric shapes, and were more able to extract properties for geometric shapes. Logo procedures seemed to facilitate the construction of geometric shapes and made relations between shapes clearer than verbal definitions. The use of turtle graphics had a positive effect on students' confidence and motivation as related to mathematics.

Another study was designed to examine the integration of Logo into the sixth-grade mathematics curriculum through its supplementary use with traditional textbook material and manipulatives. One finding was that Logo was effective in improving students' geometry achievement and spatial visualization ability. Girls in this study had a greater feeling of success when using Logo or software related to the curriculum content than when using software that included competitive games or had no relation to the geometry concepts being studied in class (35).

A second area of research is the use of computer software related to informal geometry and reasoning. One research team has developed software called the Geometric Supposer and the Geometric preSupposer (41). These are flexible tools for investigating a wide variety of concepts and relationships in geometry. They are designed to let students participate actively and to encourage them to behave like geometers—to observe patterns, make conjectures, test them, and even propose new theorems. The software enables students to carry out many constructions and offers a wealth of visual and numerical data whereby conjectures about relationships within the data can be easily tested. The measurement capabilities of the software allow students to find counterexamples for given conjectures quickly (41).

Sample Logo and Geometric preSupposer activities.

1. Many commercial publications feature Logo activities to construct shapes, to create procedures, to construct regular polygons, and to invent more complex configurations. One example is *Tessellations Using LOGO* (22) (see Fig. 11.15).

FIGURE 11.15 Logo tessellations

2. "Concept Formation in Geometry" describes the classroom use of the Geometric preSupposer in which students create "family albums" for a specific shape (21).

Problem Exploration

Problem exploration in geometry should be an underlying theme in the classroom since this helps students to go beyond the learning of isolated ideas and to formulate organized systems of relationships (e.g., make geoboard figures to meet certain criteria, find all possible figures that meet certain conditions, or solve the problem another way). The problem exploration approach can assist students in using geometry to further their understanding of other mathematical ideas, to apply mathematical thinking to explore problems that arise in other disciplines, and to value the role of geometry in our society. This addresses, in part, the NCTM curriculum and evaluation standard, Mathematical Connections.

Sample Geometry Problem-Solving Activities.

1. Creative geometry problems can lead to creative problem solvers. "'Take ye 20 paces East of the old oak tree, then 15 North and 18 West. Walk 9 paces North and another 5 East and here ye find me treasure.' How many paces in a straight line was the treasure from the oak tree?" (29, p. 70) (see Fig. 11.16).

2. In a cooperative learning activity, give each group of 4–5 students a loop of heavy yarn 4 meters long. Each student must have both hands touching the yarn at all times. The groups are challenged to make geometric figures with the yarn: figures such as isosceles triangle, square, trapezoid, regular hexagon, three equilateral triangles, and four congruent squares. The group must be able to explain and verify their solutions.

FIGURE 11.16   Treasure hunt

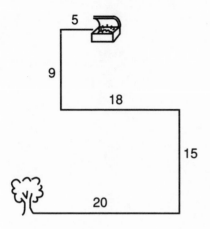

Trends in Teaching Geometry

Psychological theory has influenced approaches to the teaching of geometry. An active role for students in learning is seen in constructivist theory (see the cognition chapter in this volume) and in the increased focus on the use of manipulatives by middle school students in learning geometry. Because of the diverse cultural background of North American students, the need for multicultural activities in teaching geometry is being widely recognized.

Use of Manipulatives

Middle grade students are "especially responsive to hands-on activities in tactile, auditory, and visual instructional modes" (32, p. 87). Since the study of geometry began with observations of the world from which mathematical concepts were abstracted, students, when exploring geometry ideas, should be involved in the use of physical models and in well-designed activities with manipulatives (9) (see Fig. 11.17). A survey of geometry instructional aids indicated that traditional ruler, compass, protractor, and graph paper were the basic tools for instructional purposes. Laboratory oriented teaching materials (e.g., Miras, Reflectas, mirrors, geoboards, and models) were used infrequently. Teachers reporting greater use of a variety of instructional aids in the teaching of geometry, ratio, proportion, and percent also were able to cover more of the course content. Experienced teachers made greater use of instructional aids than did less experienced teachers. Middle grades students' geometry learning should be rich in activities with containers of different shapes, tiling patterns, pentominoes, tessellations, paper folding, model building, drawing, and mapping. These activities should be designed to focus on underlying geometry ideas, properties, and phenomena (4). A wide variety of geometry activities using instructional aids are described in detail in several publications (11, 28, 38).

FIGURE 11.17 Plexiglas mirror and geoboard

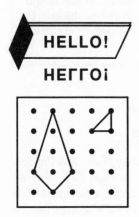

Multicultural Activities

Because of the similarity of much of the mathematics content across cultures, the role of culture is more prominent in how students learn mathematics (e.g., tools, traditions, attitudes, methods) (44). There have been a growing interest in developing well-designed multicultural activities for classroom use. Here are some multicultural activities that focus on geometry.

1. Origami, the oriental art of paper folding, is a powerful motivational tool for exploring concepts of polygons, angles, symmetry, and congruence (16).
2. Activities and games involving geometry and reasoning have their roots in different parts of the world (24).
3. Symmetry and motion geometry concepts are exemplified in African life (50).

Assessments of Teaching and Learning Geometry

Results from the geometry section of the fourth National Assessment of Educational Progress (27) show that 13-year-old students performed best on items that required identification of common geometric properties. Their next best performance was on visualization tasks. Performance was low on examples that required some understanding of underlying geometric principles (e.g., angle sum for a triangle, Pythagorean theorem). As on previous assessments, students did not perform well on application items. Certain implications for classroom instruction can be drawn from these assessments: Teachers need to have students spend more time on developing geometric concepts (concretely and using multiple embodiments) and principles (in varied settings) and not merely focus on practice involving algorithmic procedures.

> "The teacher of mathematics should pose tasks that are based on sound and significant mathematics . . . engage students' intellect, . . . stimulate students to make connections and develop a coherent framework for mathematical ideas."
> (*Professional Teaching Standards*, 33, p. 25)

Geometry Resources for Middle School Teachers

Middle school teachers of geometry need to have a wide variety of examples of geometric figures and ideas in the environment to stimulate and motivate their students. Innovative curriculum materials developed and tested by projects for the middle grades, such as the Mathematics Resource Project's *Geometry and Visualization* (28) and the Middle Grade Mathematics Project's *Spatial Visualization* (48), are major sources of interesting and challenging student activities in geometry.

Looking Ahead . . .

Results of current van Hiele research is encouraging in terms of giving new direction for geometry teaching and learning but more teaching experiments are needed, particularly with respect to the "phases" aspect of the model. Teachers should examine the role of the phases (which relate closely to their lesson planning and implementation) in assisting their students to move to higher processes (levels) of thinking in geometry. Teachers can provide important kinds of data about student abilities, difficulties, beliefs, and attitudes toward problem exploration in geometry.

> "The teacher of mathematics should promote classroom discourse in which students . . . initiate problems and questions, make conjectures and present solutions, explore examples and counterexamples to investigate a conjecture."
> (*Professional Teaching Standards*, 33, p. 45)

As middle school teachers implement recommendations of the NCTM *Curriculum and Evaluation Standards* for teaching geometry, they need to keep careful accounts and documentation of these classroom activities and then share their observations and experiences.

Teachers are on the front line of curriculum reform. They have rich collections of firsthand classroom data on the use of manipulatives, student-created models, and spatial visualization activities; on student investigations, search for patterns, conjectures, and inductive reasoning; on use of computer technology; and on explorations of real-world applications of geometry. These can provide a wealth of information for curriculum developers and researchers.

Dorothy Geddes

> "Teachers develop as professionals on an ongoing basis. Focusing on their classroom practice, they experiment with alternative approaches to engage students in mathematical ideas, possible strategies for assessment, and different ways of organization. They analyze and adapt strategies that they try, examining how well they help students develop mathematical competence and confidence. . . . They read, talk with colleagues, take the initiative to press for changes, and raise their voices to speak out on current issues." (*Professional Teaching Standards,* 33, p. 168)

In urban education there is growing emphasis on multicultural approaches to teaching mathematics. What resources are available to a teacher? An important consideration for future research is investigations into how geometry is taught in classrooms in different cultures. It is not enough for middle grades students to learn about properties of shapes and the vocabulary of geometry; they must understand what geometry is and how it relates to the real world and other topics in mathematics. Research has shown that our students must be active learners engaged in the process of discovering conjecturing, and thinking at higher levels. This is no small task for the teacher. How can research help us? We need to look beyond our textbooks for motivating and challenging activities.

Irene Fortunato

As we improve the teaching and learning of geometry, we will approach the goal set by Plato, "The knowledge at which geometry aims is the knowledge of the eternal."

About the Authors

Dorothy Geddes is a professor of mathematics education at Brooklyn College, City University of New York, Brooklyn. Before teaching at the college level, she taught mathematics in grades 7–12 for 15 years. Her research interests are geometry and higher order thinking, in particular, the van Hiele model of thinking. She has had several grants focusing on higher order thinking in mathematics for middle school teachers.

Irene Fortunato is currently the mathematics coordinator for Community School District 18, Brooklyn, and was for the past eight years a teacher of mathematics at Bildersee Intermediate School, Brooklyn. She is a member of the executive board of the Association of Teachers of Mathematics of New York City. She has been an adjunct instructor of an undergraduate mathematics course for prospective elementary and middle school teachers and of a graduate mathematics education course for teachers, grades K-9.

References

1. Assaf, S. A. (1986). The effects of using Logo turtle graphics in teaching geometry on eighth grade students' level of thought, attitudes toward geometry, and knowledge of

geometry (Doctoral dissertation, University of Wisconsin, 1985). *Dissertation Abstracts International, 46A,* 2952.

2. BALDWIN, S. (1985). Instruction in spatial skills and its effect on mathematics achievement in the intermediate grades (Doctoral dissertation, University of Northern Colorado, 1984). *Dissertation Abstracts International, 46A,* 595.

3. BEN-CHAIM, D., LAPPAN, G., & HOUANG, R. T. (1988). The effect of instruction on spatial visualization skills of middle school boys and girls. *American Education Research Journal, 25*(1), 51–71.

4. BISHOP, A. J. (1983). Space and geometry. In R. Lesh & M. Landau (Eds.), *Acquisition of mathematics concepts and processes* (pp. 175–203). New York: Academic Press.

*5. BURGER, W. F. (1982). Graph paper geometry. In L. Silvey (Ed.), *Mathematics for the middle grades (5–9)* (pp. 102–117). Reston, VA: National Council of Teachers of Mathematics.

*6. BURGER, W. F. (1985). Geometry. *Arithmetic Teacher, 32*(6), 52–56.

7. BURGER, W. F., & SHAUGHNESSY, J. M. (1986). Characterizing the van Hiele levels of development in geometry. *Journal for Research in Mathematics Education, 17*(1), 31–48.

*8. CALIFORNIA STATE DEPARTMENT OF EDUCATION. (1987). *Mathematics model curriculum guide,* pp. 24–39, 47–50, 88–100. Sacramento, CA: Author.

9. CLEMENTS, D., & BATTISTA, M. (1986). Geometry and geometric measurement. *Arithmetic Teacher, 33*(6), 29–32.

*10. CROWLEY, M. (1987). The van Hiele model of the development of geometric thought. In M. M. Lindquist (Ed.), *Learning and teaching geometry, K–12* (pp. 1–16). Reston, VA: National Council of Teachers of Mathematics.

*11. FENNELL, F., & WILLIAMS, D. (COMPILERS). (1986). *Ideas from the Arithmetic Teacher, grades 4–6, intermediate school.* Reston, VA: National Council of Teachers of Mathematics.

12. FISHER, N. (1978). Visual influences of figure orientation on concept formation in geometry. In D. Mierkiewicz & R. Lesh (Eds.), *Recent research concerning the development of spatial and geometric concepts* (pp. 307–321). Columbus, OH: ERIC/SMEAC.

13. FUYS, D., GEDDES, D., & TISCHLER, R. (1984). *English translation of selected writings of Dina van Hiele-Geldof and Pierre M. van Hiele.* Columbus, OH: ERIC, ED 287 697.

*14. FUYS, D., GEDDES, D., & TISCHLER, R. (1988). The van Hiele model of thinking in geometry among adolescents. *Journal for Research in Mathematics Education, Monograph No. 3.* Reston, VA: National Council of Teachers of Mathematics.

*15. GEDDES, D. (1992). *Geometry in the middle grades.* Reston, VA: National Council of Teachers of Mathematics.

16. HEUKEROTT, P. B. (1988). Origami paper folding—The algorithmic way. *Arithmetic Teacher, 35*(5), 4–8.

17. HIEBERT, J., & CARPENTER, T. (1982). Piagetian tasks as readiness measures in mathematical instruction: A critical review. *Educational Studies in Mathematics, 13*(3), 329–345.

*18. HILL, J. M. (Ed.). (1987). *Geometry for grades K–6: Readings from the Arithmetic Teacher.* Reston, VA: National Council of Teachers of Mathematics.

19. HOFFER, A. (1983). Van Hiele-based research. In R. Lesh & M. Landau (Eds.), *Acquisition of mathematics concepts and processes* (pp. 205–228). New York: Academic Press.

20. INSTITUUT ONTWIKKELING WISKUNDE ONDERWUS (IOWO). (1976). Ship ahoy. *Educational Studies in Mathematics, 7*(3), 211–223.

*21. Jensen, R. J. (1988). Teaching mathematics with technology: Concept formation in geometry. *Arithmetic Teacher, 35*(7), 34–36.

*22. Kenney, M. J., & Bezuska, S. J. (1987). *Tessellations using LOGO.* Palo Alto, CA: Dale Seymour.

23. Kosel, M., & Fish, M. (1984). The Factory (Diskette). Pleasantville, NY: Sunburst Communications.

*24. Krause, M. (1983). *Multicultural mathematics materials.* Reston, VA: National Council of Teachers of Mathematics.

25. Lappan, G., & Winter, M. (1982). Spatial visualization. In L. Silvey (Ed.), *Mathematics for the middle grades (5–9)* (pp. 118–129). Reston, VA: National Council of Teachers of Mathematics.

26. Lappan, G., & Schram, P. W. (1989). Communication and reasoning: Critical dimensions of sense making in mathematics. In P. R. Trafton (Ed.) *New directions in elementary school mathematics* (pp. 14–30). Reston, VA: National Council of Teachers of Mathematics.

27. Lindquist, M. M., & Kouba, V. L. (1989). Geometry. In M. M. Lindquist (Ed.) *Results from the fourth assessment of the national assessment of educational progress* (pp. 44–54). Reston, VA: National Council of Teachers of Mathematics.

*28. Mathematics Resource Project. A. Hoffer (Dir.). (1978). *Geometry and visualization.* Palo Alto, CA: Creative Publications.

*29. Milauskas, G. (1987). Creative geometry problems can lead to creative problem solvers. In M. M. Lindquist (Ed.), *Learning and teaching geometry, K–12* (pp. 69–84). Reston, VA: National Council of Teachers of Mathematics.

30. Mitchelmore, M. C. (1976). Cross-cultural research on concepts of space and geometry. In J. L. Martin (Ed.), *Space and geometry* (pp. 143–184). Columbus, OH: ERIC/SMEAC.

31. National Council of Teachers of Mathematics. (1981). *Priorities in school mathematics.* Reston, VA: Author.

*32. National Council of Teachers of Mathematics. (1989). *Curriculum and evaluation standards for school mathematics.* Reston, VA: Author.

*33. National Council of Teachers of Mathematics. (1991). *Professional standards for teaching mathematics.* Reston, VA: Author.

34. Normandia, B. R. (1982). The relationship between cognitive level and modes of instruction, teacher centered and activity centered, to the learning of introductory transformational geometry (Doctoral dissertation, Rutgers University, 1981). *Dissertation Abstracts International, 43A,* 102.

35. Olson, J. K. (1986). Using Logo to supplement the teaching of geometric concepts in the elementary school classroom (Doctoral dissertation, Oklahoma State University, 1985). *Dissertation Abstracts International, 47A,* 819.

36. Peterson, J. (1973). Informal geometry in grades 7–14. In K. Henderson (Ed.), *Geometry in the mathematics curriculum* (pp. 52–91). Reston, VA: National Council of Teachers of Mathematics.

37. Piaget, J., Inhelder, B., & Szeminska, A. (1960). *The child's conception of geometry.* London: Routledge and Kegan Paul.

*38. Reesink, C. (Ed.). (1985). *Teacher-made aids for elementary school mathematics: Readings from the Arithmetic Teacher* (Vol. 2). Reston, VA: National Council of Teachers of Mathematics.

39. Rowell, J., & Mansfield, H. (1980). The teaching of transformation geometry in grade eight: A search for aptitude-treatment interaction. *Journal of Educational Research, 74*(1), 55–59.

*40. SANOK, G. (1987). Living in a world of transformations. In J. Hill (Ed.), *Geometry for grades K–6* (pp. 50–54). Reston, VA: National Council of Teachers of Mathematics.

*41. SCHWARTZ, J. L., & YERUSHALMY, M. (1986). The Geometric preSupposer and The Geometric Supposer (Diskettes). Pleasantville, NY: Sunburst Communications.

42. SHAUGHNESSY, J. M. (1989). Visualization in mathematics. In T. Cooney (Ed.), *American perspectives on the sixth international congress on mathematics education* (pp. 48–49). Reston, VA: National Council of Teachers of Mathematics.

*43. SHAUGHNESSY, J. M., & BURGER, W. F. (1985). Spadework prior to deduction in geometry. *Mathematics Teacher, 78*(6), 419–428.

44. STIGLER, J., & PERRY, M. (1988). Cross-cultural studies of mathematics teaching and learning: Recent findings and new directions. In D. Grouws & T. Cooney (Eds.), *Effective mathematics teaching* (pp. 194–223). Hillsdale, NJ: Erlbaum; Reston, VA: National Council of Teachers of Mathematics.

45. TILLOTSON, M. L. (1985). The effect of instruction in spatial visualization on spatial abilities and mathematical problem solving (Doctoral dissertation, University of Florida, 1984). *Dissertation Abstracts International, 45A,* 2792.

46. TRAFTON, P. R., & LeBLANC, J. F. (1973). Informal geometry in grades K–6. In K. Henderson (Ed.), *Geometry in the mathematics curriculum* (pp. 11–51). Reston, VA: National Council of Teachers of Mathematics.

47. VAN HIELE, P. M. (1984). A child's thought and geometry. In D. Fuys, D. Geddes, & R. Tischler (Eds.), *English translation of selected writings of Dina van Hiele-Geldof and P. M. van Hiele* (pp. 243–252). Columbus, OH: ERIC, ED 287 697.

*48. WINTER, M., LAPPAN, G., PHILLIPS, E., & FITZGERALD, W. (1986). *Middle grades mathematics project: Spatial visualization.* Reading, MA: Addison Wesley.

*49. YOUNG, J. (1982). Improving spatial abilities with geometric activities. *Arithmetic Teacher, 30*(1), 38–43.

*50. ZASLAVSKY, C. (1979). Symmetry along with other mathematical concepts and applications in African life. In S. Sharron (Ed.), *Applications in school mathematics* (pp. 82–97). Reston, VA: National Council of Teachers of Mathematics.

*51. ZASLAVSKY, C. (1989). People who live in round houses. *Arithmetic Teacher, 37*(1), 18–24.

52. ZYKOVA, V. I. (1969). The psychology of 6th grade pupils' mastery of geometric concepts. In J. Kilpatrick and I. Wirszup (Eds.), *Soviet studies in the psychology of learning and teaching mathematics,* (Vol. 1, pp. 149–188). Palo Alto, CA: School Mathematics Study Group.

PART III

Teaching

CHAPTER 12

Technology: Implications for Middle Grades Mathematics

Robert J. Jensen and Brevard S. (Bard) Williams

B.C.

J. Hart © 1990 Creators Syndicate, Inc. By permission of Johnny Hart and Creators Syndicate, Inc.

By initially "chiseling" on the mathematics curriculum with computer software that resembled electronic workbook pages, educators have, in a sense, exhibited a closed mindset about the use of the computer that parallels Peter's use of the "pencil" in the B.C. comic shown. Over time, we have begun to realize that other learning activities can take better advantage of a computer's unique capabilities. As we continue to explore possible roles for technology in the teaching and learning of middle grades mathematics, we must remain open to innovative instructional strategies, mindful that some of these approaches may change the dynamics and culture of our classrooms in significant ways.

Teachers and researchers are now also aware that technology offers no panacea for acknowledged weaknesses in the mathematics curriculum and initially complicates rather than simplifies a teacher's life. Skill in orchestrating the overall classroom learning experiences for children will continue to be the critical factor in effective instruction.

225

Is the payback in educational gains for students worth the extra effort required to implement technology in a meaningful way? There is now evidence to suggest that skillfully guided use of computers and calculators in the middle grades mathematics classroom can accomplish the following:

- increase instructional options for teaching content areas with which students have traditionally had difficulty
- allow individualization of portions of the learning environment for students
- encourage the active participation of students in building their own knowledge and understanding
- provide students with an avenue for receiving immediate, nonjudgmental feedback on their work
- provide many opportunities for cooperative problem-solving activities
- allow us to complement our traditional role of "teacher as dispenser of knowledge" with the qualitatively different role of "teacher as facilitator of learning"
- perhaps most important, be an empowering experience for many students, improving their attitudes toward mathematics, themselves, and learning

This last benefit should not be underestimated because of the direct relationship between students' disposition to learn and their subsequent achievement.

> "Information technologies have transformed the worlds of business, science, entertainment, the military, government, law, banking, travel, medicine, and agriculture. The question is whether they will make as deep a mark on classroom learning—and how." (*Power On*, 40, p. 200)

The position of the National Council of Teachers of Mathematics on the use and availability of computers and calculators is emphatic:

- appropriate calculators should be available to all students at all times;
- a computer should be available in every classroom for demonstration purposes;
- every student should have access to a computer for individual and group work;
- students should learn to use the computer as a tool for processing information and performing calculations to investigate and solve problems. (*Curriculum and Evaluation Standards*, 25, p. 9)

Government agency reports, such as *Everybody Counts* (26) and *Power On* (40), give similar mandates.

> "Rapid developments in technology are changing (and ought to be changing) the way we teach mathematics both because they modify our goals for the mathematics education of people and because they provide new tools with which we can better achieve our goals." (42, p. 60)

Before responding in a knee-jerk fashion to the NCTM *Curriculum and Evaluation Standards'* call for the use of calculators and computers, it makes sense first to consider whether there are any consistent research findings to help guide our use of these technological tools in middle grades mathematics classrooms. Researchers have observed that using computers in classrooms affects not only the curriculum but also learning interactions, classroom management, and the assessment and monitoring of student progress (15). Access to new technology is only the first step. We must also develop the associated teaching and management skills needed to apply technology effectively if we are to begin to capitalize on its potential.

Our intent is to present an overview of the research findings to date related to the use of computers and calculators in middle grades classrooms. We will first introduce a system for reflecting on the qualitatively different teaching modes that computers can be used for. Then we will report findings related to the teaching and learning of mathematical skills, concepts, and problem solving. Implications for the use of both calculators and computers to assist instruction in each of these three broad areas will be included. Along the way we will point out where gaps exist in the research base and suggest some ways for teachers to get involved by conducting their own classroom action research—not necessarily for publication but to inform their own teaching and perhaps to share with fellow teachers in their school and county. In a final section, we will discuss orchestrating the use of technology in classrooms.

Mathematics: The Driving Force of the Curriculum

Is technology the tail that wags the dog? Wisdom based on the history of pedagogical innovations in the curriculum suggests that mathematics objectives are, and should remain, the primary drive behind any decisions you make regarding the use of technology in your classroom. Using calculators and computers is not the goal; they are resources to assist children in constructing a rich understanding of mathematics. Research is clear on this point; when a teacher uses technology without first making some conscious decisions about the curriculum objectives served, children's understanding of mathematics is not improved.

Teaching Modes for the Use of Technology

Computers can be used in a variety of ways in the middle school mathematics classroom. The appropriateness of a specific approach will depend on your goal. Taylor suggests three qualitatively different ways: as a tutor, as a tutee, or as a tool (38). These pedagogical modes can apply as well to other forms of technology used in the classroom.

Tutor.   In the mode of tutor, the computer is used as a sophisticated teaching machine. Most computer assisted instruction (CAI) software falls into the "computer as a tutor" mode. Recent advances now point the way to incorporating expert teacher characteristics into the software. This will allow a program to take advantage of "teachable moments" by prompting a student with the specific information that seems most needed at that time based on the student's response pattern (43). Future developments in this area will require more advanced computer hardware than can currently be found in most schools.

"The great hope for an intelligent tutoring system is to have the program comprehend the nature of the student's misconception and select appropriate remediation, just as is currently done by a good human teacher." (20, p. 12)

Although no technology in the foreseeable future will have the level of artificial intelligence needed to approximate a good classroom teacher tutoring a student one-on-one, this lack does not preclude a place for tutorial uses of technology in our classroom, especially since we do not often have the luxury to work individually with a student. Good tutorial software can supplement instruction with a degree of individual assistance for students that would otherwise be impossible. Motivated students can achieve a level of automaticity with procedural skills through the unlimited practice and feedback that computers can provide.

Tutee. The "computer as tutee" mode suggests a role reversal. Here, the student is in charge and programs ("teaches") the computer to perform some desired action by means of a logical sequence of steps that the student constructs and enters. Advocates of student programming justify this approach with one or more of following arguments:

- Learning to program is an important life skill that should be included in the curriculum for its own sake.
- In learning to program, students experience firsthand the process of coming to know something, gaining insights and powerful ideas that can transfer to other learning situations (27).
- Constructing a program that accomplishes some mathematical procedure encourages students to analyze the procedure more carefully than they normally would, resulting in a deeper understanding of the underlying mathematics (35).

Although these claims have logical appeal, related research findings have been mixed. In particular, gains have been hard to document with currently available assessment instruments, and successful experimental learning environments are difficult to replicate in practice. Since programming languages are rapidly evolving toward higher levels and becoming more powerful, it does not seem wise, at this time, to devote a large chunk of precious curriculum time to the study of any particular programming language as a subject in the middle grades.

Developing short programs for the sake of examining mathematics ideas and concepts seems to provide the best justification for student programming (34, 12). With short tasks, less time is needed for developing programming skills, and the connection between the steps in the written computer procedure and the mathematical concepts the task is intended to reinforce is more transparent.

> *Try This:* Ask your students to write a computer program that will print out all the factors of any number entered from the keyboard. Have students compare and discuss their approaches.

Tool. The "computer as tool" mode contains the widest range of possible applications and is currently the most active area for research and development. This mode includes software "tool kits" that display graphs, manipulate symbols, analyze data, and perform mathematical procedures. In addition to mathematics-specific tools, there are many generic software tools such as spreadsheets, word processors, data bases, and communication packages with direct applicability to the mathematics classroom. Applications such as these have the additional appeal of matching the classroom's use of technology with that of society's, thus helping students see that what they learn in school has a relevance beyond the classroom.

The use of a computer as a tool is currently an exciting area for research because certain applications permit students to experience mathematics in ways that have never been possible before. Dede suggests that although intelligent machine-based tutors will gradually become useful in school settings, "cognition enhancers" designed to combine the cognitive strengths of humans and computers will evolve much more rapidly. These tools are still in their infancy, but so far three kinds seem to be emerging: empowering environments, hypermedia, and microworlds (7).

Empowering environments use the technological capacities of a machine to handle the routine mechanics of a task permitting the user to focus on decision making and constructing higher levels of understanding. These environments can be as simple as a handheld calculator used to operate efficiently with large numbers or as complex as software that performs advanced mathematical and statistical procedures, generates graphics, or produces computer simulations to investigate (see Fig. 12.1).

Hypermedia is the delivery of information in forms that go beyond traditional list and data-base report methods. Here the machine provides the user with the means for retrieving a variety of types of information—text, graphics, images, software code—all related in a nonlinear way to a central idea. In mathematics, applications of hypermedia could include "hyperworlds" featuring button-linked ideas and concepts and a variety of interactive multimedia linking mathematics to real-world animation (23). Prototypes are being developed but research is currently limited in this area.

Microworlds are learning environments in which students experimentally control and manipulate various objects and receive immediate feedback on the consequences of their manipulations (see Fig. 12.2). A set of building blocks, for example, are objects in a simple, yet powerful, microworld that allows children to construct a rich informal knowledge of basic principles in engineering and design. In any quality microworld the child is motivated by the inherent appeal of the objects under his or her control to experiment in a natural, playful way and yet in the process construct knowledge that has importance beyond the simulated environment itself. Carefully crafted computer software can provide students with a wide assortment of micro-

FIGURE 12.1   Pythagorean theorem (based on Euclid's proof)

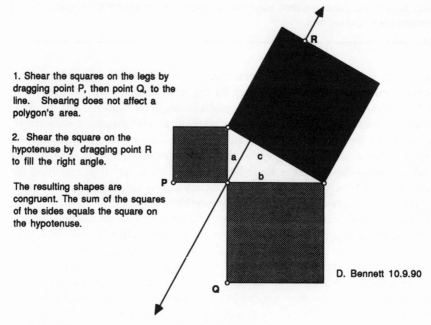

1. Shear the squares on the legs by dragging point P, then point Q, to the line.   Shearing does not affect a polygon's area.

2. Shear the square on the hypotenuse by dragging point R to fill the right angle.

The resulting shapes are congruent. The sum of the squares of the sides equals the square on the hypotenuse.

D. Bennett 10.9.90

Geometer's Sketchpad©, Key Curriculum Press, 1991 (17).

FIGURE 12.2   Tiling Microworld (18)

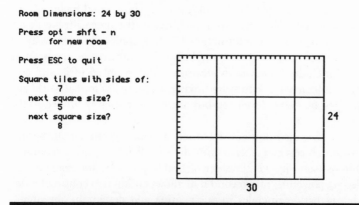

```
Room Dimensions: 24 by 30

Press opt - shft - n
      for new room

Press ESC to quit

Square tiles with sides of:
       7
  next square size?
       5
  next square size?
       8
```

24

30

8 by 8 squares can tile one dimension evenly, but not the other. To try a 24 by 30 room again, press Option-Shift-R.

  • Invent a general rule for determining the largest size square tile that will evenly tile
    rectangular rooms of integer dimensions. Use the above "Tiling Microworld" to
    experiment and collect data from rooms of various sizes.

worlds to investigate. These are made all the more powerful by the speed and accuracy by which a computer can simulate actions in these worlds.

Some applications seem to spill over into several of the tutor, tutee, or tool modes, for example, *Lego-Logo* (©LEGO Systems, Inc., 1989). Here robots can be programmed by students (tutee mode) to perform tasks (tool mode) or teach other students (tutor mode). Nevertheless, it is still helpful when planning for a lesson to consider the quantitatively different learning outcomes that are possible from the various modes.

The next sections discuss findings from research in which calculators and computers were used to assist in the teaching and learning of specific mathematics content in the middle grades. Although knowledge acquisition often involves building connections between skills and concepts through appropriate problem-solving experiences, for the sake of organization these findings have been partitioned among the areas of skill development, concept learning, and problem solving.

Teaching and Learning Procedural Skills in Mathematics

The *Curriculum and Evaluation Standards* for grades 5–8 mathematics calls for a decreased emphasis on a large portion of the procedural skills on which we have spent a great deal of time and energy in the past. Identified for decreased emphasis are

* memorizing rules and algorithms;
* practicing tedious paper-and-pencil computations;
* finding exact forms of answers; and
* memorizing procedures without understanding (25, p. 71).

This pronouncement does not mean that computational proficiency will become unimportant, just that the algorithms children use in performing complicated calculations will shift from paper-and-pencil aided to technology aided. Perhaps the most difficult aspect of implementing this recommendation will be dispelling the widely held misconception that if students are permitted to use computers and calculators to perform computations, they will not be able to perform mathematically without these crutches.

Calculators.   Research on the use of calculators has shown this fear to be ungrounded. In the last 10 years over 200 research studies have focused on the effects of calculators, especially on whether their use harms students' mathematical achievement. The evidence is overwhelmingly in favor of the use of calculators and provides little evidence of any computational debilitation (36, 28, 24).

"Rather than replacing paper-and-pencil computational procedures, calculators are more likely to reinforce them; rather than substituting for independent thought, calculators are apt to sustain it" (21, p. 32)

A summary of 79 calculator studies concluded the following:

- Students who use calculators in concert with traditional instruction maintain their paper-and-pencil skills without apparent harm.
- The use of calculators in testing produces much higher achievement scores than paper-and-pencil efforts, both in basic operations and in problem solving.
- Students using calculators possess both a better attitude toward mathematics and a better self-concept in mathematics than do those students who do not use calculators. This statement applies across all grades and ability levels (16).

Try This: Challenge your students to invent their own calculator algorithms that could be used instead of the standard paper-and-pencil procedures taught in their textbook. Be sure to have students explain why their calculator procedures work and debate the advantages and disadvantages of their method over another. Reward creativity by affixing student's names to their procedures and validate their creations by allowing their use on homework and tests.

Much of this achievement gain may be the result of an effect referred to as "time compression." In some settings and for some student populations, calculators significantly reduce the time it takes students to learn to solve problems. The use of the calculator to assist handicapped students, for instance, has allowed these students to master tasks quickly that might have taken them hours using the traditional pencil-and-paper method (37). Results of a study involving a calculator that was purposely wired to produce incorrect answers does suggest, however, that students often place too much trust in a calculator's answer (29).

Try This: Encourage students to question the reasonableness of all answers, especially those produced by a calculator or a computer.

Computers. For over 30 years, mathematics educators have been using computer-assisted instruction (CAI) to tutor and drill students in basic skills. Quality drill and practice applications carefully guide the student through problems presented at prescribed levels of difficulty, branching to help or remedial areas when objectives are not achieved. Programs can also keep records of student progress and allow teachers to set up a "prescribed learning environment." In the prescribed environment, the teacher determines which skills need work and configures the program to present the student with choices specifically linked to the objective at hand. Additionally, some programs allow the teacher to control the difficulty level, speed of presentation, and length of session from within the program.

Many research studies have been conducted over the years to assess the effectiveness of CAI in the teaching of basic skills. Syntheses of this large research base have indicated that although methodological problems exist in many of these studies, there is a high degree of consistency across studies to support the following findings (2, 4, 22):

- When CAI is used as a supplement to traditional instruction, it is more effective than traditional instruction alone.
- When CAI is used as the sole basis for instruction, results are mixed.
- CAI is more effective at raising achievement among low- and high-achieving students than among average students.
- Short daily sessions are more effective than are long and infrequent ones.
- Students complete the material faster with CAI than with traditional instruction.
- Most studies reported significant, positive change in student attendance and motivation as well as an increase in attention span. In some cases, these positive effects were found to transfer to other classroom tasks, especially with special education students.
- "Passive" students reported feeling more in control and behaved more independently.

One researcher recently raised a warning flag that CAI is most effective for capable students and therefore may actually widen the gap between high- and low-achieving students (13). This study suggests that able students displayed various qualities, unrelated to mathematics, that the less able students did not display to nearly the same degree. These included a good memory, an ability to learn from mistakes, an aggressiveness in asking for help, and task persistence.

The generally positive findings from the use of the skill development software produced to date suggest that as intelligent computer-assisted instruction (ICAI) becomes more available these findings should become even more pronounced. Software will soon be available that reinforces student progress in intermittently scheduled cycles rather than after each problem, increasing the likelihood that the student will focus more on accuracy than immediate feedback in the learning process. Additionally, teachers will be able to obtain analyses of student learning rates and difficulty areas and use the information to help guide instruction in the regular classroom.

"Students work longer on computer activities than they do on traditional activities, and talk more about the tasks." (21, p. 35)

Other Technology. The yoke of keyboarding has been reduced through alternate input devices such as a "mouse," "trackball," "light" pen, or "touch screen." Recent advances in speech synthesis technology now even allow students to "speak" their answers—convenient for the average child but a clear breakthrough for the physically disabled. Another exciting area for development is the use of videodisc technology which when coupled with a computer will branch to appropriate video segments that can introduce, demonstrate, or review, not only procedural skills but concepts as well.

Teaching and Learning Mathematical Concepts

The introduction and development of concepts forms the backbone of mathematics instruction. There is great potential for using technology to assist students in constructing a rich interconnected network of conceptual understanding.

Calculators.   Little research has been reported regarding the teaching of mathematical concepts with calculators. With the advent of inexpensive calculators that are programmable, produce graphics, and work in fractional and algebraic notation, new approaches for developing and reinforcing concepts become possible. For example, with a graphing calculator students can quickly generate a geometric base for exploring the concept of function. There is a real need here for teachers to be innovative, experiment in their own classes, and share what they learn with others.

Computers.   Computers are a natural medium for producing an unlimited number of examples and nonexamples for a given concept. The difficulties involved in constructing a "good" definition and the recognition that there may be alternate definitions that are equally appropriate are excellent experiences for middle grades students who will grapple with these same issues on a more formal level in their high school classes.

Try this: Place students in small groups and ask them to create their own definition for *convex polygon* based on examples and nonexamples that are randomly generated for them by a computer programmed to do so. Have groups share their definitions and then challenge them to see if each group's proposed definition encompasses all shapes that are convex polygons without including shapes that are not.

Student programming can help students develop links between what they know about a certain concept from its definition with what that translates to procedurally. For example, writing a Logo procedure that produces a regular hexagon by repeating the sequence—move forward 50 spaces then turn right 60 degrees—six times provides the learner with a more active perspective of a regular hexagon than its formal definition would (see Fig. 12.3).

Appropriate tasks need not be limited to geometry or Logo turtle graphics. Creating a simple BASIC program, such as one that generates the least common multiple of two numbers, would certainly enrich the student programmer's conceptual knowledge of "multiples," "common multiples," and "least common multiples."

A particularly exciting development in the area of concept acquisition is the use of computers to present linked multiple representations of a concept by means of hypermedia software, such as *HyperCard* (©Apple Computer, Inc., 1991), *Hyper-Studio* (©Wagner Pub., Inc., 1991), or *LinkWay* (©IBM Corp., 1990). Here, one area of the screen, called a window, can show the formal definition, another can show a procedural definition, while a third could produce a random example or nonexample on student command. Additional windows of information, such as historical background, applications of the concept to other areas of the curriculum, or

FIGURE 12.3   Concept: Regular hexagon

Definitional approach

A *regular hexagon* is a six-sided polygon with all angles and all sides equal.

Procedural approach

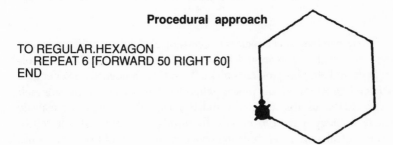

```
TO REGULAR.HEXAGON
    REPEAT 6 [FORWARD 50 RIGHT 60]
END
```

even a related microworld environment to investigate, could be accessed by clicking on-screen buttons (23).

Dynamic linking of various representational windows permits changes in one representation to cause simultaneous changes in the others. Since research has found that students differ widely in their abilities to understand and use particular representations, having several representations available allows students to develop their conceptual understanding by focusing on the representational mode or modes most effective for them. Researchers are now actively engaged in studying the educational potential of such software for the teaching and learning of concepts in geometry, algebra, and proportional reasoning (9, 19).

Other Technology.   The power of telecommunications brings untold resources to the mathematics classroom. Imagine a classroom in which students from all over the country participate in online question and answer sessions with people who can express the excitement, utility, and beauty of mathematics. An extension of telecommunications, distance learning, allows the "resident expert" to be beamed via satellite into your classroom with full two-way interaction. Pioneers in mathematics and science can present simulations and conduct experiments that help students develop concepts difficult to convey in a traditional classroom.

Problem Solving and Mathematical Reasoning

Engaging in the problem-solving process means that one is willing to invest time and energy in a problem without assurance that success will be forthcoming or even possible. Researchers have consistently found that technology can have a positive effect on both problem-solving achievement and attitudes toward the activity of problem solving.

Theories of cognitive science suggest that learning does not necessarily progress by building up knowledge one step at a time but often comes in leaps made possible by reconceiving an entire interconnected network of knowledge. These theories imply that students who have not mastered paper-and-pencil computations could still gain intellectually from problem-solving software that emphasizes higher level thinking processes. When working on problems students should have access to the same technological tools that would be natural to use in problem solving outside the classroom (see Fig. 12.4).

Calculators.   The research evidence is clear concerning calculators. When provided with calculators—the least expensive and most prevalent technological tools available—students perform better on problem-solving tasks (16). Students are better able to manage the overall problem-solving process when they are not expending so much energy on its computational aspects. Guess and test also becomes a more realistic approach when technology is used to remove the drudgery of recalculating results with different inputs. Calculators let students solve challenging problems that would otherwise take too much time with paper and pencil.

Try This: Provide students with calculators whenever they are engaged in solving problems. After a time, reflect on any changes you note with respect to level of success, persistence, and attitudes toward problem solving. Briefly interview several of your students to get their perspective.

FIGURE 12.4   Problem-solving task

Experiment with the following procedure written in *Logo*. What effect do changes in the value of the first variable "*X* have on the resulting display? What effect do changes in the value of the second variable "*A* have? The third variable "*N*? Can you figure out a combination of values to enter for "*X*, "*A* and "*N* that will result in a regular pentagon? A regular hexagon of perimeter 120? A regular quadrilateral of area 625?, etc. Be prepared to discuss your findings.

```
TO POLY :X :A :N
   REPEAT :N [FORWARD: X Left :A]
END
```

POLY 60 80 5

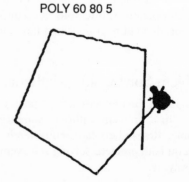

Computers.   A computer can be an invaluable tool to help the problem solver focus on generating ideas, trying out various approaches, and checking hunches. Computers put students in the position of being able to test their conjectures rather painlessly since the machine can produce an endless stream of output that students can use as data for testing and revising their conjectures (32).

Problem formulation is an important aspect of problem solving that has not received much research attention. Computer microworlds provide a powerful arena for problem posing and mucking about with mathematical ideas. Students can play "what-if" in a microworld environment in ways that would be impossible otherwise (see Fig. 12.5). In addition, investigations of microworlds allow students to see the effects of operations that they perform within this system on the overall mathematical system modeled (39). An apt analogy would be to consider microworlds as useful to your students in much the same way that "busy boxes" are useful to very young children. Both allow children to experiment with interesting objects that provide them with direct feedback on the consequences of their actions, all within a safe environment.

The ability to monitor and manage thinking processes has been established as an important, though often overlooked, aspect of problem solving. Well-conceived tutorial software can provide students with a step-by-step record, called an audit trail, of actions taken in the problem-solving process. Although little research exists in this area, exploration of systems that assist students in managing their thinking processes is a future direction for research in the metacognitive aspects of problem solving.

Other Technology.   Telecommunication stands to revolutionize information exchange in the classrooms. Through modem-accessible networks (e.g., *America Online,* ©Quantum Computer Services, Inc., 1991, and *KidsNet,* ©National Geographic Society, 1990) students can solve problems in collaborative efforts shared by students nationwide. This exciting environment presents much promise in the mid-

FIGURE 12.5   Billiards Microworld (18)

This microworld simulates the path of a ball on tables of various dimensions.

The ball starts at a 45 degree angle from the lower left corner and bounces until it hits a corner.

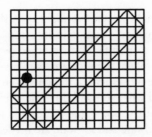

Stopped!!! in Table 16 x 14

dle grades where students are in the process of leaving the ego-centricism of early childhood and are beginning to search for meaningful connections between their lives as students and the world beyond school. Problems posed by professionals from a variety of industries can reveal the relevance of mathematics in addressing social and environmental problems and serve as a powerful response to middle grade students' inevitable questions about the usefulness of their mathematics classwork.

The Teacher Factor

Orchestrating Technology

A Rand Corporation study interviewed and visited the classroom of teachers identified by peers and administrators as successful users of computer software. A pattern of computer use, identified as "orchestration," was the one most associated with significant improvement in the academic achievement of children. Teachers in this orchestration cluster stressed both cognitive and basic-skills goals, used a variety of instructional modes to meet these goals, integrated the content of computer-based instruction with the ongoing curriculum, and changed their uses based on feedback from students. Although these teachers did use the more traditional drill and practice software, they also mixed in tutorials, simulations, microworld investigations, games, and other applications when appropriate to achieve curriculum goals (33).

Researchers have found that when placed in technology-enriched classrooms, experienced teachers undergo managerial concerns not unlike novice teachers. Their initial concern is "survival" in the new environment. Teachers at first spend considerable time trying to "fix" immediate problems. Only later do they begin to anticipate problems effectively and develop strategies for solving them. Teachers need time—typically a year or so—before they can shift their efforts from managerial to curricular concerns. At that time teachers begin to reflect on the various effects of technology on their teaching, and based on this knowledge, integrate technology in a more strategic, goal-directed fashion (31).

> "Instructional innovation [with computers] begins to emerge when teachers have achieved a significant level of mastery over management issues." (31, p. 7)

Recognizing that change will not happen overnight, you should take a proactive role in the management of instruction. Your role in these situations needs to be flexible. You may find that your role shifts from resource person to task-setter, explainer to counselor, manager to fellow pupil or any combination of these (11). Include in your plans ideas about the movement of students to and from the computers, the availability of equipment, and what you will do if the equipment fails.

Call upon trained paraprofessionals, peers, and students to help you over the hurdles that inevitably arise when hardware and software are invited into your classroom. Discuss the use of technology and specific software programs with other teachers—

learn from their experiences. Here are some hints for an effectively managed technology-assisted lesson (41):

- Provide both oral and written directions for the use of the software.
- Make sure students understand the basic on/off procedures of the computer and how to care for the media.
- Develop methods to ensure the equitable use of equipment; wall charts, computer logs, and cards are effective.
- Develop a method for a student to get your attention for help while working at the computer.

Try This: Place a plastic cup atop the monitor as a nondisruptive "help" flag and encourage students to put their hands back on the keys while waiting for you to help; often they solve their own problems.

- Try to avoid using software as a "reward" for class achievement. Not only will this discriminate against students who choose not to compete but will also send the wrong message that technology is only for the brightest students.
- Preview the software.
- Be aware of the time spent using the software. Use a timer or other method to monitor student access.
- Identify students and teachers who might be available to help you in the planning and management of your lesson.

One other important organizational decision you will need to make is how to group your students. National survey data reveal that female students, irrespective of class or ethnicity, currently have less involvement with computers in schools than do male students (5). Research pertinent to this issue suggests that girls tend to favor and perform better in collaborative and cooperative learning experiences than in purely isolated and competitive ones (1, 6). Other researchers confirm this, reporting that girls became as involved as their male peers if computer-related activities were posed within a cooperative learning format that emphasized activity-centered learning (14, 30). The Lawrence Hall of Science has produced excellent classroom-tested activities books, such as *Off and Running* (10), based on these principles.

Try This: Organize your class into cooperative learning groups when using computers. Critique the results of each group's collaborative effort separately to downplay competition among groups.

Teacher as Researcher

Most of the studies reported in the research literature are limited by the artificiality imposed on the natural learning environment by an outside researcher. As a full-time classroom teacher you have a unique opportunity to observe and document the learning outcomes of students using technology in various ways in your mathematics classroom. We have suggested a few ideas for classroom action research that you might conduct yourself. Specifics, however, are less important than a commitment to a classroom research process that seeks answers to you own questions that can in turn inform your classroom teaching.

Our message is similar to Nike's sporting shoe ad campaign: *"Just Do It."* For example, you might begin by identifying just two students who display a wide difference in behavior or learning outcome after participating in the same computer activity. What characteristics of these students seem to have been critical to their relative success in this particular learning activity? What implications does this have for the way you would organize this same activity next time? Share with others what you are learning from your own students as you experiment with various strategies for integrating technologies in your mathematics classroom.

Curriculum Change

Computers and calculators may permit us to envision sweeping changes in the curriculum and teaching of middle grades mathematics but research findings are more sobering: Initially, teachers and schools that provide students with substantial computer experiences will implement a fairly traditional program of instruction (3). It is not until teachers have had the time and training needed to appropriate these new tools that they feel comfortable in being creative in their use (8). At that point the central educational question becomes "What is important to know?" The *Curriculum and Evaluation Standards* represent the NCTM's broad-based response to this question and gives a cohesive vision for mathematics education in North America. Some uses of technology in classrooms do not fit nicely in the traditional curriculum. We must be willing to modify our curriculum if in so doing the new direction better supports the development of higher order problem-solving skills—the "basic skills" of our information age.

Looking Ahead . . .

Will there come a day when a teacher can challenge all students with computer-based instruction that is powerful, flexible, meaningful, fun, and uses real-world applications of mathematics? Will recent innovations in integrated learning systems foster or stifle creativity in the use of mathematics software? Will businesses and community leaders support mathematics instruction and help ensure student access to state-of-the-art instructional technology? What will the availability of a global telecommunications network mean to mathematics instruction? What are the possibilities of using multimedia to support mathematics instruction? In some ways "the journey is the reward" as teachers and students work together to find the best application of emerging technologies. Teachers need to join with researchers in the development and refinement of the new technology.

Bard Williams

Schools are now beginning to issue calculators in much the same way as textbooks; cost-effective clipboard-sized computers will also be made available in the near future. Will we begin to decrease the gap between technological potential and classroom reality? Access to technological tools can greatly influence patterns of teaching and learning, but a paradigm shift will be necessary if real change is to occur. Testing, under these assumptions, will shift toward student demonstrated proficiency in problem solving. The direction of future research will parallel changes in the mathematics curriculum itself as we struggle with the question: "What is most important to know?" I also envision the mathematics education community as recognizing more fully the importance of classroom teachers as equal partners in the research process.

Bob Jensen

About the Authors

Bob Jensen is currently an associate professor of mathematics education at Emory University. His interests include problem posing and the design and implementation of computer microworld investigations for middle grades. He was a middle school mathematics teacher in Stamford, Connecticut, and Miami, Florida.

Bard Williams is currently coordinator of instructional technology for the public schools in Gwinnett County, a suburb of Atlanta. His interests include integrating technology into the mathematics curriculum, Logo microworlds, multimedia, and problem-solving activities. Bard taught middle school mathematics, science, and computer applications for 12 years.

References

1. AMERICAN ASSOCIATION FOR THE ADVANCEMENT OF SCIENCE (AAAS). (1984). *Equity and excellence: Compatible goals. An assessment of programs that facilitate increased access and achievement of females and minorities in K–12 mathematics and science education* (AAAS Pub. No. 84-14). Washington, DC: Office of Opportunities and Science.

*2. BECKER, H. J. (1987). *The impact of computer use on children's learning: What research has shown and what it has not.* Baltimore, MD: Center for Research on Elementary and Middle Schools, Johns Hopkins University.

3. BECKER, H. (1990). *Effects of computer use on mathematics achievement: Findings from a nationwide field experience in grade five to eight classes.* Baltimore: Center for Social Organization of Schools, Johns Hopkins University.

4. CAPPER, J., & COPPLE, C. (1985). Computers in education: Research review and instructional implications. *The Research into Practice Digest, 1*(3).

5. CENTER FOR SOCIAL ORGANIZATION OF SCHOOLS (CSOS). (1983–84). *School uses of microcomputers: Reports from a national survey (Issues 1-6).* Baltimore: Johns Hopkins University.

6. COLE, M., GRIFFIN, P., & LABORATORY OF COMPARATIVE HUMAN COGNITION (LCHC). (1987). *Contextual factors in education: Improving science and mathematics education for minorities and women.* Madison: Wisconsin Center for Educational Research.

7. DEDE, C. J. (1987). Empowering environments, hypermedia and microworlds. *The Computer Teacher, 15*(3), 20–24,61.

*8. DWYER, D. C., RINGSTAFF, C., & SANDHOLTZ, J. H. (1991). Changes in teachers' beliefs and practices in technology-rich classrooms. *Educational Leadership, 48*(8), 45–52.

9. EDUCATIONAL TECHNOLOGY CENTER. (1988). *Making sense of the future: A position paper on the role of technology in science, mathematics, and computer education.* Cambridge, MA: Harvard Graduate School of Education.

*10. ERICKSON, T. (1986). *Off & running: The computer offline activities book.* Berkeley, CA: EQUALS, Lawrence Hall of Science.

11. FRASER, R., BURKHARDT, H., COUPLAND, J., PHILLIPS, R., PIMM, D., & RIDGWAY, J. (1987). Learning activities and classroom roles with and without computers. *Journal of Mathematical Behavior, 6*(3), 305–338.

*12. HATFIELD, L. L. (1983). Teaching mathematics with microcomputers: Junior high school. *Arithmetic Teacher* (Focus Issue: Teaching with microcomputers), *30*(6), 44–45, 68–69.

13. HATIVA, N. (1988). Computer-based drill and practice in arithmetic: Widening the gap between high- and low-achieving students. *American Educational Research Journal, 25*(3), 366–397.

14. HAWKINS, J. (1987). Computers and girls: Rethinking the issues. In R. D. Pea and K. Sheingold (Eds.), *Mirrors of minds: Patterns of experience in educational computing.* Norwood, NJ: Ablex.

15. HAWKINS, J., & SHEINGOLD, K. (1986). The beginnings of a story: Computers and organizations of learning in classrooms. In J. A. Culbertson & L. L. Cunningham (Eds.), *Microcomputers and education: 85th Yearbook of the National Society for the Study of Education* (pp. 40–58). Chicago: University of Chicago Press.

16. HEMBREE, R., & DESSART, D. J. (1986). Effects of hand-held calculators in precollege mathematics: A meta-analysis. *Journal for Research in Mathematics Education, 17*(2), 83–99.

17. JACKIW, N. (1991). *The Geometer's Sketchpad.* [Computer program]. Berkeley, CA: Key Curriculum Press.

18. JENSEN, R. J. (1992). *ICIM Project Microworlds* [Computer programs]. Atlanta: Emory University. (See *A teacher enhancement model for integrating computer microworlds in middle grade mathematics,* Final report. National Science Foundation 8751325).

19. KAPUT, J. J. (1986). Information technology and mathematics: Opening new representational windows. *Journal of Mathematical Behavior, 5*(2), 187–207.

*20. KNEZEK, G. A. (1988). Intelligent tutoring systems and ICAI. *Computing Teacher, 15*(6), 11–13.

21. KOBER, N. (1991). *What we know about mathematics teaching and learning.* Tallahassee: Council for Educational Development and Southeastern Regional Vision for Education.

22. KULIK, J. A., & KULIK, C. C. (1985). Effectiveness of computer-based education in elementary schools. *Computers in Human Behavior, 1,* 59–74.

23. LEHRER, R., KNIGHT, W., SANCILIO, L., & LOVE, M. (1989, March). *Software to link action and description in pre-proof geometry.* Paper presented at the annual American Educational Research Association meeting, San Francisco.

*24. NATIONAL COUNCIL OF TEACHERS OF MATHEMATICS. (1987). Calculators (Focus Issue). *Arithmetic Teacher, 34*(6).

*25. NATIONAL COUNCIL OF TEACHER OF MATHEMATICS. (1989). *Curriculum and evaluation standards for school mathematics.* Reston, VA: Author.

*26. NATIONAL RESEARCH COUNCIL. (1989). *Everybody counts: A report to the nation on the future of mathematics education.* Washington, DC: National Academy Press.

27. PAPERT, S. (1980). *Mindstorms: Children, computers, and powerful ideas.* New York: Basic Books.

*28. REYS, B. J., & REYS, R. E. (1987). Calculators in the classroom: How can we make it happen? *Arithmetic Teacher, 34*(6), 12–14.

29. REYS, R. E., BESTGEN, B. J., RYBOLT, J. F., & WYATT, J. W. (1980). *Identification and characterization of computational estimation processes used by in-school pupils and out-of-school adults.* Washington, DC: National Institute of Education.

*30. SANDERS, J. S., & STONE, A. (1986). *The neuter computer: Computers for girls and boys.* New York: Neal-Schuman.

31. SANDHOLTZ, J. H., RINGSTAFF, C., & DWYER, D. C. (1990, April). *Teaching in high tech environments: Classroom management revisited* (ACOT Report #10). Paper presented at the annual meeting of the American Educational Research Association, Boston.

32. SCHWARTZ, J. L., & YERUSHALMY, M. (1987). The Geometric Supposer: An intellectual prosthesis for making conjectures. *College Mathematics Journal, 18*(1), 58–65.

33. SHAVELSON, R. J., WINKLER, J. D., STASZ, C., FEIBEL, W., ROBYN, A. E., & SHARAN, Y. (1984). *"Successful" teachers' patterns of microcomputer-based mathematics and science instruction* (Report to the National Institute of Education). Santa Monica, CA: Rand Corp.

*34. SHUMWAY, R. J. (1983). Let kids write programs. *Arithmetic Teacher* (Focus issue: Teaching with microcomputers), *30*(6), 2,56.

*35. SHUMWAY, R. J. (1984). Young children, programming and mathematical thinking. In V. P. Hansen (Ed.), *Computers in mathematics education.* Reston, VA: National Council of Teachers of Mathematics.

*36. SHUMWAY, R. J. (1988). Calculators and computers. In T. R. Post (Ed.), *Teaching mathematics in grades K–8: Research based methods* (pp. 334–383). Newton, MA: Allyn & Bacon.

*37. SUYDAM, M. N. (1987). Research report: What are calculators good for? *Arithmetic Teacher, 34*(6), 22.

38. TAYLOR, R. (1980). *The computer in the school: Tutor, tool, tutee.* New York: Teachers College Press.

39. THOMPSON, P. (1985). Experience, problem solving, and learning mathematics: Considerations in developing mathematics curriculum. In E. A. Silver (Ed.), *Teaching and learning mathematical problem solving: Multiple research perspectives* (pp. 281–294). Hillsdale, NJ: Erlbaum.

40. U.S. CONGRESS OFFICE OF TECHNOLOGY ASSESSMENT. (1988). *Power on! New tools for teaching and learning* (OTA-SET-379). Washington, DC: U.S. Government Printing Office.

*41. WILLIAMS, B. S. (1989). *Managing the use of computers.* Gwinnett County, GA: Gwinnett County Schools.

*42. WILLOUGHBY, S. S. (1990). *Mathematics education in a changing world.* Alexandria, VA: Association for Supervision and Curriculum Development.

43. YAZDANI, M. (1987). Intelligent tutoring systems: An overview. In R. W. Lawler and M. Yazdani (Eds.), *Artificial intelligence and education: Vol. 1. Learning environments and tutoring systems.* Norwood, NJ: Ablex.

CHAPTER 13

Models of Instruction

William M. Fitzgerald and Mary Kay Bouck

> *Mathematics is a useful, exciting, and creative area of study that can be appreciated and enjoyed by all students in grades 5–8. It helps them develop their ability to solve problems and reason logically. It offers to these curious, energetic students a way to explore and make sense of their world. However, . . . instruction has emphasized computational facility at the expense of a broad, integrated view of mathematics and has reflected neither the vitality of the subject nor the characteristics of the students. (Curriculum and Evaluation Standards, 21, p. 65)*

This powerful paragraph is asking all of us in mathematics education to take a hard look at the instruction we are offering to students in mathematics classrooms in grades 5–8. This same concern was expressed by the National Research Council in its publication, *Everybody Counts*, when it stated, "Much of the failure in school mathematics is due to a tradition of teaching that is inappropriate to the way most students learn" (23, p. 6).

> "Students' opportunities to learn mathematics are a function of the setting and the kinds of tasks and discourse in which they participate. What students learn—about particular concepts and procedures as well as about thinking mathematically—depends on the ways in which they engage in mathematical activity in the classroom." (*Professional Teaching Standards,* 22, p. 21)

Later the same publication states:

> Effective teachers are those who can stimulate students to learn mathematics. Educational research offers compelling evidence that they construct their own

mathematical understanding. To understand what they learn, they must enact for themselves verbs that permeate the mathematics curriculum: "examine," "represent," "transform," "solve," "apply," "prove," "communicate." This happens most readily when students work in groups, engage in discussion, make presentations, and in other ways take charge of their own learning. (23, pp. 58–59)

If we are to respond to the changes called for by the NCTM *Curriculum and Evaluation Standards* and the *Professional Standards for Teaching* (21,22) we must find ways to break away from the lessons that have taken place in so many mathematics classes, review those models that are consciously designed to make mathematics exciting by presenting a broader view of the subject, and, at the same time, help students develop their ability to solve problems and reason logically.

"All students engage in a great deal of invention as they learn mathematics; they impose their own interpretation on what is presented to create a theory that makes sense to them. Students do not learn simply a subset of what they have been shown. Instead, they use new information to modify their prior beliefs. As a consequence, each student's knowledge of mathematics is uniquely personal." (*Professional Teaching Standards*, 22, p. 2)

If you are a typical teacher in a middle grade classroom today, you have come through 12 years of elementary, middle, and high school and through a four-year college in which most or all of the mathematics you have seen taught or that has been taught to you was taught in a direct instructional manner. By the time you were ready to become a middle grades mathematics teacher, you had already spent years observing the teaching of mathematics, both as a student and as a prospective teacher. The experiences you have had with mathematics undoubtedly shaped your feelings about the subject and about yourself as a student of mathematics (2).

Direct Instruction

The most commonly used model of instruction in mathematics classes at all levels is direct instruction (6). Direct instruction is generally considered to be the most effective way to promote the learning of basic skills in mathematics (5). According to Peterson, "students learn more efficiently when their teachers first structure new information for them and help them relate it to what they already know, then monitor their performance and provide corrective feedback recitation, drill, practice, or application activity" (24, p. 5).

When 2,400 principals of schools including grade 7 were asked, they reported the most frequent instructional approach in mathematics was drill and practice (13). Typical math teachers give daily drills on computation in 78% of the schools; they emphasize applications and problem solving in only 25% of the schools. In 43% of the schools, teachers rarely or never allow students to use calculators.

> "We must give up the outdated notion that one can assess the learning of mathematics solely in terms of the ability to produce correct answers." (26, p. 869)

Brophy and Good assert that direct instruction might serve to promote the development of higher order mathematical knowledge and skills as well as it promotes lower order thinking. This assertion is challenged by Peterson who suggests that direct instruction may be insufficient to develop the self-discovery and independence learners need to function at a higher level of thinking and learning (25). Doyle also suggests that less direct instruction might be needed to teach students higher level thinking skills in mathematics. They need the opportunity for self-discovery and activities unstructured enough to allow them to derive generalizations and to invent their own algorithms (12).

A Pause for Some Questions

There are specific sources giving rise to the contention that exists today in thought and discourse regarding the teaching of mathematics among teachers and mathematics educators. Some of those sources are one's conception of the nature of mathematics, what it means to learn and understand mathematics, and how to teach mathematics most effectively.

The differing views of the nature of mathematics arise from the relative value one places on the process of doing mathematics as opposed to knowing mathematics. Does one need to create his or her own mathematics to know it, or can he or she be told and allowed to practice the mathematics and simply remember it to play back on an exam? On the other hand, knowledge is sometimes classified as procedural when we only learn to do the arithmetic, or conceptual when we learn why we do arithmetic as we do (10).

When does a person understand mathematics? There are many different answers to this question and these differences are reflected in assessment procedures that are employed by middle grades teachers, school systems, employers, and Ph.D. committees. The word *understand* takes on various meanings in different settings. If you get the right answer, do you understand? Do you have to be able to explain why, or to be able to teach it to others really to understand? Richard Skemp, the renowned British psychologist, has devoted his professional life to answering this question (28).

The idea that all must construct their own mathematical knowledge from their experience with their spatial and quantitative environment suggests that the role of a teacher of mathematics might become very different from what is seen in common practice. The literature of the past few years has been broadcasting this message to all who would hear. Maybe now more teachers are in a position to learn about the implications of these different conceptions of teaching. The complete series of Research into Practice published in the 1990–91 *Arithmetic Teacher* is devoted to examples of a constructivist approach in action. Impressive specific results have been observed in New Jersey where teachers have had the advantage of several continuous

---

In changing the classroom environment, the teachers' role will need to include

- "Helping students work together to make sense of mathematics . . .
- Helping students to rely more on themselves to determine whether something is mathematically correct . . .
- Helping students to reason mathematically . . .
- Helping students learn to conjecture, invent, and solve problems . . .
- Helping students to connect mathematics, its ideas, and its applications" (*Professional Teaching Standards,* 22, pp. 3–4)

---

years of workshop experience. These results show that positive gains in mathematics learning among children in grades 7 and 8 can be measured with instruments even so crude as standardized tests (20).

The answer to the question of how best to teach mathematics depends on one's conceptions of what it means to know mathematics and the related question, how is mathematics learned by people? These questions classically appear to be answered implicitly by common practice. Most instruction is direct instruction. Most assessment is simple short-answer or multiple-choice response. If one concludes that the most common conceptions of knowing, learning, and teaching mathematics are reflected by current practice, then current practice and the *Standards* do not have the same agenda. One purpose of the *Curriculum and Evaluations Standards* is to question general thinking about knowing, learning, and teaching mathematics in the hope of improving the mathematics education of all children.

"The discourse of the mathematics class should be founded on mathematical ways of knowing and ways of communicating. The nature of the activity and talk in the classroom shapes each student's opportunities to learn about particular topics as well as to develop their abilities to reason and communicate about those topics." (*Professional Teaching Standards,* 22, p. 54)

Alternatives to Direct Instruction

There are many possible alternatives to direct instruction. These alternatives have been developed by teachers and in projects throughout the world at least since Xenophanes in the sixth century B.C. (32).

Teaching Mathematical Activities

Teaching mathematics in an active manner has had many names. The mathematics laboratory was widely discussed and sometimes practiced in the late 1960s and early 1970s. A mathematics laboratory is a classroom equipped with a rich variety of materials which children can use to explore and experiment with mathematical ideas individually or in small groups. The teacher's role in such a classroom is that of an overseer moving about helping students, asking questions, challenging conclusions, and generally encouraging inquiry. Some excellent sources for teachers were published and read widely (4,11,16). All of these voices were calling for the same approach to mathematics that is currently being called for in the NCTM *Curriculum and Evaluation Standards*. Barson reported that 75 out of 266 elementary schools in Philadelphia had active mathematics laboratories in 1971 (3). The demise of the laboratories in Philadelphia was attributed to several factors: the reduction of funding, high turnover of teachers, parent resistance, discipline problems, an increased focus on reading, and impatient principals pushing teachers to change their teaching patterns. The accountability movement developing in the mid-1970s caused teachers to have to focus on the low-level "basic" skills that were measured by the routine standardized tests. Teachers abandoned the idea of mathematics laboratories as being too expensive in terms of time, equipment, and energy.

"The picture of how students learn based on recent research is quite different from that assumed in traditional classrooms. This perspective is that learners construct knowledge, they do not simply absorb what they are told." (26, p. 859)

Another attempt heavily funded by the National Science Foundation (NSF) in the early 1970s and which also was swamped by the tidal wave of "back to basics" was the Unified Science and Mathematics for Elementary School (USMES) Project (19). This multidisciplinary approach to problem solving engaged whole classes in trying to find the solutions to long-range, complicated problems such as, "What kind of shapes make fair dice?" or "Is our lunch line as efficient as it might be?" Even though the evidence was built rather strongly in favor of positive effects on children's problem-solving behavior, when the outside incentives vanished, so did the programs.

Recently new activity-oriented programs have begun to emerge resembling strongly some of those of past times. Activities in Mathematics and Science (AIMS) grew from an NSF-funded teacher enhancement project at Fresno Pacific College in 1982 (1). The project is now under the umbrella of the AIMS Education Foundation which has produced varieties of curriculum materials to be used in elementary and middle grades, conducts many workshops, and publishes a newsletter. Very little formal evaluation or assessment has been done within the project, but the growth and the popularity of the ideas with teachers and administrators indicate that the activities developed by AIMS are worth exploring.

Teaching Integrated Mathematics and Science (TIMS) is a K–8 curriculum development project that has devised more than 80 experiments for helping students understand fundamental scientific and mathematical concepts, variables, and methods (31). TIMS is an ongoing process of research, development, and implementation that started over 13 years ago and is presently funded by the NSF. The experiments in TIMS use a simple four-step method: picture, table, graph, and questions. Like AIMS, TIMS has not attempted to justify its value by using standardized commercial measures that do not reflect the goals of the project.

> "To improve their mathematics instruction, teachers must constantly analyze what they and their students are doing and how that is affecting what the students are learning." (*Professional Teaching Standards,* 22, p. 67)

Materials produced by the Regional Math Network centered at Harvard University consist of four collections of activities focusing on common social themes (14). The four themes are Sports Shorts, Ice Cream Dreams, Quincy Market, and Math Space Mission. This project supplements the regular curriculum with activities that invite students to pose and solve problems related to each theme.

The Used Numbers Project is a K–6 project in which the students engage in activities that help them learn to deal with quantitative information in intelligent ways (27). A main concern of this project is development of the concept of what is typical (averages). One might find the students in a class counting the number of raisins in small boxes to determine the average number of raisins, the range of the distribution, and the amount of variation of the number of raisins in the boxes.

The Middle Grades Mathematics Project (MGMP) at Michigan State University has produced five units of innovative, activity-oriented curriculum materials (18). The central focus of each unit in this project is a collection of important mathematical ideas and their interrelationships. Units produced thus far are Probability, Similarity, Spatial Visualization, Factors and Multiples, and Measuring Growth (Mouse and Elephant). Each unit is a sequence of activities built around mathematical challenges. Embedded in each activity is a consistent instructional model with three phases: Launching, Exploring, and Summarizing.

> "Beyond the standard fare of number concepts and operations, the school curriculum must include serious exploration of geometry, measurement, statistics, probability, algebra, and functions." (*Professional Teaching Standards,* 22, p. 19)

The students are motivated to pursue the solution to the challenges because of the intrinsic interest of the challenge itself. They gather data in small groups, then report back to the class so all the groups' data can be organized and summarized; generalizations can then be discovered and described. The teacher's role in a classroom using the MGMP materials varies from teaching the whole class when introducing the challenge, to working with small groups during the exploration, to guiding the entire class for the summary. The unit guides provide sets of questions and probable responses of the students.

In all projects using an activity approach the central focus of the class is the pursuit of solutions to interesting problems and questions. Much less attention is given to the practice of skills for the sake of practicing. It is implicit that one practices skills by using them in real situations. Suydam and Higgins reviewed 23 research studies involving activity-based instruction in mathematics classes. They found the approach to be superior in 11 of the studies, to make no difference in 10 studies, and to be inferior in 2 studies. Their general conclusions were favorable to the use of an activity approach using concrete materials in appropriate ways (30).

"Good tasks are ones that do not separate mathematical thinking from mathematical concepts or skills, that capture students' curiosity, and that invite them to speculate and to pursue their hunches." (*Professional Teaching Standards,* 22, p. 25)

The Suydam-Higgins study focused specifically on achievement outcomes—usually measured by standardized tests. Missing from this summary, but present in most current evaluations of activity-oriented projects, are measures of students' attitudes and feelings about more active participation in the teaching-learning process. As one might guess, students generally like it very much.

Cooperative Learning

The model of instruction known as cooperative learning is another instructional strategy recommended for teachers in mathematics classrooms as well as other subject areas. It is based on the belief that humans learn best working together and that schools should deemphasize competitive and individualistic instructional methods (7). Cooperative learning involves more than just putting a few kids together in a small group and giving them problems to solve. Cooperative learning may be played out in the mathematics class as follows:

> A class period might begin with a meeting of the entire class to provide an overall perspective. This may include a teacher presentation of new material, class discussion, posing problems or questions for investigation and clarifying directions for the group activity. The class is then divided into small groups, usually with four members each. Each group has its own working space, which might include a flip-chart or section of the chalkboard. Students work together cooperatively in each group to discuss mathematical ideas, solve problems, look for patterns and relationships in sets of data, make and test conjectures, and so on. Students actively exchange ideas with one another and help each other learn the material. The teacher takes an active role, circulating from group to group, providing assistance and encouragement, and asking thought-provoking questions as needed. (7, p. 6)

"If students are to become competent in problem solving, reasoning, and communicating mathematically, instruction must allow them opportunities to engage actively and frequently in these processes." (*Curriculum and Evaluation Standards,* 21, p. 246)

The cooperative learning situation described above does not just happen. Teachers and students need to learn to work together in this type of classroom environment. Careful thought and attention must be given to both the mathematics objectives as well as various aspects of the group process. Methods of achieving this environment are given by many. Two that have received much attention include Student Team Learning Methods (29) developed at Johns Hopkins University and Learning Together developed by Johnson and Johnson (15).

The Student Team Learning methods focus on learning computational skills. The cooperative learning groups are established to help students master basic skills. Individual skill tests (or tournaments) are the means of assessment. Even though basic skills are important, this method does not appear to reflect the spirit of group work that is described in the *Curriculum and Evaluation Standards*.

Johnson and Johnson's Learning Together method involves placing students in small groups to work together to accomplish shared goals. Learning Together offers a framework for incorporating cooperative learning into the existing curriculum. Five basic conditions are needed for productive group learning: (a) Teachers must structure clearly positive interdependence with each student learning group. All cooperative efforts begin with the realization that "we sink or swim together." This may be done through common goals, division of labor, assigning students differing roles, and giving joint rewards. (b) Students must engage in promotive (face-to-face) interaction while completing math assignments. This includes assisting, helping, supporting, and encouraging each other's efforts to achieve. (c) Teachers must ensure that all students are individually accountable to complete math assignments and promote the learning of their group mates. One member of the group cannot carry another. Individual testing or random selection of one group member's work to represent the entire group are only two strategies to ensure this. (d) Students must learn and frequently use required interpersonal and small group skills. Cooperative skills include leadership, decision-making, trust-building, communication, and conflict-management skills. These must be taught just as academic skills are taught. (e) Teachers

> "Effective teachers are those who can stimulate students to *learn* mathematics. Educational research offers compelling evidence that students learn mathematics well only when they *construct* their own mathematical understanding." (*Professional Teaching Standards*, 22, p. 2)

must ensure that the learning groups engage in periodic and regular group processing. Group members need to reflect on how well the group has functioned. The Learning Together method, where students work together to accomplish shared goals, is a more flexible method whose primary goal is not mastering basic skills but having students engage in problem solving. Means of evaluating students are also more diversified. It is the authors' belief that this method is more aligned with the group work described in the *Curriculum and Evaluation Standards*.

A classroom teacher wishing to implement cooperative learning strategies into his or her teaching needs to be aware of the time factor. Cooperative learning takes additional planning and class time. Yet, it seems easy to justify the time spent when one considers the positive factors: increase in mathematical communication, the social support for learning mathematics, an opportunity for all students to experience success in mathematics, the possibility that several approaches to solving a problem might arise, and the opportunity to deal with mathematics through games and discussion of meaningful problems (7). It is worth noting that research assessing the effects of cooperative learning in classrooms appears to be positive when comparing academic achievement, self-esteem of a learner, intergroup relations, and social acceptance of mainstreamed children.

To begin to implement cooperative learning strategies into the classroom, one should start small and let the process evolve—perhaps begin with groups of two. This helps to ensure maximum participation by all students and allows the teacher a chance to ease into this instructional model. Increased noise level is often the first concern of teachers. Most teachers come to expect this and realize the benefits when they circulate from group to group and find that the noise is a result of students engaging in communication of mathematical ideas.

"Well-posed questions can simultaneously elicit and extend students' thinking. The teacher's skill at formulating questions to orchestrate the oral and written discourse in the direction of mathematical reasoning is crucial." (*Professional Teaching Standards,* 22, pp. 35–36)

Mathematics as Inquiry

Some confident teachers have set examples of treating the mathematics classroom as a setting for mathematical inquiry much as mathematicians would explore a set of new ideas. Davis demonstrated these techniques in the early days of the Madison Project as he focused on equations, variables, and graphs as the substance which a middle grade mathematics class could explore with interest and excitement. For example, in the fifth grade he would have children invent linear functions, have the rest of the class guess the rule, then graph the function. Later they would have a chance to determine the equation from the graph. All of this activity took place in a classroom where exploration and discovery were the only modes of instruction (8).

More recently Lampert has used this model extensively to learn the extent to which fifth-grade students could deal with the processes of creating and testing hypotheses (17). With this model of instruction, the ideas of what it means to know mathematics are redefined. Currently in many mathematics classrooms, to know mathematics means to be able to get the right answer. For children in the most common setting, "doing mathematics" means following the rules laid down by the teacher. "Knowing mathematics" means remembering and applying the correct rule when the teacher asks a question. Mathematical truth is determined when the answer is ratified by the teacher. This was not the definition Lampert used nor is it one that the *Curriculum and Evaluation Standards* endorses.

In a classroom where mathematics as inquiry is the model of instruction, Lampert explains how she had to change drastically the roles of the teacher and the students.

> How does a teacher go about redefining the meaning of knowing mathematics?
> In the lessons I designed and enacted, I portrayed what I wanted students to learn
> about mathematical knowing both in how I constructed my own role and in what

I expected of the class. I gave them problems to do but I did not explain how to get the answers, and the questions I expected them to answer went beyond simply determining whether they could get the solutions. I also expected them to answer questions about mathematical assumptions and the legitimacy of their strategies. Answers to problems were given by students, but I did not interpret them to be the primary indication of whether they knew mathematics. In this interaction, the words "knowing," "revising," "thinking," "explaining," and "answer" took on new meanings. (17, p. 441)

If we were to visit Lampert's classroom, we would see her presenting a problem to the class for discussion. The criterion for choosing a problem is that it has the capacity to engage all students in the class in making and testing mathematical hypotheses. The students in the class are given time to figure out how to solve the problem as well as find a solution. After that, Lampert asks the students for their solutions which she lists on the board. Once all given solutions are listed, the class engages in a discussion concerning these solutions. Discussion most often leads to revisions of the list.

The discussion often will begin with students explaining why they gave the answers they did. Other students will join the conversation, giving reasons why they questioned a given hypothesis. To guide students in their thinking and reasoning, Lampert may ask the class, "Can anyone explain what they thought so-and-so was thinking?" and "Why would it make sense to think that?" It is at these moments that we see Lampert modeling talk about thinking.

"The teacher has a central role in orchestrating the oral and written discourse in ways that contribute to students' understanding of mathematics." (*Professional Teaching Standards*, 22, p. 35)

An example from a class discussion from Lampert's class is given below. The students had already engaged in conversation about the ones digit of 7^4 when Lampert asked them about the ones digit of 7^5. The following discussion ensued.

ARTHUR: I think it's going to be 1 again.
SARAH: I think it's 9.
SOO WO: I think it's going to be 7.

The teacher wrote on the board: $7^5 = 1? 9? 7?$

TEACHER: Arthur, why do you think it's 1?
ARTHUR: Because 7^4 ends in 1, then it's times 1 again.
GAR: The answer to 7^4 is 2401. You multiply that by 7 to get the answer, so it's 7×1.
TEACHER: Why 9, Sarah?
THERESA: I think Sarah thought the number should be 49.
GAR: Maybe they think it goes 9,1,9,1,9,1.
MOLLY: I know it's 7, 'cause 7 . . .
ABDUL: Because 7^4 ends in 1, so if you times it by 7, it'll end in 7.
MARTHA: I think it's 7. No, I think it's 8.

SAM: I don't think it's 8, because it's odd number times odd number and
that's always an odd number. (17, p. 458)

It seems clear that students who are expected to engage in communication about
mathematics as described above will have a very different conception of the nature
of mathematics than students in a more standard classroom.

> "Above all, the discourse should be focused on making sense of mathematical
> ideas, on using mathematical ideas sensibly in setting up and solving problems."
> (*Professional Teaching Standards,* 22, p. 45)

I assumed that changing students' ideas about what it means to know and do mathematics was a matter of immersing them in a social situation that worked according
to different rules from those that ordinarily pertain in classrooms, and then respect-
fully challenging their assumptions about what knowing mathematics entails. Like
teaching someone to dance, it required some telling, some showing, and some doing
it with them, to say nothing of regular rehearsals. (17, p. 470)

> "Knowledge of mathematics is obviously fundamental to being able to help
> someone else learn it. In order to select and construct fruitful tasks and activities
> for their students, as well as interpret and appraise pupils' ideas flexibility, teach-
> ers must understand the mathematical concepts and procedures themselves."
> (2, p. 12)

It should be apparent from the description and discussion above that teaching
mathematics as inquiry is not only a unique model of instruction that redefines the
teacher's and students' roles but is also a model that requires a teacher to have a
strong knowledge of subject matter. The primary purpose of this instructional model
is to redefine what it means to know mathematics. The *Curriculum and Evaluation
Standards* (21) also calls for a new definition of what it means to know mathematics.
They want to move people from the tradition that "to know" means to identify the
basic concepts and procedures of the discipline, where learning is viewed as students
passively absorbing information and storing it as easily retrievable fragments as the
result of repeated practice and reinforcement. The *Curriculum and Evaluation Standards* describes knowing mathematics as doing mathematics, and doing mathematics
means a person gathers, discovers, or creates knowledge in the course of some activity
having a purpose.

To implement this model of instruction, the teacher poses problems, raises questions, and asks students for clarification. Teachers' questioning techniques are an
important feature of this model. The lesson is determined by the mathematics that
students use and the interaction that takes place in the particular classroom. The
teacher must continue to encourage conjecturing and arguing and to maintain an
environment in which students may safely express their thinking (9, 17). The desired
outcome of incorporating this model of instruction is "mathematical power" for stu-

dents. Know-how in mathematics that leads to mathematical power requires the ability to use information to reason and think creatively and to formulate, solve, and

> "Mathematical power encompasses the ability to 'explore, conjecture, and reason logically, as well as the ability to use a variety of mathematical methods effectively to solve nonroutine problems' and the self confidence and the disposition to do so." (*Professional Teaching Standards*, 22, p. 19)

reflect critically on problems. We may conclude from the short sample discussion in Lampert's class that mathematics as inquiry is an instructional model aimed at empowering students, a desired outcome of the *Curriculum and Evaluation Standards.*

The model of instruction a teacher chooses to use when teaching mathematics in the middle grades depends heavily on that teacher's conception of the nature of mathematics and the nature of learning mathematics by children. The recent literature asking for change demands that teachers improve their repertoire of possible models

> "The time for Spatial Visualization came and found me at my desk playing with blocks each day after school as I prepared one day at a time. My enthusiasm continues to spiral as my students actually try to will the bell not to ring and interrupt their work! Never have I had students so engaged with only two weeks of school left. Their perception is amazing to me and the help they give to one another and to me is fantastic." (a Florida middle grades mathematics teacher, 1990)

for instruction as well as their knowledge of recent developments in mathematics. The professional responsibility of the middle grades mathematics teacher is to make the extra necessary efforts to achieve the goal sought by the profession: good mathematics taught well.

Looking Ahead . . .

The nature of the mathematics classroom is changing very fast. What will it look like when all fifth-grade students have a graphing calculator (computer) in their hands? They will soon learn that a linear function such as $4x + 3 = 0$ has one root and the graph crosses the horizontal axis one time at $x = -3/4$. They will also learn very soon that all quadratic functions such as $(x + 3)(x - 4) = 0$ will have a graph that is a parabola which crosses the horizontal axis at -3 and 4. What will they think when they try to find the roots of $x(x + 1)(x - 1) + 4 = 0$ and see that the graph crosses the horizontal axis only once? Teachers will want to muster all the help they can get. Much of that help may come from the children themselves as they explore together the exciting mathematical ideas that surround us. Teaching mathematics in tomorrow's classrooms will be very exciting.

William M. Fitzgerald

A look to the future for mathematics teachers is exciting, challenging, and somewhat scary. With all eyes on us, it is exciting to be part of mathematics education today. It is also a challenge to respond to the current concerns and reforms. And thus it is scary to think about the role we play and how important that role is, as people look to us for solutions and results. At present we have the *Curriculum and Evaluation Standards for School Mathematics* (21) and the *Professional Standards for Teaching Mathematics* (22) as guides. Yet, just as these two current documents push our thinking as practitioners, there are likely to be others. Therefore, all of us must always remain students of teaching in this ever-evolving profession.

Mary Kay Bouck

About the Authors

William M. Fitzgerald is a professor of mathematics and teacher education at Michigan State University and is a co-director of the Connected Mathematics Project—a project to develop a complete grades 6–8 mathematics curriculum for all children.

Mary Kay Bouck has been a middle school mathematics teacher in Portland, Michigan, for 17 years. She also directs the Ionia County Mathematics Project, an inservice program aimed at helping K–12 mathematics teachers implement the NCTM *Curriculum and Evaluation Standards* in the spirit of the NCTM *Professional Teaching Standards*.

References

*1. AIMS NEWSLETTER, Box 7766, Fresno, CA 93747.

2. BALL, D. L. (1988). *Unlearning to teach mathematics*. Issue Paper 88-1. East Lansing: Michigan State University, National Center for Research on Teacher Education.

3. BARSON, A. (1974). A schoolman's view of the historical development and change of the mathematics laboratory in a large urban school system. In W. M. Fitzgerald & J. L. Higgins (Eds.), *Mathematics laboratories: Implementation, research, and evaluation* (pp. 3–33). Columbus: ERIC.

*4. BIGGS, E. E., & MacLEAN, J. R. (1969). *Freedom to learn: An active learning approach to mathematics*. Don Mills, Ontario: Addison-Wesley (Canada).

5. BROPHY, J. E., & GOOD, T. L. (1986). Teacher behavior and student achievement. In M. Wittrock (Ed.), *Handbook for research on teaching* (3rd ed., pp. 328–375). New York: Macmillan.

6. COTTON, K., & SAVARD, W. G. (1982). *Intermediate level mathematics and science instruction, research syntheses*. Portland, OR: Northwest Regional Educational Lab.

*7. DAVIDSON, N. (1990). *Cooperative learning in mathematics: A handbook for teachers*. Reading, MA: Addison-Wesley.

*8. DAVIS, R. B. (1964). *Discovery in mathematics*. Reading, MA: Addison-Wesley.

9. DAVIS, R. B. (1965). *A modern mathematics program as it pertains to the interrelationship of mathematical content, teaching methods, and classroom atmosphere*. Syracuse, NY: The Madison Project.

10. DAVIS, R. B. (1986). Conceptual and procedural knowledge in mathematics: A summary

analysis. In J. Hiebert (Ed.), *Conceptual and procedural knowledge: The case of mathematics* (pp. 265–300). Hillsdale, NJ: Erlbaum.

11. DIENES, Z. P. (1960). *Building up mathematics*. London: Hutchinson Educational, Ltd.

12. DOYLE, W. (1983). Academic work. *Review of Educational Research, 53*(2), 159–200.

13. EPSTEIN, J. L., & MAC IVER, D. J. (1990). *Education in the middle grades: Overview of national survey of practices and trends.* (Report No. 45). Baltimore: Center for Research on Elementary and Middle Schools, Johns Hopkins University.

*14. HARVARD MIDDLE SCHOOL MATHEMATICS PROJECT. (1982). Cambridge, MA: Harvard Graduate School of Education.

*15. JOHNSON, D. W., & JOHNSON, R. T. (1990). Using cooperative learning in math. In N. Davidson (Ed.), *Cooperative learning in mathematics: A handbook for teachers.* Reading, MA: Addison-Wesley.

*16. KIDD, K. P., MYERS, S. S., & CILLEY, D. M. (1970). *The laboratory approach to mathematics.* Chicago: Science Research Associates.

17. LAMPERT, M. (1988). The teacher's role in reinventing the meaning of mathematical knowing in the classroom. In M. Behr (Ed.), *Proceedings of the Tenth Annual Meeting of the North American Chapter of the International Group for the Psychology of Mathematics Education* (pp. 433–475). De Kalb, IL: Northern Illinois University.

18. LAPPAN, G. (1983). Middle grades mathematics project. Final Report. (NSF SED 80-18025).

19. LOMON, E. L., BECK, B., & ARBETTER, C. C. (1975). Real problem solving in USMES: Interdisciplinary education and much more. *School Science and Mathematics, 75*(659), pp. 53–64.

20. MAHER, C. A., and ALSTON, A. (1990). Teacher development in mathematics in a constructivist framework. In R. B. Davis (Ed.), *Constructivist views on the teaching and learning of mathematics* (pp. 147–165). JRME Monograph No. 4. Reston, VA: National Council of Teachers of Mathematics.

21. NATIONAL COUNCIL OF TEACHERS OF MATHEMATICS. (1989). *Curriculum and evaluation standards for school mathematics.* Reston, VA: Author.

22. NATIONAL COUNCIL OF TEACHERS OF MATHEMATICS. (1991). *Professional standards for teaching mathematics.* Reston, VA: Author.

23. NATIONAL RESEARCH COUNCIL. (1989). *Everybody counts: A report to the nation on the future of mathematics education.* Washington, DC: National Academy Press.

24. PETERSON, P. L. (1988). Teaching for higher-order thinking in mathematics: The challenge for the next decade. In D. A. Grouws and T. J. Cooney, (Eds.), *Perspectives on research for effective mathematics teaching* (pp. 2–26). Hillsdale, NJ: Erlbaum; Reston, VA: National Council of Teachers of Mathematics.

25. PETERSON, P. L. (1979). Direct instruction reconsidered. In P. L. Peterson and H. J. Walberg (Eds.), *Research on teaching: Concepts, findings and implications* (pp. 57–69). Berkeley, CA: McCutchan.

26. ROMBERG, T. A., & CARPENTER, T. P. (1986). Research on teaching and learning mathematics: Two disciplines of scientific inquiry. In M. C. Wittrock (Ed.), *Handbook of research on teaching* (pp. 850–873). New York: Macmillan.

*27. RUSSELL, S. J., & CORWIN, R. B. (1989). *Used numbers: Real data in the classroom.* Palo Alto, CA: Dale Seymour.

28. SKEMP, R. F. (1978). Relational understanding and instrumental understanding. *Arithmetic Teacher, 26*(3), pp. 9–15.

29. SLAVIN, R. (1990). Student team learning in mathematics. In N. Davidson (Ed.), *Cooperative learning in math: A handbook for teachers.* Reading, MA: Addison-Wesley.

30. Suydam, M. N., & Higgins, J. L. (1976). *Review and synthesis of activity-based approaches to mathematics teaching.* Final Report of NIE Contract No. 400-75-0063, Columbus, OH.

*31. TIMS Project, University of Illinois at Chicago, Box 4348, Chicago, IL 60680.

32. von Glasersfeld, E. (1990). An exposition of constructivism: Why some like it radical. In R. B. Davis (Ed.), *Constructivist views on the teaching and learning of mathematics* (pp. 19–29). JRME Monograph No. 4. Reston, VA: National Council of Teachers of Mathematics.

CHAPTER 14

Planning and Organizing the Middle Grades Mathematics Curriculum

Anne L. Madsen and Kendella Baker

Mathematics is a useful, exciting, and creative area of study that can be appreciated and enjoyed by all students in grades 5–8. . . . However, many students view the current mathematics curriculum in grades 5–8 as irrelevant, dull, and routine. Instruction has emphasized computational facility at the expense of a broad, integrated view of mathematics and has reflected neither the vitality of the subject nor the characteristics of the students. (23, p. 65)

Recent research on mathematics learning and instruction in concert with national efforts to reform school mathematics have called for changes in the curriculum and instruction of school mathematics. Advocates of such changes have suggested implementing a more conceptual approach in teaching mathematics (7, 21, 23). Adopting a conceptual approach in middle grades mathematics requires a different kind of instructional planning and a reorganization of the curriculum.

> "Educators in tomorrow's schools must put aside two fundamental conceptions of learning and teaching. The first is that teaching is telling, knowledge is facts, and learning is accumulation and recitation. The second is that basic skills develop before 'higher order skills' and must be taught first." (Holmes Group, 12, p. 1)

In spite of the recognized need to change our beliefs about learning and teaching (12), recent studies of mathematics education have noted that procedurally oriented instruction prevails in most classrooms today (4, 7, 17). Specifically, the National Research Council (24) characterized this instruction as "lecturing and listening."

"Despite daily homework, for most students and most teachers mathematics continues to be primarily a passive activity: teachers prescribe; students transcribe. Students simply do not retain for long what they learn by imitation from lectures, worksheets, or routine homework. Presentation and repetition help students do well on standardized tests and lower-order skills, but they are generally ineffective as teaching strategies for long-term learning, for higher-order thinking, and for versatile problem-solving." (*Everybody Counts,* 23, p. 23)

Since procedurally oriented instruction does not promote long-term learning, higher order thinking, and problem solving, alternative ways of planning mathematics lessons and organizing the curriculum need to be considered. This chapter deals with two issues, changing the ways mathematics instruction is planned and reorganizing the curriculum to focus on a variety of mathematics topics and concepts.

Planning for Mathematics Instruction

"The teaching of mathematics is shifting from an authoritarian model based on 'transmission of knowledge' to a student-centered practice featuring 'stimulation of learning.' The teacher of mathematics is shifting from preoccupation with inculcating routine skills to developing broad-based mathematical power" (21, p. 5). Changing middle grades mathematics to meet current and future demands of society requires changing the curriculum and instructional planning.

The Characteristics of Middle Grades Mathematics Instruction

Our beliefs about learning and teaching influence the way we plan mathematics lessons (19, 20). Results from the Second International Mathematics Study (4) portrayed mathematics instruction as procedurally oriented in most middle grades mathematics classes. Planning for instruction reflects our understanding of the content we think students need to learn and the way they learn it (19). If we believe students should learn computational procedures, then we plan mathematics lessons to include a demonstration of the procedure followed by drill and practice.

What Should Characterize Middle Grades Mathematics Instruction?

Current reform efforts in mathematics education have recognized the need to change current beliefs and practices. The *Professional Teaching Standards* presents a view of the "major arenas" (or components of instruction) which should influence the way mathematics lessons are planned and implemented. These arenas are described below.

- *Tasks* are the projects, questions, problems, constructions, applications, and exercises in which students engage. . . .
- *Discourse* refers to the ways of representing thinking, talking, and agreeing and disagreeing that teachers and students use to engage in those tasks. . . .
- *Environment* represents the setting for learning. It is the unique interplay of intellectual, social, and physical characteristics that shapes the ways of knowing and working that are encouraged and expected in the classroom. . . .
- *Analysis* is the systematic reflection in which teachers engage. It entails the ongoing monitoring of classroom life—how well the tasks, discourse, and environment foster the development of every student's mathematical literacy and power. (22, p. 20)

"A positive classroom climate is essential to the students' learning and understanding of mathematical concepts. An open attitude of acceptance and inquiry on the part of the teacher to all student responses (correct or incorrect) will encourage students to take risks and to more actively explore mathematics." (Kendella Baker)

Designing lessons to promote students' conceptual learning and optimize the time they spend engaged in mathematical activities requires careful planning with special attention to the major arenas and every component of the lesson. We will discuss the characteristics of three components of mathematics lessons which, when implemented, assist in promoting conceptual learning. These components include the presentation of the content, the task or assignment, and the summary.

Planning Lesson Presentations.   The lesson presentation is the direct instruction portion of the lesson. It focuses students' attention on a mathematical concept and sets the stage for the mathematical task or activity (29). The mathematical concept is presented to the students in the form of a mathematical problem or question. Questions promote students' thinking about the concept and encourage them to discuss the mathematical ideas related to the concept (5). Manipulatives, illustrations, and models are used by the teacher and students to assist in the understanding and development of the mathematical concept. The task to be assigned is modeled at this time. Student understanding of the concept and the task is evaluated through the teacher's questioning and controlled practice activities (5). Controlled (guided) practice activities encourage students to be involved and engage them in examining the concept (10).

The following is an example of a controlled practice activity during a lesson presentation in a fraction unit (19). The teacher, Pamela Kaye, is a general mathematics teacher who participated in a three-year instructional intervention project to improve learning and teaching in general mathematics classes. In the following observation Pamela presented a problem and waited for the students to solve it.

MS. KAYE: Let's try this one.

$$\frac{1}{2} \times \frac{1}{2} = \frac{1}{4}$$

[Jeff scowls indicating he is confused.]
MS. KAYE: Draw a picture of one half and cut it in half.

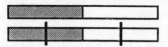

A STUDENT: They turn into fourths!
MS. KAYE: How much is half the shaded part?
A STUDENT: One fourth.
MS. KAYE: Now, draw a one third fraction bar.

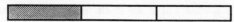

MS. KAYE: Take one half of the one third.

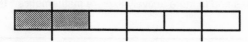

A STUDENT: [What] you get is one sixth or half of the shaded part.
MS. KAYE: Draw a two thirds fraction bar.

MS. KAYE: Take one half of the two thirds.

A STUDENT: If I take one half of two thirds, I get two sixths.
JEFF: Now I understand.
(19, p. 172–73)

Controlled practice activities need to be planned and included in every lesson. They extend the lesson development time, help the teacher become aware of the students' thinking, encourage student communication and model the task of the assignment (10).

Planning Lesson Tasks.   Mathematical tasks are planned to encourage and enhance the development of mathematical understanding (29). One factor to consider when planning tasks/assignments is how students are to be organized (1, 14, 15, 30). Student pairs may be the best arrangement for calculator activities or games. Groups of three or four students may be better in problem solving. Cooperative groups allow all students the opportunity to become actively involved in explorations. A second factor is the selection of challenging and interesting tasks that promote the development or understanding of the concept. A third factor is providing challenging activities for students who finish the assignment early (2).

The following is an example of a challenging task Pamela selected from *Teaching Problem-Solving Strategies* (6) (Fig. 14.1).

> You have a balance scale and you are trying to weigh these packages of meat. You have only four weights to work with—a 1 kg, 3 kg, 9 kg, and 27 kg weight. You have bundles of meat ranging from 1 to 40 kilograms. You have to weigh them with just these four weights. (6, p. 264)

The classroom observation (19) depicted students who were interested and intensely engaged in solving the problem. This was unusual because the students in her class were not those usually interested in solving these kinds of problems.

The assignments and tasks Pamela Kaye selected were different from the typical textbook problems she had used previously. The activities encouraged students to explore, develop, investigate, and construct their own mathematical ideas and concepts. While working on the tasks, students formulated strategies for problem solving and discussed the problems in their groups. The observation below shows the students discussing the solution to a problem.

> MS. KAYE: It takes 12 minutes to cut a log into three pieces.
> How long does it take to cut a log into four pieces?

FIGURE 14.1   The problem

[Ms. Kaye shows how to weigh 1 kg, 3kg, and 2 kg bundles.]

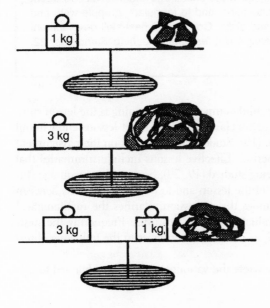

JEFF: 16 minutes.

SUE: Ms. Kaye, are there three pieces or three cuts?

MS. KAYE: She just raised a question, do we make three pieces or do we make three cuts?

[Alice draws a picture of a log on her paper, makes two cuts, and realizes two cuts form three pieces.]

DON: Well, I got the answer that 3 goes into 12 four times.

JEFF [TO DON]:   Look, I'll draw a picture for you!

[Jeff draws a picture on Don's paper and makes two cuts.]

MS. KAYE: Jeff, show us what you did.

[Jeff walks to the front of the room and draws a picture.]

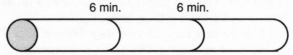

MS. KAYE: What strategy did Jeff use to show the problem?

DON: I get it now. He drew a picture.

The students were on task, interested in solving the problem, and involved in the discussion of the solution. Those students who did not have the correct answer wanted to know how and why they made a mistake.

Selecting mathematical assignments that reflect the learning and teaching goals set forth in NCTM's *Curriculum and Evaluation Standards* and *Professional Teaching Standards* requires careful planning and the identification of worthwhile assignments that encourage students to develop and construct ideas and concepts.

"The tasks in which students engage must encourage them to reason about mathematical ideas, to make connections, and to formulate, grapple with, and solve problems. Students also need skills. Good tasks nest skill development in the context of the problem solving." (*Professional Teaching Standards, 22*, p. 32)

Planning Lesson Summaries.   The third component of planning is the lesson summary. Observations of many mathematics classrooms reveal that lessons end without summaries of the mathematical ideas (19). Students usually work on their assignment until the end of the mathematics period. Effective lessons include summaries that review the mathematical concept being studied (19, 29). Summaries encourage students to reflect on the mathematics of the lesson and to make connections between mathematical ideas. The teacher guides the discussion, clarifies the mathematical ideas, extends the concepts, and evaluates students' learning. Frequently the summary includes a discussion and analysis of common errors as in the following observation (19, p. 184).

[As the students worked Ms. Kaye wrote the various answers they obtained to one problem on the chalkboard.]

$$\begin{array}{r} \dfrac{3}{5} \\[6pt] + \;\; \dfrac{3}{4} \\ \hline \end{array}$$

(a) $\dfrac{6}{9} = \dfrac{2}{3}$ (b) $\dfrac{3}{9} = \dfrac{1}{3}$ (c) $\dfrac{6}{20} = \dfrac{3}{10}$ (d) $\dfrac{27}{20} = 1\dfrac{7}{20}$

Ms. Kaye asked the students to tell her how each of the four answers could have been obtained. After the students explained each answer, she asked them to decide which was correct. The students disagreed. She then asked them to draw fraction bars for the problem.

> "This is the kind of problem checking that promotes critical thinking. It requires more student explanation of answers and processes. It gives the students an ownership in the process and helps them to rely more on their own problem-solving skills and abilities." (Kendella Baker)

Ms. Kaye told them to add the bars and determine the correct answer.

The students observed that the sum was more than one whole bar and that 1 7/20 was the correct answer.

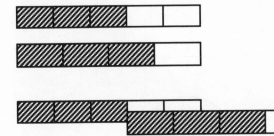

Planning and implementing lesson summaries is necessary for effective learning and instruction. Questions included in the lesson summary help students reflect on the mathematical concepts that will enable them to establish linkages between mathematical topics and across mathematical units (19, 23, 29).

What Happens When Instructional Changes Are Implemented?

Descriptions of typical mathematics classes indicate that less than 10 minutes per period is planned for lesson presentation and more than half the period is devoted to seat work assignments. When lessons are planned that involve students in mathematical explorations and discussion, there is a dramatic change in the amount of time spent in mathematical study (19). Table 14.1 compares the percentage of time spent per class period in Pamela Kaye's classes prior to and after the implementation of instructional changes such as those discussed in this chapter.

TABLE 14.1   The Percentage of Time Per Class Period Spent in
             Mathematical and Nonmathematical Activities

Percent of Time Per Class Period

Activity	Year Prior to Instructional Changes	Year After Instructional Changes
Lesson Presentation	14.2	33.3
Lesson Assignment	63.3	48.3
Lesson Summary	2.5	12.3
Nonmathematical Activities	20.0	7.1

The amount of time the students spent discussing the daily mathematical topic
had more than doubled and the time they spent working on assignments was reduced.
Time for lesson summaries increased dramatically from the first year to the last year
and the time students were engaged in nonmathematical activities decreased. Students were now spending more time in mathematical activities. Even the time before
the lesson was now used in a short five-minute "beginning of class review" (19) (see
Fig. 14.2).

FIGURE 14.2   Beginning of class review

1. Do these circles seem reasonable?
   Explain why or why not.

2. Guess what percentage of each
   circle is labeled A, B, C.

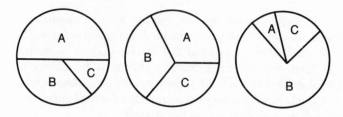

> "The majority of student time was devoted to seat work, blackboard work, or listening to lectures or explanations. A median of 40 minutes, about one class period, per week was spent taking tests and quizzes. Very little time in mathematics class was spent in individual or small group work." (4, p. 14)

Improving learning and teaching in middle grades mathematics requires changing the way lessons are planned. Planning includes the integration of the recommendations in the *Curriculum and Evaluation Standards* and the *Professional Teaching Standards* and the three major components of a lesson (presentation, assignment, and summary).

Organizing the Middle Grades Mathematics Curriculum

"We must judge schools not by remembrances of things past, but by necessary expectations for the future. Students must learn not only arithmetic, but also estimation, measurement, geometry, optimization, statistics, and probability—all the ways in which mathematics occurs in everyday life" (24, p. 46).

In the first part of this chapter we looked at reform efforts calling for changes in the ways mathematics is taught and how planning can respond to these changes. However, careful planning and effective instruction will not guarantee students' exposure to mathematics beyond that of arithmetic. Consideration also needs to be given to the planning and organization of the mathematics curriculum.

Reports (23, 24, 25) have called for the creation of a new curriculum in middle grades mathematics. This section suggests restructuring the curriculum to reflect current views of the mathematics judged important for today's students. The content of the mathematics curriculum as suggested by the National Science Board Commission (25) and the NCTM (23) is used to develop a schema for organizing the middle grades mathematics curriculum.

The middle grades mathematics curriculum is largely determined by the textbook. "The overall picture is that to a great extent the textbook defines the content of the mathematics that is taught in U.S. schools" (8, p. 18). With respect to eighth- and twelfth-grade mathematics classes, "the textbook defined the 'boundaries' for mathematics taught by teachers. Limited use was made of resources beyond the textbook for either content or teaching methods" (4, p. vii). If the textbook defines what mathematical content is covered, then the Flanders (8) findings of the analysis of three textbook series is particularly disturbing in middle grades mathematics. Flanders's research (Fig. 14.3) shows that the amount of new mathematics content in textbooks for grades 5–8 was the lowest of all grades K–9.

Teachers' reliance on the textbook to determine both the curriculum and mode of instruction limit the opportunity for students to learn, understand, and experience any mathematics beyond arithmetic. In the Second International Mathematics

FIGURE 14.3   The average percentage of new content in three
               mathematics text series (8, p. 20)

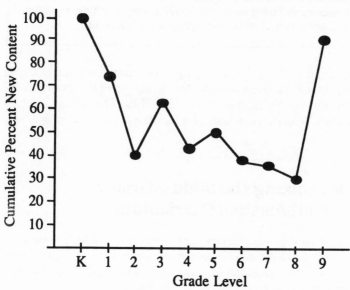

Study, eighth-grade teachers reported that arithmetic dominated the mathematics curriculum (4, p. ix). The results of international and national studies indicate middle grades mathematics is largely an arithmetic review of computational procedures (4, 7).

> "Generally speaking, topics in arithmetic predominated, with a median of 30 class periods (about one-sixth of the total eighth grade program) devoted to common and decimal fractions. Relatively little time was anticipated to be given to probability and statistics (about 4 periods per year, on average), with 90 percent of the eighth grade classes receiving 10 periods or less on this topic." (4, p. 15)

Reorganizing the Middle Grades Mathematics Curriculum

Educating Americans for the 21st Century (25), includes curriculum recommendations from the working group on elementary and middle grades mathematics. The NCTM's *Curriculum and Evaluation Standards* (23) reflect the suggestions of *Educating Americans for the 21st Century* and further recommend the inclusion of mathematical communication, reasoning, and connections. We are suggesting the curriculum contain six or seven mathematical units to be studied during the year. Students would spend from four to six weeks in units on problem-solving strategies, patterns and functions, algebra, statistics, probability, geometry, and rational num-

- Understanding number facts.
- Deemphasis of large number computations.
- Use of calculators and computers.
- Emphasis on mental arithmetic, estimation, and problem solving.
- Use of data analysis, statistics, and probability.
- Understanding relative sizes of numbers.
- Relationships of numbers to geometry.
- Understanding fractions.
- Intuitive geometric understandings.
- Concepts of sets.
- Function concepts.
- Algebraic symbolism and techniques.
- Mathematics and computers in other school subjects (*Educating Americans for the 21st Century,* 25, pp. 6–7)

bers. Strands contained within each unit are problem solving, communication, reasoning, mathematical connections, number/operations/computation, estimation/mental arithmetic, and technology. Figure 14.4 presents this structure.

No textbooks available fit the proposed curriculum plan; however, appropriate materials, activities, and resources can be obtained from publishing companies to assist teachers in the development and planning of each unit. The nature of these mathematics materials, activities, and other considerations for teachers in planning the units are presented below.

Problem Solving. A unit on problem solving includes activities and content that provides students with an experiences in using a variety of strategies such as guess and check, making tables, finding patterns, modeling, simplifying, and eliminating. Materials selected for this unit contain interesting and challenging problems

"Problem solving should be included in every mathematics unit we plan and teach. Problem solving strategies should be taught as a special content unit in which the students' attention and experiences are focused on learning specific problem solving strategies. Then students should be asked to reflect on the strategies they used to solve mathematics problems in the other units of content they study." (Kendella Baker)

that encourage student group exploration. Included in this unit are estimation, application, open search, and situational problems providing students with opportunities to develop and practice their reasoning, thinking and logic abilities. "It [problem solving] should be a cornerstone of mathematics curriculum and instruction, fostering the development of mathematical knowledge and a chance to apply and connect previously constructed mathematical understandings" (3, p. 14).

FIGURE 14.4   A curriculum for middle grades mathematics

Mathematical Strands

	Problem Solving	Communications	Reasoning	Connections	Number/ Operations/ Computation	Estimation/ Mental Arithmetic	Technology
Problem-Solving Strategies							
Patterns & Functions							
Algebra							
Statistics							
Probability							
Geometry							
Rational Numbers							

Mathematical Units

"Teaching mathematics as reasoning does not mean just including some reasons and underlying rationales when presenting mathematical material. It means involving students in activities that call on them to reason and communicate their reasoning rather than to reproduce memorized procedures and rules." (9, p. 16)

Patterns and Functions.   A unit on patterns and functions includes activities in which students study relationships in many different ways. Materials selected for this unit include calculator activities, problem solving, estimation, geometric patterning and analogies, and graphing activities. "The exploration of patterns, relationships, and functions is a thread that runs through the entire Standards document as students encounter regularities in all of mathematics, from counting and computation to underpinnings of calculus" (13, p. 23). Students are encouraged to discover, illustrate, use manipulatives, and write about patterns and relationships. Interpreting graphs is one way to help students understand the relationships between sets of data.

Algebra, Statistics, Probability.   Units in algebra, probability, and statistics include materials and activities in which students actively engage in problem identification, data collection, forms of data representation, and analysis/interpretation in order to answer a question or solve a problem they have identified.

"Students should have assignments where they work in cooperative groups to identify a question or problem they would like to study. When the question or problem is identified they should then decide what data they need and how to go about collecting it. When the data are gathered the group needs to decide how they will analyze and report their findings. It is important that student groups choose problems to study which are important to them. It is also important that they make the decisions regarding data type, collection, analysis, representation, and reporting." (Kendella Baker)

Experiences in graphing their data by using scatter plots, histograms, and stem and leaf plots help students analyze and synthesize their results. In exploring and describing their data sets students are encouraged to make generalizations and inferences. Figures 14.5 and 14.6 illustrate the results of such student activities using data collection, representation and analysis.

Activities and lessons are planned to include the use of a graphing calculator. Manipulatives and activity-based assignments included in the algebra unit promote student understanding of fundamental algebraic concepts such as distribution.

Geometry.   A geometry unit includes the study of geometric transformations from an informal and intuitive perspective. Students solve mathematical problems using geometric ideas and relationships. Activities utilizing calculators and computers to study geometric topics are an integral part of the unit. Ratio, proportion and scaling activities help students develop an understanding of similarity. Spatial visualization activities using manipulatives are also included. "Settings in which students have opportunities to explore, invent, and discuss in their own words may be the most productive for helping students attain a firm foundation in geometry" (28, p. 25).

Measurement.   A unit on measurement provides experiences in which students actively study these concepts using standard and nonstandard units. Students

> need to explore attributes and use measuring instruments. They need to explore relationships among figures to determine efficient ways to count the number of units rather than memorize formulas. They need to experience being unable to measure an attribute with inappropriate units (e.g., measuring weight with units of capacity). That is, they need to use the measurement process. (16, p. 23)

FIGURE 14.5   An example of a scatter plot

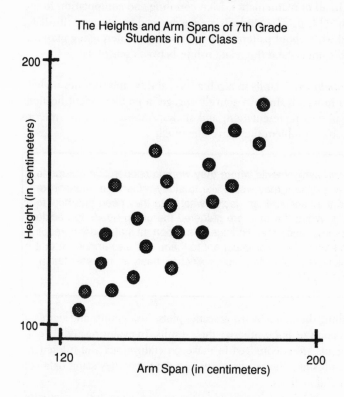

FIGURE 14.6   An example of a histogram

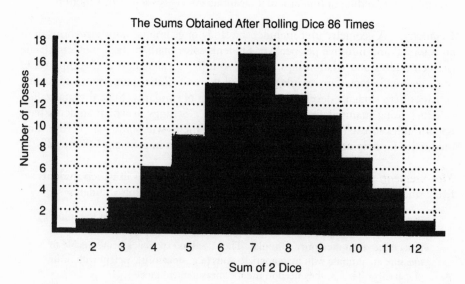

Rational Numbers. The unit on rational numbers develops conceptual under-standings of fractions, decimals, and percentages. Manipulatives are incorporated

> "The most critical part of instruction in fractions is the careful development of sound concepts of fractions and decimals prior to any computational work." (26, p. 24)

throughout the unit to allow students to study concepts such as equality, inequality, and order. Along with using manipulatives, students illustrate rational number op-erations (Fig. 14.7).

Estimation and mental arithmetic activities with rational numbers are included with the use of fraction calculators. "The study of estimation should be integrated with the study of concepts underlying whole numbers, fractions, decimals, and ra-tional numbers so that these concepts can be constructed meaningfully by the learner" (27, p. 23). Problem solving and writing activities are included throughout the unit.

Students examine rational number operations with manipulatives and illustrations after they have an understanding of rational number concepts and relationships. At all times rational number operations are connected to whole number operations. Verbalizing the problem: $3/4 \div 1/2 = ?$ ("How many one halves are there in three fourths?" (enables students to connect this operation to the whole number counter-part: $10 \div 5$ ("How many fives are there in ten?").

> "Students should be continually asked to judge the reasonableness of the an-swers they obtain. They should also be encouraged to illustrate problems in frac-tions, decimals and percents." (Kendella Baker)

Connections between fractions, decimals, and percents are made using the part-to-whole interpretation of rational numbers (Fig. 14.8). Questions such as, "What is the part and what is the whole in this rational number?" encourage students to make these connections.

Organizing the Curriculum

Reorganizing the middle grades mathematics curriculum requires an intensive lon-gitudinal effort on the part of each middle grades mathematics teacher working in concert with his or her colleagues. Such an effort has been a part of the Support Teacher Program, a comprehensive program designed to restructure junior high school science and mathematics (18). Experienced mathematics teachers (called Support Teachers) from different junior high schools worked in this way to reorganize the curriculum. After two and a half years the Support Teachers described the math-ematics curriculum at the start of and after their participation in the program.

FIGURE 14.7   Illustrating the meaning of the arithmetic
                       operations

What is the sum of one half and one fourth?

$\frac{1}{2} + \frac{1}{4}$

What is the difference between three fourths and one half?

$\frac{3}{4} - \frac{1}{2}$

What is one half of one fourth?

$\frac{1}{2} \times \frac{1}{4}$

What many fourths are there in one half?

$\frac{1}{2} \div \frac{1}{4}$

How many one halves are there in one fourth?

$\frac{1}{4} \div \frac{1}{2}$

FIGURE 14.8   Rational number connections

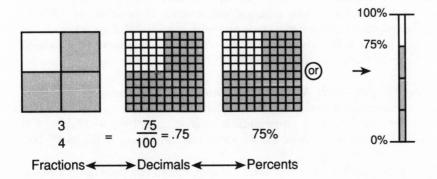

Fractions ◄──────► Decimals ◄──────► Percents

TABLE 14.2   Wilma Burns 7th-Grade
Mathematics Curriculum

1986–1987

TOPIC	WEEKS
Whole Numbers & Operations	4
Number Theory	1 1/2
Fractions	5
Decimals	3
Equations	3
Geometry	4
Ratios	1 1/2
Percents	4
Perimeter, Area, Volume	4
Integers	3
Real Numbers/Coordinate Plane	3

1990–1991

TOPIC	WEEKS
Probability Unit	6
Integers	3
Rational Numbers	7
Measurements Using Fractions	2
Mouse & Elephant Unit	7
Equivalency (Decimals/Proportion/Percent)	5
Informal Equations	2
Measurement (Metric)	2
Spatial Visualization Unit	2
Problem Solving	daily

Wilma Burns's Seventh-Grade Mathematics Curriculum. According to Support Teacher, Wilma Burns, "I went straight through the book" (18, p. 67). Her 1986–87 curriculum (Table 14.2) reflects a typical mathematics curriculum. By 1990–91 Wilma planned her curriculum to include new units of content that are activity based and concept oriented. She also extended the number of weeks spent on a topic to provide for more thorough content coverage.

Susan Day's Eighth-Grade Mathematics Curriculum. The teachers in Susan's mathematics department worked together to plan and restructure their mathematics courses. After describing their curriculum in 1986–87 and 1990–91 (Table 14.3) Susan asked, "What in the world did we spend our time doing in the past?" (18, p. 68).

Emphasis in the eighth-grade curriculum has shifted from computation to exploration of mathematical ideas and new content. In Susan's department the teachers

TABLE 14.3   Susan Day's 8th-Grade
Mathematics Curriculum

8th Grade 1986–1987

TOPIC	WEEKS
Whole Numbers	3
Decimals	3
Number Theory	2
Fractions	4
Equation Solving	3
Geometry	3
Ratio, Proportion, Percent	3
Measurement	1
Perimeter, Area, Volume	3
Integers	2
Rational Numbers	2
Graphing	2
Geometry	2

8th Grade 1990–1991

TOPIC	WEEKS
Review	2
Problem-Solving Strategies	4
Mouse & Elephant Unit	4
Probability Unit	4
Statistics	4
Spatial Visualization Unit	1
Geometry	3
Algebra	10

incorporate writing activities in their lessons to help them evaluate student understanding.

Conclusion

The changes in planning and organizing the mathematics curriculum we have suggested are indeed comprehensive; they include changing what we teach and how we teach. These changes are difficult to achieve; they need the support of the mathematics faculty, administrators, parents, students—all those involved in the learning and teaching endeavor. Yet, these changes can be realized. Through intensive efforts and close collaboration among teachers, new units and new approaches can be planned for and successfully implemented (11).

"Implementing these changes will naturally bring about an uneasiness among some parents; the kinds of activities in which their children are engaged are frequently unlike the mathematics they knew as a student and expect as a parent. It is helpful to send a letter to parents explaining that the students will be involved in activity-centered mathematics in the classroom and they are welcome to visit the class at their convenience. This is a time when short computational review assignments from the students' textbook may be used as homework to keep computational skills sharp." (Kendella Baker)

Looking Ahead . . .

Improving the ways teachers plan and organize the middle grades mathematics curriculum requires reeducation supported by intensive classroom assistance. How can teacher educators be encouraged to participate actively in such long-term endeavors? With what degree of success can we expect inservice teachers to implement these changes? What kinds of support mechanisms will encourage and sustain the changes suggested in this chapter? What are the outcomes for teachers and students when changes are implemented? These questions provide the beginning of future research and inservice work.

Anne L. Madsen

Where can I find materials to help me implement a middle grades mathematics curriculum that encourages students to share ownership in their learning and fosters the development of mathematical concepts? How do I convince parents and administrators that the most effective means of learning and instruction does not lie in a textbook? How do I convince them that drill and practice are not indicators of student learning? How do I convince them that manipulatives, cooperative learning, and interesting, challenging tasks promote the development of mathematical thinking and understanding? I am convinced, but how do I convince others?

Kendella Baker

About the Authors

Anne L. Madsen is an assistant professor in the Department of Curriculum and Instruction at the University of Texas at Austin and coordinator of the Early Adolescence Teacher Education Program. Her research interests are in improving learning and instruction in middle grades mathematics through effective staff development and teacher education programs. She was a middle school mathematics and science teacher, a mathematics specialist at a vocational high school, and a participant in several research studies at Michigan State University, including the Middle Grades Mathematics Project and the General Mathematics Project.

Kendella Baker has been a classroom teacher for 15 years. Her primary teaching focus has been on mathematics in grades 4–8. She participated in the Middle Grades Mathematics Project program for teacher leaders and staff development specialists at Michigan State University in the summers of 1989 and 1990. She presently teaches a mathematics methods course for elementary preservice teachers at the University of Texas at Austin and is providing professional development through conferences, inservice programs and workshops for teachers and administrators.

References

*1. BEHOUNEK, K., ROSENBAUM, L., BROWN, L., & BURCALOW, J. (1988). Our class has twenty-five teachers. *Arithmetic Teacher*, 36(4), 10–13.

*2. BURNS, M. (1977). *The good time math event book*. Palo Alto, CA: Creative Publications.

*3. CAMPBELL, P., & BAMBERGER, H. (1990). Implementing the standards: The vision of problem solving in the standards. *Arithmetic Teacher*, 37(9), 14–17.

4. CROSSWHITE, J., DOSSEY, J., SWAFFORD, J., MCKNIGHT, C., & COONEY, T. (1985). *Second International Mathematics Study: Summary report for the United States*. Champaign, IL: Stipes.

*5. DILLON, J. T. (1983). *Teaching and the art of questioning*. Fastback 194. Bloomington, IN: Phi Delta Kappa Educational Foundation.

*6. DOLAN, D., & WILLIAMSON, J. (1983). *Teaching problem solving strategies*. Menlo Park, CA: Addison-Wesley.

7. DOSSEY, J. A., MULLIS, I. V. S., LINDQUIST, M. M., & CHAMBERS, D. L. (1988). *The mathematics report card: Are we measuring up? Trends and achievement based on the 1986 national assessment*. Princeton, NJ: Educational Testing Service.

8. FLANDERS, J. (September, 1987). How much of the content in mathematics textbooks is new? *Arithmetic Teacher*, 35(1), 18–23.

*9. GAROFALO, J., & MTETWA, D. (1990). Implementing the standards: Mathematics as reasoning. *Arithmetic Teacher*, 37(5), 16–18.

*10. GOOD, T. L., GROUWS, D. A., & EBMEIER, H. (1983). *Active mathematics teaching*. New York: Longman.

*11. HITCH, C. (1990). How can I get others to implement the standards? I'm just a teacher. *Arithmetic Teacher*, 37(9), 2–4.

12. HOLMES GROUP. (1988). First seminar on "Tomorrow's Schools" rejects traditional precepts for learning. *The Holmes Group Forum*, 3(1), 1.

*13. HOWDEN, H. (1990). Implementing the standards: Patterns, relationships, and functions. *Arithmetic Teacher*, 37(3), 18–24.

14. JOHNSON, D. W., MARUYAMA, G., JOHNSON, R., & SKON, L. (1989, January). Effects of

cooperative, competitive and individualistic goal structures on achievement: A meta-analysis. *Psychological Bulletin*, pp. 47–62.

15. JOHNSON, D. W., JOHNSON, R. T., JOHNSON HOLUBEC, E., & ROY, P. (1984). *Circles of learning*. Alexandria, VA: Association for Supervision and Curriculum Development.

*16. LINDQUIST, M. (1990). Implementing the standards: The measurement standards. *Arithmetic Teacher*, 37(3), 22–26.

*17. MCKNIGHT, C. L. (1987). *The underachieving curriculum: Assessing U.S. school mathematics from an international perspective*. Report of the International Association for the Evaluation of Educational Achievement: Report of the study group. Cambridge, MA: Author.

18. MADSEN, A. L., GALLAGHER, J. J., & LANIER, P. E. (1991, April). *A new professional role for junior high school science and mathematics teachers*. Paper presented at the meeting of the American Educational Research Association, Chicago, IL.

19. MADSEN-NASON, A. (1988). *A teacher's changing thoughts and practices in ninth grade general mathematics classes: A case study* (Doctoral dissertation, Michigan State University, 1988). *Dissertation Abstracts International, 50*, 666–A.

20. MADSEN-NASON, A., & LANIER, P. (1986). *From a computational to a conceptual orientation: An instructional evolution of Pamela Kaye and her general mathematics class*. (Research series no. 172). East Lansing: Michigan State University, Institute for Research on Teaching.

21. MATHEMATICAL SCIENCES EDUCATION BOARD, NATIONAL RESEARCH COUNCIL. (1990). *Reshaping school mathematics: A philosophy and framework for curriculum*. Washington, DC: National Academy Press.

*22. NATIONAL COUNCIL OF TEACHERS OF MATHEMATICS. (1991). *Professional standards for teaching mathematics*. Reston, VA: Author.

*23. NATIONAL COUNCIL OF TEACHERS OF MATHEMATICS. (1989). *Curriculum and evaluation standards for school mathematics*. Reston, VA: Author.

24. NATIONAL RESEARCH COUNCIL. (1989). *Everybody counts*. Washington, DC: National Academy Press.

25. NATIONAL SCIENCE BOARD COMMISSION ON PRECOLLEGE EDUCATION IN MATHEMATICS, SCIENCE AND TECHNOLOGY. (1983). *Educating Americans for the 21st century*. Washington, DC: Author.

*26. PAYNE, J., & TOWSLEY, A. (1990). Implementing the standards: Implications of NCTM's standards for teaching fractions and decimals. *Arithmetic Teacher*, 37(8), 23–26.

*27. REYS, B., & REYS, R. (1990). Implementing the standards: Estimation—direction from the standards. *Arithmetic Teacher*, 37(7), 22–25.

*28. ROWAN, T. (1990). Implementing the standards: The geometry standards in K–8 mathematics. *Arithmetic Teacher*, 37(6), 24–28.

*29. SCHROYER, J. (1984, December). *The LES model: Launch-explore-summarize*. Paper presented at the Honors Teachers Workshop for Middle Grades Mathematics. East Lansing: Michigan State University, Department of Mathematics.

*30. SLAVIN, R. E. (1983). *Cooperative learning*. New York: Longman.

CHAPTER 15

Classroom Interactions: The Heartbeat of the Teaching/Learning Process

Mary Schatz Koehler and Millie Prior

Imagine a sixth-grade mathematics class with 25 students. The teacher has just posed a question and about ten hands are raised, eight students have puzzled looks, five are off-task, and the remainder look bored. Who should the teacher call on: Anne, who always gets the answer right; John, who is off-task; Carlos, who is very shy; or Heidi, who will most likely give the wrong answer? What should the follow-up question be? How will the teacher bring back the off-task students? How can the teacher encourage more students to volunteer?

A recent study (12) found that the above scenario (teacher asking a question) occurred an average of 24 times in a 50-minute mathematics class. Asking a question is just one type of interaction that teachers and students engage in. This chapter will explore what is known about this vital aspect of the teaching/learning process and will focus on three aspects of teacher-student interactions. The first aspect will focus on the interactions themselves and will define what is meant by classroom interactions and include a look at how interactions were and are studied. The second, but equally important aspect, is an examination of why a particular interaction occurs. This will include the influences on teachers and students that cause them to initiate or engage in particular interactions. Last, the chapter will include some strategies for improving teacher-student interactions.

What Are Classroom Interactions?

Early studies of teacher-student interactions may have included only questions that the teacher posed to an individual student. Later studies, however, broadened the definition of classroom interactions to include any interaction between the teacher and students including individuals, a small group of students, or the whole class. It included interactions initiated by the teacher as well as those initiated by students. This broader definition included questions, and also comments, praise, criticism, feedback to student responses, student requests for help, and often many other categories.

Besides noting how the definition of interactions has changed, it is important to note how research methods for examining classroom interactions have changed. In some studies, particularly earlier ones, researchers would enter a classroom and count and categorize the interactions observed. The frequency of particular interactions would then be correlated with pupils' achievement scores in an attempt to identify particular teacher behaviors with respect to interactions that might be considered "good" or "effective" teaching techniques. For example, Rowe's (27) work on wait-time indicated that a long pause (3 seconds or more) after posing a question is beneficial to students' achievement. However, there are relatively few rules that can be

---

"Try to pause after asking a question. . . . A pause of three to five seconds or even more will bring amazing results. Now the slow thinker will be able to participate. . . . The longer pause gives them time to think carefully and gain confidence before responding." (9, p. 9)

---

uncovered with this type of research. Often the categories are so detailed that the results might be applicable only to a particular grade level or a particular teacher.

"Teaching is a complex practice and, hence, not reducible to recipes or prescriptions." (*Professional Teaching Standards,* 20, p. 22)

More recent research has continued to examine classroom interactions but from a different perspective. Researchers now are interested in why a teacher decides to interact in a particular way or why students might respond in a particular way. The emphasis is not so much on Teacher A asked 30 questions, Teacher B asked 50 questions, Which is more effective?, but rather on What influenced Teacher A to ask a certain question at a particular point in the lesson? What made Teacher B decide to call on a particular student? What did the student mean by his or her response? What kind of understanding of mathematics did the response indicate? It is the understanding of why particular interactions occur and the effect of these interactions that researchers are now interested in studying.

Most would agree that teaching and learning could occur without texts, blackboards, or manipulatives, but we maintain that the learning process would exist for only a very few students if classroom interactions with teachers and peers were eliminated. Teacher-student interactions are indeed the heartbeat of the teaching-learning process.

Why Particular Interactions Occur

If one were to observe two classes at the same grade level, using the same text and covering the same topic, chances are the interactions occurring in each class would be quite different. This is because each teacher is unique as is each class of students. Even if the same question were posed initially, students might respond differently and the follow-up interactions would vary. Comments like, "My third-period class asks so many questions and my fifth-period class is so quiet" are not at all uncommon. For this reason it is important to examine the particular factors that influence teachers and students.

Influences on the Teacher

The mathematics classroom teacher is a thoughtful, reflective decision maker. There are many factors that influence the decisions a teacher makes, such as his or her beliefs about (a) how students learn mathematics, (b) what mathematics is, (c) the characteristics of the students, and (d) teaching itself (see Fig. 15.1). Each of these factors will be examined in terms of its influence on classroom interactions.

FIGURE 15.1   A teacher's beliefs influence
                      decision making

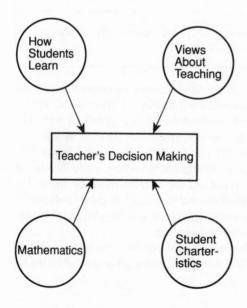

Teachers' Beliefs about How Students Learn. Theories of learning have influenced teaching for many years. Years ago some believed that in order to learn students needed to have much repetition, thus drill and practice techniques were used in our classes. (See the chapter on cognition for more details on the influence of learning theories on teaching.) Currently, research done by cognitive psychologists and mathematics educators (24, 28) suggests that learning takes place in a constructivist manner. That is, "Students construct knowledge for themselves by restructuring their internal cognitive structures" (3, p. 87). Students' minds are not an empty box for teachers to fill. Students have preconceived ideas about many mathematical phenomena and are most apt to learn when they are able to fit the new ideas into their already existing structure. Students are not passive absorbers of information; they are active constructors of knowledge.

Romberg (26) elaborates on knowledge by stating that to know mathematics is to do mathematics and that doing mathematics involves the four activities of abstracting, inventing, proving, and applying. Teachers who view learning and knowing mathematics from this perspective provide students with opportunities to explore different mathematical ideas and encourage them to think about their thinking processes in order to facilitate their construction of their own knowledge. (See 22 for a discussion of knowing mathematics.)

"If the process of coming to know mathematics in the classroom is going to have some relationship to the process of coming to know mathematics in the discipline, then teaching will involve getting students to reveal and examine the assumptions they are making about mathematical structures, and it will involve presenting new material in a way that enables them to consider the reasonability of their own and teacher's assertions. Lessons will be in the form of a mathematical argument, which students accept or reject on the basis of their own reasoning." (13, p. 136)

Teachers' Beliefs about Mathematics. A variety of mathematical topics are usually covered in the middle school grades. A traditional sequence might include continued work on multiplication and division, fractions, decimals and percents, prealgebra, and for some students, algebra. Additional topics might be geometry, probability, and statistics. The mathematics background of middle school teachers is probably more varied than that of a group of elementary or secondary teachers. Some middle school teachers were trained as elementary teachers with only a few college-level mathematics courses, and some might have been trained as secondary teachers with a college major in mathematics. Regardless of the amount of formal training in mathematics, however, it is how one views mathematics as a discipline that has the greatest influence on classroom interactions. For example, if one views mathematics as a set of procedures or algorithms to follow, then the classroom interactions will consist mostly of an attempt to have students understand and perform those procedures. However, if mathematics is viewed as a dynamic discipline that encompasses the studying of patterns (29), then the interactions will be much more open-ended and

> "Mathematics is the science of patterns. The mathematician seeks patterns in number, in space, in science, in computers, and in imagination. . . . In this way mathematics follows its own logic, beginning with patterns from science and completing the portrait by adding all patterns that derive from the initial ones." (29, p. 240)

will undoubtedly include explorations, lively discussions, and written expressions of students' thinking procedures and conclusions.

Teachers' Beliefs about Student Characteristics.   Teachers today are faced with a much more diverse student population than teachers of years ago (21). Students vary

> "In the long run, the most important factor affecting education is the changing profile of students. By the year 2000, one in every three American students will be minority; by 2020, today's minorities will become the majority of students in the United States. . . . Already the ten largest school districts in the United States are 70 percent Black and Hispanic . . . For as far ahead as we can reliably project, the percentage of minority children in America will continue to grow." (*Everybody Counts*, 21, p. 18)

widely in abilities, study habits, previous mathematics background, and motivation. Teachers have certain beliefs about or expectations of each of their students, either based on past experience with that particular student or on a preconception of students of a particular "type" (gender, race, or socioeconomic level). These beliefs, acted on consciously or unconsciously, affect teachers' interactions with students.

Research done on the elementary, middle, and secondary levels has shown that, in general, teachers of either sex interact more with boys than with girls during mathematics instruction (1). This pattern holds even when interactions for discipline purposes are not included in the counts. The sheer number of interactions with girls and with boys may or may not be a critical factor in girls' and boys' performance in mathematics. A more worrisome finding is that teachers often ask boys the more difficult or thought-provoking questions (those at a higher cognitive level) and ask

> Consider the cumulative effect of questioning patterns such as these:
>
> TEACHER: Joey, can you think of a story problem which you would use 2/3 × 12 to solve?
> TEACHER: Elizabeth, what is 2/3 × 12?

girls the easier ones. Why is this occurring? Do teachers have lower expectations for girls? Since there are some differences in achievement between boys and girls, are these expectations just a reflection of reality? What is the effect of these discrepant interactions? Do the girls and boys notice that the girls rarely get asked the difficult questions? Does this give the girls lower expectations of themselves? Sorting out the

---

The views of a female middle school student:

"INTERVIEWER: Do you think that teachers tend to call on boys more or on girls more in a math class?
STUDENT: Probably on boys more.
INTERVIEWER: Why do you think this is?
STUDENT: Well, they'll probably think that, um, since the guy is, um, you know, supposed to be the man of the house and stuff, he should know how to do a lot of stuff too and learn a lot of math and stuff . . . understand it better." (17, p. 84)

---

complexities of why interactions occur and their effects is not a simple task. However, teachers should be aware of such differential treatment and consider the possible consequences of their interactions. (See 6, 11, and 15, for more information on this topic.)

Research has also shown that teachers act differently with students of differing ability levels. In a study of teachers who taught both a regular algebra class and also a ninth-grade general math class, Lanier (14) found that these teachers "give their general math students much less direct instruction; general math students spend most of their class time doing homework and problems at their seat. Teachers also give general math students less assistance with seatwork, less encouragement, and less opportunity for discussion" (p. 1).

Good and Brophy (7) note, "A particular danger is that low expectations combined with an attitude of futility will be communicated to certain students, leading to erosion of their confidence. . . . This will confirm or deepen the students' sense of hopelessness and cause them to fail even when they could have succeeded under

---

"At the higher grades, failure to teach is sometimes seen in teachers who have low expectations . . . about the learning abilities of a particular class. Where homogeneous grouping is practiced in a junior high or high school, for example, teachers assigned to a period with a low-achieving class may sometimes abandon serious attempts to teach their subject. They may, perhaps, attempt to entertain the class, or else merely act as a sort of proctor who is interested only in seeing that the noise does not get out of hand. . . . It represents a total surrender to failure expectations." (7, p. 92)

---

different circumstances" (p. 100). If teachers have high expectations for students who have previously been low achievers, they will encourage student autonomy, independence, self-direction, and persistence in learning, and they will teach higher level cognitive processes and strategies. Some teachers simply will not allow their students to adopt a passive learning style and will not accept failure as an option.

Teachers' Beliefs about Teaching.   Teachers bring with them their own philosophical views of what teaching is all about and exactly what the role of the teacher should be. Some teachers view themselves as dispensers of knowledge, and as such, their

---

"The notion that a teacher could just have math knowledge and give that to the students is erroneous."

"Quite often the teacher is a transmitter, sending out information which the student is expected to receive. I think that mathematics must be much more than that. Mathematics is not just the science of learning the 'rules' and applying those rules to problems. Mathematics is much more dynamic, and there are many discoveries to be made not only by me, but my students." (unpublished written comments made anonymously by preservice teachers, fall 1989, in Mathematics Curriculum and Instruction taught by M. Koehler at San Diego State University)

---

interaction pattern would probably reveal many interactions involving "teacher telling." It would be the students' role to "catch" the information being given out. Other teachers view themselves as mediators between the discipline and the student, and their interactions would reveal much "teacher explaining" or efforts to make the discipline very clear and explicit to the student. Last, the teacher might view his or her

---

"As a teacher, I should be an organizer of ideas and a facilitator of learning, not a dispenser of information as were many of my mathematics teachers."

"Teaching math means guiding students toward number power and its application. It means helping them to discover the path on their own, but keeping them out of the deep pits along the way. . . . I see learning as a dynamic condition along a path, with students in front and the teacher behind holding a lantern." (unpublished written comments made anonymously by preservice teachers, fall 1989, in Mathematics Curriculum and Instruction taught by M. Koehler at San Diego State University)

---

role as "co-explorer." This teacher still maintains a leadership role but allows students much more autonomy in the learning situation and explores various facets of the discipline with them. The interactions in this case would be much more open-ended.

In summary, many factors influence how a teacher interacts with his or her students in the classroom. Often, these factors are combined in different ways for different sets of circumstances. Some teachers vary their style of teaching depending on the perceived ability level of their students. Some teachers might feel they can be co-explorers with an advanced group of students but will allow lower ability students much less autonomy and will assume the role of knowledge dispenser with these students.

Influences on the Student

We know from research that students learn and retain more if they are actively involved in the learning process rather than being passive absorbers of information.

Students are individuals, however, and they interact or participate in a mathematics class in varying degrees. Two factors affecting student participation are their views of themselves as learners of mathematics and of the discipline of mathematics.

Students' Views of Themselves as Learners of Mathematics. How students feel about their ability to learn and do well in mathematics plays an important role in their actual achievement. (A detailed discussion of affective variables is contained in another chapter in this volume. A few affective variables will be highlighted here.) Confidence in one's ability to do well in mathematics is critical to succeeding in mathematics. In terms of classroom interactions, a student who is more confident will be more likely to take a risk and attempt to solve a difficult or unfamiliar problem or volunteer to respond to or ask a difficult question. Success at a difficult problem leads to more confidence. In addition, a teacher is often more inclined to call on more confident students, thus giving them more opportunity to interact (25). Finding

---

To bolster confidence:

TEACHER: Christine, would you like to work #27 out on the board for us today?
CHRISTINE: (looks frightened and reluctant) Not really.
TEACHER: You can take a friend to the board with you, if you like.
CHRISTINE: Oh. Okay, I'll do it.

---

a way to encourage the less confident student to participate more in class without feeling threatened is indeed difficult. Using small group learning is one technique that might meet this need. Questions or tasks that are open-ended and involve more than one right answer also may stimulate the less-confident student.

Another important affective variable that influences how a student interacts in class is the student's attributional style. This refers to the reasons the student gives as the causes of her or his success or failure. Students with a mastery-oriented attributional style believe that their success is due to their ability and to their effort. They also believe their failure results from lack of effort. On the other hand, students exhibiting learned helplessness attribute their success to the ease of the task or to luck and their failure to lack of ability or effort (10). Mastery-oriented students feel that they are in

---

Interaction involving attribution statements:

STUDENT: Wow! This is my lucky day! I just aced that test.
TEACHER: Yes, Jerry you did very well—but it wasn't luck. You have a lot of ability, and you've been studying hard lately. That's a winning combination!

---

control of their own mathematical destiny. Students whose attributional style is learned helplessness believe that success is out of their control and will therefore be elusive. The mastery-oriented students will be more likely to put forth effort in class and participate actively in classroom interactions. The learned helplessness students feel that they have little influence on their situation, so it does not matter whether they participate or not. This type of student is most likely to be a passive absorber of information rather than one who tries to construct personal knowledge. When a teacher is aware of these different attributional styles he or she is better able to encourage all students to be active participants.

Students' Views of Mathematics. The perception that students have of mathematics influences how they choose to participate in a mathematics class. If they see mathematics as a collection of rules, they will be less inclined to conjecture, question, or explore. Instead they will wait to be told the rule, and then they will want

---

According to the Fourth Mathematics Assessment of the NAEP (31), seventh-grade students had somewhat mixed views of mathematics.

- 88% believed that knowing how to solve a problem is as important as getting the solution
- 83% believed that there is always a rule to follow in solving mathematics problems
- 78% believed that doing mathematics requires lots of practice in following rules
- 50% felt learning mathematics is mostly memorizing
- 35% believed that new discoveries are seldom made in mathematics

---

to apply the rule in similar problems. The most common question asked by students with this perception of mathematics will be "Is this right?" Their reaction to a teacher's explanation will be, "Just tell me the steps, and I'll do it." On the other hand, if students have the view that mathematics is a dynamic discipline and that they can discover particular facets of it, they are more likely to be inquisitive, asking, "What would happen if . . . ?" It appears that the students' view of mathematics is most likely to influence the quality of the interactions they engage in rather than the quantity.

In summary, when teachers are trying to improve the quality of classroom interactions, it is important for them to be aware of a student's confidence level, attributional style, and perception of mathematics. If these aspects are not considered, even the most perfectly phrased question by the teacher may not elicit a thoughtful student response.

Improving Classroom Interactions

The NCTM *Curriculum and Evaluation Standards* (19) suggests five goals for all students: "(1) that they learn to value mathematics, (2) that they become confident in their ability to do mathematics, (3) that they become mathematical problem solvers, (4) that they learn to communicate mathematically, and (5) that they learn to reason mathematically" (p. 5). If students are to realize these goals, they must have the opportunity to practice them in daily classroom interactions. Teachers can help by improving their use of three classroom strategies: questioning, responding to student-initiated interactions, and monitoring peer-peer interactions.

Questioning. Although there are many types of teacher-student interactions, the most frequent is the teacher-initiated question. As questioning is a fundamental teaching device, teachers should use it for the maximum instructional benefit. In most teacher education programs some basic features of questioning are discussed. Posamentier and Stepelman (23) discuss a variety of question types that should be avoided. These include (a) yes-no or guessing questions such as, "Is triangle ABC isosceles?" (p. 29), (b) leading questions such as, "Seven is a factor of 35, isn't it?" (p. 31), (c) whiplash questions such as, "The slope of the line is, what?" (p. 30), and (d) teacher-centered questions such as, "Give *me* the solution set of $3x - 5 = 2$" (p. 31). Johnson (9) points out other poor questioning techniques that even the best teachers sometimes use. These include answering your own questions, showing giveaway facial expressions, and labeling a question as easy or hard before it is asked.

> "Try not to label the degree of difficulty of a question. How many times have I said, for example, 'Here's an easy one!' . . . A student who answers the question correctly can't feel much satisfaction, thinking, 'So what? It was easy.' A student who can't answer the question is going to feel even worse: 'Why try? I can't even answer an easy question!'" (9, p. 12)

Another way to categorize questions is by cognitive level. Questions on a low cognitive level might ask students to recall a fact, perform a simple computation, or carry out an algorithm. At a higher cognitive level, questions would call for a deeper comprehension of the mathematical situation and an explanation of the mathematics involved. Such questions might require students to know why a particular process works, to analyze a problem, or to use applications correctly. The goals of the *Curriculum and Evaluation Standards* aimed at increasing students' reasoning ability and their ability to communicate mathematically would be enhanced by asking more questions of this type. Questions at higher cognitive levels might involve asking students why a particular answer was given, or to explain a process used, or to find another way to solve a problem, or to convince another student of their reasoning. Burns (2) illustrates other appropriate questioning techniques to stimulate student thinking.

Research has shown that teachers ask many more questions at low cognitive levels than at high cognitive levels. For example, Suydam (32) reports on a large observational study of junior high mathematics classes in which 80% of questions asked by teachers were at a low cognitive level. In a study conducted at the seventh-grade level, Hart (8) made detailed observations of interaction patterns. She found that on the average, each day there were about five times as many interactions at low cognitive levels than at high cognitive levels. In a study of fourth-grade classes, Fennema and Peterson (6) also observed interaction patterns and found that low cognitive level interactions occurred about 5.3 times more often than high cognitive level interactions. It is sometimes more illuminating to consider raw data rather than percentages.

Low cognitive level questions that do not help the students' understanding:

MR. JOHNSON: Shelley, do you have the answer to number 10?
SHELLEY: π/3.
MR. JOHNSON: No, that's not right. Mark, what do you have?
MARK: π/6.
MR. JOHNSON: No, but that's close. Vicky, what do you have?
VICKY: I didn't get that one.
MR. JOHNSON: Nick?
NICK: I only worked up to number 8.
MR. JOHNSON: Kristen?
KRISTEN: π/7.
MR. JOHNSON: That's right, Kristen. Now, does everyone understand? (9, p. 22)

In a study of 8 ninth-grade algebra classes, Koehler (12) found an average of 64.1 interactions in a class period (50 minutes). Of these, an average of 50.3 interactions involved low-level mathematics, 1.0 involved high-level mathematics, and the remaining interactions were not mathematics related.

Several reasons can be suggested for the small number of high cognitive level interactions that take place. First, teachers may not realize the importance of asking such questions. Second, teachers may think they are asking high cognitive level questions more frequently than they actually are. (One interesting self-evaluation technique is to tape-record yourself while teaching, and then later try to categorize your questions as high or low level). Last, high-level questions might be more difficult to think of "on your feet." They often require advance preparation and may need to

---

Changing low cognitive level questions into high-level ones:
  Low cognitive level questions:

(a) Find the perimeter and area of a rectangle with sides of 6 and 9 inches.
(b) Round these numbers: 5.75   5.83

High cognitive level questions:

(a) A rectangle has a perimeter of 30 units. What might be its area?
(b) What numbers could be rounded off to 5.8? (30)

---

become part of the actual plan for the lesson. A teacher needs to make a conscious effort to ask high-level questions. One technique is for the teacher to give himself or herself "wait-time" before asking a question in an effort to formulate a more meaningful one.

Many of the reports of the 1980s, including the *Curriculum and Evaluation Standards* (19) and *Everybody Counts* (21), point out the importance of having our students improve their higher order thinking skills. Assessments such as the National

Assessment of Educational Progress (16) reveal how poorly our students are performing at problem solving and at higher cognitive level thinking.

Problem posing is one form of asking higher cognitive level questions. In order to become adept at problem posing, teachers need to have a collection of problems to pose, and they need to develop their problem-posing skills. Since the appearance of

> "Posing problems which engage students in using their mathematical knowledge is central to the act of teaching." (13, p. 156)

NCTM's *Agenda for Action* (18), which stated as its first recommendation that "problem solving must be the focus of school mathematics in the 1980s" (p. 2), many problems and sources of problems have appeared in the NCTM yearbooks and journals. In terms of casting a problem in a cognitively rich setting, Romberg (26) suggests three aspects of such instructional activities: "(a) a complex task to be solved whose solution is not intended to be obvious; (b) the concepts and procedures needed to solve the task are known by the student; and (c) the 'problem' is to find a strategy (or heuristic) that can be used to connect the known ideas with the unknown" (p. 189). Lampert (13) based on her research as a teacher-scholar in fourth- and fifth-grade

> "The problems that were used served to mediate between what the students already knew and what I wanted them to learn." (13, p. 142)

classes, suggests the attributes of a good problem for teaching mathematics: creating a learning environment in which students are inclined to express their thinking about the mathematical structures underlying computational procedures and leading students into unfamiliar and important mathematical territory.

Responding to Student-Initiated Interactions. Thus far this chapter has focused primarily on interactions such as questioning and problem solving that are initiated by the teacher. However, a great number of classroom interactions are student-initiated. In one study (12), about half of the classroom interactions observed were student initiated. The most common of these interactions, as most teachers will testify, is a request for help or for clarification of procedure or directions. Teachers need to be aware that as they are responding to a request for help, they need to be as thoughtful as they are when forming their own questions. What kind of response will help most to stimulate the thinking of this particular student? In order to answer this, teachers need to know as much as they can about what a student understands. Often a request for help is fairly broad as in "How do you do number 5?" or "I don't get this" or "I'm lost" or "Is this right?" As a first response, the teacher should try to clarify where the difficulty lies. By probing a bit, a teacher might be able to pinpoint a difficulty. To the student who asks, "Is this right?" the teacher would want to identify whether the student lacks estimation skills to check for reasonableness of result, or lacks knowl-

The teacher of mathematics should orchestrate discourse by—

* posing questions and tasks that elicit, engage, and challenge each student's thinking;
* listening carefully to students' ideas;
* asking students to clarify and justify their ideas orally and in writing;
* deciding what to pursue in depth from among the ideas that students bring up during a discussion;
* deciding when and how to attach mathematical notation and language to students' ideas;
* deciding when to provide information, when to clarify an issue, when to model, when to lead, and when to let a student struggle with a difficulty;
* monitoring students' participation in discussions and deciding when and how to encourage each student to participate (20, p. 35).

edge of how to check calculations, or is displaying a lack of confidence. The teacher would then be able to respond to the specific difficulty and empower the student to be more independent in understanding and judging the correctness of her or his own work. A response such as "Tell me what you did" might be revealing. In contrast, if a teacher simply responds, "Yes, it's right—good job," he or she is not helping the student increase in knowledge or understanding.

In responding to students' requests for help, teachers should focus on the goals stated in the *Curriculum and Evaluation Standards*. In helping students to clarify exactly what their questions are, we will be helping them to communicate mathematically. In helping them to determine if their answers are correct, we will be helping them to reason mathematically.

Teachers should foster the development of autonomous learning behaviors. An autonomous learner is one who can work independently, is persistent in the face of difficulty, and who chooses to or has a willingness to attempt higher cognitive level problems. A more complete discussion is given by Fennema and Peterson, (5). In one study, Koehler (11) looked primarily at the influence of different classroom processes on gender differences in mathematics achievement. The study findings suggest that teachers whose students, particularly their female students, developed an improved sense of autonomy were those who limited the amount of help they gave

"When to let students struggle to make sense of an idea or decision about a problem without direct teacher input, when to ask leading questions, and when to tell students something directly are crucial to orchestrating productive mathematical discourse in the classroom." (*Professional Teaching Standards*, 20, p. 36)

students. That is, females performed best in a class in which they had less opportunity to seek help and where they were not encouraged to do so. The processes in this type of class forced the females to become more independent and autonomous in their learning of mathematics. In some instances, then, teachers might consider redirecting, rather than personally addressing, their students' requests for help, and thus might be helping them to become more independent.

Monitoring Peer-Peer Interactions.   The interaction patterns that we have discussed thus far have involved the teacher and the students. Another important type occurring within the mathematics classroom is exchanges between students. This type of

> "Students must talk, with one another as well as in response to the teacher. . . . When students make public conjectures and reason with others about mathematics, ideas and knowledge are developed collaboratively, revealing mathematics as constructed by human beings within an intellectual community." (*Professional Teaching Standards,* 20, p. 34)

interaction occurs most frequently in small group instruction, an effective teaching strategy that has recently become more popular. Even though the teacher is not directly involved in the interactions that occur within the small group, he or she should be aware of these exchanges and their possible implications.

Small groups work cooperatively; the members ask for and give help to one another. Research has shown, however, that not all students are equally adept at getting their questions answered using this peer process. Webb (33) and Webb and Kenderski (34) investigated peer interactions within small groups in both high- and low-achieving eighth-grade classes. In the high-achieving classes, they found that females' requests for help went unanswered at a rate double that of males. However, females were more responsive than males to their peers and gave help more frequently. Females often asked questions that were more general, whereas males asked questions that were more specific. Students of both sexes addressed their questions to males more often than to females. When a group was composed of three males and one female, often the female was virtually ignored. It is interesting to note that in the lower achieving classes, the researchers did not notice different interaction patterns on the part of males and females.

Although the research on this phenomenon is not extensive, it should alert teachers to monitor closely the interactions occurring in small groups. Some students need help in being sensitive to the needs of other students, while other students need help in knowing how to ask a question so that they are successful in receiving an explanation. Students also need to be encouraged to be somewhat independent and to ask questions only when they really need to.

A teacher can help students work in groups in a manner that benefits all. One way is to ask them to characterize those they like to work with. Usually, descriptions such as listeners, turn takers, and helpers are given. The teacher can then have students strive to be the kind of group member they like to work with. See Davidson (4) for more suggestions on cooperative groups.

Classroom Reality.   Besides the specific recommendations made above, there are some additional aspects to consider that deal directly with the reality of life within the classroom. These ideas are not based on empirical research but come from the wisdom of the classroom teacher. First, it is important that teachers develop a style of interacting that involves respect for the student and he or she use this style throughout the day and with all students. If a teacher interacts with students in an authoritarian way during certain periods of the day and then tries to establish more student

---

SCENE: It is the beginning of the class period, and the teacher is attending to many details.

TEACHER: (in a scolding tone) Mark, Sit down! This is not the time to sharpen your pencil!

MARK: (sits down, but appears embarrassed and angry)

SCENE: A few minutes later, discussing the homework.

TEACHER: Mark, would you share with us how you did the third proof?

MARK: I didn't get that one (but Mark's homework paper is in front of him, and it is complete).

---

thinking and cooperation during mathematics class, the strategy will most likely not be successful. Boys and girls are very perceptive and will notice when a teacher treats students differently or is insincere. For example, if a teacher uses a demeaning, critical tone when making behavior-related comments, students may be unwilling to cooperate with the teacher in answering high-level mathematics questions for fear of also being publicly criticized for an incorrect answer.

A second aspect of classroom reality regards the demands of implementing changes. The above paragraphs have made suggestions regarding the improvement of classroom interactions. It is important that we realize that teachers are thoughtful and reflective decision makers. They will ultimately decide how they will implement these suggestions in their individual classes. Without question, however, many of the suggestions given (e.g., asking more high cognitive level questions, using more problem posing, fostering mathematical communication, developing autonomous learning behaviors, and encouraging good peer interactions) take quite a bit of out-of-class time in terms of planning and developing methodologies. Many classroom teachers

---

A typical middle school teacher's load might include

- teaching 5 periods, with 35 students per class
- making 3 different preparations
- acting as moderator of the mathematics team
- tutoring 2 days a week after school
- serving on the School Restructuring Committee
- serving on the Race and Human Relations Committee
- attending professional conferences
- planning major curriculum changes in summers
- attending to personal concerns (e.g., as spouse, parent)

are not given adequate planning time or resources to enable them to develop modifications to their existing classroom interaction patterns. Aggressively seeking planning time and time to work with colleagues in an ongoing process is one of a teacher's professional responsibilities. A serious revamping of classroom interaction patterns involves many aspects. Teachers cannot be expected to alter their patterns without the time and opportunity to explore and learn about some of the options mentioned briefly in this chapter.

One technique that might facilitate the implementation of some of the above ideas is the practice of pairing teachers for "peer-coaching." Teachers can observe each other and give each other suggestions for improving certain strategies. This can be done in a nonevaluative manner, and both teachers benefit.

A final aspect involves recognizing the importance of the "critical incident"—a singular event that stands out in a student's mind and may alter his or her success in mathematics. This event might be positive or negative. One intervention strategy for dealing with people who are "math anxious" or who are "math avoiders" is to have them write their "math autobiography." In many instances, students are able to trace the origin of their anxiety (or dislike for, or poor performance in mathematics) to an event that happened to them in some particular grade. They might have been embarrassed because they did not know an answer, or were criticized by the teacher in front of the class, or froze while doing a problem at the board. Even though these events might seem minor in the eyes of a teacher, compared to the many hours students spend in a mathematics class over the course of 12 years of schooling, they are often major in the eyes of the students.

Sometimes a teacher may not be aware that an incident is critical until a student comes back a year or many years later and relates the incident. One seventh grader told a teacher, "You can't teach me fractions. No one has ever been able to teach me fractions, and I'll just never learn them." The teacher replied, "But you've never had *me* for a teacher. I'm the best fraction teacher that ever lived, and when we're through, you'll know fractions." The student came up at the end of the year and reminded the teacher of the interchange and added, "You taught me fractions."

Some readers might dismiss the notion of critical incidents as being important only in the lives of mathematics low achievers. However, this is not the case. When several classes of preservice secondary mathematics teachers were asked to write their "mathematics histories" many described a singular event that stood out in their memory as influencing their mathematics learning thereafter. Some events described were positive and some were negative. The events included instances of criticism or praise (especially in front of peers); unfair grading practices; individual teacher attention, time, and interest; being called on or being ignored; or being the winner or loser of a mathematics competition (informal, in-class competitions rather than mathematics contests). Many of these students survived their critical incidents, went on to become mathematics majors, and are planning to teach. Many other students, however, might have been lost.

As classroom teachers we need to consider every interaction we have with students in terms of short-term goals as well as possible long-term effects. A positive or careless negative remark may have a lasting impact.

Summary

Three themes have been discussed in this chapter: a definition of classroom interactions, influences on teachers and students in participating in interactions, and suggestions for improving classroom interactions. Interactions are indeed the heartbeat of the mathematics classroom. Mathematics is learned best when students are actively participating in that learning, and one method of active participation is to interact with the teacher and peers about mathematics. The nature of classroom interactions needs to change as we learn more about how students learn and as we examine what it means to know mathematics. NCTM has presented the mathematics education community with challenging documents in the *Curriculum and Evaluation Standards* (19) and the *Professional Standards for Teaching Mathematics* (20). To implement these standards fully will take much in the way of resources and coordinated effort. However, besides changes in texts or equipment, classroom interactions will also need to change in both subtle and major ways. After all, it is what goes on in each individual class that really makes a difference in students' lives.

Looking Ahead . . .

The entire teaching/learning process is extremely complex, and classroom interactions are a large and vital component of that process. Researchers need to continue to investigate the effect of particular interactions in terms of mathematical achievement and understanding, affective variables, and differential effectiveness based on gender or race. In the past this research was done mostly by observing willing teachers. While this has provided us with a good knowledge base, future research might be done with the teacher as a more active participant. Having teachers help to analyze and interpret the results will add keen insight to a complex issue.

Mary Schatz Koehler

The teacher is the heartbeat of the classroom—the master magician who inspires, guides, and rewards the efforts of students as they explore the dimensions of mathematical power. The teacher provides the atmosphere for observing patterns, making connections, and enjoying the beauty of mathematics. This is an awesome responsibility that requires persistence, reflection, creativity, and genuine respect for students and their divergent thinking. An excellent teacher is one who provides the opportunity for all of his or her students to make an A, clearly defines objectives, looks beyond isolated concepts, models mathematical questioning and thinking, makes the students the central focus in the classroom, and instills confidence. Students mirror the attitudes and beliefs of teachers. I wonder what the future would hold for us if this philosophy were shared by all.

Millie Prior

About the Authors

Mary Schatz Koehler is an associate professor in the Mathematical Sciences Department at San Diego State University where she teaches classes for preservice elementary and secondary teachers. Her research interests include gender-related issues in mathematics and the effects of various teacher behaviors on student learning.

Millie Prior, resource teacher at Bell Junior High in San Diego and mentor teacher, is affiliated with the Greater San Diego Mathematics Council, the San Diego Mathematics Project, the California Mathematics Demonstration Schools, and the California Assessment Program. She was named Outstanding Junior High Mathematics Teacher in 1987.

References

1. BROPHY, J. (1985) Interactions of male and female students with male and female teachers. In L. C. Wilkinson & C. B. Marrett (Eds.), *Gender influences in classroom interaction* (pp. 115–142). New York: Academic Press.
*2. BURNS, M. (1985). The role of questioning. *Arithmetic Teacher,* 32(6), 14–16.
3. COBB, P. (1988). The tension between theories of learning and instruction in mathematics education. *Educational Psychologist,* 23(2), 87–103.
*4. DAVIDSON, N. (Ed.). (1990). *Cooperative learning in mathematics: A handbook for teachers.* Menlo Park, CA: Addison-Wesley.
5. FENNEMA, E., & PETERSON, P. L. (1985). Autonomous learning behavior: A possible explanation of gender-related differences in mathematics. In L. C. Wilkinson & C. B. Marrett (Eds.), *Gender influences in classroom interaction* (pp. 17–32). New York: Academic Press.
6. FENNEMA, E., & PETERSON, P. L. (1986). Teacher-student interactions and sex-related differences in learning mathematics. *Teaching and Teacher Education,* 2(1), 19–42.
7. GOOD, T. L., & BROPHY, J. E. (1978). *Looking in classrooms.* New York: Harper & Row.
8. HART, L. E. (1989). Classroom processes, sex of student, and confidence in learning mathematics. *Journal for Research in Mathematics Education,* 20(3), 242–260.
*9. JOHNSON, D. R. (1982). *Every minute counts: Making your math class work.* Palo Alto, CA: Dale Seymour.
10. KLOOSTERMAN, P. (1990). Attributions, performance following failure and motivation in mathematics. In E. Fennema & G. C. Leder (Eds.), *Mathematics and gender* (pp. 96–127). New York: Teachers College Press.
11. KOEHLER, M. S. (1990). Classrooms, teachers, and gender differences in mathematics. In E. Fennema & G. C. Leder (Eds.), *Mathematics and gender* (pp. 128–148). New York: Teachers College Press.
12. KOEHLER, M. S. (1986). Effective mathematics teaching and sex-related differences in algebra one classes (Doctoral dissertation, University of Wisconsin, 1985). *Dissertation Abstracts International,* 46, 2953A.
13. LAMPERT, M. (1988). Connecting mathematical teaching and learning. In E. Fennema, T. P. Carpenter, & S. J. Lamon (Eds.), *Integrating research on teaching and learning mathematics* (pp. 132–167). Madison: University of Wisconsin, Wisconsin Center for Education Research.
14. LANIER, P. (1981, Fall). Ninth-grade general mathematics adds up to trouble. *Institute for Research on Teaching Communication Quarterly.* East Lansing: Michigan State University.
15. LEDER, G. C. (1990). Teacher/student interactions in the mathematics classroom: A different perspective. In E. Fennema & G. C. Leder (Eds.), *Mathematics and gender* (pp. 149–168). New York: Teachers College Press.
16. LINDQUIST, M. M. (Ed.). (1989). *Results from the fourth mathematics assessment of the*

National Assessment of Educational Progress. Reston, VA: National Council of Teachers of Mathematics.

17. MEYER, M. R., & KOEHLER, M. S. (1990). Internal influences on gender differences in mathematics. In E. Fennema & G. C. Leder (Eds.), *Mathematics and gender* (pp. 60–95). New York: Teachers College Press.

18. NATIONAL COUNCIL OF TEACHERS OF MATHEMATICS. (1980). *An agenda for action*. Reston, VA: Author.

*19. NATIONAL COUNCIL OF TEACHERS OF MATHEMATICS. (1989). *Curriculum and evaluation standards for school mathematics*. Reston, VA: Author.

*20. NATIONAL COUNCIL OF TEACHERS OF MATHEMATICS. (1991). *Professional standards for teaching mathematics*. Reston, VA: Author.

21. NATIONAL RESEARCH COUNCIL. (1989). *Everybody counts*. Washington, DC: National Academy Press.

22. PUTNAM, R. T., LAMPERT, M., & PETERSON, P. L. (1990). Alternative perspectives on knowing mathematics in elementary schools. *Review of Research in Education, 16*, 57–150.

*23. POSAMENTIER, A. S., & STEPELMAN, J. (1986). *Teaching secondary school mathematics*. Columbus, OH: Charles Merrill Publishing Company.

24. RESNICK, L. B., & FORD, W. W. (1981). *The psychology of mathematics for instruction*. Hillsdale, NJ: Erlbaum.

25. REYES, L. H. (1981). Classroom processes, sex of student, and confidence in learning mathematics (Doctoral dissertation, University of Wisconsin, 1981). *Dissertation Abstracts International, 42*, 1039A.

26. ROMBERG, T. A. (1987). A common curriculum for mathematics. In T. A. Romberg & D. M. Stewart (Eds.), *The monitoring of school mathematics: Background papers*. Madison: Wisconsin Center for Education Research.

27. ROWE, M. B. (1986). Wait-time: Slowing down may be a way of speeding up! *Journal of Teacher Education, 37*, 43–50.

28. SCHOENFELD, A. H. (1987). *Cognitive science and mathematics education*. Hillsdale, NJ: Erlbaum.

29. STEEN, L. A. (1988, April 29). The science of patterns. *Science, 240*, pp. 611–616.

*30. SULLIVAN, P., & CLARKE, D. (1991). Catering to all abilities through "good" questions. *Arithmetic Teacher, 39*(2), 14–18.

31. SWAFFORD, J., & BROWN, C. (1989). Attitudes. In M. M. Lindquist (Ed.), *Results from the fourth mathematics assessment of the National Assessment of Educational Progress* (pp. 106–116). Reston, VA: National Council of Teachers of Mathematics.

*32. SUYDAM, M. (1985). Questions? *Arithmetic Teacher, 32*(6), 18.

33. WEBB, N. M. (1984). Sex differences in interaction and achievement in cooperative small groups. *Journal of Educational Psychology, 76*(1), 33–44.

34. WEBB, N. M., & KENDERSKI, C. M. (1985). Gender differences in small-group interaction and achievement in high- and low-achieving classes. In L. C. Wilkinson & C. B. Marrett (Eds.), *Gender influences in classroom interaction* (pp. 209–236). New York: Academic Press.

CHAPTER 16

Assessment and Evaluation for Middle Grades

Norman L. Webb and Carol Welsch

We must ensure that tests measure what is of value, not just what is easy to test. If we want students to investigate, explore, and discover, assessment must not measure just mimicry mathematics. (31, p. 70)

$\mathbf{E}$valuation and assessment are valuable tools to help teachers and others meet students' mathematical needs. Evaluation is using standardized tests, surveys, demographic analyses, and other means to determine the value of a program. Assessment is using classroom tests, observations, questioning, projects, portfolios, and other means to determine what a student knows, can do, feels, and believes. In this chapter, research and other developments are reported on how evaluation and assessment can be applied to teaching mathematics in the middle grades.

Evaluation and assessment in the middle grades have the challenge of balancing high academic standards and expectations with encouragement and building self-confidence. They must also take into consideration the fact that students vary greatly in their ability to work with abstract information and in their mathematical knowledge. Instruction in grades 5–8 actively engages students through exploring, questioning, discussing, and investigating mathematics; evaluation and assessment must do the same.

Reasons for Evaluation and Assessment

Two reasons for evaluation and assessment are decision making and communication. Evaluation and assessment provide information for making decisions about students and programs. Students in the middle grades can vary greatly in mathematical achievement, have the potential for rapid changes in intellectual growth, and require

---

Assessment and evaluation help to answer questions such as

- What is the student's conception of area?
- Can the student represent situations using a variety of means (tables, graphs, verbal rules, and equations)?
- Does the student have the confidence to take a risk in attacking a difficult problem?
- Can the student correctly use common terms such as *and, or, all,* and *if . . . then*?

---

their emotional development to be considered along with other factors. Data and information collected through student assessment and program evaluation can help teachers juggle these many factors.

Evaluation and assessment can communicate what is expected and what has been achieved. Students whose minds are constantly whirring with thoughts of how they relate to their peers and dealing with their self-image need to know where they stand. Assessment results can give students productive feedback about their mathematical achievement if these are presented in such a manner as to reassure students and to help develop their self-esteem, so critical to preadolescence. Assessment information is also important for communicating with parents or guardians about their children's progress. In grades 5–8, teacher-parent conferences are still viable means of communication, a means whose effectiveness is greatly reduced in high school. But caution is needed. Adults need help in understanding what is normal development for this age group. And, for the first time in their schooling career, a number of students can reach a level of mathematical achievement that exceeds that of their parents or

---

Parents need to know what mathematics is important for their child to know as much as what progress their child is making.

---

guardians. Learning to do mathematics using technology is only one of many such examples. For effective communication with parents, assessment and evaluation information needs to be in a form that is understandable to them.

Evaluation and Assessment for Decision Making

Evaluation and assessment help to make decisions for directing, selecting, grading, and motivating students (32). The information provided helps to structure student experiences, develop criteria for judging performance, and encourage further learning.

Directing Student Learning.   Directing student learning requires constant decision making by the teacher and by students. Teachers gather information by observing students, making conjectures about their knowledge of mathematics, testing these suppositions, considering what students are to know, and then using this information to help students learn mathematics. Through this process evaluation and assessment become integral to instruction. Thompson and Briars (47) identify three important features of informed decision making.

1. Know what students need at any given moment considering content, circumstances, the structure of the students' knowledge, and good teaching practices.
2. Ask thought-provoking questions to determine student perceptions about important ideas.
3. Listen thoughtfully and interactively, probing and analyzing the meaning students attach to mathematical concepts, procedures, and thinking.

Cooperative learning groups can help students in middle grades become more accountable for their own learning and for helping other students (22). For this to happen, adequate time is needed for the learning groups to process and assess how

---

One example of students directing their own learning is fifth-grade students working in cooperative groups designing a park.

---

well they worked together and what improvements they can make to be more effective. When students are given the responsibility to share their knowledge and reasoning with each other, to confirm each other's answers, and to devise procedures for their group to become more effective, they are directing their own learning.

Tests can be a sound source of information for making instructional decisions. However, the dominant form of testing, teacher-constructed tests, is generally restricted to short-answer items requiring low-order knowledge. Information gained from such tests does not provide useful information on students' problem solving and higher order thinking skills. Silver and Kilpatrick (41) stress that teacher-constructed tests are not nearly so useful as they might be in providing information to guide problem-solving activities. Instead, they recommend using tests that (a) measure the ability to recognize problems with similar mathematical structure, (b) are open-ended and require students to generate numerous conjectures, and (c) require students to

---

Twin primes are two prime numbers that only differ by two (e.g., 5 and 7, 11 and 13, 17 and 19). Make conjectures about the numbers that occur between twin primes for primes greater than 3. Explain how you would validate your conjectures." (30, p. 82)

---

develop appropriate mathematical models to represent situations. Such tests ask students to analyze, explain, conjecture, contrast, and model rather than only to solve, find, or compute.

Selecting Students.   Assessment has been used to place students in particular mathematics programs or to group them with the belief that students will perform better when working with students at a learning level similar to their own. For example, in middle schools, tests and other assessment procedures have been used to determine algebra readiness. Test scores have also guided the selection of students for special programs such as those for the talented and gifted. However, there is little evidence to support tracking as being educationally sound (34, 35). Dividing students into separate classes for high, average, and low achievers and developing different curriculum paths have a negative effect by exaggerating initial differences rather than providing a means to overcome them. Also, mathematics learning is not strictly hierarchical. Students having difficulty with one topic at one level can do mathematics

> **Assessment should be used for inclusion not exclusion.**

at other levels or in other topics. Middle grade students who are still struggling to master computation skills, for example, can learn about and successfully use algebraic concepts such as variable and linear relationships. Making wrong decisions about students can be reduced by using multiple means of assessment.

Grading or Certifying Students. Grading generally assumes two forms: norm-referenced or "grading on the curve" and criterion-referenced or "grading for mastery" (32). Available research does not lead to a clear interpretation of how these two different reward structures relate to performance. There is some evidence that the higher achieving students—the top third—perform better when they know they will be graded under individual competition rather than by use of a curve. There also is

> **Some teachers have given students group projects and group tests on which all members receive the same grade and have found this to work well. (13)**

evidence that indicates students who perform poor initially are given assurance by a criterion-referenced scheme that enables some to improve their performance. In other studies, however, students who did well initially became over-confident and lowered their achievement expectations (50). The grading process used will affect students differently according to their levels of achievement.

Motivating Students. Assessment as a motivating factor for students can be weakened when a grade is assigned to a test. Instead, informal assessment that explores student knowledge and that creates interesting and perplexing situations can build on intrinsic motivation that will lead to deeper understanding of mathematics (19). Some research has shown that requiring students to explain, elaborate, or defend their positions to others has made them evaluate, integrate, and elaborate knowledge in new ways (2). Reciprocal teaching seems to enhance the engagement and motivation of middle grades students, helping them to become more self-directed learners. Motivation and adjustment to student knowledge as well as cognitive functioning are important in the assessment process (39).

> Needed are ways for using evaluation and other means to encourage students to value learning for its own sake rather than competing for grades or teacher recognition. (33)

Evaluation and Assessment as Forms of Communication and Influence

Assessment instruments reflecting the curriculum and instructional goals provide a concise way for a teacher to communicate what he or she values to students, parents, and other teachers (10). These instruments translate curriculum goals and expectations into specific examples and delineate need as well as accomplishments. Beyond

> The use of fixed (multiple) choice items, regardless of validity, as the only means of assessing mathematics achievement communicates the wrong message about a curriculum that stresses problem solving, application, and investigation.

communicating expectations, the conditions and the results of assessment, particularly tests, can have a profound influence on student performance and curriculum.

Influences on Students. In a review of 120 research studies on the effects of non-content variables on mathematics test performance, Hembree (20) reports that test conditions affect student test performance. Some of the conditions that enhance performance are work space located adjacent to test items, an easy-to-hard arrangement of items on timed tests, pictures with word problems, a "proper" ordering of data in word problems, and in test taking.

Hembree found that unannounced and frequent testing (more than once a week) can encourage a positive learning environment. Caution needs to be taken in interpreting Hembree's findings, however because the content tested was not indicated. These conclusions may be inappropriate for assessing higher order knowledge. If testing is done too frequently, objectives may be restricted to those that can be covered during the period between tests, thereby inhibiting the development of problem-solving experiences and the ability to solve more complex tasks over extended periods of time. The length of a test can also be an issue for middle school students if the time to take the test exceeds their attention span.

Influences on Teachers. Teachers spend a significant amount of their professional time—as much as 20% to 30%—in assessment-related activities (46). Certain tests can strongly influence teaching practices and the curriculum. The influence of tests on teachers and what they teach depends on the value attached to the tests. Test results used for evaluating teacher performance, certifying students for graduation, or determining budgetary allocations can significantly influence teachers. In a national survey of eighth-grade mathematics teachers (38), 80% reported giving mandated tests in grades 7, 8, or 9. The same percentage of teachers indicated that they had made some instructional changes because of district- or state-mandated tests. Mandated tests influenced at least a quarter of the teachers to increase their emphasis on basic skills and pencil-and-paper computation. Some teachers, because of mandated tests, decreased their emphasis on extended project work (19%) and activities involving calculators (16%). Mandated tests do influence instructional content, emphasis, and time allocation.

What to Evaluate and Assess

Middle grades mathematics programs should evaluate (a) what mathematics students know and can do; (b) student's dispositions towards mathematics, including their attitudes, interests, and beliefs; (c) program equity (assuring that all students have equal opportunity for reaching their potential in learning mathematics); and (d) program effectiveness for meeting the goals of a quality mathematics program.

Assessing Mathematical Knowledge

One important principle is that knowledge of mathematics should be assessed over the full range of goals. A framework specifying content ensures that assessment provides an adequate coverage of goals. This framework could be a list of strands, a content-by-behavior matrix, or a cognitive map. The choice of framework will influence the information obtained from the assessment and needs to be selected

---

All aspects of students' mathematical knowledge—problem solving, communication, reasoning and analyzing, concepts, and procedures—and their integration with each other need to be assessed to have a comprehensive understanding of what students know.

---

carefully (49). The NCTM *Curriculum and Evaluation Standards* (30) stresses that assessment must determine students' ability to integrate different aspects of mathematics with each other and with other subject matter. Figure 16.1, for example, illustrates an assessment task based on a situation from social studies.

A second principle is that the emphasis in assessment should reflect the emphasis placed on specific curriculum goals, objectives, and mathematical content. This is important because different situations, such as using a story or even varying the wording in a story, in which mathematical knowledge is assessed can result in different outcomes. If curriculum goals strongly emphasize that students should be able to solve real-world problems, then these need to be emphasized in assessment.

There is some indication that even changing the wording of a task by making the situation more concrete or more abstract can change the difficulty of the task. Problems such as those in Figure 16.2 have similar mathematical structure, but those presented in an abstract form were more difficult for junior high students than the

FIGURE 16.1   An assessment task related to
social studies (30, p. 206).

Pretend you are a pilot for a major airline-
transport company. You have been assigned
to a trans-Pacific flight from Denver
to Hong Kong. You are curious about the
shortest route between the two cities, but all
you have is a regular globe and a piece of
string. You know that the distance around the
earth along the equator is 25,000 miles.
With only these two items, how can you figure the
shortest distance? What is this distance?

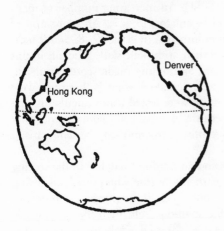

FIGURE 16.2   Concrete factual word problems were less difficult for junior high
school students than abstract hypothetical word problems with
similar mathematical structure (3, p. 189)

A sample concrete factual word problem:
   A young farmer has eight more hens than dogs. Since hens have two legs
   each, but dogs have four legs each, all together the animals have 118 legs.
   How many dogs does the young farmer own?

A sample abstract hypothetical word problem:
   A given number is six more than a second number. If the first number were
   four times as large and the second two times as large, their sum would be
   126. What is the second number?

problems with the same structure presented in a concrete and factual form (3). One reason students found the concrete factual problems easier was that over 75% of problems appearing in textbooks were of this type. This and other research (17) emphasize the importance of situational factors. These factors relate to assessment results and appear to relate to the curriculum. For assessment to be aligned with the curriculum, the emphasis given to situational factors in assessment needs to reflect the instructional goals.

Assessment also may not reflect the curriculum emphases because of the degree in which technology is used in both. If calculators are used in instruction but excluded from assessment, then the alignment between the two is in question. Research has shown that sustained calculator use in the mathematics class tends to improve students' attitudes as well as achievement (21, 51). An increasing number of mandated tests are requiring at least some use of calculators (5, 25). An evaluation of students in the *Transition Mathematics* curriculum (16) in grades 7, 8, and 9 indicates that the use of calculators does not affect their arithmetic skill. Students in this curriculum who used calculators in instruction and testing made scores similar to those of comparison students who did not use calculators when both groups were tested without calculators. When the two groups were tested using calculators, the *Transition Mathematics* students, perhaps because of enhanced manual dexterity at data entry for the calculator users, consistently, outperformed the comparison students.

Another way of comparing the assessment and curriculum match is in the scoring and reporting of assessment results. This is particularly true when problem-solving and higher order thinking skills are important outcomes. If the means and processes for deriving a solution are as important as the solution itself, then the scoring and reporting should reflect these. Charles and Lester (8) used a scheme that reported scores on understanding the problem, planning a solution, and getting an answer. The School Mathematics Project (40) used log sheets for students to record their work and queries, and for teachers to write notes about their students' work on open-ended tasks. In both cases, students' thinking was assessed because of the importance given to it in the curriculum. The results of students' thinking were recorded and reported along with indications of correct solutions. In using cooperative learning groups, Slavin (42) reports giving team scores based on students' improvement points. These are assigned to each student by comparing his or her current quiz score with a base score determined from previous work. The higher the student's current score rises above his or her base score, the more improvement points the student will earn. What is scored and reported in assessment should reflect what is emphasized by the instructional goals.

Assessing Student Disposition Toward Mathematics

What students believe about mathematics, what they believe about themselves doing mathematics, how they get excited about mathematics, and how they value mathematics all play a central role in mathematics learning and instruction (27) and should be assessed. The NCTM *Curriculum and Evaluation Standards* (30) provides seven areas to consider when assessing disposition toward mathematics: (a) confidence in using mathematics; (b) flexibility in exploring mathematical ideas; (c) willingness to persevere in mathematical tasks; (d) interest, curiosity, and inventiveness in doing mathematics; (e) inclination to monitor and reflect on their own thinking and performance; (f) valuing of the application of mathematics; and (g) appreciation of the role of mathematics in our culture. Students in grades 5 through 8 are at a critical stage in forming a positive disposition, which adds credence to the importance of

> **At a time when peer thinking is such a strong influence on students' disposition in general, monitoring how students are relating to mathematics is important.**

including this focus for assessment. Systematically observing students, talking with students, and recording information using checklists based on the above seven areas are means for assessing mathematical disposition.

Evaluating Program Equity

Many studies report differences in mathematics achievement and expectations for different groups of students (a) by gender (18, 26); (b) by race (1, 23, 24, 48), and (c) by ethnicity, language backgrounds, or socioeconomic status (SES) (20). In the previous three national assessments, African American and Hispanic 13-year-olds have consistently scored below white 13-year-olds; however, the gap narrowed in the 1986 assessment (14). While the achievement level of middle-grade underrepresented students is improving, this gain seems to be dissipated by these students being channeled away from higher level mathematics. Some have observed that African American students now have less access to college preparatory courses in mathematics than before the mid-1960s (44). Because of the changing demographics and strong evidence of inequities, programs at all levels—classroom, school, district, state, and nation—need to evaluate equity.

Evaluation needs to go beyond identifying differences to providing insight into causes and methods for reducing them. For example, evaluation can help determine whether some students are being systematically excluded from access to the full range of mathematics courses. Enrollment data by gender, SES, or ethnicity can identify inequities that may be explained in more detail by information on entry procedures. Discovery of inequities may necessitate evaluating the beliefs and attitudes of those who are responsible for the mathematics program and biases embedded in instructional and assessment materials.

How to Evaluate and Assess

The diversity of students and objectives requires a wide variety of evaluation and assessment tools and techniques. The NCTM *Curriculum and Evaluation Standards* (30) emphasizes using multiple methods to assess all aspects of mathematical

> "Effective means of assessing operational knowledge of mathematics must be . . . broad, reflecting the full environment in which employees and citizens will need to use their mathematical power." (*Everybody Counts,* 31, p. 69).

knowledge and their connections. A variety of techniques is particularly relevant in assessing students in the middle grades as they continue their transition in mathematics from concrete experiences to abstract reasoning. The means to determine what students know and their dispositions toward mathematics must be as interesting and relevant to the middle grade student as the curriculum. Means of assessing students are testing, questioning, observing, and other alternatives.

Using Tests

Nearly all teachers, in some reports over 95% (53), use some form of testing—more in mathematics than in other content areas. The percentage of teachers using tests increases by grade level. Teachers use tests for grading, grouping, diagnosing, evaluating, and reporting. More teachers (44%) use tests for grading than for any other single purpose, although at least a third of the mathematics teachers use tests for each of the other purposes (45).

Different types of tests are used in different ways. Teachers are more comfortable with published tests and have more concern with those they construct themselves when considering test effectiveness, potential for improving learning, focus on real skills, and challenge to the students (45). Criterion-referenced tests are more appropriate than norm-referenced tests for relating achievement to what a person should know, testing competence rather than general ability, and providing useful feedback to students. Criterion-referenced tests are usually administered under less rigorous conditions than norm-referenced tests (52).

In constructing tests, many factors are important. Students' reading ability is a major factor in solving word problems. This does not imply that reading difficulty should be reduced. Word problems written in a terse, bare-bones form are more difficult because of fewer contextual clues (28). Yet the text, situation, and mathematical representation or model do contribute to the complexity in solving and then interpreting the mathematical solutions to word problems, for example, those shown in Figure 16.2. It is important to understand the relationship among these elements. Researchers are applying and developing cognitive theories to help explain the relationship between the mathematics and situations, but explicit findings have yet to evolve.

> Asking students to explain a procedure can be an excellent test exercise using writing.

New forms of testing are being researched. Collis, Romberg, and Jurdak (12) have developed items that include a mathematical situation and a structured set of questions about a situation based on a model for cognitive development. An example of these "super items" is shown in Figure 16.3. The model, *Structure of the Learned Outcomes or Responses* (SOLO), has been influenced by Piaget's cognitive development stages. A series of increasingly complex tasks is used to assess the student's level of mathematical knowledge. The tasks increase in complexity by using more information and requiring the information to be put together in deeper ways. The *unistructural* level requires the use of one obvious piece of information. The *multistructural* level requires the use of two or more discrete inferences related to separate pieces of information. The *relational* level requires the use of two or more inferences directly related to an integrated understanding of information in the situation. The *extended abstract* level requires the use of an abstract general principle or hypothesis.

Other studies have expanded traditional forms of testing that require only one number response or a short answer. Figure 16.4 shows an open-ended question used by the California Assessment Program to assess students' higher order thinking (4). Student responses or scores on this question reveal students' ability to delete and

FIGURE 16.3   An example of a super item with the different stages (12, p. 212)

[There] is a machine that changes numbers. It adds the number you put in three times and then adds 2 more. So if you put in 4, it puts out 14.

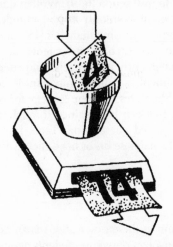

If 14 is put out, what number was put in? [Unistructural question level]

If we put in a 5, what number will the machine put out?
[Multistructural question level]

If we got out a 41, what number was put in? [Relational question level]

If *x* is the number that comes out of the machine when the number *y* is put in, write a formula that will give us the value of *y* whatever the value of *x*. [Extended abstract question level]

FIGURE 16.4   An open-ended problem assessing the ability to detect and explain faulty reasoning (4, p. 21)

James knows that half of the students from his school are accepted at the public university nearby. Also, half are accepted at the local private college. James thinks that this adds up to 100 percent, so he will surely be accepted at one or the other institution. Explain why James may be wrong. If possible, use a diagram in your explanation.

describe a condition in which two groups can each be half of the total and still not be mutually exclusive. The mathematical language used in students' responses helps to assess their mathematical sophistication. Those who use Venn diagrams in their responses indicate another form of understanding. Responses to one well-written open-ended question generally give more information on what students know about mathematics than responses to a short answer question.

Using Questioning

A second means of assessing students' knowledge is through verbal or written questioning. Using the response to help determine student comprehension and skill level is a form of assessment that is integral to instruction (6, 9). Written questionnaires or surveys can be used to gather information on opinions, student attitudes toward problem solving (7), student attitudes toward learning mathematics (15), or attitudes about students from other sources such as former teachers and parents. Scarr (39) stresses that schools have a responsibility to match curricula to each child's needs and talents and to consider motivation and adjustment as equally important to cognitive functioning in determining competence. She notes that one strategy for assessing motivation is student self-report measures that can be obtained through different forms of questionnaires. Another means is guided questioning. Table 16.1 shows an ordered set of questions to ask a student to diagnose his or her difficulty in solving problems (11).

Making Observations

Observing and assigning some meaning to these observations is an essential part of assessment. Performance assessment involves observing students demonstrating their proficiency and judging the outcomes in some context. Stiggins and Bridgeford (45) distinguish between *structured performance assessment*, which is planned and systematically designed, and *spontaneous performance assessment*, which arises naturally from the classroom environment. Nearly all (96%) mathematics teachers questioned reported using spontaneous performance assessment and 86% reported using structured performance assessment. Mathematics teachers seem to be more comfortable with spontaneous observation than with other forms of assessment, including teacher-made and published tests.

TABLE 16.1   An Example of a Sequence of Questions for Diagnosing Difficulty in
Solving Word Problems (11, p. 123)

Find one problem that you cannot do.

Procedure	Purpose
1. Read the question to me. If you don't know a word, leave it out.	To identify reading errors
2. Tell me what the question is asking you to do.	To identify errors in comprehension
3. Tell me how you are going to find the answer.	To identify transformation errors
4. Show me what to do to get the answer. Tell me what you are doing as you work.	To identify errors in the use of process skills
5. Now write down the answer to the question.	To identify encoding errors

Teachers are not as careful in considering quality control when doing structured performance assessment (45). Most (84%) mathematics teachers will specify reasons for assessment prior to conducting the assessment. Fewer (46% to 68%) teachers plan scoring before the observation, define levels of performance before rating, inform students of scoring criteria before assessment, observe and rate more than once before judging, and write down the scoring criteria before assessment. Less than 15% of the teachers reporting rely on more than one rater such as a colleague, students rating one another's performances, and students rating their own performance.

In evaluating programs, a number of sources exist for rating forms or other structures for making observations. Pechman (36) provides a series of forms for mathematics classroom observations as well as for conducting schoolwide observations. These have been field tested for the purpose of evaluating middle school mathematics programs. The NCTM *Curriculum and Evaluation Standards* (30, pp. 235–236) displays forms that can be used to make informal observations of students' mathematical disposition. Teachers need to be aware, however, of the middle school student who becomes "invisible" and avoids being noticed. Middle school students are unusually good at this, especially the more self-conscious ones.

Using Alternative Forms of Assessment

One alternative form of assessment currently receiving attention is the use of portfolios (29, 43). In a portfolio the teacher and the student choose items to collect as a record of the student's progress in mathematics. A portfolio might include samples of the written descriptions of the results of practical or mathematical investigations, extended analyses of problem situations, descriptions and diagrams of problem-solving processes, and group reports and photographs of student projects. The content of the portfolios can be reviewed by groups of teachers to reflect on what has been accomplished. Teachers who have used portfolios have reported that the procedure has helped them to understand what students were thinking and to gain ideas for improving instruction (43).

Students may be asked to prepare a narrative to explain why the selected material was included in the portfolio or to let the material speak for itself, illustrating a

---

Categories for evaluating portfolios:

- evidence of mathematical thinking
- quality of activities and investigations
- variety of approaches and investigations (29).

---

particular view of mathematics held by the student. One issue that arises with portfolios is how to evaluate them in assigning a grade. Portfolios are promising as a form of assessment for considering the work of students over an extended period of time; however, many practical details are yet to be worked out.

Asking students to list all they can about a concept, procedure, or mathematical situation can help assess how the student connects the concept, procedure, or situation with other ideas.

Another alternative form of assessment is to have students do a project or investigation that may extend from a class period to one or two weeks. Projects can be both instructional and valuative. Examples of projects include conducting an opinion survey of the student body on music group preference and analyzing the data, collecting

---

"Topics for possible investigations include gears and ratios, maps, sound waves and music, collecting and analyzing litter, and consensus studies." (43, p. 13)

---

data on pulse rate as related to different forms of exercise and states of rest, or evaluating living conditions on a distant planet. Pirie (37) stresses that processes and thinking should be the focus when assessing investigations and extended projects.

The two general approaches to rating projects are giving an overall impressionistic grade or allocating numerical marks to observed features. The features can be the approach taken to solve the task, implementation, use of argument, interpretation of results, and overall use of communication ability as well as mathematical knowledge demonstrated. Other assessable student characteristics, though requiring more judgment, are work habits, thoroughness, curiosity, and persistence. As with other alternative forms of assessments, the use of projects and investigations for assessment is still in the developmental stage with new questions being raised as others are answered.

Conclusion

Not all past research is relevant to evaluating the expanded view of mathematics knowledge that is currently being proposed. New forms of evaluation and assessment are called for and are to be encouraged, with teachers taking a leading role in using new techniques to determine their students' full range and depth of mathematical knowledge, their disposition toward pursuing the learning of mathematics, and the relevance and equity of the programs.

Evaluation and assessment, essential to education, are closely linked to instruction and must change concurrently. The research and literature reported here, primarily from the last decade, are only a sample of the information available and have been selected to make specific points. But in that time mathematics education has changed significantly as new reforms have been instituted. Research and literature from the past that reports on evaluation need to be reviewed with careful attention to the mathematics content and goals. Problem solving, higher order thinking, communicating, and integrating knowledge are now being emphasized.

Looking Ahead . . .

Evaluation and assessment are tools, not ends in themselves. Changes in assessment practices are called for because what students are to know about mathematics and to do with mathematics are changing. In looking toward new forms of assessment, questions remain unanswered. Classroom teachers are the people to research these questions in small, deliberate steps: trying an essay question, organizing a test differently (one third on skills, one third on concepts, and one third on open-ended problem solving), having students devise their own test, or doing other small experiments. With teachers as researchers, meaningful assessment practices can be developed.

Norman L. Webb

Research has provided much information. What is missing is information about gathering data on the student's enjoyment of mathematics, eagerness to pursue the topic, and confidence in his or her abilities. It is still difficult to find an evaluation technique that is appropriate for the middle school student who is enduring the stresses of intense physical and psychological changes. Teachers need measurements that enhance student confidence, do not cause self-consciousness, temper assessment with understanding, and encourage students to continue their study of mathematics through an appropriately sequenced program. We need to find more answers to what is motivating our students.

Carol Welsch

About the Authors

Norman L. Webb is a senior research scientist for the Wisconsin Center for Education Research, University of Wisconsin-Madison. His work is in the area of evaluation and assessment.

Carol Welsch is a seventh-grade mathematics teacher at Orchard Ridge Middle School, Madison, Wisconsin. She has been active in the University of Wisconsin-Madison College of Engineering and Mathematics Academic Industrial Teacher Internship Partnership, National Aeronautics and Space Administration Educational Workshop for Mathematics and Science Teachers, Teachers Teaching Teachers, and Improving Mathematics for Minority Students.

References

*1. BRADLEY, C. (1984). Issues in mathematics education for native Americans and directions for research. *Journal for Research in Mathematics Education, 15*(2), 96–106.

*2. BROWN, A. L. (1988). Motivation to learn and understand: On taking charge of one's own learning. *Cognition and Instruction, 5*(4), 311–321.

*3. CALDWELL, J. H., & GOLDIN, G. A. (1987). Variables affecting word problem difficulty in secondary school mathematics. *Journal for Research in Mathematics Education, 18*(3), 187–196.

*4. CALIFORNIA STATE DEPARTMENT OF EDUCATION. (1989). *A question of thinking.* Sacramento, CA: Author.

5. CARTER, B. Y., & LEINWAND, S. J. (1987). Calculators and Connecticut's eighth grade mastery test. *Arithmetic Teacher, 34*(6), 55–56.

6. CAZDEN, C. B. (1986). Classroom discourse. In M. C. Wittrock (Ed.), *Handbook of research in teaching* (3rd ed.) (pp. 432–463). New York: Macmillan.

*7. CHARLES, R., LESTER, F., & O'DAFFER, P. (1987). *How to evaluate progress in problem solving.* Reston, VA: National Council of Teachers of Mathematics.

*8. CHARLES, R. I., & LESTER, F. K. (1984). An evaluation of a process-oriented instructional program in mathematical problem solving in grades 5 and 7. *Journal for Research in Mathematics Education, 15*(1), 15–34.

9. CLARK, C. M., & PETERSON, P. L. (1986). Teachers' thought processes. In M. C. Wittrock (Ed.), *Handbook of research on teaching* (3rd ed.) (pp. 255–296). New York: Macmillan.

10. CLARKE, D. J. (1988). *Assessment alternatives in mathematics.* A Mathematics Curriculum and Teaching Program professional development package. Canberra, Australia: Curriculum Development Centre.

*11. CLARKE, D. J., CLARKE, D. M., & LOVITT, C. J. (1990). Changes in mathematics teaching call for assessment alternatives. In T. J. Cooney (Ed.), *Teaching and learning mathematics in the 1990s* (1990 Yearbook, pp. 118–129). Reston, VA: National Council of Teachers of Mathematics.

*12. COLLIS, K. F., ROMBERG, T. A., & JURDAK, M. E. (1986). A technique for assessing mathematical problem-solving ability. *Journal for Research in Mathematics Education, 17*(3), 206–221.

*13. DAVIDSON, N. (1990). Small-group cooperative learning in mathematics. In T. J. Cooney (Ed.), *Teaching and learning mathematics in the 1990s* (1990 Yearbook, pp. 52–61). Reston, VA: National Council of Teachers of Mathematics.

14. DOSSEY, J. A., MULLIS, I. V. S., LINDQUIST, M. M., & CHAMBERS, D. L. (1988). *The mathematics report card: Are we measuring up?* Princeton, NJ: Educational Testing Service.

15. FENNEMA, E., & SHERMAN, J. A. (1976). Fennema-Sherman mathematics attitude scales: Instruments designed to measure attitudes toward the learning of mathematics by females and males. *Journal for Research in Mathematics Education, 7*(4), 324–326.

16. FLORES, P. V., GENIESSE, R., GISKEN, O., KLEINE-KRACHT, P., MATHESON, D., MATHISON, S., & SELTZER, M. (1986). *Transition mathematics: Field study.* Evaluation Report 85/86-TM-2. Chicago: University of Chicago School Mathematics Project.

17. GOLDIN, G. A., & McCLINTOCK, C. E. (Eds.). (1984). *Task variables in mathematical problem solving.* Philadelphia: The Franklin Institute Press.

18. HANNA, G. (1986). Sex differences in the mathematics achievement of eighth graders in Ontario. *Journal for Research in Mathematics Education, 17*(3), 231–237.

19. HATANO, G., & INAGAKI, K. (1987). A theory of motivation for comprehension and its application to mathematics instruction. In T. Romberg & D. Stewart (Eds.), *The monitoring of school mathematics: Background papers. Volume 2: Implications from psychology; outcomes of instruction* (pp. 27–46). Madison: Wisconsin Center for Education Research.

20. HEMBREE, R. (1987). Effects of noncontent variables on mathematics test performance. *Journal for Research in Mathematics Education, 18*(3), 197–214.

21. HEMBREE, R., & DESSART, D. J. (1986). Effects of hand-held calculators in precollege mathematics education: A meta-analysis. *Journal for Research in Mathematics Education, 17*(1), 83–99.

*22. JOHNSON, D. W., & JOHNSON, R. T. (1990). Using cooperative learning in math. In N. Davidson (Ed.), *Cooperative learning in mathematics* (pp. 103–125). Menlo Park, CA: Addison-Wesley.

23. JONES, L. V., BURTON, N. W., & DAVENPORT, E. C. (1984). Monitoring the mathematics achievement of black students. *Journal for Research in Mathematics Education, 15*(2), 154–164.

24. LLABRE, M. M., & CUEVAS, G. (1983). The effects of test language and mathematical skills assessed on the scores of bilingual Hispanic students. *Journal for Research in Mathematics Education, 14*(4), 318–324.

25. LONG, V. M., REYS, N., & OSTERLIND, S. J. (May, 1989). Using calculators on achievement tests. *Mathematics Teacher, 82*(5), 318–325.

*26. MARSHALL, S. P. (1983). Sex differences in mathematical errors: An analysis of distracter choices. *Journal for Research in Mathematics Education, 14*(4), 325–336.

27. McLEOD, D. P. (1987). New approaches to research on attitude. In T. Romberg and D. Stewart (Eds.), *The monitoring of school mathematics: Background papers. Volume 2: Implications from psychology; outcomes of instruction* (pp. 279–290). Madison: Wisconsin Center for Education Research.

*28. MOYER, J. C., MOYER, M. B., SOWDER, L., & THREADGILL-SOWDER, J. (1984). Story problem formats: Verbal versus telegraphic. *Journal for Research in Mathematics Education, 15*(1), 64–68.

*29. MUMME, J. (1990). *Portfolio assessment in mathematics.* Santa Barbara: California Mathematics Project, University of California-Santa Barbara.

*30. NATIONAL COUNCIL OF TEACHERS OF MATHEMATICS. (1989). *Curriculum and evaluation standards for school mathematics.* Reston, VA: Author.

31. NATIONAL RESEARCH COUNCIL. (1989). *Everybody counts.* Washington, D.C.: National Academy Press.

32. NATRIELLO, G. (1987). The impact of evaluation processes on students. *Educational Psychologist, 22*(2), 155–175.

*33. NOLEN, S. B. (1988). Reasons for studying: Motivational orientations and study strategies. *Cognition and Instruction, 5*(4), 269–287.

*34. OAKES, J. (1986a). Keeping track, part 1: The policy and practice of curriculum. *Phi Delta Kappan, 68*(1), 12–17.

*35. OAKES, J. (1986b). Keeping track, part 2: Curriculum inequality and school reform. *Phi Delta Kappan, 68*(2), 148–154.

36. PECHMAN, E. M. (1989). *Mathematics program assessment for the middle grades.* Field-test edition. Carrboro, NC: Center for Early Adolescence.

37. PIRIE, S. (1988). *The formal assessment of investigational work and extended projects in mathematics.* Paper presented at the International Congress of Mathematics Education, Budapest, Hungary.

38. ROMBERG, T. A., ZARINNIA, E. A., & WILLIAMS, S. R. (1989). *The influence of mandated testing on mathematics instruction: Grade 8 teachers' perceptions.* Madison: National Center for Research in Mathematical Science Education, University of Wisconsin.

39. SCARR, S. (1981). Testing for children: Assessment and the many determinants of intellectual competence. *American Psychologist, 36,* 1159–1166.

40. SCHOOL MATHEMATICS PROJECT. (1989). *MEG mathematics (SMP) mode 2 with coursework teachers handbook.* 1989–90 Edition. Southampton: The University.

*41. SILVER, E. R., & KILPATRICK, J. (1988). Testing mathematical problem solving. In R. Charles & E. Silver (Eds.), *Teaching and assessing mathematical problem solving* (pp. 178–186). Hillsdale, NJ: Erlbaum.

*42. SLAVIN, R. E. (1990). Student team learning in mathematics. In N. Davidson (Ed.), *Cooperative learning in mathematics* (pp. 69–102). Menlo Park, CA: Addison-Wesley.

*43. STENMARK, J. K. (1989). Assessment alternatives in mathematics: An overview of assessment techniques that promote learning. A document prepared by the EQUALS staff and the assessment Committee of the California Mathematics Council *Campaign for Mathematics.* Berkeley: University of California.

44. STIFF, L. V. (1990). African-American students and the promise of the Curriculum and Evaluation Standards. In T. J. Cooney (Ed.), *Teaching and learning mathematics in the 1990s* (1990 Yearbook, pp. 152–158). Reston, VA: National Council of Teachers of Mathematics.

*45. STIGGINS, R. J., & BRIDGEFORD, N. J. (1985). The ecology of classroom assessment. *Journal of Educational Measurement, 22*(4), 271–286.

46. STIGGINS, R. J. (1988). Revitalizing classroom assessment: The highest instructional priority. *Phi Delta Kappan, 69*(5), 363–372.

*47. THOMPSON, A., & BRIARS, D. (1989). Assessing students learning to inform teaching: The message in the NCTM evaluation standards. *Arithmetic Teacher, 37*(4), 22–26.

48. TSANG, S. L. (1984). The mathematics education of Asian Americans. *Journal for Research in Mathematics Education, 15*(2), 114–122.

49. WEBB, N. L. (1992). Assessment of students' knowledge of mathematics: Steps toward a theory. In D. A. Grouws (Ed.), *Handbook of Research on Mathematics Teaching and Learning* (pp. 661–683). New York: Macmillan.

50. WILLIAMS, R. G., POLLACK, M. J., & FERGUSON, N. A. (1975). Differential effects of two grading systems on student performance. *Journal of Educational Psychology, 67,* 253–258.

*51. WILSON, J. W., & KILPATRICK, J. (1989). Theoretical issues in the development of calculator-based mathematics tests. In J. W. Kenelly (Ed.), *The use of calculators in the standardized testing of mathematics* (pp. 7–15). New York: College Entrance Examination Board.

52. WOOD, R. (1986). The agenda for educational measurement. In D. L. Nuttall (Ed.), *Assessing educational achievement* (pp. 185–203). London, England: Falmer Press.

53. YEH, J., HERMAN, J., & RUDNER, L. M. (1980). A survey of the use of various achievement tests. *Testing in our schools.* Washington, DC: National Institute of Education.

Classroom Research

Part IV

Classroom Research

CHAPTER 17

Teacher As Researcher

Gillian Clouthier and Darlene Shandola

If I set out to find an answer to some classroom matter, I am a learner; but in engaging in the inquiry, I am initiating a small piece of research: I am both learner and researcher—two sides of the same coin. (16, p. 23)

Teacher researchers are teachers interested in improving educational practices within their own settings. To do this, they undertake research in order to get a better understanding of events in their particular environments. Although all educational researchers have as their goal the improvement of instructional practice, teacher researchers differ from traditional researchers in that their findings are immediately translated into practice within the same setting that the research was done. They are motivated by a need to construct their own knowledge about the things that are important to them. In this chapter, we will talk about the teacher as researcher in the middle grades mathematics classroom. First, however, the origins of classroom inquiry will be reviewed briefly. Then we will offer suggestions for planning and structuring classroom inquiry so that advantage can be taken of the ongoing, but tacit investigations that form part of everyday classroom practice. Finally, we will present our views on why classroom inquiry should be a component of every teacher's professional repertoire.

Action research saw its beginnings in education in the 1950s. Corey saw collaborative research as a means to improve school practices by modifying the behavior of all those involved in an institutionalized change effort (9). Motivation for this research stemmed from the involvement of practitioners in the definition of problems to be solved and the identification of workable solutions.

Action Research

Action research is characterized by the collaborative efforts of teachers to identify an important problem and to develop a workable solution (10). It is on-site inquiry aimed at problem resolution rather than the production of research data and reports (15).

Historically, much educational research evolved from a comparison of treatments with different groups of students. Findings are often reported statistically, with the goal of generalizing from a random sample to an entire population. Educational research of this type has produced a large quantity of data but little information about the way education operates in naturalistic settings. Consequently, it appears to have had little effect in changing classroom practice. Because it is conducted in isolation, university-generated research is often seen as impractical and inaccessible to classroom teachers (7, 20).

Generally speaking, in the 1950s action research was not fully accepted by the scientific establishment in the United States. It was believed that social science investigations should proceed by controlled testing (24). Problems and descriptions of researchers were seen to have more value than those of practitioners (13). Since then, however, action research has experienced a resurgence of interest. This occurred when qualitative methods and ethnographic techniques were being developed in social science research (24).

Naturalistic studies in education, rooted in the experience of those who are actually involved, have become more common. The classroom is seen as the key, with teachers and students being the essential information providers. They are both the chief source of questions and the best source of data to investigate those questions. The relationship between teaching and learning from this standpoint is seen as a complex, interactive process involving many variables. With this perspective comes a change in direction toward a study of individual case histories rather than group responses to planned interventions (16).

According to Wallace, action research is now a well-established strategy whereby teachers may improve their work in classrooms (24). Their role is that of researcher. Stenhouse uses the phrase *teachers as researchers* to describe teachers who are developing their art as practitioners through a reflective approach to and ongoing inquiry about the activities of their classroom (22).

Inquiry is an interesting way to describe the research of teachers in their teaching-learning environments. It implies a sense of discovery, a curiosity, an openness to explore different phenomena observed in the classroom. Although they are not always doing formalized research, teachers constantly assess and modify their actions and behavior in order to make student learning more meaningful. The inquiry view of research is tremendously liberating because it validates the everyday work of classroom teachers; it emphasizes the importance of teacher and student interaction as a source of information on learning and teaching.

> If research is seen primarily as a process of discovery, then "every lesson should be for the teacher an inquiry, some further discovery, a quiet form of research." (5, p. 15)

Classroom Inquiry: Who Can Do It?

Any and all teachers can be involved in classroom inquiry. Any teacher who asks questions such as "What if?" or "Why is this happening?" or who is interested in improving teaching and learning in the classroom can be a teacher researcher.

Classroom teachers are in the best position to ask questions about learning, to accumulate data, and to take up teaching directions based on the learning patterns that emerge (16). It is not enough that classrooms be researched; they need to be researched by teachers. Educational research will not count as valid knowledge of practice unless it feeds teachers' understanding of their own practical day-to-day problems (15).

Two different models of teacher research are evident in the literature: teacher/professor and teacher/teacher. Each will be described briefly in the next section.

> Some models of teacher research are individual, some collaborative. In all cases one important element remains constant: the research must be personally or collectively owned by the teacher or teachers involved. "We are not researchers in other people's classrooms, looking for proofs or generalizable truths, but reflective practitioners in our own classrooms, searching for insights that help us understand and improve our practice" (4, p. 775).

Teacher/Professor Collaboration

Having significant numbers of teachers involved in classroom inquiry would improve the quality of educational research in terms of the relevance of the questions addressed, the methods of inquiry, the interpretation of results, and the implementation of change (19). Since the time and depth of research training and the collegial network available to university faculty is not likely to be as accessible to individual classroom teachers, some may not engage in classroom inquiry. Research teams that include teachers and university personnel could overcome some of the difficulties.

Strickland discusses research teams and details four reasons for the trend toward collaboration between classroom teachers and university professors (23). First, new trends in research have stimulated an increased desire to conduct research in natural contexts: classrooms. The second reason is a shift in focus toward process. Information on children's thinking processes and the strategies they use in different learning situations is best collected in actual classroom settings. The third reason is an increased use of qualitative research methods such as interviews and systematic observations which are best carried out in the classroom. Fourth, there is a trend toward collaboration in every aspect of research. Investigators from different fields are working on topics of mutual interest, bringing their various points of view to bear upon problems and research questions.

An important point must be made regarding teacher/researcher collaboration. Often the classroom teacher implements other people's research. A successful partnership, however, involves the active participation of the teacher in posing the questions and deciding on parameters as well as in collecting data. Anzul and Ely were involved in such a team approach initiated by the classroom teacher (2). Anzul was interested in improving the quality of discussion in her literature groups and in encouraging her students to express themselves while exploring literature in more depth. Ely was a teacher of teachers who acted as a mentor, supporting Anzul, offering methodological advice, and encouraging her to share her work with others.

In the pursuit of such collaboration, Asher used seven principles that guided the work of one particular teacher/researcher project (3). These principles embody experiential learning, peer support, and discovery in the learning process. With this approach, learners have control and ownership of their work. They apply not only to beginning writers or beginning researchers, but to all learners.

Asher identified seven principles that guided the work of one particular teacher-researcher project (3).

1. The university researcher should act as a model and share his/her own processes of doing research;
2. Seminar sessions should be generated by participant questions, ideas, and concerns;
3. Participants should be allowed and encouraged to change the focus of their inquiry if another question becomes more important;
4. Researchers should be given support at every stage of the research process, from defining a research question and developing a methodology to collecting data, analyzing it and writing it up;
5. Opportunities should be provided for team members to work together;
6. Teacher researchers are given the right to make decisions about their own studies;
7. Teacher researchers should be encouraged to learn about doing research by engaging in all the struggles in which any researcher would engage.

Teacher/Teacher Collaboration

A second scenario for teacher as researcher is that of teacher/teacher collaboration. In this situation, teachers engage in classroom inquiry with other teachers without input from universities. A common experience, question, or concern may initiate the classroom inquiry. Colleagues then work together planning instruction, collecting data, and interpreting it in order to enhance their classroom practices. Time for reflection is important. Teachers must have a chance to discuss their findings and then directly relate them to practice.

One project involved approximately 50 elementary teachers who formed a research community (1). Although there was university involvement, the teachers themselves initiated, planned, and implemented research on literacy-related topics. They met regularly to discuss insights, problems, and concerns. University researchers offered advice and guidance at different points in the teacher research process. The group became a support system, supporting each other in different ways at different times.

Teacher/teacher collaboration may occur at the school level where a staff has identified an area of common interest. Professional development funds can be used to pay for substitute teachers so that small groups of teachers can meet to discuss their work and share findings. Teachers can be released to visit one another's classrooms to observe or co-teach a lesson. Dialogue should follow the lesson(s) so that teachers have opportunities to consider their findings in light of a full range of contextual and pedagogical factors before making further instructional decisions. This model for professional development is powerful because teachers are actively pursuing answers to questions directly related to the everyday life of the classroom.

In an example of individual inquiry, McConaghy collected data from her daily interactions with children to determine how they were experiencing literature and how this experience was contributing to their becoming more literary readers and writers. As the year went by "the teacher-researcher duality dissolved as the researching became a natural part of her interaction and being as a teacher." (14, p. 727)

How Do I Start?

In all likelihood, a teacher interested in conducting a research investigation would not require an extensive search for a topic. At any given moment in the day, classroom teachers face puzzles and dilemmas in both teaching and learning. The identification of any one problem or question often leads to another. Classroom inquiry is cyclical and ongoing in nature; each investigation conducted may result in possible solutions to a question but will most likely uncover yet another avenue to explore.

Bringing an interesting question to a forum of one's peers broadens the perspective in which it can be viewed and assists the individual in determining the significance of the problem. It is an excellent first step toward classroom inquiry.

Problem Setting

In contrast to traditional research, classroom inquiry need not begin with a set of hypotheses about which an experimental teaching program is designed. The motivation for a study may come from observations an individual teacher makes about students. Often colleagues compare and discuss observations about student behavior, identifying common concerns or queries. For example, as a teacher of grade 7 classes for a number of years, I often wondered why division posed such a problem for students who had studied the concept over a period of at least 3 years. Even students who had apparently mastered the concept with whole numbers seemed to lose all understanding when presented with division of decimal fractions. In discussing this difficulty with a colleague, we found we had had common experiences and shared similar concerns. Corroboration of this type gives rise to both relief and consternation: relief because "it's not just you" and consternation because the problem is apparently widespread. Bringing an interesting question to a forum of one's peers broadens the perspective in which it can be viewed and assists the individual in determining the significance of the problem. It is an excellent first step toward classroom inquiry.

Systematizing or formalizing the research we already do as classroom teachers brings a sense of rigor to our work. The quest for rigor may bring to mind the search for a carefully designed research question and a tidy set of hypotheses that clearly articulate a study. There are many differences between traditional research and classroom inquiry, but the timing and importance of developing the question and the hypotheses may be the greatest one.

Reflective decision making is part of being a teacher researcher. A reflective teacher "makes instructional decisions consciously and tentatively, critically considers a full range of pertinent contextual and pedagogical factors, actively seeks evidence about the results, and continues to modify these decisions as the situation warrants." (20, p. 20)

Because classroom inquiry is done for personal reasons, it need not conform to guidelines commonly associated with formal research projects conducted to satisfy requirements for a graduate degree. While defining a problem is often viewed as the first step in formal research, this is not always a simple task. In classroom inquiry teachers will sometimes begin collecting data before they are entirely sure of their research question (3). This may appear to be a somewhat disorganized way to approach an investigation, but in fact problems do not generally present themselves as givens. They must be constructed, as Schön notes, from the materials or problematic situations that are puzzling, troubling, and uncertain (18). When open to surprise, a teacher interprets an unusual occurrence as a puzzle to be solved by becoming curious about it. Then on-the-spot experiments to explore the puzzle are invented— Schön's notion of reflection-in-action. This is not to say that a problem is never defined; rather, it may not become clear until an investigation is underway and it may change during the course of investigation.

Data Collection

How can we as classroom teachers begin to collect the data that will lead to better understanding of teaching and learning? Observations, interviews, and written artifacts combine to provide us with a rich source of information.

Observations can be recorded in a journal or a diary. In addition to taking notes during and after class, videotapes and audiotapes can be used to record discussions in which students reveal their thinking about concepts and procedures. Teachers can then look back on the lesson and reflect on what has transpired. Students should be encouraged to express their ideas without judgment, to challenge each other's thinking, and to justify statements they make. Acknowledging students' comments made in such a forum should be done in as neutral a manner as possible to ensure maximum participation.

Formal interviews conducted with individual students yield a wealth of information, especially when videotaped or audiotaped. While they do require a quiet setting

---

In this excerpt from videotape transcripts, students explain how they think the question 2.8 ÷ 0.7 might be approached. One student has just explained multiplying both terms by 10 and then dividing.

JOANI: Yeah, but Geoffrey, if you times that by 10 at the start of the equation, what do you do at the end? Do you divide the answer by 10 at the end of the question?

GEOFFREY: I think you divide by 100.

TEACHER: Joani says if you multiply these numbers by 10 at the beginning, then isn't the answer that you get going to be too large? Reaction?

DARIN: No. Well at the end you just put the decimal points back in.

TEACHER: Do you want to follow that through?

DARIN: Well, after you times it by 10 and you've done the question, you put the decimal points back in and you move the decimal point up.

TEACHER: Tell me exactly where I should put the decimal points.

DARIN: In between the 2 and the 8. And then back in front of the 7. And then you move that decimal point up in front of the 4.

TEACHER: So this is what I'd want here? $7\overline{)28}$ = $.7\overline{)2.8}$ Have a look at it. Think about it. Then I'd like to hear some reactions. That's an interesting way of thinking it through.

JUSTIN: Isn't there two numbers after the decimal points?

TEACHER: Yes, in the original question.

JUSTIN: Then the answer is 0.04.

TEACHER: Instead of the 0.4, you think we should be seeing 0.04? Why?

JUSTIN: There is one number behind the decimal point here (.7) and one there (2.8).

ANTHONY: I agree with Justin because with the whole 7 dividing 2.8, the answer is 0.4, so that's 0.7 dividing 2.8 so you can't get the same answer. And they're not whole numbers.

and often have to be conducted during nonteaching time, interviews reveal both unsuspected weaknesses and surprising strengths in students' mathematical thinking (13). Informal interviews with individuals or small groups are possible when the remainder of the class is directed to independent tasks or to center work. We may not be able to glean as much detailed information from this method as in an individual interview, but it does reveal important thinking about processes and shows the range of understandings within a group. A convenient way to collect data in this setting is the use of adhesive notes for recording anecdotal comments. These notes can later be added to student files.

Second only to the individual interview, having students write about problems enables teachers to assess the processes employed and the thinking by which they were driven. Work samples and learning logs can be used to assess understanding if students have been taught to justify their work and include their thoughts with their written responses. Student reflection in this form can range from asking students to rate problems according to difficulty (easy, just right, difficult), to asking them to write about how and why they chose to solve a problem the way they did. Recording the "how" of problem solution is much easier than the "why"; over time, students gradually become more adept at expressing their reasoning through discussions in small and whole class groupings.

In our quest for detailed information about students' thinking, it is important to remember they will tire if we always insist on written explanations of their thinking. Rating problems gives teachers a reading on the appropriateness of problem difficulty and is a quick check on student perception. Comparing students' ratings and exploring similarities and differences through discussion can be very revealing.

The goal of research should be to uncover potential meanings, tentative solutions, and working theories. (7)

Interpreting the Data

Central to the definition of classroom inquiry is the importance of putting research findings into practice within the setting where the data were collected (23). At the culmination of a more traditional form of inquiry, we may be left with test scores indicating the degree of success of an intervention upon which teaching recommendations can be made. This is not necessarily true with classroom inquiry. Videotapes and audiotapes, anecdotal comments, and student artifacts cannot and should not be treated statistically to determine significance. If this is the case, how can we make sense of the reflections, reactions, and surprises that are the result of our investigations?

As the motivation for conducting research of this nature is very personal, so must be the interpretation of its results. What is discovered may frequently lead to further investigation rather than conclusions of any form. According to Schön, two kinds of usable knowledge are produced in reflective teaching: carefully documented stories that contribute to usable repertoire, and theories that offer perspective on practice (17).

In the first case Schön refers to our increased depth of understanding of teaching and learning and how that will affect instructional decision making, present and future. For Schön, the classroom is a "swamp" in which we must forsake rigor in the traditional sense if we are to be able to engage in important and challenging problems (18). The stories we collect in this setting contribute to our experience, an combined with trial and error and intuition, serve to form what Schön calls "tacit knowing-in-action" (18, p. 49).

Schön's second form of usable knowledge is the development of theories that assist us in understanding practice. Contrary to traditional research, which is often theory driven, classroom inquiry may result in the generation of theories that can then be tested.

As with much classroom inquiry, there are no hard and fast rules for dealing with the wealth of data that result from an investigation. The personal motivations that initiated the research will also guide its interpretation. If we keep this forefront in our minds as we attempt to interpret our data, we will come to conclusions, however temporary, that hold personal meaning.

The Case for Mathematics

In an article that examines the impact of research in mathematics education, Kilpatrick suggests a number of possible explanations for the apparent ineffectiveness of studies conducted in the recent past, including insufficient funds, insufficient knowledge, and especially the lack of teachers in a participatory research role (12). As researchers move out into the classroom and work in close contact with teachers, he suggests teaching, learning, and research will all benefit.

> Cobb and Steffe outline three main reasons for researchers acting as teachers. First, researchers cannot rely solely on theoretical analysis to understand children's mathematical realities. Second, experiences children gain through their interactions with adults in a teaching situation greatly influence their construction of mathematical knowledge. Third, the context within which the child constructs the knowledge is crucial to understanding this knowledge." (8)

Some of the most exciting studies in recent years are those in which the researcher has attempted to understand children's mathematical thinking. Cobb and Steffe argue there is no substitute for the intimate interaction involved when teachers explore children's construction of mathematical knowledge (8). Based on this belief, the researchers gather information about children's mathematical understanding during teaching episodes. Occasional clinical interviews are conducted at selected points in the teaching experiment in order to update models of the children's current mathematical knowledge.

When we begin delving into students' mathematical thinking within the classroom setting, many interesting and surprising outcomes result. For example, in an investigation into problem-solving strategies used by elementary and junior high students, Sowder found six immature strategies that were commonly used (21). Even a seventh grader in a school's gifted program used the immature, computation-driven strategy of trying all operations and choosing the most reasonable answer when presented with a story problem.

Immature Strategies Commonly Used by Students (21, p. 26)

Coping Strategies

1. Find the numbers and add.
2. Guess at the operation to use.

Immature, Computation-driven Strategies

3. Look at the sizes of the numbers; they "tell" you what to try.
4. Try all the operations and choose the most reasonable answer.

Other Strategies of Limited Usefulness

5. Look for isolated key words or phrases that signal the operation.
6. Decide whether their answer should be larger or smaller than the given number. If larger, try addition and multiplication and choose the more reasonable answer. If smaller, make similar computations with subtraction and division.

Burns found that students who are successful at computation frequently are not able to reason through their own responses (6). When asked why there was a zero in the second row of a two-digit by two-digit multiplication question, children responded: "Nobody in our group can remember why we put the zero in the second line. We told you before that it is a rule to put the zero in the second line" (6, p. 35).

Weiland argues that teachers need to begin with the child's own thinking of a particular mathematical concept when planning instruction of standard algorithms (25). Weiland advocates the use of interviews to find out how children describe the actions they used to solve word problems involving operations such as division. When introducing standard algorithms, teachers can then match their instruction to children's mathematical realities.

Children do not learn by being "told" about mathematics; they are active participants in the construction of their own knowledge. Similarly, teachers cannot understand solely by being told about research; we must construct personal knowledge about children's understandings through our own inquiries. As researchers in our own classrooms, we are in excellent positions to determine children's understandings of mathematical concepts. We must access children's prior knowledge in order to link new knowledge to their present conceptual frames. Any beliefs or incomplete conceptions held by children that may interfere with the acquisition of new knowledge must be revealed and confronted.

> We must construct personal knowledge about children's understandings through our own inquiries. As researchers in our own classrooms, we are in an excellent position to determine children's understandings of mathematical concepts. We must access children's prior knowledge in order to link new knowledge to their present conceptual frames.

Detailed below are two examples that illustrate how teachers might become involved in classroom inquiry.

Children's Conceptions of Division—D. Shandola

My research began with questions about division and the difficulty grade 7 students had with this concept in both calculation and problem-solving contexts. I decided that it was important to gather some information concerning students' conceptions of division involving both whole numbers and decimal fractions. To me, the best way to gain insight into children's mathematical thinking is to talk to them. Consequently, I interviewed some grade 7 students while they worked on a variety of calculations and problems involving division. It was during these interviews that I gained many valuable insights—insights not only about children's conceptions of division but also about their beliefs concerning decimals and their approaches to

> Many students hold the belief that "dividing makes smaller." Here is a situation where a student knew that the final response would be less than $1.05 but had difficulty choosing the corresponding operation.
>
> One litre of special gasoline costs $1.05. How much will it cost to fill up a small lawnmower tank that can hold only 0.53 litres?
>
> KATHY:
> $$.53)\overline{1.05}$$
> with quotient 1.09, and below: 1.05, 52, 52
>
> KATHY: Somehow that doesn't look right to me.
> TEACHER: How come?
> KATHY: Because the number I got is bigger than how much it costs for one litre.
> TEACHER: What do you think you will have to do?
> KATHY: I think maybe it cost part of that. It will only cost about 52¢ because it is half a litre.
> TEACHER: So how do you think that will work out? Any ideas?
> KATHY: Not really.
> TEACHER: So you just have this thought that it will be about 52¢?
> KATHY: Yes.

problem solving. I discovered how some children's beliefs about division involving decimal fractions influenced decisions in problem solving. Some of my findings were particular to one child, but more were common to many of the seventh graders. I was fascinated to find similar findings in the research literature. Bridges between theory and the real life of the classroom were developing.

Following this initial gathering of information, questions concerning effective instruction were formulated. The importance of eliciting children's ideas and beliefs about mathematical topics was revealed to me, and I became interested in finding different ways to do this in the classroom setting. Although formal interviews yield valuable information, they are not practical in a busy classroom on a regular basis and I wanted to find out about children's mathematical thinking in other topic areas. As well, I wanted to explore instructional strategies that would challenge beliefs and naive conceptions and aid in the full development of mathematical concepts. As a result, more questions for further examination were generated and the cycle of classroom inquiry began.

A Classroom Investigation—G. Clouthier

As a middle grades teacher of 10 years' experience, I had always found it interesting that students who had studied division for some time continued to have a great deal of difficulty understanding division and its application. Not only did it seem that students were reluctant to choose this operation in the solution of problems, but that even in doing so were frequently unable to decide which number was the divisor and which was the dividend. To investigate this problem in a grade 7 setting, I chose division of decimal fractions and related problem solving.

Despite the large number of studies concerned with making links between conceptual and procedural knowledge, particularly in problem solving, there is little mention of practical suggestions that could be implemented in the classroom to nurture these links. The general purpose of my study was to use and document an instructional approach to problem solving involving division that would attempt to begin from the conceptions held by students and move toward linking their concepts to problem representation. While a general map of the instructional program was in place before the study began, the methods used and approaches taken evolved from the events experienced in the classroom.

Throughout the investigation, some interesting student beliefs and conceptions were uncovered. These were generally revealed in a discussion format. Often students were presented with a problem and asked to work on it independently. They were then to discuss their approaches in small groups. This provided an opportunity for me to circulate and note students' ideas. Following the small group work, a whole class discussion provided a forum for students to express their views and question each other. As they had no clear understanding of what should be done, they often pieced together bits of knowledge relating to multiplication of decimal fractions and other mathematical "truths" in which they believed. For example, when attempting the question $0.7\overline{)2.8}$ some students believed there should be two digits following the decimal in the answer because there were two digits in the question. Others believed that if both terms were multiplied by 10 to "get rid of the decimals" then the resulting answer would have to be divided by 10 to "make it equal."

Another fascinating belief was revealed when students were asked to write story problems to accompany open division sentences. Here is a sampling of the problems written to accompany 4 ÷ 20.

- If you had 20 dollars that you wanted to divide evenly among 4 people how much would each person get?
- If Mr. Cooper bought 4 grams of sugar for 20¢ how much did each gram cost?

When we looked at these problems as a class it became apparent that most students believed you could not divide a smaller number by a larger one. Even students who formed plausible representations of the problem, as in the second example, were unable to carry them through to fractional answers and had to make adjustments to obtain whole number answers. Through the use of base-10 blocks, discussion, and practice in small groups, students developed the ability to find problem examples for division questions involving whole numbers.

As we were nearing the completion of our unit of study, I experienced yet another surprise. I had been careful to present division of decimal fractions with varying physical models and pictorial representations, moving from concrete to abstract and back again. We had justified our thinking, challenged each other's thinking, and reached group consensus. I thought the students were developing understanding until one morning when the students were asked to write a story problem that indicated division. They were to use any two numbers, one of which had to be a decimal

---

None of the students noticed the terms in the division for the jeans problem should have been 4.5 ÷ 22. In the excerpt below, students explain why they subconsciously reversed the terms in the jeans problem:

TEACHER: How many people recognized right away that we had the numbers reversed? (No hands.) Why do you think that happened?

STAN: Sometimes a word problem, you get it switched around, depending on the way you hear it. You kind of ignore what's being divided.

TEACHER: If you ignore what's being divided, what do you focus on?

STAN: The other number. You tend to focus on the other number and you put it into what's being divided.

TEACHER: Joani, why do you think this happened?

JOANI: I guess I just wasn't thinking. Some people tend to divide the bigger number by the smaller number, instead of the small number by the big number. You just reverse them because you think the big number should be divided by the small number.

TEACHER: It feels better to do this? 4.5)$\overline{22}$.

STUDENTS: It looks better.

TEACHER: This looks weird? 22)$\overline{4.5}$.

STUDENTS: Yeah.

STAN: Yeah, 'cause you'll get a decimal (less than one).

fraction. One student volunteered her problem: Mary had 22 pairs of jeans to trim and turn up. When she finished, she had 4.5 meters of material leftover. How much fabric did she trim off each pair?

We began our investigation of the problem. Once we had established that the problem met the conditions, the students set out to explain how it might be solved. Without argument, the students agreed with one boy's suggestion that it be solved by dividing 22 by 4.5. They estimated an answer of about five. When I asked what the "five" referred to, answers ranged from five meters (which they quickly ruled out), through five decimeters, to five centimeters. Here was another example of students adapting the problem to fit their thinking: If it doesn't make sense in the way you think it should, change some part of it so there is no conflict in logic.

When we completed the unit, students had a better conceptual understanding of the meaning behind the algorithm and were more successful with division of whole numbers and decimal fractions in exercise and problem formats. I had developed a sense of the beliefs and conceptions students held that may have been partly responsible for a lack of success in the past, and I had discovered some strategies that seemed to help move students from one representation to another. Finally, I had yet another list of questions to investigate.

What Makes This Go?

Teachers who have been involved in classroom inquiry report that the most important condition for meaningful research was that it be "owned" by the teacher or teachers involved (4, 5). Regardless of the model for teacher research, teachers must be participants in the true sense of the word, intimately involved in decision making at every step of the research process.

Bridging the gap between theory and practice is another important aspect of classroom inquiry. Martin believes that this bridging is facilitated through deliberate study of specific theoretical works (16). She advocates the discussion of related research by teachers involved in classroom inquiry in order that they may inform their own decision making and bring theory and practice closer together. This viewpoint is not uncommon. Many teachers have sought information to aid in their research, either in planning or analyzing findings. Allen, Combs, Hendricks, Nash, and Wilson report that they were involved in an ongoing literature review that was essential to every element of the inquiry (1).

Support groups contribute greatly to the success of classroom inquiry. Allen et al. use the term "research community" to indicate a support group that meets regularly to discuss findings and problems and to share resources (1). Martin speaks of networks of support, some type of collaborative support among teachers in the school or the district (16). Central to her notion of support groups is the idea that each teacher needs to have both critics and listeners. Each has a major influence on the thinking involved in planning and carrying out classroom inquiry. Critics become sounding boards for new ideas. They point out alternate ways of thinking about learning and teaching. Listeners become more than sounding boards, celebrating in successes and sharing in setbacks. Simmons and Schuette remind us that there is a delicate balance between support and risk taking (20). These support groups may at times be "therapy groups" dealing openly with the notion that change can be difficult on both professional and personal levels.

A final point to be made about the conditions for continuing classroom inquiry involves value and recognition (23, 7). It is important that teachers be able to share their findings with others and receive some recognition for their efforts. If colleagues value the work being done, it becomes easier for the teachers themselves to believe that classroom inquiry is valuable and important.

> "As teachers begin to reflectively analyze their own practices, change is potentially occurring in areas such as teacher role definition, pedagogical language, metacognitive processes, classroom teaching practices, and collegial interaction." (20, p. 23)

Why Become Involved in Classroom Inquiry?

Classroom inquiry empowers teachers. When the classroom is the key to educational change, teachers become informed decision makers, more authoritative in their assessment of curricula, instructional methods, and materials. The establishment of support networks also provides opportunities to develop powerful collegial relationships.

Classroom inquiry empowers students. When students are involved in the research, fully informed about the purposes of the classroom inquiry, they see the teacher as a lifelong learner. They become more reflective about their own learning and understand that teachers care about the quality of that learning.

Classroom inquiry bridges the gap between theory and practice when teachers become theorists, articulate their questions, test their hypotheses, and link findings with practice. This seamless, ongoing approach to classroom inquiry, rather than research-to-practice, becomes research-as-practice (11).

Looking Ahead . . .

Individual teachers can and should take advantage of the opportunities afforded by classroom research. Becoming a researcher in one's own classroom adds a vital dimension to teaching and learning. Viewing "surprises" in our classrooms as intriguing elements of practice (18) transforms potential difficulties into opportunities to inform practice. Every teacher should have a personal professional development plan. Classroom research can form the basis of this plan. Whether through the pursuit of a particular interest across different groups of students or investigating several areas of interest with one group of students, a classroom teacher can work towards discovering ways to improve personal practice.

How can we involve our colleagues in classroom research? Sharing discoveries with a teacher enrolling a similar grade in your school might prompt that teacher to begin some investigations of his or her own. In the staffroom, the resulting professional dialogue can pique the interest of others. Beyond the school setting we can take advantage of structures such as mathematics specialist groups. District curriculum committees, local specialist associations, or networks of teachers interested in mathematics can serve as support groups for exploring classroom research. Some groups of classroom teachers have been successful in obtaining funding from provincial or state agencies to facilitate this type of research.

What else can be done to help raise awareness of the rewards associated with classroom research? Write an article for a regional mathematics journal describing your experiences with classroom inquiry. Make a presentation at a conference with a colleague. Allow plenty of time for questions! Offer to sponsor a student teacher. In addition to helping the student teacher become a reflective practitioner, you will create a learning environment characterized by collaborative interaction.

Open your classroom to classroom inquiry. This dynamic approach to teaching and learning will have benefits for both you and your students.

Gillian Clouthier and Darlene Shandola

About the Authors

Gillian Clouthier is a vice-principal and teacher in an elementary school in North Vancouver, British Columbia. She has presented mathematics workshops for teachers of grades 1 through 8. She has recently completed a master of arts in mathematics education at the University of British Columbia.

Darlene Shandola is a teacher consultant on the Learning Services Team for the Richmond School District, Richmond, British Columbia. In this capacity, she works with individual teachers and school staffs in the area of professional development. She also teaches an elementary mathematics methods course for the University of British Columbia.

References

1. ALLEN, J., COMBS, J., HENDRICKS, M., NASH, P., & WILSON, S. (1988). Studying change: Teachers who become researchers. *Language Arts, 65*(4), 379–387.
2. ANZUL, M., & ELY, M. (1988). Hall of mirrors: The introduction of the reflective mode. *Language Arts, 65*(7), 675–687.
3. ASHER, C. (1987). Developing a pedagogy for a teacher-researcher program. *English Education, 19*(4), 211–219.
4. BISSEX, G. (1988). On learning and not learning from teaching. *Language Arts, 65*(8), 771–775.
5. BRITTON, J. (1987). A quiet form of research. In D. Goswami & P. Stillman (Eds.), *Reclaiming the classroom* (pp. 13–19). Upper Mountclair, NJ: Boynton Cook.
6. BURNS, M. (1986). Teaching "what to do" in arithmetic vs. teaching "what to do and why." *Educational Leadership, 43*(7), 34–38.
7. BURTON, F. (1986). Research currents: A teacher's conception of the action research process. *Language Arts, 63*(7), 718–723.
8. COBB, P., & STEFFE, L. (1983). The constructivist researcher as teacher and model builder. *Journal for Research in Mathematics Education, 14*(2), 83–94.

9. COREY, S. (1953). *Action research to improve school practices.* New York: Teachers College Press, Columbia University.
10. GLATTHORN, A. A. (1987). Cooperative professional development: Peer-centered options for teacher growth. *Educational Leadership, 45*(3), 31–35.
11. GOODMAN, Y. (1978). Kid Watching: An alternative to testing. *National Elementary Principal, 57*(4), 41–45.
12. KILPATRICK, J. (1981). The reasonable ineffectiveness of research in mathematics education. *For the Learning of Mathematics, 2*(2), 22–29.
13. LABINOWICZ, E. (1987). The interview method. *Arithmetic Teacher, 35*(3), 22–23.
14. McCONAGHY, J. (1986). On becoming teacher experts: Research as a way of knowing. *Language Arts, 63*(7), 724–728.
15. McKERNAN, J. (1988). Teacher as researcher: Paradigms and praxis. *Contemporary Education, 59*(3), 154–158.
16. MARTIN, N. (1987). On the move. In D. Goswami and P. Stillman (Eds.), *Reclaiming the classroom* (pp. 20–28). Upper Mountclair, NJ: Boynton Cook.
17. SCHÖN, D. (1988). Coaching reflective teaching. In P. Grimmett & G. Erickson, (Eds.), *Reflection in teacher education* (pp. 19–29). New York: Teachers College Press.
18. SCHÖN, D. (1983). *The reflective practitioner.* New York: Basic Books.
19. SHAPIRO, P., & SHAPIRO B. (1988). The classroom teacher as researcher. In F. Brownlie (Ed.), *Teacher as Researcher, 3*(1), 2–3.
20. SIMMONS, J., & SCHUETTE, M. (1988). Strengthening teachers' reflective decision making. *Journal of Staff Development, 9*(3), 18–27.
21. SOWDER, L. (1989). Story problems and student strategies. *Arithmetic Teacher, 36*(9), 25–26.
22. STENHOUSE, L. (1975). *An introduction to curriculum research and development.* London, England: Heinemann.
23. STRICKLAND, D. (1988). The teacher as researcher: Toward the extended professional. *Language Arts, 65*(8), 754–764.
24. WALLACE, M. (1987). A historical review of action research: Some implications for the education of teachers in their managerial role. *Journal of Education for Teaching, 13*(2), 97–115.
25. WEILAND, L. (1985). Matching instruction to children's thinking about division. *Arithmetic Teacher, 33*(4), 34–35.

Research Ideas for the Classroom: Early Childhood Mathematics

Contents

Research Ideas for the Classroom: High School Mathematics

Contents

Index